The Psychology of
the Courtroom

The Psychology of the Courtroom

EDITED BY

Norbert L. Kerr

Department of Psychology
Michigan State University
East Lansing, Michigan

Robert M. Bray

Center for the Study of Social Behavior
Research Triangle Institute
Research Triangle Park, North Carolina

 1982

ACADEMIC PRESS

A Subsidiary of Harcourt Brace Jovanovich, Publishers
New York   London   Toronto   Sydney   San Francisco

ACADEMIC PRESS, INC.
111 Fifth Avenue, New York, New York 10003

United Kingdom Edition published by
ACADEMIC PRESS, INC. (LONDON) LTD.
24/28 Oval Road, London NW1 7DX

Library of Congress Cataloging in Publication Data
Main entry under title:

The Psychology of the courtroom.

  Includes bibliographies and indexes.
  1. Psychology, Forensic. I. Kerr, Norbert L.
II. Bray, Robert M.
KF8922.P78   347.73'66   81-14884
ISBN 0-12-404920-6   347.30766   AACR2

PRINTED IN THE UNITED STATES OF AMERICA

82 83 84 85   9 8 7 6 5 4 3 2 1

Contents

III. COURTROOM DECISION MAKERS

7

8

9

IV. PROBLEMS AND PROSPECTS FOR RESEARCH ON THE PSYCHOLOGY OF THE COURTROOM

10

11

List of Contributors

Numbers in parentheses indicate the pages on which the authors' contributions begin.

Robert M. Bray (1, 221, 287), Center for the Study of Social Behavior, Research Triangle Institute, Research Triangle Park, North Carolina 27709

Judee K. Burgoon (169), Department of Communication, Michigan State University, East Lansing, Michigan 48824

Anthony Champagne (257), Department of Political Science, University of Texas at Dallas, Richardson, Texas 75080

Francis C. Dane (83), Department of Psychology, State University of New York at Oswego, Oswego, New York 13126

Valerie P. Hans (39), Division of Criminal Justice and Department of Psychology, University of Delaware, Newark, Delaware 19711

Martin F. Kaplan (197), Department of Psychology, Northern Illinois University, De Kalb, Illinois 60115

Norbert L. Kerr (1, 221, 287), Department of Psychology, Michigan State University, East Lansing, Michigan 48824

E. Allan Lind[1] (13), Research Division, Federal Judicial Center, 1520 H Street, NW, Washington, D.C. 20005

[1]Present address: Department of Psychology, University of Illinois, Champaign, Illinois 61820

Elizabeth Loftus (119), Department of Psychology, University of Washington, Seattle, Washington 98105

Gerald R. Miller (169), Department of Communication, Michigan State University, East Lansing, Michigan 48824

Stuart Nagel (257), Department of Political Science, 361 Lincoln Hall, University of Illinois, Urbana, Illinois 61801

Steven Penrod (119), Department of Psychology, University of Wisconsin, Madison, Wisconsin 53706

Michael J. Saks (325), Department of Psychology, Boston College, Chestnut Hill, Massachusetts 02167

Garold Stasser (221), Department of Psychology, Miami University, Oxford, Ohio 45056

Neil Vidmar (39), Department of Psychology, University of Western Ontario, London, Ontario, Canada N6A 4V2

John D. Winkler (119), Social Science Department, Rand Corporation, Santa Monica, California 90406

Lawrence S. Wrightsman (83), Department of Psychology, 426 Fraser Hall, University of Kansas, Lawrence, Kansas 66045

Preface

During the last decade or so, social scientists have shown tremendous interest in the scientific study of legal institutions. One good index of this interest is the large number of books recently published and forthcoming that have focused on psychology and the law.[1] The current volume contributes to this rapidly growing literature. However, whereas previous work consists largely of original research reports, theoretical papers, "perspective papers" (lawyers and judges looking out from and social scientists looking into the legal system), and occasional reviews, the present volume consists primarily of comprehensive and integrative reviews that critically examine the psychology of the courtroom.

[1] For example, G. Bermant, C. Nemeth and N. Vidmar (Eds.), *Psychology and the law* (Lexington, Massachusetts: Lexington, 1976); S. L. Brodsky, *Psychologists in the criminal justice system* (Urbana: Univ. of Illinois Press, 1973); B. Clifford and R. Bull, *The psychology of person identification* (London: Routledge & Kegan Paul, 1978); R. Hastie, S. Penrod and N. Pennington, *Inside the jury* (Cambridge, Massachusetts: Harvard Univ. Press, in press); V. Konečni and E. B. Ebbesen (Eds.), *Social-psychological analysis of legal processes* (San Francisco, California: Freeman, 1980); P. D. Lipsett and B. D. Sales (Eds.), *New directions in psycholegal research* (New York: Van Nostrand-Reinhold, 1979); E. F. Loftus, *Eyewitness testimony* (Cambridge, Massachusetts: Harvard Univ. Press, 1979); M. Saks and R. Hastie, *Social psychology in court* (New York: Van Nostrand-Reinhold, 1978); B. D. Sales (Ed.), *Perspectives in law and psychology, Volume I: The criminal justice system* (New York: Plenum, 1977); B. D. Sales (Ed.), *Psychology in the legal process* (New York: Spectrum, 1977); B. D. Sales (Ed.), *Perspectives in law and psychology, Volume II: The trial process* (New York: Plenum, 1980); R.

Our motivation for preparing this volume stemmed from two sources: a personal need for an integrative and broad-based text in some of our classes and a recognition that the expanding empirical literature focusing on various courtroom participants and problems was in need of summary and critical review. The present volume meets both of these needs. It provides a book suitable for advanced undergraduate and graduate courses that require a comprehensive, up-to-date, and fairly high-level review of psychological theory and research bearing on the courtroom trial.

We may note several descriptive and perhaps distinctive features of this book. First, all the chapters have been written by behavioral scientists who are or have been actively engaged in research in the area that they review. Second, the general emphasis is on breadth of coverage within topic areas, rather than on in-depth coverage of the authors' own work. Third, the range of topics is intentionally narrower than that of many other current books; it excludes legal processes that precede and follow trials (e.g., arrests, plea-bargaining, parole decisions, corrections). Finally, the chapters all aim to organize and integrate existing work, to identify gaps in knowledge, and to highlight important topics for future research.

The themes of the chapters are either common courtroom roles (defendant and victim, juror, jury, judge, witness) or problems (court procedures, methodological problems for research, problems of innovation in the courts). Some other obvious topics have not been included, either because there was too little focused research upon which to base a review (e.g., attorney behavior) or because the research literature was too diffuse, nonthematic, or speculative (e.g., expert testimony on competency to stand trial).

This book should be of greatest value to social scientists interested in the psychology of the courtroom and to advanced undergraduates or graduate students in the social sciences. At these levels, it would be appropriate for courses in forensic psychology, applied psychology, criminal justice, or social psychology. It might also be useful as a reference book for lawyers and judges or as a text for law students. The chapters have been written and edited to minimize the reader's need of extensive background in statistics, research methods, psychology, or the law. However, a basic familiarity with these areas, particularly research methods, would be helpful.

In our role as editors, we would like to note that the order of editorship is totally arbitrary; we shared equally the editorial work and must, therefore, share equally the responsibility for any shortcomings. We would also like to express our appreciation to the number of people who have aided in this project:

J. Simon (Ed.), *The jury system in America* (Beverly Hills, California: Sage, 1975); R. J. Simon, *The jury: Its role in American society* (Lexington, Massachusetts: Lexington, 1980); J. L. Tapp and F. J. Levine (Eds.), *Law, justice, and the individual in society: Psychological and legal issues* (New York: Holt, 1977); J. Thibaut and L. Walker, *Procedural justice: A psychological analysis* (Hillsdale, New Jersey: Erlbaum, 1975); H. Toch (Ed.), *Psychology of crime and criminal justice* (New York: Holt, 1979); A. D. Yarmey, *The psychology of eyewitness testimony* (New York: Free Press, 1979).

These include the staff of Academic Press for their guidance, enthusiasm, and support; our contributors for doing such thorough, timely, and professional jobs; and our wives, Jeanne and Phyllis, for their patience as yet another of our "little" projects turned into something that consumed a great deal of both our time and attention.

The Psychology of the Courtroom: An Introduction

Norbert L. Kerr
Robert M. Bray

The workings of the courtroom have fascinated behavioral scientists since the turn of the century, when the science of psychology was still in its infancy. During the first half of the century, however, research studies were relatively narrowly focused, concentrating almost entirely upon problems of eyewitness reliability (e.g., Burtt, 1931; Marston, 1924; Münsterberg, 1908). Furthermore, these early efforts were sporadic and unsustained due, in part, to lack of theory, resources, and, to some degree, acceptance of such work by the legal community (e.g., Wigmore, 1909). The Jury Project of the University of Chicago (Broeder, 1958), which began during the 1950s, marked the beginning of sustained research attention to the psychology of the courtroom. It produced several landmark works (e.g., Kalven & Zeisel, 1966; Simon, 1967) and signaled a revival of interest among psychologists and other social scientists in courtroom functioning. Since that time the amount and scope of research on the psychology of the courtroom has increased dramatically and steadily.

Several observers, most notably Tapp (1969, 1971, 1976, 1980), have speculated on the forces that have produced this growing fascination with courtroom behavior. Among the plausible contributing factors that have been suggested are the following: (*a*) the public's growing concern with crime, (*b*) the resul-

1

THE PSYCHOLOGY
OF THE COURTROOM

tant expansion of research funds, primarily from the federal government, for the study of the criminal justice system, (c) the more general trend in the social sciences, and particularly in psychology, to shift focus from basic to applied research, (d) the allure of the courtroom drama as an object of inquiry, and (e) an apparent receptivity to psychological theory and research by legal decision makers (e.g., *Ballew* v. *Georgia*, 1978; McCrystal, 1977).

To this plausible list of incentives we would add one additional factor: Many of the most fundamental assumptions underlying courtroom trials are psychological assumptions. For example, the entrusting of ultimate decision-making powers to untrained groups of citizens—that is, juries—is not only an embodiment of a democratic ideal, a safeguard against judicial tyranny, and, perhaps, a hidebound tradition; it is also a policy that assumes that such groups can understand their task, set aside personal prejudices, reliably judge the credibility of witnesses, and collectively apply the law to reach a just verdict. Another psychological assumption underlies the common reliance upon the testimony of eyewitnesses: that they accurately perceived and can accurately recall the events about which they testify. Unfortunately, this assumption has sometimes been made even when these events may have been of brief duration, occurred during periods of great stress, or happened far in the past. Even the choice of an adversarial system of justice makes important psychological assumptions concerning the relative advantages of different methods of adjudication for motivating disputants to present all relevant evidence and for enhancing the perceived fairness and justness of the legal process. In short, the operation of the courts is predicated upon a host of psychological assumptions about just how the key actors in the court (judges, attorneys, defendants, witnesses, and jurors) can and will behave under a variety of conditions.

As the psychological bases of courtroom practice have become more evident, spurred in part by several court rulings (e.g., *Johnson* v. *Louisiana*, 1972; *Williams* v. *Florida*, 1970), so has the recognition that psychologists and other social scientists are probably the best equipped, theoretically and methodologically, to test these fundamental assumptions. Psychologists, for example, have studied and developed theories of memory, cognition, information processing, attitude change, attitudes and behavior, prejudice, social influence processes, conformity, group dynamics, and decision making, all of which have clear relevance to courtroom events. In addition, both traditional and innovative social science methodologies now routinely employ sophisticated analytic techniques, many only recently developed, that make possible the study of questions that have long been considered unassailable. In fact, it has been suggested that advances in technical areas have outstripped parallel theoretical developments (Tapp, 1980).

The purpose of this book is to review the attempts that have been made thus far to scientifically study the psychology of the courtroom. Before describing the book's structure and content in more detail, however, it might be useful to comment briefly on what the book does not attempt to do. First, it is not a description of psychology *in* the courtroom. For reasons elaborated on in Chapter 10, we do not subscribe to the belief that knowledge of courtroom behavior must be based largely on in-court observation. Rather, we believe that a great deal of laboratory and simulation research, some of which has been undertaken without any reference to courtroom behavior, may shed light on such behavior and thus merits inclusion here. Secondly, this book is not a handbook for legal professionals or a "how to" manual for using psychological knowledge to help win cases. As will become apparent to the reader, in most instances our knowledge of the psychology of the courtroom is too sketchy to confidently advise attorneys or litigants.

This volume does attempt to critically review the empirical work bearing on the psychology of the courtroom. As such, it draws on both basic and applied research and considers relevant psychological theory as well as atheoretical descriptive work. The book provides a broad, current overview of the kind of questions posed by social scientists, the approaches that have been employed in addressing these questions, the tentative answers suggested by the existing research, some of the more glaring gaps of our knowledge, and suggests potentially fruitful directions for future research on the psychology of the courtroom.

The book is divided into four major sections. Part I, Courtroom Procedures and Key Actors, addresses the ground rules—the procedures—that govern courtroom trials and introduces us to some of the major actors of the trial: jurors, defendants, and victims. In Chapter 2, The Psychology of Courtroom Procedure, E. Allan Lind reviews three procedural issues that have attracted considerable research attention. He first considers the psychological consequences of employing an adversarial system of justice. For example, is it perceived as fairer by litigants and attorneys? Does it actually encourage more thorough preparation of cases by attorneys and more vigorous presentation of opposing views than alternative systems? He next examines a problem of longstanding interest to psychologists that has one of its most practical applications in the courtroom—the ffects of the order of presenting information. Does the prosecution, for example, gain an advantage by presenting its side first, or does the defense enjoy that advantage by presenting last? Although the literature is not totally consistent, Lind shows that the order of presentation does have consequences for the recall and impact of evidence. Lind then turns to the much discussed problem of the comprehensibility and effectiveness of judicial instructions to jurors. He concludes with a consideration of several less thoroughly investigated but vital procedural questions.

Valerie P. Hans and Neil Vidmar take up the issue of juror selection in Chapter 3. They first describe the fundamental principles governing jury selection—the requirements that juries be representative, drawn from the local community of the crime, and impartial. Hans and Vidmar first review the reasons—historical, legal, and psychological—for each of these requirements. They then delve into the key empirical issues that have engaged the attention of social scientists. For example, just how representative are juries generally, given the typical methods of jury pool composition and exemption? What kind of empirical evidence has proven adequate to demonstrate unrepresentativeness? What kind of psychological data have been marshaled to support motions for change of venue and with what success? How effective are standard juror examination and challenge techniques, in principle and in practice? Recurrent themes in Chapter 3 are the promise and practice of involvement by psychologists in jury selection. These themes are particularly relevant to their final section, which reviews and evaluates efforts at "scientific" jury selection.

The juror, of course, is only one key actor in the psychology of the courtroom. In criminal cases, the defendant and victim play prominent roles as well. In Chapter 4, Francis C. Dane and Lawrence S. Wrightsman focus on the effects of defendants' and victims' personal characteristics on the trial outcome. To organize and integrate this rather large literature, they employ Abelson's theory of scripts (1976). Within this framework, they point out that defendant and victim characteristics may have differential effects, since jurors' vignettes of trial events may occur at varying levels of abstraction. Using the script approach, Dane and Wrightsman review research on defendant and victim effects for six characteristics: gender, socioeconomic status, moral character, general attractiveness, race, and attitude similarity. The influence of such extralegal factors has been a popular object of research because it often constitutes a clear judgmental bias or prejudice.

The second major section of the book focuses on the general issue of testimony. The first chapter of Part II, Chapter 5, by Steven Penrod, Elizabeth Loftus, and John Winkler, examines the long-standing question of the reliability of the eyewitness. Drawing extensively from research on memory and cognition, they enumerate the many sources of unreliability affecting the acquisition, retention, and retrieval of witnessed material. These sources include such things as stimulus events (e.g., exposure time, event complexity, event stressfulness), witness factors (e.g., expectations, information processing strategies), the length of the retention interval, distortion and changes in memory that occur over time, question biases, and lineup instruction biases. They also examine literature dealing with facial recognition and its implications for eyewitness performance. Finally, they review studies dealing with eyewitness activities related to identification of suspects (e.g., photo spreads, mug shots, facial composites) and evaluate several possible means of improving or extending eyewitness performance, including use of different modes of questioning, hyponosis, and lie detectors.

Regardless of how well witnesses can reliably recall and recount what they saw or know, the actual impact of their testimony may depend in large part on how credible their testimony is perceived to be by the trier of facts. In Chapter 6, Gerald R. Miller and Judee Burgoon examine the factors which affect this judgment of credibility. Two primary and complementary questions are addressed: What behaviors are reliably associated with honest and deceptive messages? What behaviors are perceived as signaling honest and deceptive messages? The authors pay particularly careful attention to the role of nonverbal behaviors for these two questions. The chapter concludes with an assessment of the general ability of perceivers (that is, jurors or judges) to accurately detect deception, and the effects of the mode of presentation (e.g., live versus video recordings versus audio recordings) on such accuracy.

Once all the testimony has been given, the final arguments have been made, and the jury has been instructed, the actual process of decision making must begin. Part III's three chapters review the research on the decision-making process for the individual juror, the jury, and the judge. In Chapter 7, Martin F. Kaplan examines the decision-making process of the individual juror. Using Anderson's (1974) integration model as an organizing framework, he begins with a discussion of the major factors involved in the judgment process. He then applies the model to judgments made by jurors (such as verdicts) and examines the sources and kinds of information that contribute to these judgments. Here he gives special emphasis to factors that contribute to juror bias both from legal and extralegal sources (e.g., juror's personal biases, defendant characteristics, pretrial publicity, and inadmissible evidence). He then turns to a consideration of the reduction of these biases, drawing on the judgment model and its implications, and suggests some needed research. He concludes with a discussion of the related process of juror criterion setting, for example, deciding how much doubt is needed to reach the threshold of a reasonable doubt.

The process whereby individual juror preferences are combined to form a jury verdict is the subject of Chapter 8, which we coauthored with Garold Stasser. Chapter 8 examines the structure, process, and product of jury deliberations. The primary structural issue concerns the factors related to the selection of a jury foreman. The primary process issue concerns the patterns of verbal communication during deliberation: Who speaks, who is spoken to, and what is said? We also consider some of the ways in which a foreman may exert special influence. The chapter then looks at the outcome or product of deliberations. The primary product issues are the prediction of the final verdict and the examination of the bases for two consistent consequences of deliberation: the power of majorities and a leniency bias.

Judges typically have a number of discretionary decision-making powers, including ruling on challenges of potential jurors for cause, enforcing the rules of evidence, dismissing or severing charges, acting as trier of fact in bench trials, and sentencing convicted criminal defendants. The psychology of judging is the topic of Chapter 9 by Anthony Champagne and Stuart Nagel. Unlike jurors, judges occupy relatively permanent positions in the courts. As such, they are much more subject to political, organizational, and occupational forces at work in the legal system. Champagne and Nagel describe these forces by outlining the structure of the courts and the nature of the judicial environment. They then review several traditional approaches to the study of judicial behavior, along with much of the research generated by each of these approaches. More recent work has employed sophisticated quantitative models to predict and, ultimately, explain judicial behavior. Champagne and Nagel provide a general characterization and survey of such models, followed by more detailed descriptions of some specific models of interest.

The final section, Part IV, focuses on the study of the psychology of the courtroom—its prospects for stimulating innovation in the criminal justice system, its problems, its past, and its future. The first chapter in this section, Chapter 10, grew out of a recent methodological paper on jury simulations (Bray & Kerr, 1979). Chapter 10 focuses on the most common methodological criticism of research on the psychology of the courtroom—what might simply be termed the problem of realism. We begin by documenting just how pervasive this problem is and then proceed to a comparison of the relative strengths and weaknesses of more versus less realistic research methods. Several recurrent themes of methodological criticism are then identified and discussed. The central conclusion is that a number of methods and settings, including highly "unrealistic" ones (e.g., laboratory and simulation studies), can inform us about courtroom behavior. Therefore, we reject the growing counsel for a restriction of "acceptable" methods for the study of the psychology of the courtroom.

Michael J. Saks, in Chapter 11, addresses the problem of innovation and change in the courtroom. He first discusses innovations—both generally and specifically in the courts—as a scientific-technical problem and as a legal-organizational problem. He then considers three prominent examples of court innovations fueled, at least in part, by behavioral research: (a) reductions in jury size and relaxation of jury decision rule, (b) provision of sentencing guidelines to judges, and (c) introduction of video technology into the courtroom. Saks identifies many of the forces promoting and opposing these innovations, reviews the relevant empirical literature, comments on the prospects for implementation of these innovations, and mentions a number of dilemmas surrounding policy-oriented research.

The courtroom is not only a formal institution designed to resolve some of society's most difficult conflicts, it is also an incredibly complex behavioral setting. It is an institution that, like most others, is ultimately governed by the capacities, limitations, and proclivities of the human beings that function within it. If our goal is to narrow the gap between how the courts actually function and how we would have them function, an essential first step must be to improve our understanding of the psychology of the courtroom. It is our hope that the following chapters will not only document the sometimes halting progress made thus far, but will also help direct our succeeding steps in informative directions.

The following paragraphs provide a brief background sketch of the contributors. Their names appear in alphabetical order.

Robert M. Bray received his doctorate in social psychology from the University of Illinois in 1974. He is currently a Research Psychologist at the Center for the Study of Social Behavior at Research Triangle Institute in North Carolina. His principal research interests concern small group behavior, psychology and law, and the relationship between attitudes and behavior.

Judee K. Burgoon is Associate Professor of Communication and Director of Graduate Studies at Michigan State University, where she has taught since 1978. She earned her doctorate from West Virginia University in the joint areas of Communication and Educational Psychology. She is the author of over 40 articles and chapters and three books, including *The Unspoken Dialogue.* Her research interests include nonverbal and interpersonal communication and public assessment of mass media. She has received eight national awards for research excellence and the Teacher−Scholar Award at Michigan State University.

Anthony Champagne received his doctorate from the University of Illinois and is currently Associate Professor of Political Science at the University of Texas at Dallas. He has published a number of articles on poverty of law and judicial behavior. At present he is writing a political biography of Samuel Rayburn.

Francis C. Dane received his doctorate in social psychology from the University of Kansas in 1979 and is currently Assistant Professor and Director of the Graduate Program in Psychology at the State University of New York College at Oswego. His research interests involve decision processes, measurement, and mathematical modeling, and currently include investigations of the quantification of reasonable doubt as a decision criterion in jury trials and the application of script processing to courtroom events.

Valerie P. Hans received her doctorate in social psychology from the University of Toronto in 1978. She is currently Assistant Professor of Criminal Justice and Psychology at the University of Delaware. She has conducted research on the jury and has served as an advisor to the Law Reform Commission of Canada on jury reform. One of her current research interests is the effects of pretrial questioning of prospective jurors.

Martin F. Kaplan is Professor of Psychology at Northern Illinois University, where he has taught since receiving his doctorate from the University of Iowa in 1965. He also teaches courses in juror behavior at Northern Illinois University's College of Law. Dr. Kaplan is the author of over 50 research articles and chapters, and was co-editor of *Human Judgment and Decision Processes* and *Human Judgment and Decision Processes in Applied Settings.* His research lies primarily in social judgment, with current work involving juror decision-making, morality judgment, and evaluation of contestants in old-time fiddling contests by expert judges and inexpert listeners.

Norbert L. Kerr received his doctorate in social psychology from the University of Illinois. He is presently Associate Professor of Psychology at Michigan State University. His primary research interests are in small group decision making, motivation in task-performing groups, and psychology and the law.

E. Allan Lind received his doctorate in social psychology from the University of North Carolina at Chapel Hill and is presently Assistant Professor of Psychology at the University of Illinois. In addition to his work on procedural justice, he has published articles on social perception and witness speech styles and on intergroup conflict, attitude formation and change, and methodology. His current research includes evaluation studies of federal court programs and laboratory studies of the role of participation and control in reactions to conflict resolution rules.

Elizabeth F. Loftus received her doctorate in psychology from Stanford University in 1970. She is currently Professor of Psychology at the University of Washington. A former Fellow at the Center for Advanced Study in the Behavioral Sciences at Stanford, her major research interests focus on human cognition, particularly memory and eyewitness performance. She has published numerous articles and five books. Her recent book, *Eyewitness Testimony*, received a National Media Award from the American Psychological Foundation. Professor Loftus has testified and consulted frequently as an expert on eyewitness testimony.

Gerald R. Miller is Professor of Communication at Michigan State University. His major research interests are in the areas of interpersonal communication, persuasion, and communication in the legal setting. Dr. Miller is a Fellow and Past President of the International Communication Association, and a former editor of the journal, *Human Communication Research*. The author of numerous books and articles, he has recently co-authored a book, *Videotape on Trial: A View from the Jury Box*, with Professor Norman E. Fontes. This volume summarizes the results of a 4-year research program aimed at determining the effects of videotaped trial materials on juror response, a project that won him a Joint Resolution of Tribute from the Michigan Legislature.

Stuart S. Nagel is Professor of Political Science at the University of Illinois and a member of the Illinois bar. He is the author or co-author of *Decision Theory and the Legal Process, Legal Policy Analysis: Finding an Optimum Level or Mix, Improving the Legal Process: Effects of Alternatives*, and *The Legal Process from a Behavioral Perspective*, as well as numerous articles for journals in political science, criminology, and the law. He is currently completing two books, entitled *Policy Optimizing Models* and *Optimizing Analysis: Goals, Methods, and Applications*.

Steven Penrod received his JD from Harvard Law School and his doctorate from Harvard University. He is currently Assistant Professor of Psychology at the University of Wisconsin. His research interests include eyewitness reliability, legal decision making, modeling and simulation of jury behavior, trial advocacy techniques, and jury selection. He is a co-author of the forthcoming book, *Inside the Jury*.

Michael J. Saks is Associate Professor in the Department of Psychology at Boston College. He has also taught at the Boston College Law School and for 2 years was Senior Staff Associate at the National Center for State Courts. He is the author or editor of four books, including *Social Psychology in Court* and *Advances in Applied Social Psychology*.

Garold Stasser received his doctorate in social psychology from the University of Illinois. He is presently Associate Professor of Psychology at Miami University, Oxford, Ohio. His research interests include the role of normative and informational influence in decision making groups and the effects of competition and evaluation on individual performance.

Niel Vidmar is Professor of Psychology and Associate Professor of Law at the University of Western Ontario, London, Canada. He received his doctorate from the University of Illinois in 1967 and was a Russell Sage Fellow at Yale Law School in 1973–1974. He has published articles on various legal topics in social science journals and in law reviews. He has served as a legal consultant, lecturer, and expert witness in the United States and Canada. His current research projects include the study of attitudes toward punishment and social psychological dynamics in the civil dispute process.

John Winkler received his doctorate in social psychology from Harvard University. He is currently Associate Social Scientist at the Rand Corporation, Santa Monica, California. His interests include social perception and judgment, and the application of social science research to policy problems.

Lawrence S. Wrightsman is Professor and Chairman, Department of Psychology, University of Kansas. He received his doctorate in 1959 from the University of Minnesota. In addition to teaching there, he has also been on the faculty of Hamline University, The University of Hawaii, and George Peabody College for Teachers. In 1978 he served as president of the Society for the Psychological Study of Social Issues (SPSSI); his presidential address dealt with the psychological and legal assumptions behind jury behavior. He directs the Jury Research Project at the University of Kansas.

REFERENCES

Abelson, R. P. Script processing in attitude formation and decision making. In J. S. Carroll & J. W. Payne (Eds.), *Cognition and social behavior*. Hillsdale, New Jersey: Erlbaum, 1976.

Anderson, N. H. Cognitive algebra: Integration theory applied to social attribution. In L. Berkowitz (Ed.), *Advances in experimental social psychology* (Vol. 7). New York: Academic Press, 1974.

Ballew v. Georgia. United States Reports, 1978, 435, 223–246.

Bray, R. M., & Kerr, N. L. Use of the simulation method in the study of jury behavior: Some methodological considerations. *Law and Human Behavior*, 1979, 3, 107–119.

Broeder, D. The University of Chicago jury project. *Nebraska Law Review*, 1958, 38, 744–761.

Burtt, M. E. *Legal psychology*. Englewood Cliffs, New Jersey: Prentice-Hall, 1931.

Johnson v. Louisiana. United States Reports, 1972, 406, 356–403.

Kalven, H., & Zeisel, H. *The American jury*. Boston, Massachusetts: Little, Brown, 1966.

McCrystal, J. The promise of prerecorded videotape trials. *American Bar Association Journal*. 1977, 63, 977–979.

Marston, W. M. Studies in testimony. *Journal of Criminal Law and Criminology*, 1924, 15, 5–31.

Münsterberg, H. *On the witness stand: Essays on psychology and crime*. New York: Clark, Boardman, 1908.

Simon, R. J. *The jury and the defense of insanity*. Boston, Massachusetts: Little, Brown, 1967.

Tapp, J. L. Psychology and the law: The dilemma. *Psychology Today*, 1969, 2, 16–22.

Tapp, J. L. Reflections. *Journal of Social Issues*, 1971, *27*, 1–16.

Tapp, J. L. Psychology and the law: An overture. In M. R. Rosenzweig & L. W. Porter (Eds.), *Annual review of psychology* (Vol. 27), Palo Alto, California: Annual Reviews, 1976.

Tapp, J. L. Psychological and policy perspectives on the law: Reflections on a decade. *Journal of Social Issues*, 1980, *36*, 165–191.

Wigmore, H. H. Professor Münsterberg and the psychology of evidence. *Illinois Law Review*, 1909, *3*, 399–445.

Williams v. Florida. United States Reports 1970, *399*, 78–145.

COURTROOM PROCEDURES
AND KEY ACTORS

chapter 2

The Psychology of Courtroom Procedure[1]

E. Allan Lind

> *No person shall be . . . deprived of life, liberty, or property, without due process of law.*

> —Amendment V, United States Constitution

[1]. The opinions expressed in this chapter are those of the author; they do not necessarily represent the position of any institution.

13

THE PSYCHOLOGY
OF THE COURTROOM

Virtually all courts, and certainly those of the United States and other Western countries, are governed by quite complex and strict rules of procedure. The due process specifications of the United States Constitution, of which the Fifth Amendment clause quoted is but one example, raise to the status of a fundamental right the requirement that accepted rules of procedure be used. It is well beyond the scope of this chapter to attempt a complete discussion of the procedural rules now in use; that is an endeavor that has filled law texts and casebooks. Rather, an attempt will be made to discuss three aspects of trial procedure that have received considerable attention from psychological researchers: the overall procedural model, the order in which evidence is presented, and the techniques used to communicate the law to a lay jury.

It is important to keep in mind, though, that the psychological investigation of procedure has just begun. Like much of the law, the law of procedure is based to a large extent on untested assumptions about how people behave. Most of these assumptions are open to empirical testing; such testing is essential for the scientific improvement of legal institutions. Legal procedure is the methodology of the law, and it is by understanding and improving this methodology that we can best hope to make our justice system more reliable and fair.

PROCEDURAL MODELS

If one observes the trial of a civil or a criminal case in a United States court, it is evident that the procedures employed are based on open and active contention between the two sides of the case. Both sides are generally represented by attorneys who are experts in argument and persuasion and are obviously attempting to convince the judge or jury to render a verdict favorable to their client. The choice of what evidence is to be presented is left, within limits, to the discretion of the disputing parties and their attorneys. The judge and jury listen more or less passively to the testimony and arguments; the judge may occasionally ask a question of a witness, but for the most part this is done by the partisan attorneys.

Contrast this general approach to hearing and deciding a case to that used in a French court. In a French trial, the questioning of witnesses is conducted almost exclusively by the presiding judge. The judge interrogates the disputing parties and witnesses, referring frequently to a dossier that has been prepared by a court official who investigated the case. Although the parties probably have partisan attorneys present at the trial, it is evident that control over the presentation of evidence and arguments is firmly in the hands of the judge.

These differences in trial procedures arise from the different procedural models used in the two nations. Most trial courts in the United States and in other countries that have based their legal systems on English law follow what is termed the *adversary model* of procedure. This model calls for certain roles for and relationships between the individuals who are involved in the trial. It specifies, for example, that the investigation and presentation of evidence is properly done by the parties to the dispute and their attorneys, and it encourages argument between the representatives of the parties over the meaning and accuracy of the evidence presented to the court. In contrast, in the *nonadversary model* followed in most French trial courts there is an investigation of the dispute by an impartial representative of the court, which considerably lessens the parties' control over what evidence is presented at trial and over the interpretation of its meaning. The use of one model or another has vital implications for legal procedure with regard both to how the trial is conducted and how the case is researched and developed before it reaches trial.

As might be expected, each model of justice is supported by arguments and hypotheses about its consequences. Supporters of the Anglo–American adversary model contend that it leads to less biased decisions, to a more thorough investigation of the case, and to decisions that are more likely to be seen as fair by the disputing parties than does the nonadversary model, which they often refer to as an *inquisitorial* approach to justice. Supporters of the nonadversary model argue that the adversary model promotes competitive forces that can distort the truth about the dispute, and that these competitive forces decrease the likelihood of cooperative resolutions of the dispute. Only in recent years have empirical methods been applied to the investigation of the validity of these opposing arguments.

Perceptions of Procedural Justice

Much of the research on the consequences of using one procedural model or another has focused on the effects of procedural models on disputants' perceptions that the procedure is fair (Thibaut & Walker, 1975). In the first such study, Walker, LaTour, Lind, and Thibaut (1974) sought to test the claim advanced by supporters of the adversary model that it results in procedures that are seen as more fair than nonadversary procedures. In this experiment, male undergraduates were told that they would be participating in a simulation of a business competition. One of the options in the simulation allowed the subject's assistant, actually an accomplice of the experimenters, to engage in industrial espionage against an opposing company. The espionage option could backfire, however: if the opposing company suspected that it had been spied upon, it could demand a trial and, if the charge was supported, could have the subject's company disqualified. In all conditions of the experiment, the subject's company was charged with espionage. In some sessions, the subject received private information that led him to believe that his assistant had in fact spied; in other sessions the subject received information that led him to believe that his assistant had not spied; in still other sessions he received no information about the guilt or innocence of his assistant. Trials were held, structured according to either the adversary or the nonadversary model. In adversary trials, the subject's side of the case was presented by an attorney whom he had chosen and whose payment depended on the successful outcome of the case, the other company was similarly represented by an attorney whose payment depended on its winning the case. In nonadversary trials, the same evidence was presented by a single attorney who worked for the judge and who was to receive the same payment regardless of which side won. These manipulations of the subject's beliefs about his company's guilt and of the procedural model used in the trial were crossed with a third manipulation: in half the cases the subject was told that he had lost the case and in half he was told that he had won.

The results of the this experiment were quite straightforward. The subjects believed that the adversary procedure was more fair and they were more satisfied with the verdict from an adversary trial. This positive reaction to the adversary procedure was not affected by whether the subjects succeeded in the trial or by their pretrial belief concerning their company's true guilt or innocence. Of course, the subjects were much more satisfied with an innocent verdict than with a guilty verdict, but the procedure used had an effect in addition to this verdict effect, reducing dissatisfaction with a guilty verdict and increasing satisfaction with an innocent verdict. The researchers also found that impartial observers (other undergraduates who simply watched the trial without having a personal interest in the outcome) believed that an adversary trial was more fair to the defendant than was a nonadversary trial. Later research showed that each of three procedural factors that distinguish adversary from nonadversary procedures—the presence of two attorneys, the alignment of an attorney with one of the disputing parties, and the provision that the parties can choose their attorneys—contributed to disputants' favorable reactions to the procedure (LaTour, 1978), and that there was a preference for adversary procedures whether the disputant had a strong case, a weak case, or did not know whether the case was strong or weak (Thibaut, Walker, LaTour, & Houlden, 1974). On the basis of these and other studies, Thibaut and Walker (1975) concluded that procedures that afford the disputants control over the presentation of evidence and arguments are seen as high in procedural fairness and engender greater satisfaction with the verdict.

Walker et al. (1974) found that adversary procedures produced more satisfaction and perceived procedural fairness than did nonadversary procedures regardless of the verdict the disputant received. Two other studies have raised some doubt about this overall effect, however. LaTour (1978) reports that the positive effects of adversariness appeared to be stronger when the verdict was unfavorable to the disputant than when the verdict was favorable. In contrast, Austin, Williams, Worchel, Wentzel, and Siegel (1979), report a roleplaying study that showed adversary presentation increased satisfaction when the verdict was more favorable to the disputant but decreased satisfaction when the verdict was less favorable.

In order to resolve the issue of whether the adversary procedure enhances perceived procedural fairness and satisfaction under both positive and negative verdicts, Lind, Kurtz, Musante, Walker, and Thibaut (1980) replicated the Walker et al. study with some additional measurement devices and conditions. The Lind et al. (1980) study assessed perceptions of the procedure before or after the verdict was announced and used multiple scale indices of satisfaction with the verdict and perceived procedural justice. The results were congruent with those of the original Walker *et al.* study: the adversary procedure resulted in more satisfaction and greater perceived fairness than did the nonadversary procedure both when the verdict was favorable and when it was unfavorable. Further, Lind *et al.* (1980) found no evidence that subjects revised their perceptions of the structural aspects of the procedure when they learned the verdict. Thus, this study supports the indication from the Walker *et al.* experiment that the effect of adversariness on disputant perceptions is not limited by the verdict resulting from the adjudication; the reason for the contrary findings of LaTour (1978) and Austin *et al.* (1979) remains unclear.

The Thibaut and Walker group examined the possibility that the positive reactions to adversary procedures might have resulted from the use of American college students as subjects in the studies cited above. Americans may react more positively to adversary than to nonadversary procedures simply because such procedures are used routinely in American courts and are therefore more familiar. Thibaut, Walker, and their colleagues carried out two experiments comparing the responses of American subjects to those of European subjects, whose courts use nonadversary models. If the results of the Walker *et al.* (1974) study were due to some intrinsic characteristic of the adversary model, one would expect to observe a preference for adversary procedures in the European as well as in the American sample. On the other hand, if the results were simply showing that people prefer whatever procedural model is most commonly used in the courts of their nation, one would expect to observe a preference for adversary procedures in the American sample and a preference for nonadversary procedures in the European sample.

LaTour, Houlden, Walker, and Thibaut (1976) examined the preferences and perceptions of American and West German students concerning a number of conflict resolution procedures. Some cross-national differences were found in preferences for procedures, but when a procedure called for a binding third-party decision (as is the case in courtroom procedures) subjects from both nations preferred adversary to nonadversary models. Lind, Erickson, Friedland, and Dickenberger (1978) focused on adjudication procedures (procedures that require a binding verdict from a decision maker) and assessed the preferences of students and young professionals in the United States, England, France, and West Germany. The results of this investigation are of particular interest here because of the focus on courtlike dispute resolution procedures.

In the Lind *et al.* (1978) study, the respondents were given "barebones" descriptions of four procedural models that vary along a continuum of increasing adversariness: (*a*) an *inquisitorial* model that specified that a decision maker would question the parties to the dispute and reach a verdict, (*b*) a *single investigator* model that included one nonpartisan professional who would investigate the dispute and report to the decision maker, (*c*) a *double investigator* model that assigned a different nonpartisan professional to investigate and

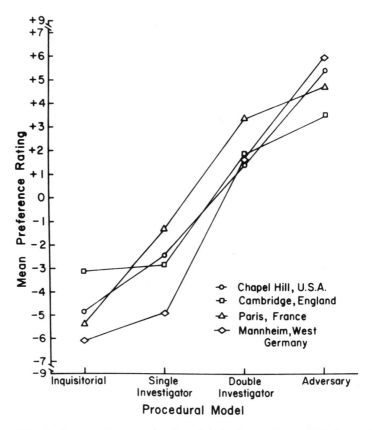

Figure 2.1. Preferences for procedural models in four nations. [This figure drawn from "Reactions to Procedural Models for Adjudicative Conflict Resolution: A Cross National Study" by E. Allan Lind *et al.*, is reprinted from *Journal of Conflict Resolution*, Vol. 22, No. 2 (June 1978).]

present each side of the case, and (*d*) an *adversary* model that specified that each side of the case would be investigated and presented by a partisan, adversary representative of the party. The respondents were asked to rate their preference for using each of the models if they were themselves involved in a lawsuit. Figure 2.1 shows the average preferences observed at each of the four sites of the study. It is apparent from Figure 2.1 that the subjects in all four countries showed a marked preference for more adversary procedures over less adversary procedures. Similar results were obtained on ratings of the fairness of the procedural models. Because these preferences were demonstrated by the subjects from the countries with nonadversary legal systems (France and West Germany) as well as by those from countries with adversary legal systems (the United States and England), there is little support for the idea that the original results of the Thibaut and Walker project (1975) were due to a cultural bias on the part of American subjects in favor of adversariness in legal procedures. A further demonstration of the pervasiveness of the preference for adversary procedures is found in a study by Kurtz (1978). She found that inmates in a United States Army prison also preferred more adversary procedures to less adversary procedures.

Walker, Lind, and Thibaut (1979) examined the relationship between the perceived fairness of a legal *procedure* and the perceived fairness of the *outcome* produced by that procedure. Walker *et al.* identified three common roles in the legal system: the role of participating disputants, who are personally involved in the trial process and are affected by the outcome of the trial; the role of nonparticipating disputants, who are not personally involved in the trial process but are nonetheless affected by the outcome of the trial; and the role of observers, who do not participate personally in the trial process and are not affected by the outcome of the trial. These three roles correspond respectively to the situations confronting litigants in simple criminal and civil trials, members of a class in class action litigation, and the general public watching a trial. Walker *et al.* placed subjects in one of these three roles, and exposed them to either an adversary or a nonadversary trial and to either a favorable or an unfavorable verdict. Subjects in all three roles were asked to rate the fairness of and their satisfaction with the procedure and the verdict. The results showed that subjects in all three roles perceived the adversary procedure to be fairer than the nonadversary procedure, but only the participating disputants perceived the adversary verdict to be fairer than the nonadversary verdict. This experiment indicates that the knowledge that an adversary procedure is used is sufficient to heighten the feeling that procedural justice has been done, but that personal involvement is necessary for this perception of procedural justice to increase the perceived fairness of the verdict.

In general, the research on the subjective consequences of procedural models has produced results very favorable to the adversary model. The bulk of the research on perceptions of procedural models has supported the proposition that parties to a dispute prefer adversary procedures, view adversary procedures as more fair, and experience greater satisfaction with the outcome of adversary trials; only a very few studies have failed to support this general effect.

Other Effects of Procedural Models

The research described above shows that parties to a dispute prefer adversary procedures and think that such procedures are more fair than nonadversary procedures, but questions remain about the effects of adversary procedures on other major roles in the courtroom. How does adversariness affect the behavior of judges, juries, attorneys, and witnesses? Does adversariness promote or limit bias in the decisions of those who must render a verdict? Does the adversary model lead to a more thorough investigation of the case, as its supporters claim? Do witnesses report their observations as accurately after exposure to adversary attorneys as they do after exposure to nonadversary attorneys? These questions have been addressed in several studies.

Thibaut, Walker, and Lind (1972) tested the claim, advanced by supporters of the adversary procedural model (Fuller, 1961), that an adversary trial reduces a natural human bias to judge a new case in terms of expectancies from past cases. It is an uncontested principle of law that each case should be judged on its own merits, and it would be desirable to use procedures that promote such individual judgment, if indeed any procedures could be shown to decrease this expectancy bias. Thibaut *et al.* exposed one-half of their subjects to an experimental manipulation that had been found to create an expectancy bias. These subjects judged a series of assault cases before judging the lawfulness of a defendant's actions in an additional, similar case. The "experience" cases were constructed so that most of them clearly indicated that the correct judgment was that the defendant had acted unlawfully. The remaining subjects rendered judgments on the final case, but they were not exposed to the biasing experience. In the final case the subjects either received the evidence in a nonadversary format, with a single attorney presenting the evidence for both sides, or they received the evidence in an adversary format, with each side presented by a different attorney. Of course, the evidence was the same regardless of which format was used.

The results were in line with the claimed advantage of the adversary model: Subjects who had been exposed to the biasing experience were less likely to render biased judgments when the presentation was adversary than when the presentation was nonadversary. A later replication of the experiment in France (Lind, Thibaut, & Walker, 1976) produced the same results, ruling out the possibility that the original finding was caused by the American subjects' familiarity with adversary trials. It appears that the presentation of evidence by attorneys aligned with the various parties in a case helps combat expectancy biases.

Kaplan and Miller (1978) reported two studies that they interpreted as showing that adversary procedures may increase, rather than decrease, the likelihood that decision makers will judge a case in terms of preexisting biases. In their studies, the subjects, who had been asked to act as jurors, had been found to hold either harsh or lenient attitudes toward the punishment of criminals. The subjects were given summaries of cases and required to make judgments of guilt and recommendations of punishment for the defendants. The cases varied in terms of the apparent reliability of the evidence. In one experiment, some subjects were told that the evidence was from a highly reliable source, while others were told that the evidence was from an unreliable source and had been challenged by opposing attorneys. In the other experiment, the subjects were given cases with mixed evidence (some favoring one side and some favoring the other) and were told either that they should discount some of the evidence or that they should weigh all evidence equally. The results of the first experiment showed that the subjects gave responses more in line with their preexperimental attitudes when the evidence was described as unreliable; the results of the second experiment showed that subjects whose attitude was lenient but not those whose attitude was harsh, demonstrated their bias more when they were instructed to discount some of the evidence than when they were instructed to weigh all the evidence equally.

Kaplan and Miller did not manipulate presentation of the case in an adversary or nonadversary fashion. They argue, however, that the contentiousness that characterizes adversary trials leads to an appearance of unreliability in the evidence and that this, according to their findings, should in turn lead to judgments more in line with preexisting biases. These conclusions are, of course, contrary to those that one would draw from the Thibaut *et al.* (1972) study. There are many differences between that study and the Kaplan and Miller study: the former manipulated the use of adversary or nonadversary presentation, while the latter based a conclusion about adversary presentation on the untested assumption that it would produce an appearance of unreliability in the evidence; the former used experimentally induced biases, while the latter used preexisting differences between subjects; and the former asked the subjects to assume that all the evidence was reliable, while the latter manipulated the reliability of the evidence. In the face of such differences, the claimed advantage of the adversary model must be subjected to further testing. Until additional experiments can be conducted it seems best to conclude tentatively that some features of the adversary model induce decision makers to overcome expectancy bias, but that other features of the model may result in the expression of attitudinal bias.

There is some evidence that use of an adversary model of justice produces another sort of bias. Critics of the adversary model often contend that adversariness is not a particularly good method of seeking out facts needed to find the truth in a case, because adversary attorneys have no interest in finding and presenting facts that might be damaging to their clients. Proponents of the adversary model answer by arguing that the self-interest of adversary attorneys, who often receive higher fees if their clients win cases, will lead to a more thorough investigation of the case than would occur if the case were investigated by a nonadversary investigator. Lind, Thibaut, and Walker (1973; see also Lind, 1975) had law students participate in a legal game that required them to invest resources in the investigation of a case and decide which of the facts they found should be presented to the judge who would decide the case. The law students were placed in either an adversary role, in which they were told they were working for one of the disputing parties, or a nonadversary role, in which they were told they were working for the judge. The experiment also manipulated the nature of the case on which the subjects were to work. Some subjects were given a balanced case, with half the facts favoring each side of the dispute, while others were given an unbalanced case, in which 75% of the facts favored one side and 25% of the facts favored the other side. The major dependent variables were the number of facts found by the subjects, the number of facts presented to the judge, and the extent to which the facts presented to the judge reflected accurately the true nature of the case.

The results of the study showed that the adversary role attorneys conducted more complete investigations of the case only when the case was unbalanced in such a way as to be unfavorable to their clients. When the case was balanced or when it favored the attorney's client, there was no difference between the number of facts discovered by adversary and nonadversary attorneys. As a result of this extra effort in investigation by adversary attorneys with clients who were disadvantaged by the evidence, a particular type of bias appeared in the facts reaching the judge. Although the facts presented by pairs of adversary attorneys reflected the true nature of the case when the case was balanced, the facts were biased in favor of the party disadvantaged by the evidence when the case was unbalanced. That is, the adversary model produced a consistent effect that made unbalanced cases look more balanced than they in fact were. In contrast, the facts presented by pairs of nonadversary attorneys reflected the true nature of the case whether the evidence in case was balanced or unbalanced.

Another form of bias, also related to the effect of adversariness on the information reaching the judge or jury, has been demonstrated by Sheppard and Vidmar (1980). In two experiments, undergraduates saw a slide presentation of an incident that may have involved unlawful assault, and were then interviewed by other undergraduates who had been assigned the roles of adversary or nonadversary attorneys. The witnesses were later given a chance to tell what they had seen. It was found that, at least in some situations, their testimony was more biased when they had been interviewed by an adversary attorney than by a nonadversary attorney.

In general, the research on the effects of procedural models on the development and transmission of evidence and on the verdicts of decision makers has shown that, relative to nonadversary procedures, adversary procedures reduce some types of bias and enhance other types of bias. The Thibaut *et al.* (1972) and Lind *et al.* (1976) studies show that adversary presentation can counteract some types of judgmental bias, but the Kaplan and Miller (1978) study raises questions about how extensive this effect is. The Lind *et al.* (1973) study and the Sheppard and Vidmar (1980) study show definite information biases in the development of evidence by adversary attorneys. These findings, when considered together with the research on perceived procedural justice, suggest that some additional theoretical work is needed to arrive at a general understanding of the strengths and weaknesses of various procedural models. It is to such theoretical development that we now turn.

Theoretical Development

Some of the research described above has been criticized on the grounds that it has not closely simulated actual courtroom settings, materials, and populations (e.g., Damaska, 1973, 1975; Hayden & Anderson, 1979; Sheppard & Vidmar, 1980), but when it is understood that most of the studies were intended to test existing theories of legal procedure, it is clear that the body of research on procedural justice has contributed much by showing that some of the conventional beliefs about adversariness are accurate and others inaccurate (Lind & Walker, 1979). The appropriate scientific response to such a state of affairs is the development of new theory that accounts for the existing data and that yields new predictions that are amenable to further research testing (cf. Bray & Kerr, 1979; Henshel, 1980; Kruglanski & Kroy, 1976). Thibaut and Walker (1978) undertook the creation of a revised theory of procedural models.

Their theory of procedure had to account for two general findings from the early research on adversariness. First, it had to explain the pervasive tendency of disputants and observers to see adversary procedures as more fair than nonadversary procedures. Second, it had to recognize that adversariness can introduce bias into the gathering and presentation of evidence, and that adversary procedures are thus limited in their capacity to aid in the determination of the true facts of a case. Their theory begins by pointing out that interpersonal disputes can be classified into two general categories on the basis of the major disputed issue: disputes that concern which of a number of views about the state of the world is accurate (termed *truth conflicts*), and disputes that concern the distribution of goods and costs (termed *conflicts of interest*). An example of a truth conflict would be a scientific dispute about the accuracy of a formula relating levels of radiation to the frequency of cancer; an example of a conflict of interest would be a dispute about the distribution of goods in an estate. Although most disputes have elements of both truth conflict and conflict of interest, usually one element predominates. Thibaut and Walker (1978) contend that in most legal disputes the major element is the conflict of interest between the disputants. In criminal cases the dispute is essentially an argument between the state and the accused over what degree of freedom the accused should enjoy after the trial; in civil cases the dispute is at heart an argument between the disputing parties about the distribution of goods.

Thibaut and Walker argue that the overall goal in the resolution of truth conflicts is the attainment of an accurate representation of the nature of the world, and that this goal is best served by employing nonadversary procedures to resolve such conflicts. As previously noted, nonadversary procedures are less likely than adversary procedures to introduce bias in the information-gathering and information-presenting stages of the conflict resolution. Because bias is harmful to the major goal of truth conflict resolutions, and because the major advantages of adversary procedures lie in their promotion of the goal of fairness, adversary procedures are not particularly appropriate for trying truth conflicts.

In contrast, the overall goal in the resolution of conflicts of interest is the attainment of a fair distribution of the disputed goods. In conflicts of interest the proper resolution of the dispute depends not so much on knowledge of the accuracy of some general statement as on a division of outcomes along the lines dictated by equity norms. Social psychological studies of equity have shown that such norms usually specify that the outcome of the participants in a social relationship be proportional to their contributions to the relationship (cf.

Adams, 1965; Homans, 1961). A division of outcomes in an equitable fashion requires that the decision maker—the judge or jury—have information on the contributions of each party to the relationship in which the dispute arose. This information on contributions is best accumulated and considered, according to Thibaut and Walker, if the disputants exercise substantial control over the gathering and presentation of evidence, as they do when the procedure is adversary. Further, the disputants will *perceive* the procedure to be most fair when it is adversary, because they will see the adversary procedure as promoting the consideration of evidence relevant to equity, a goal that disputants in conflicts of interest are assumed to value.

The Thibaut and Walker theory has received some experimental confirmation. Houlden, LaTour, Walker, and Thibaut (1978) found that disputants facing an adjudication said they would prefer that the adjudication procedure contain provision for high disputant control over the trial process, a provision that they believed favored the presentation of equity relevant, as opposed to legalistic, evidence. Furthermore, this preference for disputant control existed even when the disputant's own case was based on legalistic arguments. Some recent research (Musante, 1979; Rusbult, Musante, & Solomon, 1978) has suggested, however, that the use of only equity relevant presentation can have some shortcomings. It appears that equity-oriented presentations enhance the satisfaction disputants feel with positive outcomes, but that such presentations lead to decreased satisfaction with negative outcomes as compared to what occurs with legalistic presentations. Such a finding, if supported by additional research, would call for a qualification or elaboration of some of the general statements advanced by Thibaut and Walker (1978) and would require additional theorizing on the factors involved in disputant satisfaction.

The development of theory on the psychology of procedural justice is of major importance for our understanding of this area, because it permits the standard scientific cycle of theory testing and theory revision to progress. More testing of the Thibaut and Walker theory is needed, of course, but the theory has already suggested new applications of the research findings on procedural justice (see the later discussion on science courts). Our knowledge of procedural justice is expanding rapidly.

ORDER OF PRESENTATION OF EVIDENCE

Cound, Friedenthal, and Miller (1974, p. 784), in a law text on civil procedure, note that the courts have discretion to order the trial as they wish, but they usually use the following order in civil cases:

1. Plaintiff's opening statement
2. Defendant's opening statement
3. Plaintiff's presentation of direct evidence

4. Defendant's presentation of direct evidence
5. Plaintiff's presentation of rebuttal evidence
6. Defendant's presentation of rebuttal evidence
7. Opening final argument by plaintiff
8. Defendant's final argument
9. Closing final argument by plaintiff
10. Giving instructions to the jury

A similar order of presentation is used in criminal cases, with the prosecution preceding the defense in most instances. Psychologists have long been interested in the effects of order of presentation on attitudes and perceptions, and it is not surprising that the effect of the trial order has received some attention from psychologists interested in legal procedure.

Basic social psychological research on order effects is relevant to the question of what effects variation in order of presentation might have in trials. In fact, one of the most commonly used sets of stimulus materials in basic research on order effects is grounded on legal materials because they generate high subject involvement and allow the researcher to create new attitudes in the laboratory (cf. Insko, 1964; Miller & Campbell, 1959.) The general approach to the study of order effects in attitude formation has been to present subjects with evidence and arguments favoring one side of an issue, then the other, and to assess the subjects' attitudes, either immediately or after some period of time has elapsed.

Most of the attitude studies have shown that, when attitudes are assessed immediately after presentation of the second set of arguments and evidence, the attitudes show what is termed a *recency effect:* the second set of materials has more influence on subjects' final attitudes than does the first set. This recency effect tends to increase in strength if there is some delay between the presentation of the first set and the presentation of the second set, and to decrease in strength if there is some delay between the presentation of the second set and the assessment of the subjects' attitudes (Insko, 1964; Insko, Lind, & LaTour, 1976, Miller & Campbell, 1959). To the extent that these findings are applicable to the attitudes that jurors and judges form about a case, they suggest that there should be a substantial advantage for the party presenting arguments last. This advantage should increase if there is a delay between the two presentations and decrease if there is a delay between the presentation of the last argument and the final judgment in the case.

There is another set of basic research studies on order effects that is relevant to courtroom judgments, however, and these studies may limit the previously mentioned conclusions. Specifically, a number of experiments have shown that when people are asked to process information about other people, rather than information relevant to general attitudes, a *primacy effect,* favoring the earlier information, often occurs (Anderson & Jacobson, 1965; Jones, Rock, Shaver, Goethals, & Ward, 1968). From this research it would be expected that in trials in which a substantial issue involves perceptions of a particular person (for example, where the character of the defendant or the credibility of a particular witness becomes a central issue) the recency effect predicted by the attitude literature will be lessened or reversed.

There have been a number of studies designed specifically to test order effects in legal decision making. In one of the very early studies of the psychology of the courtroom, Weld and Roff (1938) had jurors in a law school moot court trial indicate their beliefs about the case at intervals during the trial. When the effects of hard evidence were excluded, they found that the jurors' attitudes tracked the direction of the evidence, moving toward guilt or innocence depending on the last evidence they had heard. A similar recency effect was found in the Thibaut, Walker, and Lind (1972) study on adversariness and bias, which manipulated whether the prosecution or the defense evidence was presented first. Thibaut *et al.* found that their subjects' beliefs about the lawfulness of the defendant's actions tracked the evidence, moving progressively in the "unlawful" direction during the presentation of the prosecution evidence and in the "lawful" direction during the presentation of the defense evidence. The subjects' final judgments showed a recency effect.

Walker, Thibaut, and Andreoli (1972) varied not only the overall order of evidence presentation (prosecution followed by defense or defense followed by prosecution), but also the order of strong and weak evidence for each side of the case (strong followed by weak or weak followed by strong). They found a recency effect both for the overall ordering and, with one exception, for the internal ordering (so that weak followed by strong was usually more effective than strong followed by weak). Walker *et al.* also compared the results of each condition in their study to an external standard of the final opinions that would be expected if all evidence were considered equally, and concluded that the overall ordering now used in courts (prosecution followed by defense) and the use of the most effective internal ordering by each side produces a trial with the fewest undesirable order effects.

However, there are some other studies and commentaries that must be considered before it is concluded that recency effects are pervasive in courtroom decision making. Some experiments have not shown a recency effect (Stone, 1969; Weld & Danzig, 1940), and at least one study has supported an information integration theory that would predict primacy effects in some cases (Kaplan & Kemmerick, 1974). Davis, Bray, and Holt (1977) have noted that all of the recency effect studies described above have had subjects make repeated judgments over the course of the trial, and they argue that this procedure, which does not occur in real trials, may itself have produced the recency effects. However, Kassin and Wrightsman (1979) found no significant differences in a mock-trial test of repeated versus final-only measurement.

In general, then, the research has often shown recency effects for the order of presentation of evidence, but there have been exceptions. Perhaps the best explanation is that mentioned earlier in the discussion of basic research on order effects: recency effects can be expected when the decision maker is focusing on general issues, but not when personal characteristics become important to the verdict.

JURY INSTRUCTIONS

In civil and criminal jury trials in the United States, the closing phase of the trial involves the judge's delivery of instructions to the jury. The judge, as the courtroom authority on the rules of law in the case, must inform the jury, the final decision maker in matters concerning the facts in the case, on the law relevant to its decision. In criminal trials, the jury's instructions include a description of the elements that must be proved if the defendant is to be found guilty; in civil trials the instructions include a description of the legal issues involved in the dispute. For example, the jury in a murder trial would be told the legal definitions of various types of homicide and the findings of fact that imply each type of homicide. The jury in a civil tort case might be told the legal definitions relevant to the finding of negligence. In both civil and criminal trials the instructions also include a general commentary on how the jury is to regard the evidence (e.g., what issues are and are not to be considered in deciding whether a witness is credible) and instructions on how convinced the jury must be in order to reach a verdict (e.g., the "beyond a reasonable doubt" criterion required to convict in criminal cases).

The specific instructions given to the jury are usually left to the discretion of trial judges, although they may consult with the attorneys in the case. During the last several decades there has been a movement to the use of "pattern" or standardized instructions, which are written by judicial or bar groups to cover the most common trial situations and issues in a particular jurisdiction. Many of the states and some federal courts now have sets of pattern instructions.

Psychologists have conducted a number of studies on the comprehensibility of jury instructions and on the obedience of juries to their instructions. For the most part these studies have focused on pattern instructions. This research has pointed to some substantial problems in making the instructions clear to the jury and in inducing the jury to follow the instructions.

Comprehensibility of Jury Instructions

Because the instructions given the jury may form the basis for an appeal of the verdict, trial judges often use instructions that conform to previous appellate court decisions. The most reliable way to assure that instructions will be acceptable to the appellate courts is to use language that follows closely that used in previous appellate decisions. This practice has the unfortunate effect of producing jury instructions that use terms and grammatical constructions that are quite unusual in everyday speech, and that are likely to be quite confusing to the typical lay juror. The following example of a common civil pattern instruction illustrates the "legalese" that often occurs in jury instructions:

> One test that is helpful in determining whether or not a person is negligent is to ask and answer whether or not, if a person of ordinary prudence had been in the same situation and possessed of the same knowledge, he would have foreseen or anticipated that someone might have been injured by or as a result of his action or inaction. If such a result for certain conduct would be foreseeable by a person of ordinary prudence with like knowledge and in like situation, and if the conduct reasonably could have been avoided, then not to avoid it would be negligence [California Jury Instructions—Civil—Book of Approved Jury Instructions, #3.11, 1969.]

Several researchers, including Charrow and Charrow (1979) and Sales, Elwork, and Alfini (1977), have pointed out that commonly used jury instructions contain many elements that psycholinguists have identified as difficult to process and understand. Among these potentially troublesome elements are the use of uncommon and archaic words and constructions, difficult sentence structure, and multiple negations within a single sentence, to name only a few. Much of the research on jury instructions has sought to determine whether these elements prevent jurors from understanding their instructions and, if so, whether it is possible to recast the instructions in language that is easier to understand.

Charrow and Charrow asked individuals who had been called for jury duty to listen to a set of pattern jury instructions and to paraphrase each instruction. They found that, on the average, about 45% of the important elements of the instructions were not understood. The results showed that some linguistic elements were particularly likely to cause problems in comprehension: nominalizations (the use of nouns constructed from verbs), misplaced phrases, relative pronoun and complement deletions, problematic lexical items, lists of more or less synonymous words, and the use of passive voice in subordinate clauses. Two elements were found to be especially well understood: the use of the passive voice in main clauses and the use of modal verbs (e.g., *must, should*).

Sales, Elwork, and Alfini (1977; Elwork, Sales, & Alfini, 1977) investigated potential improvements in the comprehensibility of jury instructions. Basing their analyses of current instructions on psycholinguistic research and theory and on recommendations from style guides, these investigators identified features that might make the instructions difficult to understand. They then rewrote the instructions to remove the potentially troublesome features. Subjects in their study, drawn from the community at large, saw a videotaped reenactment of a trial. The subjects were given either the rewritten instructions or the conventional instructions, or they were given no instructions at all. When the subjects were tested on their memory and understanding of the material contained in the instructions, it was found that those who had received the conventional instructions did no better than did those who had received no instructions. In contrast, the subjects who had received the rewritten instructions showed significantly better memory and understanding. The rewritten instructions also appeared to result in a better congruence between the subjects' attitudes about the case and their final verdicts than did the conventional instructions.

Charrow and Charrow (1979) also found that rewriting jury instructions to remove potentially difficult linguistic features resulted in substantially better understanding. When the pattern instructions used in the paraphrase study described above were rewritten to remove the elements that had been found to be difficult to understand, the instructions were rendered significantly more comprehensible. Another benefit of instructions written for clarity has been found in studies by Strawn, Buchanan, Pryor, and Taylor (Strawn, personal communication, 1979). Jurors were shown a videotaped trial and their deliberations were taped. It was found that juries that had received standard instructions spent most of their time in deliberation talking about their own personal experiences and knowledge, while juries that had received instructions rewritten and restructured for improved clarity spent most of their time discussing the case and the law.

In general, then, the research on the comprehensibility of jury instructions shows that the types of instructions now in use in many jurisdictions are very difficult to understand, and that it is possible to improve the instructions considerably by removing features that are likely to detract from understanding. Whether the research findings will stimulate improvement in jury instructions remains in question, though. The research has yet to deal with the cause of the comprehensibility problem—the trial judges' belief that instructions rewritten for clarity will not state the law in a form acceptable to appellate courts. Additional research is needed to show that understandable instructions can be as accurate in stating the law as are conventional instructions. Such research may encourage the prior approval of appellate courts for sets of understandable pattern instructions.

Obedience to Instructions

Even if jury instructions can be rewritten to improve their comprehensibility, the question remains whether jurors will obey even understandable instructions. The research on this topic suggests that some instructions may not be followed. For example, Doob and his colleagues (Doob, 1976; Doob & Kirshenbaum, 1972; Hans & Doob, 1976) studied whether jurors will follow instructions concerning how information on a defendant's prior offenses should be used. The law of evidence permits a defendant's prior record to be introduced when the defendant testifies, but requires that such information be used only to judge the defendant's credibility, not to judge the defendant's guilt per se. The experiments cited were constructed so that the defendant did not offer any unique information about the case, thus making it impossible for a record of prior offenses to influence the verdict only by affecting the defendant's credibility. Nevertheless, jurors who knew of the prior offenses and who were instructed not to use the information to assess the defendant's guilt were more likely to believe the defendant guilty than were those who did not know of the prior offenses.

Sue, Smith, and Caldwell (1973) also found that instructions to disregard certain evidence sometimes are not obeyed. Their subjects read a summary of a robbery–murder case in which the evidence against the defendant was either strong or weak. For some of the subjects the case summary contained rather compelling information favoring the prosecution but which was said to have been ruled inadmissible; for others the same evidence was presented and was said to have been ruled admissible; for still others the controversial information was not included in the summary at all. Sue et al. found that the information in question was apparently used by subjects whether it was ruled admissible or inadmissible, but only when the case was weak. When the case against the defendant was strong, there were no differences between the three information conditions. Another study about instructions to disregard information arising in a trial is reported by O'Barr and Lind (1981), who found that the possibly prejudicial effects of a witness's speech style could not be removed by instructing jurors to consider that this characteristic is not related to credibility.

There do appear to be some circumstances in which instructions to disregard are effective. Simon (1966) exposed jurors to pretrial publicity that was either "sensational" or "conservative," and found that, although the sensational publicity produced stronger pretrial attitudes than did the conservative publicity, an instruction early in the trial to lay aside such attitudes wiped out the publicity-induced differences. However, this study has some methodological problems. Mitchell and Byrne (in a study cited in Davis et al., 1977) found that instructions to disregard some information were effective with low authoritarians, but not with high authoritarians. Sealy and Cornish (1973) found that British jurors followed instructions concerning the inadmissibility of information on prior convictions.

When the instructions under consideration are concerned with the criteria that jurors should use in reaching a judgment, rather than with their duty to disregard certain types of information, the research has found greater obedience to the instructions. Kerr, Atkin, Stasser, Meek, Holt, and Davis (1976) exposed subjects to a simulation of a rape trial and gave them one of three instructions on the beyond a reasonable doubt criterion used in criminal trials. The criterion was either defined in a stringent or lax manner, or it was left undefined but was still mentioned to the jurors. Kerr et al. found that the manner in which the criterion was defined did indeed affect the decisions of individual jurors and of deliberating juries: The stringent definition resulted in the lowest percentage of guilty verdicts, followed by the undefined mention of the criterion, followed by the lax definition. Kassin and Wrightsman (1979) manipulated the timing of instructions on the presumption of innocence, burden of proof, and the beyond a reasonable doubt criterion. The instructions were found to reduce conviction rates, relative to those of uninstructed jurors, when the instructions were delivered before the presentation of evidence, but not when the instructions were delivered after the presentation of evidence. Finally, Simon (1967) found that instructions on criteria for insanity verdicts affected juror judgments; different insanity criteria led to different verdicts.

The research on obedience to the judge's instructions shows that some instructions, especially those on criteria for judgments, are followed, while others, on the jurors' responsibility to disregard some information, are often ignored. There are some issues that require further research, however. First, the timing of instructions to disregard should be studied. It is probably unreasonable to expect anyone to retroactively discount information that may appear to be quite important to the task with which he or she is charged, but this is what is required of jurors receiving instructions to disregard. A fruitful line of inquiry is suggested by the Kassin and Wrightsman (1979) study: It may be that jurors should be warned early in the trial that they may be asked to disregard some information that arises in the trial. With respect to the instruction to use information on prior convictions only for credibility decisions, it is, as Doob (1976) points out, easy to sympathize with the disobedient jurors. It is hard to see how prior offenses are more indicative of credibility than of present guilt, although it is reasonable to argue that prior offenses are indicative of neither credibility nor guilt.

Also needed is some research on the effectiveness of what is probably the most important part of criminal jury instructions: the description of the elements of the offense. These instructions are often quite complex, especially when there are several lesser included offenses (e.g., various types of homicide) involved in the case, and there is some research that suggests that there are complex psychological issues involved in jurors' reactions to offense instructions (Vidmar, 1972; see also Kaplan, Chapter 7, this volume). Although we have made some progress in our understanding of the jury instruction process, there remain some unanswered questions.

CURRENT ISSUES IN THE PSYCHOLOGY OF PROCEDURE

It was noted at the beginning of this chapter that the psychological study of courtroom procedure has just begun. Given that, it is useful to consider the issues that are now arising in the law that might benefit from research. The remainder of this chapter is devoted to the discussion of two of these issues.

Should Juries Be Eliminated?

At first glance it appears that the institution of lay juries in civil and criminal cases is well protected by the United States Constitution. There has recently been some movement away from jury trials in the United States, however, and the experience of the jury in Great Britain, where it is now seldom employed in civil cases, is noteworthy. Trial by jury is, after all, an expensive and time-consuming enterprise, and it is not surprising that judges and legislators, pressed by crowded court calendars and budgetary concerns, might begin to ask whether juries are doing the job they are supposed to be doing.

A recent focus for the debate about the need for jury trials is the propriety of the institution for civil cases that are concerned with complex questions or that promise to have very long trials (Burger, 1980). To understand the issues involved in proposals to eliminate juries from trials of such cases, it is necessary to appreciate some recent reasoning concerning the Seventh Amendment. The amendment mandates a right to trial by jury in civil cases that involve more than $20 and that, in 1796, would have been considered cases in "law" rather than cases in "equity." The distinction between law and equity, based on the practices of the double court system that arose in England, is crucial to the debate, because it was a provision of the equity system that cases that could not be decided in the common law system were automatically cases in equity. It is therefore possible to argue that, if a case is too complex to be understood by a lay jury, it would not be possible for the case to be resolved in law, and that the case therefore would have been one in equity, to which the Seventh Amendment right to trial by jury does not apply. If this rather complicated reasoning is followed, it yields the result that a trial judge may decide that a case is too complex for trial by jury and may deny a request by one of the disputants for a jury trial. The debate is far from resolved; the Supreme Court has yet to rule on this question.

The justification for the removal of the jury, as described, poses many questions that are ripe for psychological research. What constitutes too much complexity for resolution of a dispute by a lay jury? When the issue is complex because of its technological or economic content, is a law-trained judge more qualified to decide the dispute than a lay jury? What procedural mechanisms might be employed to contribute to the clarification and presentation of the evidence if a jury is to be used? What is the effect of the length of the trial on jurors' attention and comprehension of the evidence? Such questions are closely related to the issues that psychologists have been researching for years under such rubrics as group productivity or cognitive processing.

The movement to reduce the use of juries raises another important question that has received no research attention: What is the role of the jury in perceptions of procedural justice? Psychologists have done much work on how juries function, but they have neglected the jury as an institution that is supposed to contribute to the acceptability of the final outcome of the dispute. We have devoted a great deal of effort to studying the effects of other factors or trial participants on the jury, but have not yet considered the effects of the jury on other aspects of the legal system.

Alternatives to Trial

Jury trials are certainly expensive and time-consuming, but even a bench trial, with the judge serving as the decision maker with respect to both the law and the facts, can consume substantial resources. The legal community continues to devote much attention to alternatives to trial. Among these alternatives are negotiation, including plea bargaining in criminal cases, and arbitration.

Plea bargaining is a common practice, and is seen by many as essential to the criminal justice system. If it were necessary to dispose of cases only by un-negotiated guilty pleas or by trial, the cost and delay involved would become much greater. The plea bargaining process has been studied by other social scientists, but has not received much attention from psychologists. A notable exception is the work of Houlden (1979), who has begun to study perceptions of procedural justice in plea bargaining. She has found that some of the same factors that affect perceptions of procedural justice in the courtroom, including and in particular the extent to which defendants can exercise control over the conflict resolution process, also affect such perceptions in plea bargaining. There are certainly many applications of the social psychological literature on bargaining and conflict resolution that can be made to problems in plea bargaining, but these applications have yet to be developed. Part of the reason for the neglect of this important area by psychologists may lie in the popular conceptions of criminal justice which tend to ignore the view of the criminal justice system as an institution that resolves disputes between the state and particular individuals in much the same way that the civil justice system resolves disputes between individuals or groups.

Negotiated settlement is, of course, a common practice in civil litigation; for many types of cases more than 90% settle before trial. Although psychologists have devoted some attention to the civil negotiation process (e.g., Erickson, Holmes, Frey, Walker, & Thibaut, 1974; Walker & Thibaut, 1971), there are many questions that remain to be studied. Particularly intriguing are the effects of the threat of trial and of the discovery process on legal negotiations. Rubin (1980) has offered an analysis that points out the importance of viewing negotiation as only one step in the total conflict resolution process, a perspective that may be very fruitful for research on legal bargaining.

In spite of the high rate of negotiated settlement in many types of civil cases, overcrowded trial calendars have prompted courts to examine arbitration as a possible process for reducing further the number of cases that reach trial. Several states have civil rules that require certain types of cases to undergo nonbinding arbitration before they can reach trial, and recently three federal courts have adopted similar rules on an experimental basis. Evaluation of the federal arbitration programs (Lind & Shapard, 1981) suggest that the effects of arbitration rules may be quite complex: Arbitration seems to induce prearbitration negotiated settlement, but it appears also that a substantial proportion of the cases actually reaching arbitration are not resolved by nonbinding arbitration judgments. The interest in arbitration points to a need for more study of this process and, as Rubin (1980) has noted, for a greater understanding of third-party resolution processes in general.

Among the most radical suggestions for alternatives to trial are those for a science court to resolve scientific and technological controversies (Task Force of the Presidential Advisory Group, 1976). The proposal for a science court is motivated by the problems associated with resolving scientific questions (especially those relevant to public policy) in the two forums currently available: the adversary legal system and governmental bodies that are often closed to public scrutiny. The proposed science court would make use of expert decision makers and public hearings. Thibaut and Walker (1978) have suggested a similar procedure for what they term *mixed conflicts*, disputes that have strong elements of both truth conflicts and conflicts of interest. They suggest a bifurcated procedure that would conduct more or less nonadversary hearing before an expert decision maker to resolve scientific or technical questions and a subsequent adversary hearing before nonexpert decision makers to decide the outcome conflict. The legal community has shown little willingness to make use of a science court, but this may simply reflect a natural conservatism in the face of such radical procedural change. The incidence of policy-relevant scientific disputes in a society as complex as ours may make the adoption of some such procedure necessary. There is certainly a need for psychological research on this topic, as there is for continuing research on more traditional legal procedures.

REFERENCES

Adams, J. S. Inequity in social exchange. In L. Berkowitz (Ed.), *Advances in experimental social psychology* (Vol 2.). New York: Academic Press, 1965.

Anderson, N. H., & Jacobson, A. Effect of stimulus inconsistency and discounting instructions in personality impression formation. *Journal of Personality and Social Psychology*, 1965, 2, 531–539.

Austin, W., Williams, T. A., Worchel, S., Wentzel, A. A., & Siegel, D. *Effect of mode of adjudication, presence of defense counsel, and favorability of verdict on observers' evaluation of a trial proceeding: An empirical study of procedural justice.* Unpublished manuscript, University of Virginia, 1979.

Bray, R. M., & Kerr, N. L. Use of the simulation method in the study of jury behavior: Some methodological considerations. *Law and Human Behavior*, 1979, 3, 107–119.

Burger, W. E. *Year end review.* Washington, D.C.: U.S. Supreme Court, 1980.

California jury instructions—Civil—Book of approved jury instructions. St. Paul, Minnesota: West, 1969.

Charrow, R. P., & Charrow, V. R. Making legal language understandable: A psycholinguistic study of jury instructions. *Columbia Law Review*, 1979, 79, 1306–1374.

Cound, J. J., Friedenthal, J. H., & Miller, A. R. *Civil procedure: Cases and Materials.* St. Paul, Minnesota: West, 1974.

Damaska, M. Evidentiary barriers to conviction and two models of criminal procedure. *University of Pennsylvania Law Review*, 1973, 121, 578–589.

Damaska, M. Presentation of evidence and factfinding precision. *University of Pennsylvania Law Review*, 1975, *123*, 1083–1106.

Davis, J. H., Bray, R. M., & Holt, R. W. The empirical study of decision processes in juries: A critical review. In J. L. Tapp & F. J. Levine (Eds.), *Law, justice, and the individual in society: Psychological and legal issues*. New York: Holt, 1977.

Doob, A. N. Evidence, procedure, and psychological research. In G. Bermant, C. Nemeth, & N. Vidmar (Eds.), *Psychology and the law*. Lexington, Massachusetts: Heath, 1976.

Doob, A. N., & Kirshenbaum, H. M. Some empirical evidence of the effect of Section 12 of the Canada Evidence Act upon the accused. *Criminal Law Quarterly*, 1972, *15*, 88–96.

Elwork, A., Sales, B. D., & Alfini, J. J. Juridic decisions: In ignorance of the law or in light of it? *Law and Human Behavior*, 1977, *1*, 163–189.

Erickson, B., Holmes, J., Frey, R., Walker, L., & Thibaut, J. Functions of a third party in the resolution of conflicts: The role of a judge in pretrial conferences. *Journal of Personality and Social Psychology*, 1974, *30*, 293–306.

Fuller, L. The adversary system. In H. Berman (Ed.), *Talks on American law*. New York: Vintage, 1961.

Hans, V. P., & Doob, A. N. Section 12 of the Canada Evidence Act and the deliberations of simulated juries. *Criminal Law Quarterly*, 1976, *18*, 235–253.

Hayden, R. M., & Anderson, J. K. On the evaluation of procedural systems in laboratory experiments: A critique of Thibaut and Walker, *Law and Human Behavior*, 1979, *3*, 21–38.

Henshel, R. L. The purposes of laboratory experimentation and the virtues of artificiality. *Journal of Experimental and Social Psychology*, 1980, *16*, 466–478.

Homans, G. C. *Social behavior: Its elementary forms*. New York: Harcourt, 1961.

Houlden, P. *Evaluation of procedural modifications of plea bargaining by state's attorneys, public defenders, community residents, and inmates*. Unpublished manuscript, University of Illinois at Chicago Circle, 1979.

Houlden, P., LaTour, S., Walker, L., & Thibaut, J. Preference for modes of dispute resolution as a function of process and decision control. *Journal of Experimental Social Psychology*, 1978, *14*, 13–30.

Insko, C. A. Primacy versus recency as a function of the timing of arguments and measures. *Journal of Abnormal and Social Psychology*, 1964, *69*, 381–391.

Insko, C. A., Lind, E. A., & LaTour, S. Persuasion, recall, and thoughts. *Representative Research in Social Psychology*, 1976, *7*, 67–78.

Jones, E. E., Rock, L., Shaver, K. G., Goethals, G. R., & Ward, L. M. Pattern of performance and ability attribution: An unexpected primacy effect. *Journal of Personality and Social Psychology*, 1968, *10*, 317–340.

Kaplan, M. F., & Kemmerick, G. D. Juror judgment as information integration: Combining evidential and nonevidential information. *Journal of Personality and Social Psychology*, 1974, *30*, 493–499.

Kaplan, M. F., & Miller, L. E. Reducing the effects of juror bias. *Journal of Personality and Social Psychology*, 1978, *36*, 1443–1455.

Kassin, S. M., & Wrightsman, L. S. On the requirements of proof: The timing of judicial instruction and mock juror verdicts. *Journal of Personality and Social Psychology*, 1979, *37*, 1877–1887.

Kerr, N. L., Atkin, R. S., Stasser, G., Meek, D., Holt, R. W., & Davis, J. H. Guilt beyond a reasonable doubt: Effects of concept definition and assigned decision rule on the judgments of mock jurors. *Journal of Personality and Social Psychology*, 1976, *34*, 282–294.

Kruglanski, A. W., & Kroy, M. Outcome validity in experimental research: A re-conceptualization. *Representative Research in Social Psychology*, 1976, *7*, 166–178.

Kurtz, S. T. *Preference and determinants of preference for modes of conflict resolution by post court-martial military personnel*. Unpublished master's thesis, University of North Carolina, Chapel Hill, 1978.

LaTour, S. Determinants of participant and observer satisfaction with adversary and inquisitorial modes of adjudication. *Journal of Personality and Social Psychology*, 1978, *36*, 1531−1545.

LaTour, S., Houlden, P., Walker, L., & Thibaut, J. Procedure: Transnational perspectives and preferences. *Yale Law Journal*, 1976, *86*, 258−290.

Lind, E. A. The exercise of information influence in legal advocacy. *Journal of Applied Social Psychology*, 1975, *5*, 127−143.

Lind, E. A., Erickson, B. E., Friedland, N., & Dickenberger, M. Reactions to procedural models for adjudicative conflict resolution. *Journal of Conflict Resolution*, 1978, *22*, 318−341.

Lind, E. A., Kurtz, S., Musante, L., Walker, L., & Thibaut, J. W. Procedure and outcome effects on reactions to adjudicated resolution of conflicts of interest. *Journal of Personality and Social Psychology*, 1980, *39*, 643−653.

Lind, E. A., & Shapard, J. E. *Final evaluation report on court-annexed arbitration in three federal judicial districts.* Washington, D.C.: Federal Judicial Center, 1981.

Lind, E. A., Thibaut, J., & Walker, L. Discovery and presentation of evidence in adversary and nonadversary proceedings. *Michigan Law Review*, 1973, *71*, 1129−1144.

Lind, A., Thibaut, J., & Walker, L. A cross-cultural comparison of the effect of adversary and inquisitorial processes on bias in legal decisionmaking. *Virginia Law Review*, 1976, *62*, 271−283.

Lind, E. A., & Walker, L. Theory testing, theory development, and laboratory research on legal issues. *Law and Human Behavior*, 1979, *3*, 5−19.

Miller, N., & Campbell, D. T. Recency and primacy in persuasion as a function of the timing of speeches and measurements. *Journal of Abnormal and Social Psychology*, 1959, *59*, 1−9.

Mitchell, H. E., & Byrne, D. *Minimizing the influence of irrelevant factors in the courtroom: The defendant's character, judge's instructions, and authoritarianism.* Paper presented at the meeting of the Midwestern Psychological Association, Cleveland, 1972.

Musante, L. *Reactions to type of evidence presented within an adversary procedure.* Unpublished master's thesis, University of North Carolina, Chapel Hill, 1979.

O'Barr, W. M., & Lind, E. A. Ethnography and experimentation—Partners in legal research. In B. D. Sales (Ed.), *Perspectives in law and psychology* (Vol. 2): *The trial process.* New York: Plenum, 1981.

Rubin, J. Z. Experimental research on third-party intervention in conflict: Toward some generalizations. *Psychological Bulletin*, 1980, *87*, 379−391.

Rusbult, C. E., Musante, L., & Solomon, M. *The effect of clarity of decision rule and favorability of verdict on satisfaction with resolution of conflicts.* Unpublished manuscript, University of North Carolina, 1978.

Sales, B. D., Elwork, A., & Alfini, J. J. *Improving comprehension for jury instructions.* In B. D. Sales (Ed.), *Perspectives in law and psychology* (Vol. 1): *The criminal justice system.* New York: Plenum, 1977.

Sealy, A. P., & Cornish, W. R. Juries and the rules of evidence. *Criminal Law Review*, 1973, April, 208−223.

Sheppard, B. H., & Vidmar, N. Adversary pretrial procedures and testimonial evidence: Effects of lawyer's role and machiavellianism. *Journal of Personality and Social Psychology*, 1980, *39*, 320−332.

Simon, R. J. Murder, juries, and the press. *Trans-action*, 1966, *3*, 40−42.

Simon, R. J. *The jury and the defense of insanity.* Boston, Massachusetts: Little, Brown, 1967.

Stone, V. A. A primacy effect in decisionmaking by jurors. *Journal of Communication*, 1969, *19*, 239−247.

Sue, S., Smith, R. E., & Caldwell, C. Effects of inadmissible evidence on the decisions of simulated jurors: A moral dilemma. *Journal of Applied Social Psychology*, 1973, *3*, 344−353.

Task Force of the Presidential Advisory Group on Anticipated Advances in Science and Technology. The science court experiment: An interim report. *Science*, 1976, *193*, 653−656.

Thibaut, J., & Walker, L. *Procedural justice: A psychological analysis.* New York: Erlbaum/Halstead, 1975.

Thibaut, J., & Walker, L. A theory of procedure. *California Law Review*, 1978, *66*, 541−566.

Thibaut, J., Walker, L., LaTour, S., & Houlden, P. Procedural justice as fairness. *Stanford Law Review*, 1974, *26*, 1271−1289.

Thibaut, J., Walker, L., & Lind, E. A. Adversary presentation and bias in legal decisionmaking. *Harvard Law Review*, 1972, *86*, 386−401.

Vidmar, N. Effects of decision alternatives on the verdicts and social perceptions of simulated jurors. *Journal of Personality and Social Psychology*, 1972, *22*, 211−218.

Walker, L., LaTour, S., Lind, E. A., & Thibaut, J. Reactions of participants and observers to modes of adjudication. *Journal of Applied Social Psychology*, 1974, *4*, 295−310.

Walker, L., Lind, E. A., & Thibaut, J. The relation between procedural and distributive justice. *Virginia Law Review*, 1979, *65*, 1401−1420.

Walker, L., & Thibaut, J. An experimental examination of pretrial conference techniques. *Minnesota Law Review*, 1971, *55*, 1113−1137.

Walker, L., Thibaut, J., & Andreoli, V. Order of presentation at trial. *Yale Law Journal*, 1972, *82*, 216−226.

Weld, H. P., & Danzig, E. R. A study of the way a verdict is reached by a jury. *American Journal of Psychology*, 1940, *53*, 518−536.

Weld, H. P., & Roff, M. A study of the formation of opinion based on legal evidence. *American Journal of Psychology*, 1938, *51*, 609−623.

chapter

3

Jury Selection[1]

Valerie P. Hans
Neil Vidmar

1. The contribution of the second author was facilitated by grants from the Russell Sage Foundation and by the Social Sciences and Humanities Research Council of Canada.

The jury selection process has long been considered an essential component of trial by jury (Gutman, 1972–1973; Holdsworth, 1938; Okun, 1968). Because of a widespread conviction that the composition of the jury can be a major determinant of a trial's outcome, a number of legal rules and practices have evolved to govern the selection of jury members. The intent of these rules and practices has been to produce fair and unbiased juries.

The issues associated with jury selection encompass many problems which fall within the domain of psychological inquiry. The legal concept of an unbiased juror refers to a psychological state of mind and behavioral disposition which will allow the juror to weigh the evidence in an impartial way. The selection of jurors involves methods intended to detect and eliminate those persons who do not possess requisite states of mind and behavioral dispositions.

The purpose of this chapter is to provide a review and analysis of jury selection issues. The task, however, is a complicated one for a number of reasons. First, it involves the analysis of psychological assumptions in law and legal procedures. The jury serves more than a single function as well, making criterion analysis complicated. In addition, jury selection cannot be understood apart from the adversary legal process in which it is embedded. Finally, the chapter must deal not only with basic research designed to shed light on legal behavior but also with the impact that psychological research has had when it has been injected, directly or indirectly, into the jury selection process. Although many selection rules and practices evolved long before psychoanalysis and modern social psychology, these bodies of knowledge have been, and continue to be, assimilated into legal assumptions and practice. Moreover, in recent years, psychologists and other social scientists have become directly involved in the adversary process and have used their methods and knowledge of human behavior to assist with jury selection in specific cases. The chapter must consider the impact of such social engineering. Throughout the review, therefore, we will necessarily have to deal with some interrelated questions. What are the legal principles which govern composition of the jury? What are the psychological assumptions implicit within these principles? Are those legal rules and practices which have been developed to implement the principles accomplishing their intended goals? What is the impact of psychological research on the selection process? What problems remain to be investigated and what is the best way of investigating them?

The review focuses mainly upon the criminal rather than upon the civil jury, primarily because that is where most of the research has been conducted. In addition, it is for the most part concerned with the American jury, although we will have occasion to refer to the jury systems of both Canada and England.

The jury serves a number of vital functions in helping to resolve the legal disputes of contemporary society. It acts as the arbiter regarding conflicting facts and evidence presented at trial. At the same time it provides a means by which community norms and sentiments are injected into the trial process. In addition, its role in informing the public about the justice system and increasing the acceptability of legal decisions must be taken into account (Brooks & Doob, 1975; Kadish & Kadish, 1971; Kalven & Zeisel, 1966; Law Reform Commission of Canada, 1980). The principles governing jury selection are designed to further these multiple purposes of trial by jury.

The chapter is organized around three central principles that control the selection of jurors in criminal cases. Jury Panel Composition, the first section, focuses on the first principle, namely that the jury panel must consist of a representative cross section of the community. After considering some of the psychological reasons why jury panel representativeness is desirable, we briefly discuss and evaluate those rules which attempt to ensure jury representativeness. In certain cases social scientists have been asked to help demonstrate that jury panels have failed to meet this standard. We review these efforts and explore some of the definitional and methodological difficulties of proving this claim in the courts.

Our second section, Venue of the Trial, deals with a second principle: The requirement that the trial be held in the district in which the offense occurred. After briefly considering some of the reasons why local trials may be desirable, the focus turns to instances where they are not. In trials where it is felt that a substantial proportion of the local community may be biased against an accused, lawyers have attempted through change of venue proceedings to move the location of the trial. Psychologists have been called to provide empirical support for change of venue motions. These efforts are examined with an evaluation of the kinds of contributions that have been and might be made in this area.

The final principle, discussed in the last section, Jury Selection, involves the mandate for rejecting potential jurors who may not be able to judge the case with an open mind. Determination of a prospective juror's impartiality, or lack thereof, is a challenging task. The courts have provided specific mechanisms, such as peremptory challenges and challenges for cause, to eliminate potential jurors who may not be impartial. We examine the way lawyers and judges typically employ these mechanisms and consider contributions that social scientists have made in this area with the development of "scientific" jury selection methods.

JURY PANEL COMPOSITION

The Legal Rationale for a Representative Jury

In a series of decisions (see Kairys, Schulman, & Harring, 1975), the United States Supreme Court established the requirement that the pool or panel from which the jury is selected must constitute a representative cross section of the community. There are two main policy reasons, both entailing psychological assumptions, that underlie the cross section requirement: fact-finding ability and jury legitimacy.

FACT-FINDING ABILITY

The first reason for the representativeness requirement is that it is assumed to improve the jury's prowess as a fact finder. There are two interconnected assumptions underneath this reason. The first is that if the panel from which the jury is drawn represents a broad cross section of the community, the resulting juries will be more heterogeneous. The statistical logic behind the assumption is sound, although as Kuhn (1968; see also Kairys *et al.*, 1975) has pointed out, the peculiarities of adversary procedure may invalidate pure statistical reasoning; however, that criticism will be ignored here. The second assumption is that more heterogeneous juries will be better problem solvers (see e.g., Babcock, 1975; "Note: The Case for Black Juries," 1970; Van Dyke, 1977; Zeisel, 1971). Three main arguments are advanced for this assumption. First, it is contended that a jury composed of members with a range of individual experiences, knowledge, and abilities will result in a variety of perspectives that will generate more ideas and more robust deliberations, resulting in better fact finding (problem solving). Second, a heterogeneous jury is more likely to result in a mutual cancellation of any randomly distributed biases or prejudices that the members might hold (see Babcock, 1975; Zeisel, 1971). The third argument asserts that nonrandom biases are also more likely to be cancelled. More heterogeneous juries are more likely to include minority group members; the presence of such members may inhibit majority group members from expressing prejudice, especially if the defendant is from the same group as the minority group jurors (see, e.g., Broeder, 1965a; see also Lempert, 1975, p. 670; "Note: The Case for Black Juries," 1970).

There has been little direct investigation of the claim that heterogeneous juries possess superior decision-making abilities in comparison to juries with a more homogeneous composition. However, there exists some indirect evidence from psychological research on group problem solving that supports the notion that a more heterogeneous group has an advantage in problem-solving tasks. A number of studies have examined the relative abilities of groups composed of homogeneous and heterogeneous members. In a review of research in this area, Hoffman (1965) cited several studies in which heterogeneous groups, differing on dimensions such as sex, age, personality characteristics, decision-making approaches, or religious and political attitudes, were superior to homogeneous groups in problem-solving performance. However, a few studies have not found the expected superiority of heterogeneous groups in problem-solving tasks (Clement & Schiereck, 1973; Fiedler & Meuwese, 1963; Ruhe, 1972). Indeed, in some instances, the existence of heterogeneity may create special problems of tension or coordination between group members that impede effective problem solving (Fenelon & Megargee, 1971; Fiedler & Meuwese, 1963; Shaw, 1976; see also Hackman & Vidmar, 1970; Lempert, 1975, pp. 689–698).

Although the majority of the group problem-solving studies indicate that heterogeneous groups are likely to perform better than homogeneous groups, the relevance of this research for jury decision making is not clear. The tasks confronting the subject in a problem solving experiment and a juror in a court-room are markedly different. Furthermore, determination of the quality of performance or the accuracy of decision making by the jury is no mean feat (see discussions by Hans, in press; Kalven & Zeisel, 1966; Simon, 1980). The jury's functioning cannot be evaluated solely on the basis of the speed or "correctness" of its decision, as might be the case in a problem-solving study. Other more difficult to measure aspects of jury functioning must also be considered. While there are some hints that heterogeneity may promote the fact-finding function of the jury, definitive research on this problem has yet to be conducted.

There are clearly some instances, however, where carefully selected homogeneous juries may possess greater decision-making abilities, compared to more heterogeneous juries. Consider, for example, the advantage that a jury of accountants might have in a complicated business fraud trial. Just such an argument was used to defend the existence of "blue-ribbon" juries and jury panels whose members had demonstrated that they possessed sufficient "intel-ligence" and "common sense" to adequately discharge their fact-finding func-tion as jurors (Van Dyke, 1977). There are, however, three serious drawbacks associated with a blue-ribbon jury selected in this manner. The first obstacle is that, as has become clear in the controversy surrounding IQ tests (Hyman, 1979), it is extremely difficult to differentiate individuals on the basis of intelli-gence without drawing invidious distinctions between various segments of soci-ety. The informal and subjective assessment of intelligence in the courtroom lends itself to discrimination against minority groups, the poor, persons with accents, and so forth. A second disadvantage is that even if such an intelligence test could be conducted fairly, performance on it need not necessarily predict adequate juror performance. A final problem, the most crucial insofar as the legal system is concerned, is that specially selected juries and jury panels that deviate from the fair cross section requirement may undercut the jury's role as the voice of the entire community and threaten the jury's legitimacy. This prob-lem leads us to the second argument for representative juries, which follows.

JURY LEGITIMACY

Proponents of jury representativeness also argue that, independent of the effects on fact-finding ability, juries must be drawn from a panel representative of the community in order to preserve the legitimacy of the jury and the legal process (e.g., "Note: The Case for Black Juries," 1970). An essential function of the jury is to serve as the voice of the community; when the jury cannot reflect the composition of the community because the jury panel does not include all segments of it, the jury's role is fundamentally undermined (Farmer, 1976; Ginger, 1975; "Note: The Case for Black Juries," 1970).

There are at least two interrelated consequences which flow from jury panel nonrepresentativeness and which may weaken the jury's legitimacy. First of all, members of underrepresented groups (blacks, youths, the elderly, the poor) are much less likely to participate via jury service in the legal system; it has been demonstrated that such participation has a positive effect on attitudes toward the jury (Doob, 1979; Farmer, 1976; Ginger, 1975). Indeed, even indirect contact with the jury may enhance attitudes toward it. For example, in a recent survey, Doob (1979) found that in comparison to persons having no direct or indirect contact with jury service, Canadians who had served on a jury or knew at least one other person who had served believed that juries were more likely than judges to arrive at a just and fair verdict. Because of their relative lack of participation in and contact with jury service, members of underrepresented groups are likely to hold more negative attitudes toward the jury and toward the criminal justice system in general.

A second consequence of a nonrepresentative jury panel is that the acceptability of the verdict may be decreased. A defendant who is convicted by a jury drawn from a nonrepresentative panel is less likely to accept the validity of the verdict, especially if the defendant is a minority group member. The legitimacy issue may be likely to extend to other members of the community as well. Groups who have been largely excluded from the jury panel may feel that they had no opportunity even to present their unique perspective within the jury context; thus, the resultant jury verdict is not perceived as a legitimate expression of the community's sentiments. An example of the ramifications of an "illegitimate" verdict is given in Gillespie (1980), who describes how an all white, all male jury acquitted four white police officers in Dade County, Florida of the murder of a black insurance salesman, an event that sparked 3 days of rioting in Miami. While the trial jury is a more visible body whose composition consequently has a greater impact on public perceptions of the jury as an institution, the composition of the jury panel is also critical since the panel serves as the source of the trial jury: The limitations of the jury panel thus become the limitations of the trial jury.

Defining a Representative Jury Panel

In a number of decisions, courts in the United States have found that the right to a jury drawn from a representative cross section of the community has not been compromised unless a cognizable group can be shown to be significantly underrepresented. In general, a group is defined as *cognizable* when it is perceived as a group by the community, when its members share distinctive experiences and attitudes, and when the group's absence from the jury may have an impact in the specific case before the court. Groups may be labeled cognizable because their exclusion may directly affect the fact-finding function of the jury (*United States* v. *Guzman*, 1972) or because their absence would undermine the legitimacy of the jury (*Ballard* v. *United States*, 1946). Because the right to a representative cross section stems from several constitutional and statutory sources, judicial definitions of what constitutes a cognizable group have varied. The reader is referred to Zeigler (1978) for an extended discussion of group cognizability.

While the criteria for a group's cognizability have at least been articulated, there has been no general ruling about the point at which a cognizable group becomes substantially underrepresented in the jury panel. Deciding what constitutes a substantial disparity is a perplexing problem. It is worth noting in this context that almost all of the cases successfully arguing violations of representation have been characterized by, first, extremely large disparities between a group's proportion in the population and its representation on jury lists and, second, significant opportunities for discrimination to occur during the panel selection process (Daughtrey, 1975). In the absence of guidelines from higher courts, the responsibility for determining the amount and importance of disparity has been relegated to trial court judges, who for the most part have been unwilling to employ statistics more sophisticated than percentage data to assist them in decision making (cf. Daughtrey, 1975; Finkelstein, 1978; Suggs, 1979).

Procedures for Assembling a Representative Jury Panel

Compounding the definitional problem already discussed are the practical difficulties inherent in assembling representative jury panels. There are typically several stages in the selection of a jury panel, and at each stage the representativeness of the panel is diminished.

The initial stage consists of selecting names from one or more lists of members of the community. A variety of source lists have been used, although today voter registration lists are the most widely employed (Kairys, Kadane, & Lehoczky, 1977). Prior to the passage of the Jury Selection and Service Act of 1968 in the United States (a federal act held applicable to the states through the Fourteenth Amendment of the Constitution), a frequent method of obtaining prospective jurors had been the *key man system*, whereby key members of the community were asked to submit names of potential jury members to those in charge of jury selection (Summer, 1972). The typical outcomes of the key man system were jury pools that deviated markedly from representativeness. The 1968 Act required that voters' lists be used as the primary source of jury pool selection in order to maximize the degree of jury panel representativeness. Since that time, a number of investigators have demonstrated that while voter registration lists are superior to the key man system, they still fall short of providing a representative cross section of the population. In particular, voters' lists drastically underrepresent such groups as young persons, blacks, other racial minorities, and the poor (see generally Kairys et al., 1975, 1977; Summer, 1972; Van Dyke, 1977). As a result, some authors have argued (e.g., Kairys et al., 1977) that the voters' list should be supplemented by additional lists such as welfare rolls or driver's license lists that are likely to include those not already represented. A number of jurisdictions have implemented this policy (see Kairys et al., 1977, for a more thorough discussion of the issue).

After names have been selected from the source lists by the jury commissioner's staff, a jury questionnaire is typically sent to each person chosen, inquiring about the individual's qualifications and ability to serve as a juror. While name selection from source lists is often (though not always) done randomly, and under these conditions need not affect the representativeness of the panel, it has been demonstrated that the differential return rate of jury questionnaires results in further underrepresentation of racial minorities, the poor, and other individuals with high mobility (Van Dyke, 1977).

Returned questionnaires are screened by the jury commissioner's staff to select only those persons qualified for jury service. On the basis of their responses to the questionnaire, potential jurors may be disqualified (not permitted to serve at all) or exempted (permitted to decline serving) from jury service. The criteria for disqualifications and exemptions vary from jurisdiction to jurisdiction. Typically, specific characteristics that in the minds of legislators and policymakers preclude an individual from being an unbiased and competent juror will result in disqualification (e.g., inability to understand and speak the language, involvement by occupation in the administration of justice, possession of a criminal record). Those characteristics which imply that jury service would pose an undue hardship may be grounds for exemption (e.g., physicians, nurses, or those with domestic obligations). Even though persons qualifying for an exemption may choose to serve as jurors, studies indicate that the vast majority of those offered an exemption take it (*Taylor v. The State of Louisiana*, 1975). Thus, the end result of offering an exemption to a specific category of persons is virtually to eliminate the category from the jury panel. In addition, there are a number of documented instances in which the jury commissioners' or sheriffs' staffs have purposefully avoided sending out jury questionnaires to members of some exempted groups, effectively precluding them from service (Chevigny, 1975; Foster, 1979; *People v. Attica Brothers*, 1974). Even if individuals do not meet the formal requirements for disqualification or exemption, they may still be excused from jury service by the trial court judge if they can demonstrate that jury service would constitute a hardship in their particular circumstances.

In summary, it can be seen that at each of the stages in the selection of the jury panel there is opportunity for compromising both the randomness of selection and the representativeness of the jury panel. Deviations from representativeness first arise because the source lists do not adequately represent the community; the problem is then exacerbated by differential return rates of jury questionnaires. While discretionary or discriminatory action at any of these stages may further compromise the representativeness of the jury panel, researchers have demonstrated that even a fair and straightforward application of a jury selection plan may discriminate against the poor, the young, racial minorities, women, and persons with high or low educational attainment (Alker, Hosticka, & Mitchell, 1976). In fact, the ideal of the jury panel as a representative cross section of the community is seldom realized (Van Dyke, 1977).

Social Science and Jury Panel Selection

The issue of panel representativeness has received less attention from social psychologists than the change of venue and impartiality issues that are discussed in the remainder of this chapter. In part, this is because the problem of demonstrating statistical underrepresentation is more within the domain of the demographer. To show underrepresentation, statistical comparisons of the community and jury panels need to be performed to assess the magnitude of the underrepresentation and to determine whether any observed differences are likely to be due to chance alone.

Nevertheless, this discussion has established that underlying these statistical questions are psychological assumptions of considerable import. Once a disparity of representation has been established, it is still necessary to persuade a trial judge that the disparity is an important one. First, it must be demonstrated that the underrepresented group constitutes a cognizable group that is perceived by the community as a group whose members share distinctive experiences and attitudes. Second, it is usually important to show that the group's absence from the jury may have an impact on the case before the court. Since the standard for judging the magnitude of disparity that legally constitutes underrepresentation is largely subjective, this information about potential impact may be a decisive factor in the ultimate decision.

Social psychologists and sociologists have participated in exploring issues of jury representativeness by tendering expert opinion about the potential impact of excluding groups of persons (see, e.g., Blauner, 1976; Ginger, 1969; 1975). In some future case, empirical evidence pertaining to the cognizable groups issue might be obtained by conducting survey research demonstrating that attitudes and judgments relevant to the case are significantly different in the underrepresented group (see Zeigler, 1978).

There are, however, opportunities to make important contributions through more general research studies. We noted that there is little evidence about the impact of heterogeneous versus homogeneous composition on the quality of jury deliberations and decision making. There is also no systematic research bearing directly on Broeder's observation (1965a) that the presence of a minority group member will inhibit subtle or not so subtle expressions of prejudice in majority group members. The issue of jury legitimacy could also be explored through field studies or experiments where people evaluate the fairness of a legal outcome as a function of whether the jury was representative of the community. Answers to many of these questions, of course, obviously have implications beyond the issue of jury representativeness.

VENUE OF THE TRIAL

Drawing the Jury from the Community Where the Offense Occurred

The practice of drawing a trial jury from the district where the crime occurred developed in part out of a tradition of geographical organization of the criminal justice system (cf. Radzinowicz, 1948, 1957) and in part out of the early form of the English jury trial that employed as jurors the individuals who had witnessed the events in dispute (Darr, 1974). In contemporary times, the law has required that the jury be drawn from the local community, a requirement that in addition to its obvious practical benefits is likely to enhance both jury fact finding and the legitimacy of the jury. A jury composed of a representative group from the community will be aware of local standards and norms that form the context of the defendant's behavior. Knowledge of these norms may alter jury members' interpretation of the defendant's actions, or in civil cases may suggest damage awards consistent with community standards. In addition to its effects on jury fact finding, the location of a trial may have a broader impact on the community at large by making the operation of the legal process more salient. The legitimacy of the jury and in fact of the whole criminal justice system may be strengthened when community members who are most concerned about an offense are able to observe, either directly or by media coverage, that justice is being done in their local courtroom. The increased prominence of the operations of criminal justice also may heighten the moral or educative influence of the law (Andenaes, 1971).

Procedures for Gaining a Change of Venue

While in most cases it may be preferable to conduct the trial and draw the jury from the community in which an alleged offense has occurred, the courts have recognized that in some instances it may be difficult or impossible to select an impartial jury from that community. In both the United States and Canada, the law provides that a trial may be moved from one jurisdiction to another—a change of venue—under such circumstances.

Examination of case law indicates legal recognition of a number of circumstances under which it would be difficult to obtain an impartial jury, thereby justifying a change of venue (for United States cases see: Kairys *et al.*, 1975; McElroy, 1976; Pollock, 1977; for Canadian cases see: Arnold & Gold, 1978–1979; Vidmar & Judson, 1979). The most common instance is when the case itself or one of the parties involved has become so notorious that many persons in the community would hold such negative attitudes that they would be unable to make a judgment based on legal merit. A second kind of bias can result from the fact that segments of the community hold important knowledge about the case that under the rules of evidence would ordinarily be withheld from the jury (e.g., a defendant's history of mental illness or criminal activity unrelated to the case at issue; a confession that is inadmissible). Such prejudicial attitudes or extralegal knowledge may arise from mass media coverage, or in the instance of smaller communities, from informal communication networks. Bias may also be presumed where large segments of the community have direct personal ties to one of the persons involved in the case, as in a small community where many potential jurors may be related to a victim.

Though the criteria for gaining a change of venue may vary slightly among specific jurisdictions, it always must be demonstrated to the trial judge's satisfaction that there is a fair and reasonable probability that a panel of impartial jurors cannot be found in the local jurisdiction. The case law has established some additional guidelines for determining what constitutes prejudice, bias, or lack of impartiality. Mere knowledge about a case or a defendant is not sufficient to show bias; the knowledge must be prejudicial. Mere abhorrence of the crime itself or dislike of a defendant is not enough; rather, extraordinary prejudice with respect to a specific crime and defendant must be demonstrated. It must be shown that the prejudice or knowledge is a continuing phenomenon, not something that may have existed once but has dissipated prior to the trial, and is so strong that jurors would probably be unable to follow the judge's instructions to set their prejudices aside and render an impartial verdict.

Traditionally, two basic types of evidence about the bias or impartiality of the community have been set forth by the parties in change of venue applications: (a) affidavits about the state of public opinion sworn to by persons supposedly in touch with the pulse of the community, and (b) affidavits and documents regarding coverage of the event by the mass media (i.e., the amount of newspaper or television coverage and the content of that coverage). Both sorts of evidence, of course, constitute very indirect proof of bias. Opinions of community leaders are at best unsystematic samplings of opinion, and the existence of inflammatory newspaper articles does not mean that people have read them, that they instilled prejudicial attitudes, or that any prejudicial effects were long lasting. Yet judges have typically been required to make inferences about community attitudes or knowledge from this indirect evidence.

The difficulties of assessing the state of public opinion from such indirect and tenuous evidence were recognized by Justice Frankfurter in *Stroble* v. *The State of California* (1952) when he complained that "Science with all its advances has not given us instruments for determining when the impact of such newspaper exploitation has spent itself or whether the powerful impression bound to be made by such inflaming articles as here preceded the trial can be dissipated in the mind of the average juror by the tame and often pedestrian proceedings in court [p. 181]." Social scientists, of course, are capable of providing such evidence through direct assessment of community attitudes by means of systematic surveys. The tools and techniques were available at the time of Justice Frankfurter's writing, but the idea did not gain legal acceptance for over a decade.

Survey Evidence in Change of Venue Motions

Almost contemporaneous with Justice Frankfurter's recognition of the need for better evidence of community attitudes, several attempts were made to introduce opinion polls in court for this purpose. In the Alger Hiss case, the defense produced polls which purported to show that people in Vermont were more open-minded with respect to Hiss' guilt or innocence than people in New York City, where the trial was to be held. Although the government itself had been successful in having opinion polls admitted into evidence in two prior cases, the prosecution successfully argued that such polls constituted hearsay and, therefore, were inadmissible (see Pollock, 1977). In *The United States* v. *Irvin* (1953), a case involving a black defendant on trial for rape, the Roper polling organization was commissioned to conduct an opinion survey (see Woodward, 1952). Surveys of four Florida counties were undertaken: the county where the alleged crime had taken place; the adjoining county where the trial was to be held; and two additional *control* counties located a considerable distance away. The data showed that in comparison to the control counties, greater numbers of people in the first two counties believed that the defendants were guilty and expressed prejudice on a number of other indices. This suggested that people within the trial venue had prejudged the case. Though the researchers were allowed to testify in court about the basic methodology of the survey, the judge ruled that the results were inadmissible hearsay evidence because the interviews were anonymous, the respondents had not testifed under oath, and their answers were not subject to cross-examination.

Pollock's (1977) review notes that for over a decade following *Irvin* few attempts were made to use opinion polls in change of venue applications. In the late 1960s, however, changes in legal attitudes made further attempts possible. First, opinion polls began to be understood and viewed as having more scientific legitimacy. Second, the hearsay objection was partially eroded by the admission of survey evidence in other types of cases. Third, in *Sheppard* v. *Maxwell* (1966) the United States Supreme Court recognized the principle that grounds for a change of venue did not require the demonstration of actual prejudice, only the reasonable likelihood of prejudice, thus clearing the way for a decision based on demonstrated *probability* of prejudice rather than *actual* prejudice.

A new group of change of venue applications using survey evidence arose after 1966. Pollock (1977) concluded that "Almost without exception, however, the reported cases in which public opinion sampling was introduced for change of venue purposes have either denied the motion while attributing little or no weight to the poll, or if granting the motion, have still attributed little weight to the poll [p. 280]." As one example, in the Angela Davis trial, the court granted a change of venue, at least partly on the grounds of an opinion survey. Somewhat perversely, however, the trial was sent to another county in which the survey data had indicated community bias was as great as in the original venue (see Faber, 1973). Thus, the success rate of survey evidence has been less than impressive despite these facts:

1. Judges and legal commentators in both the United States and Canada have acknowledged the difficulty of assessing public opinion.
2. Some judges and lawyers have recognized the potential of direct assessment of opinion through systematic survey techniques.
3. Polls have gained acceptance in other areas of law.

A number of factors may account for the poor rate of success of opinion surveys. Some of these derive from problems inherent in the legal system while others can be ascribed to limitations of methodology and conceptualization associated with the surveys. One set of somewhat interrelated reasons arises from basic judicial conservatism and the tendency to protect established legal principles. A form of this conservatism relates to the hearsay objection. Despite the latter day courts' greater acceptance of survey evidence and the existence of legal techniques for avoiding the hearsay problem, such as using the researcher as a qualified expert who gives expert testimony using the survey results as a data base, individual judges who do not understand polls may simply rely on the hearsay exclusion as a convenient means of avoiding the issue (see Arnold & Gold, 1978−1979). Judges may also be reluctant to relinquish their discretionary power and intuitive judgment in making a decision (see, e.g., Fox, 1972; Lamont, 1972−1973). After all, the conclusions to be drawn from polls are essentially probability statements, and there has always been, and probably should be, a reluctance to make legal decisions purely on cold statistical grounds (Hart & McNaughton, 1959). Rather than viewing the survey results as one more piece of evidence to weigh in their decision, some judges may perceive it as preempting their decision-making function altogether.

A closely related issue involves the criterion to be used in deciding what constitutes an unacceptable level of prejudice in the community. Is it, for example, when 60% of the population indicate prejudice, or when 39% do (see Pollock, 1977, p. 280)? The more judges rely on statistical evidence, the more they may feel compelled to specify a criterion level; yet an absolute standard is inappropriate when so many other variables may enter into a particular case. To avoid what Tribe (1971), in another context, has called "trial by mathematics," a particular judge may simply shun statistical evidence altogether.

Another set of reasons for the lack of success of opinion surveys combines problems caused by judicial skepticism with inherent weakness in survey methodology. Survey responses, whether obtained by telephone or in-person interviews, are given under conditions different from those in the courtroom. Respondents are anonymous, are not under oath, and are not in the formal atmosphere of the courtroom. The survey respondent confronts more hypothetical and abstract conditions than the prospective juror in the courtroom, who is faced with the concrete and immediate conditions of trial service. The general problem of correspondence between expressed attitudes and actual behavior (Fishbein & Ajzen, 1975; Wicker, 1969) may be magnified in a survey concerning a legal case because of the respondents' nearly total lack of experience with the stimulus conditions under which they are being asked to predict their attitudes and behaviors. Although in fact a survey may result in more honest and reliable answers than those produced by questioning jurors under the heavy conformity pressures of the courtroom (see Vidmar & Judson, 1979, pp. 30−35), the opposite possibility also exists. That is, people who say they feel prejudice in a survey might be able to set their prejudices aside when required to do so by a trial judge. In short, judges' concerns about the correspondence between answers given in a survey and in a courtroom are by no means completely unfounded. It is, therefore, not surprising that judges, even though they may be unfamiliar with the attitude–behavior literature, might discount or dismiss survey results.

Nevertheless, the poor success rate of survey evidence in contemporary cases should not be ascribed solely to legal conservatism or to inherent weaknesses in methodology. A review of the cases indicates that many surveys have been seriously flawed from a social science as well as a legal perspective. Some surveys have utilized inadequate or biased sampling procedures. For example, Pollock (1977) points out that in one survey the total sample consisted of 64 persons, and another survey had only 84 respondents. In other cases it is obvious that the respondents constituted a biased sample that was unlikely to reflect the varied attitudes of the entire community. These are hardly samples from which to generate reliable estimates of the attitudes of the people residing in a venue or to inspire a judge, even one without social science training, to have confidence in the representativeness of the survey (*State v. Kramer*, 1969; see Pollock, 1977, p. 280).

Other weaknesses in the surveys have resulted from the kinds and forms of questions asked of respondents. Frequently, the questions have been superficial and/or not directly relevant to the legal issues, or limited to inquiries about general attitudes or case knowledge. A survey by Arnold and Gold (1978–1979), for example, asked respondents to indicate whether they recognized the defendant's name (along with some other names in the news) and, subsequently, to indicate their degree of liking for, or affect toward, the defendant. The assumption behind such items is that if an individual has general knowledge about or general negative affect toward the defendant or the crime, that person will be likely to be prone to convict. It is an assumption that should be carefully scrutinized from the vantage points of both the judge and the social scientist (see Constantini & King, 1980–1981, for a recent attempt to empirically examine this assumption). It may be preferable to first ask people open-ended questions regarding the case and then provide them with more specific questions about how they might behave as jurors in such a case: For example, if you were chosen as a juror in this case and instructed by the presiding judge to put all preconceived views aside, would you be able to do so and decide the case solely on the evidence presented at trial? (For other examples, see Vidmar & Judson, 1979; 1981). Such precise questions comport with judges' intuitive assumptions about human behavior and are consistent with the social psychological research showing that assessments of specific behavioral intentions are more likely to predict behavior than assessments of general affect (Ajzen & Fishbein, 1980; Fishbein & Ajzen, 1975). Additionally, surveys often have not ascertained good comparison or base-line data by which any responses to the case under consideration can be compared.

It is difficult to say how much each of these various reasons contributed to denial of the change of venue application, despite survey evidence of prejudice, in a particular case. Since judicial attitudes have become less negative toward survey evidence in recent years, it is possible to speculate that the major cause lies with poorly conceived and conducted surveys. It is, therefore, instructive to examine two applications for change of venue that were successful.

Two Successful Attempts

McConahay, Mullin, and Frederick (1977) have reported on the successful change of venue application in the Joan Little trial. Defense lawyers relied heavily on survey data to support their arguments.

Joan Little, a black woman, was to be put on trial in Beaufort County, North Carolina in 1974 for the ice-pick murder of her jailer, who she claimed had forced her to have sexual relations with him. Defense lawyers were of the opinion that Ms. Little could not get an impartial hearing in that county due to massive pretrial publicity and the belief that the rural inhabitants held conservative, sexist, and racially prejudiced attitudes.

To test these hypotheses, McConahay *et al.* conducted a systematic random telephone survey of Beaufort and 24 other North Carolina counties. Ultimately, the defense team focused on the data from Beaufort, an adjacent county, and a county located in a more urban area of the state. While the data indicated there were no differences among these counties with respect to people's perceived level of exposure to the case (roughly 75% indicated "a lot" of exposure), there were substantial differences on other issues. For example, in comparison to inhabitants of the urban county, persons in Beaufort and the adjacent county were twice as likely to hold a preconception of Ms. Little's guilt and nearly twice as likely to hold racist and sexist views. These survey data were presented in court and supplemented by a content analysis of newspaper coverage, expert testimony regarding pretrial publicity, and expert testimony on word-of-mouth communication in rural areas. Finally, over 100 affidavits from persons in the Beaufort area, testifying that opinions in the community were already formed, were introduced as evidence.

In granting the change of venue application, the judge's oral comments indicated he had been influenced by the survey data on racism as well as by the pretrial publicity. However, his written decision mentioned only the pretrial publicity.

Survey evidence was also used successfully in a Canadian case reported by Vidmar and Judson (1979, 1981). In that case, *Regina v. Brunner*, the defendant was on trial for misrepresentation and overpriced selling of home improvement materials and services by fraudulent means. The trial came in the wake of another fraud trial, popularly known as the Bevlen Conspiracy Trial, that had been highly publicized. In the Bevlen case, the owners and employees of an established and respected local home improvement company were convicted of fraudulently selling overpriced products and services to senior citizens. During a period of 18 months, the charges, trial, and sentencing of the Bevlen defendants received spectacular media coverage. The defense lawyer speculated that because of the massive publicity in the Bevlen case and the fact that Brunner had also been convicted in it, a fair and impartial jury in the Brunner case could not be obtained in the county. He therefore applied for a change of venue.

Two interrelated telephone surveys of the county were conducted in support of the change-of-venue motion. The surveys consisted of open-ended questions about the case as well as more specific questions about whether respondents felt they could be impartial jurors.

Though 4 months had elapsed since the sentencing of the Bevlen defendants, according to the surveys, at least 75% of people in the county reported knowledge of the case. The surveys also showed at least 50% of the population expressing doubts that they could be impartial jurors in a similar fraud case, even if a trial judge instructed them to set aside any preconceived biases and to decide the case solely on the evidence presented at trial. In order to determine whether this bias was due to the nature of the Bevlen case or was simply the result of bias against any defendant with a prior criminal record or any defendant accused of defrauding elderly citizens, a within-subjects experiment was included in the second survey. All respondents in the second survey were asked to judge their ability to be impartial jurors in the case of a defendant who was charged with defrauding elderly citizens (as Brunner was) in four randomly ordered conditions: where the defendant had no prior criminal record; had a conviction for assault; had a conviction for fraud; or had a conviction for fraud in the Bevlen case. Expressed inability to serve as an impartial juror was related to a defendant having a criminal record, with the conviction for fraud in the Bevlen case condition evoking the highest level of expressed bias. These experimental results indicated that Brunner's conviction in the Bevlen fraud trial would be prejudicial to him above and beyond the bias accruing to other defendants with records.

These survey results were introduced into evidence through expert testimony of the researcher. In roughly 6 hours of examination and cross-examination, the survey findings were presented and integrated with other bodies of psychological literature bearing on jury behavior. An affidavit documenting more than 100 articles about the Bevlen case in the county's leading newspaper was also produced as evidence. In addition, an official of another local building products company was called to testify about the effects of the adverse publicity from the Bevlen case on his company and its salespersons; this testimony served to corroborate the survey findings.

The change of venue was granted. In his decision, the presiding judge relied almost exclusively on the expert testimony about the survey results and the corroborative testimony by the company official.

Social Science and Change of Venue: Summary

Ironically, even though motions for changes of venue would appear to be one of the most fertile areas for social science to aid in problems relating to the jury, the track record for such attempts has been poor. Some of the lack of success may be attributed to judicial conservatism or problems inherent in survey methodology. However, especially in recent years, when judicial conservatism has lessened and survey data might be more acceptable, the reason for continued reluctance to use such data may more often lie with the poor conceptualization and methodology associated with the surveys themselves. With effort and inventiveness the faults in these surveys can be corrected for future cases.

JURY SELECTION

Once the place of trial has been fixed and a jury panel has been assembled from the community, the next task is to choose an unbiased jury from that panel. As previously noted, the legal system recognizes that individuals may differ in their attitudes and that some people may hold biases that preclude them from deciding a case objectively (see Gutman, 1972–1973; Holdsworth, 1938; Howe, 1939). Therefore, the legal systems of the United States, Canada, and England all explicitly recognize that the right to an impartial jury requires mechanisms whereby certain persons from the jury panel can be rejected as jurors.

While the right is recognized, determining when impartiality has or has not been achieved is problematic. In a landmark United States case, Chief Justice Hughes stated that impartiality is "not a technical conception," rather it is a "state of mind," a "mental attitude of appropriate indifference [*U.S.* v. *Wood*, 1936, pp. 145–146]." Yet the courts have provided no tests for determining precisely when a prospective juror may be called appropriately indifferent. In earlier times, impartiality was typically assumed if a juror swore that he or she would judge a case solely on its merits. Unless prospective jurors would be personally affected by a case's outcome, they were taken at their word. Thus, assessments of juror impartiality depended on blatantly obvious biases or jurors' own admissions of bias. Since the turn of the century, however, the influence of unconscious biases on jurors has been increasingly recognized by the courts. This shift is at least in part a function of our increasing sophistication in psychology (Babcock, 1975). The virtual explosion of psychology and law research and the practical involvement of psychologists and lawyers on many fronts within the past decade portends even greater recognition of unconscious biases. Nevertheless, it is apparent that a number of currently used pretrial procedures for detecting bias in jurors, and their underlying assumptions, are based on outdated models of human behavior.

The notion of an impartial jury rests on two explicit assumptions: first, that some prospective jurors will be able to judge a case fairly on the evidence presented at trial; and, second, that the court will be able to differentiate between those who are biased and those who are not and select only the latter for the jury. A third less explicit but equally important assumption is associated with the adversary nature of common law legal procedure. It is assumed that prosecuting and defense lawyers will each attempt to select jurors who are favorable to their respective sides, and that these opposing biases will cancel one another: that is, a juror highly favorable to one side will be rejected by the opposing side. We will provide an overview of the psychological data bearing on the first assumption before turning to consider three topics associated with the second assumption: formal procedures to eliminate biased jurors; the behavior of traditional legal practitioners in jury selection; and, finally, the recent technological–legal development usually labeled "scientific" jury selection. The reader should keep in mind throughout the discussion the third assumption— that each attorney will reject jurors most favorable to the opposing side, and thus form a balanced jury.

Sources of Bias in Jurors

Conceptually, there are several sources of bias that might render one particular juror more susceptible to prejudice than another. Certain jurors may have dispositions, resulting from personality or experience, that would bias them one way or another, regardless of the particular case in question. Alternatively, there may be elements associated with the type of case, such as the defendant or type of crime, that render a juror susceptible to bias. Finally, a juror may have particular attitudes or knowledge about the specific case in question that render him or her incapable of hearing the evidence with an open mind. These biases may manifest themselves through a number of different modes: encoding and storage of information during a trial, assessments of witness credibility, retrieval of information and reconciliation of inconsistent facts during decision making, or susceptibility to unwarranted influence by other jurors during jury deliberations. Both common sense and a more sophisticated social psychological perspective lead to the prediction that prospective jurors may differ along a number of these dimensions, any one of which might preclude them from being impartial.

Especially within the past decade, social psychologists have investigated a number of personality and demographic dimensions that might be associated with bias in jurors. That research has been reviewed in a number of places (e.g., Davis, Bray, & Holt, 1977; Gerbasi, Zuckerman, & Reis, 1977; Nemeth, 1981; Saks & Hastie, 1978) and does not need to be reviewed in detail here. Such variables as the juror's authoritarianism, moral reasoning ability, race, ethnic background, sex, age, politics, education, and previous jury service have been found to be related to verdicts in jury simulation studies. However, only the dimension of authoritarianism seems to yield fairly consistent data: High authoritarians are typically more inclined to convict than low authoritarians, especially in murder cases (e.g., Bray & Noble, 1978). However, this tendency may be reversed in cases involving a defendant who is in a position of authority, such as a police officer, or whose defense is that he or she was acting under orders (see Hamilton, 1978; Mitchell, 1972).

While generally supportive of the legal assumption that some people may not be impartial jurors, the body of literature on personality−demographic−experience effects on simulations of juror decision making evidences a number of problems. Reviews of jury simulation research have criticized the methodological features characteristic of the studies, including college student subject populations, short trial summaries, absence of group deliberation, inappropriate dependent measures, and hypothetical nature of decisions (Gerbasi et al., 1977; Weiten & Diamond, 1979). To this list of methodological shortcomings we want to add one that is crucial to research on juror bias. In the jury simulation studies, judicial admonishments to set aside biases and render a verdict solely on the evidence have rarely been included (cf. Chapter 10), while in real trials such instructions are always given. The law assumes that admonitions from lawyers and judges have the desired effect on jurors; and while this assumption may be questioned in a number of specific areas (e.g., Broeder, 1959; Doob & Kirshenbaum, 1972; Hans & Doob, 1976), there is no direct psychological data to contradict the assumption as a general proposition. Until enough data are produced to refute the assumption, a skeptical legal practitioner has no reason to abandon the belief that admonitions might cancel individual biases. At the very least, simulation studies should incorporate this element of trial realism into the trial stimulus materials.

The literature is plagued with a major conceptual problem as well. Most of the studies have been based upon the assumption that if personality or demographically based dispositions exist, they will override the evidentiary and situational factors associated with types of cases. For example, researchers in the area of simulated jury behavior have tended to ignore trial characteristics as a variable, apparently trusting that personality differences will be expressed with even a haphazard choice of stimulus materials. Such assumptions are clearly out of step with the currently prevailing view that personality dispositions interact with situations in complex ways (e.g., Bem & Allen, 1974; Epstein, 1979; Mischel, 1968). Should it be expected, for example, that the age of the juror will relate to the verdict in the same way in a drug trial involving a youthful defendant and in a trial involving a corporate executive accused of price fixing? Or should sex of juror be considered related to rape cases in the same way as to murder cases? Similarly, even within one type of case, such as murder, there are important dimensions that might cause various personality types to respond differently. Authoritarianism, for instance, might well be differentially related to murder charges involving the following dimensions or elements: homicide in the course of a felony, child abuse, insanity or self-defense, or a black versus a white victim.

In brief, then, a theory of case characteristic dimensions needs to be developed and then integrated with a theory of personality dimensions before any clear-cut predictions can be drawn about the effects of personality on juror behavior. In addition, theoretical understanding would be enhanced if researchers attempted to discover where and how bias manifests itself: for example, in pretrial dispositions, in interpreting or recalling evidence, in following judicial instructions, or in susceptibility to persuasion from other jurors during the deliberation process. A study by Berg and Vidmar (1975) suggests that high and low authoritarians may recall evidence differently; Christie (1976) reports results that are consistent with the hypothesis that high and low authoritarians are differentially susceptible to persuasion attempts during deliberation.

Rather than focusing on general personality dispositions, a more fruitful approach to the study of juror bias would be to look at the situationally specific characteristics of jurors that may cause them to be biased in a particular type of case. Feild (1978) reports a study along these lines that centered on the crime of rape. A sample of 896 white adults were asked to make simulated jury decisions in response to a six-page summary of a rape case. The following factors were systematically varied in the versions given to the various "jurors": type of rape (precipatory/nonprecipatory), race of the victim (black/white), attractiveness of victim (attractive/unattractive), sexual experience of the victim (experienced/inexperienced), race of defendant (black/white), and strength of evidence (strong/weak). Demographic characteristics of the jurors (age, sex, education, marital status, personal acquaintance with a rape victim, previous jury service, and occupational prestige) as well as their attitudes on an eight-factor Attitude Toward Rape Questionnaire were obtained and correlated with juror decisions. Case characteristics and variables of jurors' demographic backgrounds contributed negligibly to the prediction of juror decisions. While the attitude variables were related to jurors' decisions, the largest multiple correlation obtained with eight attitude predictors was .51, accounting for only 26% of the variance. It should also be noted that although the subjects made decisions about guilt and indicated confidence in their verdicts, the reported correlations are, unfortunately, with a third dependent variable, the recommended prison sentence. Not only does this fact reduce generalizability to real juror decision making (see, e.g., Vidmar, 1979), but it could be suspected that the correlations with the dichotomous guilty/not guilty verdict were probably lower.

In a similar study, Penrod (1980a) obtained demographic and attitudinal information from a sample of 367 actual jurors. The jurors then rendered verdicts in four simulated cases involving first-degree murder, rape, robbery, and damages against a common carrier arising from an accident (a civil case). Regression analyses were then performed to determine the extent to which verdict preferences could be predicted from the other information. The regression models were able to account for only 5–16% of the variance, depending on the case.

Hepburn (1980) conducted a simulation study which correlated juror demographic characteristics and attitudes relevant to the case with verdicts in a felony–murder case. Nine demographic variables accounted for only 8% of variation in verdicts. Clusters of attitudes toward the police and toward punishment each accounted for less than 10% of the variation in verdicts. These attitude clusters did relate more strongly to post verdict ratings of the strength of prosecution and defense evidence, but on the whole the statistical associations were not very high in the sense of generating practical predictions of juror verdicts.

These three studies by Feild, Penrod, and Hepburn are the most sophisticated ones in the literature. Yet examination of the attitude scales indicates that for the most part these authors only assessed somewhat general attitudes relevant to the case on which the person acting as a juror was eventually asked to render a verdict. Attitudes toward the particular case at hand and the specific evidence to be tendered were not assessed. Literature from the field of attitude prediction (e.g., Fishbein & Ajzen, 1975; Rokeach & Kliejunas, 1972) suggests more precise measurement involving a potential juror's attitudes toward a specific and immediate case would probably improve prediction. Indeed, this kind of data is frequently obtained by the lawyer in voir dire questions (see, e.g., Blauner, 1975; Christie, 1976), as we will show. Thus, asking a potential juror who is in the witness box, under oath, and faced with imminent jury service if he or she knows the defendant or witness in the case at hand, if he or she has formed an opinion about the case or the defendant, and so on, can potentially yield better predictive accuracy than questions about more general attitudes. Real world trials are complex, and jurors are exposed to idiosyncratic stimulus arrays in the form of trial evidence that may evoke prejudices that can best be uncovered by asking jurors about their behavioral intentions for the case at hand.

We have drawn attention to this fact for several reasons. First, normative data obtained from simulation studies or retrospective accounts of jurors, as is typically collected by social and personality psychologists, could be seriously underestimating the degree of prejudice held by potential jurors in a particular trial. Second, legal procedures are more conducive to idiographic analysis. Third, while normative data, even about personality or background effects, can be helpful in indicating where to look for bias, two useful research avenues are suggested. One avenue involves systematic field studies of prejudice expressed by potential jurors in the courtroom. A second avenue involves research directed toward types of questions which could be utilized in a courtroom and which might more accurately uncover biases than those questions frequently asked by lawyers and judges (see, e.g., Rokeach & Vidmar, 1973).

In-Court Selection Procedures: Challenges for Cause and Peremptory Challenges

After a jury panel is assembled, a clerk randomly selects a subset of names from this larger group. Then the lawyers from the opposing sides proceed to exercise challenges against the inclusion of certain jurors until a petit jury composed of persons satisfactory to both sides is formed. The challenges are of two kinds: for cause and peremptory.

CHALLENGES FOR CAUSE

In the United States, a pretrial examination process called the voir dire helps to shed light on the impartiality of prospective jurors. During the voir dire, jurors may be asked about their qualifications, relationship to people involved in the case, and attitudes toward the defendant or about issues involved in the case. If it is demonstrated to the trial judge's satisfaction that the potential juror is biased, the judge may dismiss that person for cause. Depending on the particular jurisdiction and the judge's discretion, the examination of the jurors may vary from relatively narrow questions centered on the trial (e.g., familiarity with the attorneys or witnesses) to broad-ranging questions intended to ascertain more general or more subtle prejudices (see Blauner, 1975; Ginger, 1975; Gutman, 1972–1973).

Although the voir dire procedure predates the United States Constitution and is considered a right accorded to defendants in the United States (Bermant & Shapard, 1980; Gutman, 1972–1973), jury panel members in Canada and England do not typically undergo such questioning unless the unique circumstances of the particular case warrant it. In these countries, the burden of proof for a challenge lies with the party that requests it, usually the defense counsel. Challenges are not allowed very often; even when they are, the latitude of questioning tends to be narrower and restricted to specific, psychologically unsophisticated questions bearing directly on the trial (see Law Reform Commission of Canada, 1980; *Regina* v. *Hubbert*, 1975; Vidmar & Judson, 1979). Thus, for the so-called "English Jury" (or Canadian jury), the lawyers must normally choose or reject jurors on the basis of their age (based largely on appearance), sex, occupation, and demeanor in the courtroom by means of peremptory challenges.

In recent years, the voir dire procedures in the United States have become controversial and in many jurisdictions the scope of questioning has been severely curtailed, or judges have undertaken the questioning instead of allowing the lawyers to do it (see Bermant & Shapard, 1980; *Ham* v. *The State of South Carolina*, 1973). The reasons for these changes are several. It is argued that lawyers frequently abuse the practice of voir dire by attempting to indoctrinate jurors to favor their side, that voir dire is administratively costly and time consuming, that it is ineffective in weeding out biased persons (see Bermant & Shapard, 1980; Broeder, 1959; Levit, Nelson, Ball, & Chernick, 1971). On the opposite side of the controversy, it is contended that there is nothing wrong with indoctrination if its effect is to sensitize jurors to their responsibility to set aside prejudices and judge the case impartially, that the cost and time involved in the voir dire is small in comparison to the rest of the trial, that cost is a less important consideration than providing justice, and that the voir dire is effective in eliminating biased jury panel members (see, e.g., Gutman, 1972–1973; Okun, 1968).

Some empirical data have been collected on the issues involved in the controversy but these data have been more anecdotal than systematic (e.g., Broeder, 1959). Clearly, however, social psychological research could shed light on some aspects of the controversy. One issue is which of the varying types of voir dire questioning, ranging from the Canadian–English procedure of no preselection questioning, to the broad and detailed examination and cross-examination about nonspecific bias, results in a better jury. Padawer-Singer, Singer, and Singer (1974) attempted one such study. In their simulation experiment, persons called for jury duty in New York State were exposed to either prejudicial or nonprejudicial pretrial publicity and subsequently viewed a videotaped trial, deliberated in groups, and rendered verdicts. Approximately one-half of the simulated juries were selected by practicing lawyers by voir dire while the rest of the juries were selected randomly. The juries selected by voir dire did not differ much demographically from the juries chosen at random. Yet voir dire juries whose members had been exposed to prejudicial pretrial publicity were less likely to convict the defendant than their non-voir dired counterparts. However, the juries exposed to newspaper clippings that contained nonprejudicial trial publicity evidenced the reverse pattern, with voir dired juries convicting more often than juries selected randomly. While the results of the study are puzzling and leave us uncertain about the general effects of voir dire questioning, the experimental design shows one way that issues associated with the voir dire could be investigated.

Another issue is whether the judge or the attorneys should conduct the questioning of jurors (Bermant & Shapard, 1980; Bigam, 1977; Kairys et al., 1975; Stanley, 1977). One study of federal courts indicated that many judges conducted the examination by themselves (Bermant, 1977); yet, Kairys et al. (1975) argued that the attorneys should ask the questions. They claim that judges ask leading questions, indicate proper answers, and fail to probe further in response to suggestive answers. Further, they contend, because of their status, judges may evoke socially desirable responses from jurors, while adversary questioning by two opposing attorneys is superior in uncovering the real attitudes hidden behind initial responses. In contrast, however, Stanley (1977) has argued that the presence of trial lawyers prohibits the judge from asking perfunctory questions and that prospective jurors are not so "overawed by the bench or the black robe that they would 'shape' their responses in violation of their oaths to answer all questions truthfully [p. 73]." No data exist on this controversy, but systematic field observations of different courts or realistic simulation studies varying whether the questions are asked by judges or lawyers could be undertaken.

The final issue to be discussed here actually involves two problems: Namely, what should be acceptable grounds for challenging and eliminating a juror and what types of questions are most likely to uncover existing biases? As noted earlier, there exists no precise legal definition of an impartial juror. In earlier times, impartiality was assumed if it could be demonstrated that there was no consciously held bias on the part of a prospective juror; but in recent times increasing weight has been given to the possibility of unconscious bias. Despite this shift, however, potential jurors are typically asked whether they hold any biases which would preclude them from being fair and impartial jurors, and if they do, whether or not they can set these biases aside when judging the case before them (see, e.g., *Ham v. The State of South Carolina*, 1973; Rokeach & Vidmar, 1973). A prospective juror who admitted bias but stated that he or she could set this bias aside might well survive a challenge for cause. There is a heavy reliance on the prospective juror's admission of bias in the successful challenge for cause. This strikes psychologists as a somewhat naive expectation.

The study of prejudice has been a classic area of concern for social psychologists from the very beginnings of the discipline. As a consequence of this interest, a good deal of research on techniques and methods for detecting prejudice is available. A recent review paper (Crosby, Bromley, & Saxe, 1980) on techniques for discovering the extent of interracial prejudice notes that survey methods in which subjects are baldly asked to indicate their racial attitudes have been viewed with increasing dissatisfaction by psychologists. Part of the discontent has arisen with the discovery that attitudinal measures do not always accurately reflect or predict related behavior, since the variables controlling the expression of a specific attitude often differ considerably from those variables controlling behavior toward the attitude object (Fishbein & Ajzen, 1975; Wicker, 1969). Another reason, of course, relates to the problem of socially desirable responses. Thus, for example, a prospective juror may be afraid to admit during voir dire the prejudice and bias that later causes him or her to vote against a minority defendant in the privacy of the jury room.

An obvious difficulty with the reliance on the prospective juror's admission of bias for a challenge for cause is that in many situations, especially unusual ones in which people would have little experience on which to form judgments, potential jurors may be unable to estimate the effects of bias on their own behavior (see Nisbett & Ross, 1980), a problem we mentioned earlier. In addition to this general issue, individuals may differ in the extent to which they recognize and admit prejudice or bias within themselves.

For the reasons described, researchers in the area of attitudes, racism, and prejudice have grown wary of the survey method as a completely valid research tool and have begun increasingly to rely on more unobtrusive measures of behavior (Crosby *et al.*, 1980; Gaertner, 1976; Webb, Campbell, Schwartz, & Sechrest, 1966). Few of these methods are easily adapted to the courtroom setting, however, and are of limited usefulness in jury selection. The development of new measures of bias which would be appropriate for the selection of jurors is clearly a worthwhile and much needed venture (see, e.g., Christie, 1976).

THE PEREMPTORY CHALLENGE

The most widely used method of eliminating unwanted individuals from the jury is the peremptory challenge. Usually, both defense and prosecuting attorneys have a prescribed number of these challenges, (for example, 6 or 12), the number depending upon the jurisdiction, the number of defendants, or the seriousness of the crime. No reason need be stated for the exercise of this challenge. Peremptory challenges thus allow lawyers fairly wide and unchecked latitude in their choices; they may eliminate a juror on the basis of hunches about prejudice even when the judge is satisfied from the voir dire that the juror is impartial. Babcock (1975) argues that the peremptory challenge serves the valuable function of allowing defendants some additional choice in the jury that will decide their fate, a choice unfettered by the requirements of legal tests or rationales for exclusion. This choice may enhance defendants' positive feelings toward juries and consequently their perception of the legitimacy of the verdict.

Peremptory challenges are not without controversy, however. Some writers have argued that in the context of the adversary system, potential jurors might be eliminated because of race or other characteristics (see Kuhn, 1968; "Note: The changing role of the jury in the nineteenth century," 1964). Indeed, Van Dyke (1977) studied challenges in one New Mexico county over a 2-year period (1972 to 1974) and found that prosecutors challenged blacks, Hispanics, and young jurors in disproportion to their numbers. Thus, peremptory challenges may provide a vehicle for the covert exercise of discrimination, a factor which in turn affects the representativeness and legitimacy of the jury. The problem could be especially acute where minority members represent only a small portion of the population and thus can be almost entirely excluded from serving on petit juries by this method. More systematic field observation studies similar to that of Van Dyke are clearly needed to determine if it is commonplace for cognizable classes of persons to be systematically excluded through peremptory challenges. Supplemented with social psychological studies on the effects of such elimination on the various functions of the jury, such research could be used in legal challenges to the representativeness of juries.

Attorneys and Traditional Selection of Jurors

Another facet of the problem involved in selecting an impartial jury is that associated with the lawyer. By ascertaining what lawyers believe and observing what lawyers actually do in the voir dire, we can begin to gain indirect evidence about the extent to which selection procedures are effective.

ATTORNEY BELIEFS

Trial tactics handbooks used in the training of lawyers provide us with some indirect evidence about the theories of "good" jurors and "bad" jurors that guide selection practices. The handbooks (e.g., Ginger, 1975) consist of a mixture of legal lore, streamlined social science findings, and common sense. Some of the advice extended to lawyers betrays an obvious trafficking in stereotypes. A case in point is provided by Bailey and Rothblatt (1971), who suggest that defense lawyers choose women for the jury if the principal witness against the defendant is female, since women are "somewhat distrustful" of other women; they also caution that the occupation of a prospective woman juror's husband is of importance, since generally a woman "will feel and think in the same manner as her husband [p. 105]." Given that the information about jurors is often minimal, the trial tactics manuals do display a remarkable ingenuity in developing generalizations about those characteristics typically available to lawyers, such as occupation. For example, Bailey and Rothblatt maintain that salesmen, actors, artists, and writers are highly desirable as defense jurors, reasoning that because their occupations have exposed them to varied aspects of life, these individuals are not so easily shocked by crime as are people in less adventuresome occupations. Piel (1978) warns defense lawyers to beware of individuals who are employees of large bureaucratic organizations, since these persons are less inclined to sympathize with the nonconforming behavior of the defendant. Also of note in the trial tactics manuals is an emphasis on fitting juror characteristics to the details of the specific case (e.g., women jurors for an attractive male defendant but male jurors when the offense is rape).

In addition to providing a wealth of information about demographic predictors of the sympathetic juror (information that is of dubious value), trial manuals also suggest strategies for the conduct of the voir dire. Lawyers are advised to use the voir dire not only to ferret out those who are unfavorable to their case but also to ingratiate themselves with the jury. Some of the strategies suggested for voir dire are notable for their psychological insight. Bailey and Rothblatt (1971) suggest, for example;

> Approach matters of prejudice delicately. Suppose the defendant is a Negro. . . . You would be wasting your time if you asked: "Will you be prejudiced against the accused because he is a Negro?" The "no" you receive is meaningless, as few will admit to their prejudices. Instead, you might inquire: "Have you had any experience—such as with Negroes, or with anybody who has used a knife—that might keep you from sitting in impartial judgment on this case?" The juror's answer and the way it is given (tone, hesitancy, etc.) will give you insight into his true feelings. [pp. 84–85].

To summarize, examination of the trial tactics manuals do provide us with some indirect information about the approaches lawyers may take to the in-court selection of jurors.

Two studies have attempted to assess lawyers' beliefs about "good" jurors more directly by providing practicing attorneys with lists of hypothetical juror profiles and asking them to indicate their choice of jurors for different kinds of trials. Hawrish and Tate (1974–1975) presented 43 Canadian lawyers with a hypothetical jury list and information about the age, sex, occupation, and appearance of each prospective juror. The lawyers were asked to rate each of the prospective jurors from the defense point of view for four types of trials (fraud, rape, false prospectus, and murder). In this sample of lawyers, male jurors were preferred to female jurors for all four types of trials, but the pattern was accentuated for the rape trial. Persons 60 years of age and older were chosen less often than people from other age groups for all four trials, while occupational status and appearance made a difference only in one type of trial. The overall impression we get from Hawrish and Tate's study is that lawyers are affected by simple demographic information in their selections, but that the specific effects may vary between cases.

A more sophisticated experiment in the same vein has recently been conducted by Penrod (1980b). He first interviewed 19 attorneys about what juror characteristics they looked for and what questions they typically asked during voir dire. He then presented them with a set of juror profiles, which included information about the prospective juror's age, gender, marital status, ethnic background (Italian versus Anglo name), attitude about whether few or many defendants escape conviction on legal technicalities, liberal or conservative orientation, political party affiliation, high versus low status residential area, head-of-household occupation, appearance, and intelligence. Lawyers were asked to rate the similarity of the prospective jurors, as well as the extent to which each person would be biased in favor of defense or prosecution in a murder case and in a rape case. From both multidimensional scaling of the juror similarity ratings and analyses of variance of the bias ratings, Penrod found that a juror's gender and age, and the legal technicalities question appeared to be important determinants of the attorneys' judgments, although there was considerable variation among attorneys in the factors affecting their preferences.

Variation among attorneys was also apparent in the interviews. Attorneys mentioned they looked for the following characteristics in jurors: intelligence, age, appearance, occupation, open-mindedness, and gender. Each of these features was mentioned by six to eight attorneys, and no other characteristic was cited by more than four attorneys. The voir dire questions attorneys reported asking most often were about a prospective juror's general attitude toward the specific crime (mentioned by 12 lawyers), general attitude toward the police (10 lawyers), exposure to prejudicial pretrial publicity (7 lawyers), and previous experience as a crime victim (5 lawyers).

While the data are suggestive, there are problems with making inferences from the Hawrish and Tate and Penrod studies. What people state in the abstract and what they do in actual practice may be quite different; they may not be fully cognizant of the decision rules they use when many input variables present themselves simultaneously. Ebbesen and Konečni (1975) have demonstrated this point quite well in their study of how judges set bail. Data obtained from responses to hypothetical cases and gleaned from subsequent courtroom observations of those same judges were quite different. A logical next step, therefore, would be to follow lawyers into the courtroom and determine whether their stated preferences as to jurors are manifested in their behavior.

ATTORNEY BEHAVIOR IN VOIR DIRE SELECTION

Several articles in the literature have involved courtroom observation of the lawyers during the voir dire. One study by Broeder (1965b) involved observation of 23 jury trials conducted in the late 1950s, as well as interviews with all lawyers and 225 of the jurors in the cases. Broeder stated that the typical voir dire in these cases consisted of a perfunctory examination of prospective jurors that lasted less than half an hour. He summarized the findings of his study: "*Voir dire* was grossly ineffective not only in weeding out 'unfavorable' jurors but even in eliciting the data which would have shown particular jurors as very likely to prove 'unfavorable' [p. 505]." Broeder also described a number of juror interviews in which jurors told him they had purposefully suppressed or distorted damaging personal information during voir dire questioning. Lack of time resulting from court administrative pressures and lack of juror candor may both have contributed to lawyers' apparent ineffectiveness in weeding out objectionable jurors. Lawyers in the trials observed by Broeder spent only an estimated 20% of the time on questions designed to differentiate prejudiced and unprejudiced jurors. The remaining 80% of the time was spent on what Broeder called *indoctrination*: commenting on points of law, preparing the jurors for the trial, forewarning jurors about negative pieces of evidence, and ingratiating themselves with the jurors (Broeder, 1965b). From posttrial interviews with jurors, Broeder concluded that with a few notable exceptions, these indoctrinational strategies were generally unsuccessful. It should be stressed that Broeder's conclusions were based on rather unsystematic observation of the voir dire proceedings and retrospective posttrial interviews; thus, the conclusions have obvious limitations. However, his work does provide an interesting descriptive account of the voir dire process in one locale. Blauner (1972) has also provided an interesting case study of the voir dire in the Huey Newton murder trial. In contrast to Broeder, Blauner describes several striking examples of one lawyer's ability to uncover subtle biases and is generally positive in evaluation of the voir dire.

A more detailed observational scheme was used in another study of the voir dire by Balch, Griffiths, Hall, and Winfree (1976). These researchers did a content analysis of voir dire examinations from three trials. Balch *et al.* found that about 36% of the statements and questions made by members of the court (judge and lawyers) during the voir dire related to prospective jurors' personal and biographical characteristics, while 43% were instructional statements. Within this latter group were the types of comments Broeder referred to as indoctrination. In these instructional comments, court personnel informed the prospective jurors about procedural and legal issues in the trial process. Many of these comments were specifically concerned with prospective jurors' abilities to fulfill their role (e.g., "Can you resist the temptation of identifying with the accused?"), and called for a public commitment of impartiality from prospective jurors (e.g., "Yes, I can resist the temptation."). Balch *et al.* state that only twice did prospective jurors fail to provide the "expected" answers to questions of this sort. While such questions, therefore, may not function effectively as a vehicle for weeding out biased jurors, they might well reduce the overall level of bias by sensitizing jurors to areas where they may be less than impartial. Further, public commitments to be impartial may increase jurors' ability to set biases aside. Indeed, the pretrial voir dire period may be the optimal time to introduce instructions to disregard specific evidence. Kassin and Wrightsman (1979) and Cavoukian (1980), for example, have demonstrated that cautionary instructions are more effective when they precede damaging evidence than when they follow it.

Information about lawyers' beliefs and behavior is only partially helpful in answering the ultimate question: To what degree are lawyers effective in selecting impartial jurors? Certainly, many attorneys are convinced that they have won or lost cases because of particularly brilliant or inept jury selection, but their comments have the ring of "fireside inductions." Almost no systematic empirical data exist. As noted above, the Broeder (1965b) and Blauner (1972) studies were more anecdotal than systematic and the results of the Padawer-Singer *et al.* study (1974), discussed earlier, were uninformative.

One recent study by Zeisel and Diamond (1978) does provide some tentative empirical data about the effectiveness of lawyers' exercise of their peremptory challenges. It is usually impossible to know how effective lawyers' challenges are, since prospective jurors who are challenged never get to vote in the jury room. In their ingenious experiment, however, Zeisel and Diamond arranged for the challenged jurors in twelve criminal trials to serve as shadow jurors who remained in court throughout the trial and voted at the trial's conclusion. The information about the challenged jurors' votes, in conjunction with knowledge obtained from posttrial interviews of the real jury's first ballot vote, allowed Zeisel and Diamond to "reconstruct" what the vote of the jury would have been without peremptory challenges. Comparing the reconstructed jury's vote with the real jury's vote allowed them to estimate the lawyers' effectiveness in using peremptory challenges to create more favorable juries. Zeisel and Diamond report that in 7 of the 12 trials, the effect of the lawyers' challenges was minimal; the verdict of the reconstructed jury and the real jury were likely to have been identical. In the remaining five cases, however, the differences in first ballot votes of the two juries were more substantial, and in two or three of these cases might well have resulted in different verdicts. In all five cases the real jury was less likely to convict the accused than was the reconstructed jury. Zeisel and Diamond also calculated an attorney performance index, which revealed that the prosecutors as a whole "made about as many good challenges as bad ones [p. 517]," while the defense attorneys' overall performance was better. Most notable from the analysis of performances, however, was the great variation in effectiveness between the attorneys. While some difficulties arise regarding the assumptions underlying Zeisel and Diamond's estimate of lawyer effectiveness (see Bermant & Shapard, 1980, for a critique), these researchers have nevertheless provided us with a novel methodological approach to the study of jury selection by lawyers.

CRITIQUE AND RESEARCH NEEDS

There is, therefore, scanty concrete information about the effectiveness of lawyers' selection techniques although what we do know indicates that generally selection strategies may be only minimally effective. From a psychological perspective, it seems unlikely that future studies of lawyer effectiveness would substantially alter the current conclusion that attorney strategies have minimal impact on the jury's verdict. The selection of jurors is primarily based on clinical type judgments and a host of studies comparing clinical and actuarial predictions present a dim view of the reliability and validity of clinical judgments (see, e.g., Mischel, 1979). Especially in situations where there is only a small amount of information about individuals, it is difficult to predict their behavior accurately. While there is substantial literature documenting the effects of attitudes and individual characteristics on behavior, the relationships between demographic and attitudinal variables and verdicts in specific cases are typically not strong enough to be useful in prediction. Recall our earlier discussion of the studies by Penrod (1980a) and Feild (1978) showing that regression analyses were able to account for only relatively small proportions of the variance. In real jury trials, the voir dire may be effective in eliminating openly prejudiced persons, but we cannot expect too much more.

On the other hand, the most useful function of the voir dire may be its ability to indoctrinate and sensitize jurors about the need to set aside prejudices and participate in the trial with an impartial mind. This function of the voir dire has been discussed in some detail by Suggs and Sales (1978) and Blunk and Sales (1977) but awaits systematic empirical examination.

Systematic ("Scientific") Jury Selection

In the late 1960s and early 1970s, social scientists became directly involved in jury selection in a series of political trials evolving out of racial protests and the Vietnam War. Variously labeled "scientific" or "systematic" jury selection, the techniques provide the defense with an alternative to traditional jury selection.

HISTORICAL BACKGROUND

The use of experts to help the lawyer select jurors dates at least to the early 1950s, when such notable attorneys as F. Lee Bailey and Melvin Belli retained the services of a "hypnoanalyst" in a number of famous trials, including those of Drs. Carl Coppolino and Sam Sheppard (Bryan, 1971). More traditional social science expertise was brought to bear on the problem of uncovering bias in potential jurors in the 1968 trial of Black Panther Huey Newton. Defense counsel Charles Garry enlisted the support of a number of eminent psychologists and sociologists to develop sophisticated voir dire questions and tactics which he successfully utilized to uncover racism and prejudice (see Blauner, 1972; Ginger, 1969). Similar advice from social scientists was sought in a number of other trials (see Rokeach & Vidmar, 1973). The trial of black Communist Angela Davis for murder, kidnapping, and conspiracy also engaged social scientists in an expanded role (see Sage, 1973). A team of five clinical psychologists helped Ms. Davis and her defense counsel frame questions, and during the voir dire at least two of the psychologists scrutinized potential jurors for prejudice and advised the defense.

Major changes in social scientists' involvement, however, began in 1972 when the Berrigan Brothers and others were brought to trial on charges of conspiracy to raid draft boards, blow up heating tunnels in Washington, D.C., and kidnap Secretary of State Henry Kissinger. For that trial, a team of social scientists brought more sophisticated social science methods and technology to bear on the problems of selecting a jury (see Schulman, Shaver, Colman, Emrick, & Christie, 1973). Methods employed included the use of surveys to assess community opinion, the subsequent construction of juror profiles, the establishment of information networks to gather data on the jury panel, and clinical observation in the courtroom.

The Berrigan case, with its attendant publicity, set off a whole new field of applied research involving social science and jury selection. Teams of social scientists using refinements on the Schulman et al. (1973) techniques have aided defense counsel in an increasingly large number of trials. These include such highly publicized cases as the Vietnam Veterans Against the War trial, the Attica Prison riot trials, the Wounded Knee trial, the trial of John Mitchell and Maurice Stans, and the trial of Joan Little (see Berk, 1976; Christie, 1976; Kairys et al., 1975; McConahay et al., 1977; Saks, 1976a; Shapley, 1974; Tapp & Kenniston, 1976; Zeisel & Diamond, 1976) as well as many lesser known cases.

THE ARSENAL OF DATA

Systematic jury selection involves a number of social science methodologies and bodies of data. Several or all of them are used to supplement the trial lawyer's judgment about a potential juror. The specific techniques and their use have been described in some detail in the following sources: Berk, Hennessy, and Swan (1977); Berman and Sales (1977); Christie (1976); McConahay et al. (1977); Schulman et al. (1973); Suggs and Sales (1978). We will briefly review each of the techniques, provide examples from various trials, note the interrelationships between various methods, and comment on other functions that they serve.

Community survey

The major tool of systematic jury selection is a survey of the community population from which the jury panel will be drawn. For reasons of cost and time, an initial survey may be conducted by telephone and then be followed by in-depth interviews with a selected subsample to confirm the telephone results and explore other issues in greater detail. The survey is geared to the particular case at hand. For example, the survey would attempt to find out how the respondent feels about Defendant X who is being brought to trial for the murder of Y in this county and is pleading self defense rather than about a defendant charged with murder. Assessment of such specific attitudes should lead to better prediction than assessment of more general attitudes (Fishbein & Ajzen, 1975).

The data obtained is used to develop demographic profiles of "good" and "bad" jurors. Thus, for a particular case a "good" juror might be a female under 30 years of age, who holds a high school degree and is a registered Democrat, while a "bad" juror might be a female over 40 years of age, who is a homemaker and a registered Republican. The importance of specialized surveys focusing on a specific trial and from a specific community can be illustrated by data from the trials of the Berrigan Brothers and the Vietnam Veterans Against the War. While both cases involved radical protest about the same issue, the former was held in Pennsylvania and the latter was held in Florida. While women were most likely to be open-minded toward such defendants in the North, they were least likely to be open-minded in the South (see Christie, 1976).

The surveys are constructed in conjunction with the defense lawyers. Sometimes the data simply help to confirm the lawyers' hunches about what types of jurors will be best for their clients. On the other hand, the data may disconfirm these hunches. In addition to these functions, the survey data may help lawyers in other ways, in shaping voir dire questions, for example, by pinpointing areas where prejudices may reside. Surveys also may be used in developing trial strategy. In a civil case known to one of the present authors, a survey found most people were opposed to the plaintiffs and their ideology; on the other hand, most subscribed to the belief that nevertheless the plaintiffs should receive a fair trial. Plaintiff attorneys began organizing their trial strategy around the concept of fairness rather than the original strategy that had been planned.

A final use of the survey, outlined by McConahay *et al.* (1977), is to obtain an estimate of the percentage of persons likely to be favorable or unfavorable to a side even before the voir dire begins. Using the estimates derived from their data, the defense team in the Joan Little trial rejected some moderately acceptable jurors early in the voir dire because they knew it was probable that more acceptable jurors would appear farther down the list (McConahay *et al.*, 1977).

Information networks

While survey profiles are derived from the population as a whole and involve projections based on statistical probabilities, information networks focus on the jury panel members themselves. Direct contact with members of the jury list would likely bring charges of jury tampering, but there is no prohibition against talking to someone who might have personal knowledge or information about that juror. In fact, investigation of persons on jury lists has a rather lengthy tradition and is practiced by both prosecuting and defense attorneys (Okun, 1968). Prosecuting attorneys may routinely have jurors' names processed through police files; there is evidence that confidential tax information about veniremen has been obtained; and police officers have been mobilized to investigate potential jurors (see Okun, 1968). Defense attorneys, for the most part, have relied primarily on informal contacts. Information networks utilize knowledge from community research showing that the structure of the community is not random and therefore enable a researcher to efficiently find persons who know potential jurors (see Christie, 1976). Christie notes some problems with information networks: Persons with knowledge will not cooperate; reputational information may be erroneous; the potential juror may resent being investigated and become hostile (if he or she finds out); and the judge may prevent such investigation by not releasing the list of jurors until the last moment. Nevertheless, Christie indicates that information networks have on occasion provided information valuable to making a decision.

Juror ratings

The jurors' expressed attitudes and behavior during the voir dire questioning may also be systematically observed. Working on the assumption that authoritarianism (Adorno, Frenkel-Brunswick, Levinson, & Sanford, 1950) should be positively related to proprosecution tendencies in most criminal trials and also to conformity behavior in jury deliberations, Christie (1976; also see McConahay et al., 1977) has devised a reliable scale for rating juror authoritarianism that has been used in a number of trials. Systematic observations of prospective jurors' body language—kinesic and paralinguistic cues—during voir dire have provided another source of data.

Small group research literature

The larger body of research on group dynamics is used to help predict status formation, alliances, and conformity processes among the jury members. Christie (1976), for example, relates the information that in the trial of the Vietnam Veterans Against the War, the defense team chose some authoritarian jurors, reasoning that while their attitudes would probably be hostile to the defense, they would be less influential members of the jury and would be likely to conform to the majority of the other members who, it was hoped, would want to bring in a verdict of not guilty. Follow-up interviews conducted after the trial confirmed that the prediction was correct. Similarly, several potentially favorable high status males were rejected on the grounds that they would be potential rivals of a female the defense hoped would be jury foreperson. In some other case an attempt might be made to provide a chosen jury member with allies on the basis of Asch's classic finding that a minority opinion is more likely to be expressed and listened to if the member holding that opinion is not alone.

Intuition of attorneys, defendants, and others

The lawyer and the defendant, of course, have the power to make the ultimate decision about selection or rejection of jurors, but their opinions are solicited for another purpose as well, namely, to incorporate more data into the decision equation. Trial lawyers bring their own unique experience to the process of jury selection, and in fact a good trial lawyer may well be better than a whole team of social scientists because of his or her past experience with jurors' reactions to trial procedures, witnesses, and other types of evidence. Finally, on occasion other special types of persons, for example, a medicine man and a psychic, have also been consulted in selecting a jury (e.g., see McConahay *et al.*, 1977).

The decision process

Christie (1976) and especially McConahay *et al.* (1977) have outlined the basic techniques by which the varied data may be combined into a mathematical prediction equation. Although the various estimates are not independent of one another (e.g., both the defense counsel and the assessor of authoritarianism are usually familiar with the survey and information network data), evaluations are made in written form before discussion to minimize the influence of one source of ratings on another. In the Joan Little trial, for example, the sources compared data and on the basis of the degree of agreement made a decision to accept or reject a juror or obtain more information (McConahay *et al.*, 1977). The decision process, therefore, may be described as a "multiple indicator" assessment of juror attitudes requiring agreement or near agreement among all the indicators before a juror is found acceptable (Cook & Selltiz, 1964).

EFFECTIVENESS OF SYSTEMATIC SELECTION

If one simply takes the batting average of the publicized cases where systematic selection techniques have been used, the success rate is impressive. Most of the trials have resulted in acquittals or convictions on less serious charges. While the mass media and the lawyers involved in the process have attributed success to the use of scientific jury selection, its effectiveness is debatable, and a number of authors have expressed doubts about its efficacy (see Berman & Sales, 1977; Saks, 1976a, 1976b; Saks & Hastie, 1978; Suggs & Sales, 1978; Vidmar, 1976; Zeisel & Diamond, 1976).

There are a number of reasons for having these doubts. One set of reasons suggests that success had nothing to do with selection: most of the trials had political overtones; they involved charges of conspiracy, which are difficult to prove under most conditions anyway and may be peculiarly odious to Americans (see Bermant, 1975); they appear to have involved weak prosecution evidence. Zeisel and Diamond's (1976) analysis of selection techniques in the Mitchell and Stans trial supports this interpretation; the techniques were demonstrably useless but the defendants were nevertheless acquitted. Additionally, it can be speculated that any defense lawyer who goes so far as to engage social scientists in the first place probably works exceptionally hard on all aspects of the trial; thus it can be argued that exceptional defense efforts which just incidentally included use of scientific techniques of jury selection, may have accounted for the outcome of the trials.

A second set of explanations suggest that the selection process had side effects, and these side effects, rather than selection per se, produced the success rate. McConahay et al. (1977) propose that a "placebo" effect may have been operating in the Joan Little trial. The lawyers believed systematic selection was effective, raising the morale of the defense team and causing them to work harder; at the same time the morale of the prosecution team was lowered, with a resultant decrease in effort. McConahay et al. (1977) also speculate that the process made the jurors feel special because they had been chosen by "experts," and thus they responded with favorable attitudes toward the defense. McConahay et al. also suggest that it could be that the selection process increased group cohesion amongst the jurors, which, in these cases, worked in favor of inherent acquittal tendencies. In addition, the exceptionally detailed voir dire may have indoctrinated the jurors to an unusual degree about being impartial.

The final reason for suspecting the efficacy of scientific jury-selection techniques is the assumption that the selection may very well have eliminated biased jurors but asks: in relation to what. A good lawyer working alone, using traditional selection techniques, probably can eliminate some biased jurors, so the real issue involves ascertaining the degree to which systematic jury selection makes a difference. In brief, if it were possible to do an experiment, the "control" condition for assessing effectiveness of the systematic method would not be random assignment of jurors but rather selection by traditional methods (see Vidmar, 1976).

Saks (1976a, 1976b) offered some reasons why social scientists might be unable to select unbiased jurors effectively. He pointed to the fact that studies of clinical judgment have shown psychologists to be very poor at predicting behavior, especially in comparison to statistical or actuarial prediction (see, e.g., Gough, 1962; Meehl, 1954; Mischel, 1968) He also suggested that because of trial experience, the lawyer's judgment is likely to be better than the psychologist's. In turning to some of the other indices that have been used in juror prediction, such as "body language" and handwriting analysis, Saks notes that empirical research has demonstrated that they are highly unreliable in predicting attitudes and behavior. Another problem, not addressed by Saks, is the fact that the selection takes place in an adversary system. Thus, the most acceptable jurors may be chosen by the defense team but rejected by the prosecutor through peremptory challenges. This is a handicap not normally encountered in clinical prediction.

There are counters to these arguments, however. Criticisms about the unreliability of certain predictors, while valid in themselves, miss the broader picture. First, systematic selection does not pit clinical prediction against statistical prediction or social science and other techniques against lawyer intuition and judgment; it utilizes all indices available. Moreover, the decision procedures by which the indices are combined more nearly resemble statistical prediction than clinical prediction. Also, the clinical versus statistical prediction controversy in psychology has involved the predictions of clinicians acting alone, while in scientific jury selection the human predictor is more properly conceptualized as a team of clinicians. Second, the social scientists (see Christie, 1976; McConahay *et al.*, 1977) report that the various predictor sources tend to go in the same direction. The high agreement may result from the fact that the predictors are not totally independent, but, as already described, attempts are made to keep them relatively independent. Third, postverdict follow-up studies, while few and not without methodological problems, indicate that the selection decisions have some validity (see Christie, 1976; McConahay *et al.*, 1977). Fourth, it is indisputable that the community surveys and information networks provided information that would not normally have been available to a lawyer. Fifth, it is possibly unfair to emphasize the role of body language and handwriting experts, an Indian medicine man, or a psychic. Even if such sources are highly unreliable and suspect, the fact is that they may serve purposes other than selection of jurors: for example, provide moral support for the defendants; contribute to jurors' feelings of being specially selected; help to "psych out" the prosecution team; and gain publicity for the trial (see McConahay *et al.*, 1977). It must be remembered that in an adversary system, the trial becomes a drama whose outcome may depend on things other than factual evidence, especially when the charges have political overtones.

Several additional points bearing on effectiveness should also be raised. The first is that systematic selection techniques should not be discounted simply because social science was used incompetently in a particular case or cases, as, say, in the Mitchell—Stans trial (see Zeisel & Diamond, 1976). The second point involves the argument that evidence and case presentation is typically far more important than jury characteristics in determining trial outcome. McConahay *et al.* noted that the techniques have usually been applied in political and other controversial trials. They report an estimate by lawyers (admittedly unscientific) suggesting that 85% of ordinary criminal trials are decided on the evidence, while the outcome in the remaining 15% may be influenced, in part, by characteristics of the jurors. In controversial trials, however, juror characteristics may influence about 50% of outcomes. In brief, systematic selection may be more useful in some trials than others. The third point is that the scientists involved in selection have recognized another limitation, specifically, the degree of homogeneity of the population from which the jury panel is drawn. Christie (1976), for example, suggests that survey research, and other techniques for that matter, are probably not of much help if the population is largely homogeneous, as is often the case in rural communities. Fourth, in cases where the voir dire is severely restricted by the trial judge, the data gleaned from surveys gives the lawyer some grounds for making decisions, at least if there are moderate or strong relationships in the data. With traditional selection techniques, there would be virtually nothing to base a decision on at all under such circumstances where voir dire is limited.

A recent simulation study by Horowitz (1980) suggests the potential strengths and weaknesses of social science techniques. Law students were given one of two kinds of training in jury selection: the conventional method derived from trial practice manuals and other sources; and the social science method, which involved instructions on empirical verification, demographic and personality data, nonverbal cues, and so on. Each law student was then assigned to one of four cases: a sale of illegal drugs; a court martial; murder; drunk driving. Subsequently, the law students observed voir dire interrogations of prospective jurors (college students) conducted by third year law students, and then made judgments about how jurors were likely to render verdicts in their case. The dependent variable was the jurors' actual verdicts after listening to the case. In comparison with law students trained in the conventional method, those trained in the social science method were more effective in estimating the decisions of jurors in the drug and court martial cases but less effective with respect to the murder trial. Both methods were relatively ineffective in the drunk driving case. These results could be partially predicted from the fact that a prior survey of students showed demographic and personality variables to be fairly strongly related to attitudes toward the drug and court martial cases but not to the murder and drunk driving cases.

In summary, the effectiveness of systematic jury selection is debatable at this point. An answer to the question of its effectiveness will require more follow-up studies, though they are difficult to do and will likely be methodologically flawed. There are, however, logical reasons for believing that systematic selection may be more effective than traditional techniques, at least for certain cases.

THE ETHICS OF SCIENTIFIC SELECTION

Scientific jury selection is controversial on ethical as well as effectiveness grounds. Detailed discussion of the ethical issues is beyond the purview of this chapter but the reader is encouraged to refer to the following sources: Bermant and Shapard (1980); Berk et al. (1977); Berman and Sales (1977); Christie (1976); Etzioni (1974); McConahay et al. (1977); Saks (1976a, 1976b); Shapley (1974); Spector (1974). From this literature, the ethical arguments that can be made against the scientific selection of jurors include the following:

1. It is deceptive because social scientists cannot select jurors.
2. It makes a spectacle of the trial and the trial loses legitimacy.
3. Social science loses credibility when it is used in a blatant adversary attempt to choose jurors biased toward the defendant rather than impartial jurors.
4. It may eventually be used by prosecutors.

Those persons in favor of selection argue that it does work. They assert that the problems of such techniques making a spectacle of the trial and creating unpalatable adversary involvement of scientists must be viewed in the context of the political nature of the trials where the techniques typically have been employed. They believe every legal means available should be used to counter government oppression. Furthermore, scientific selection only systematizes what lawyers do anyway. The government already has an advantage over most defendants in terms of resources, including the fact that prosecutors frequently utilize police resources and F.B.I. records and have even been known to scrutinize juror tax returns in attempts to select jurors favorable to the prosecution (see Okun, 1968).

These ethical issues cannot be resolved by empirical means. Nevertheless, they constantly haunt scientific jury selection and must be given consideration in any research undertaken, whether it is directed toward the actual selection of jurors or the evaluation of the efficacy of scientific jury selection.

SUMMARY AND CONCLUSION

This chapter has been organized around three areas defined by the broad topic of jury selection: drawing a representative jury panel, obtaining changes of venue, and selection of individual jurors. In each of these areas we have attempted to portray the psychological issues and review literature which bears on them.

The review has identified important gaps in knowledge about jury selection and suggested avenues of research which can produce the data needed to fill those gaps. It has also noted that sometimes the conceptual and methodological approaches used in studies directed to jury selection issues lag behind more current developments in the field of personality and social psychology. On the other hand, if one steps back and views the literature from a broad chronological perspective, it becomes apparent that within the past 2 or 3 years basic and applied research efforts have become increasingly more sophisticated in both legal and psychological conceptualization. And, despite the gaps and weaknesses in the literature, it can also be asserted that a useful body of social psychological knowledge about jury selection issues does exist. One task now is to expand it. Another task is to educate judges and other legal decision makers so that the knowledge will be put to better use.

ACKNOWLEDGMENTS

Portions of this chapter were written while the first author was at the Department of Criminology at Simon Fraser University. She would like to express her gratitude to her colleagues and to the secretarial staff at Simon Fraser for their encouragement and assistance in the early stages of writing.

The authors would like to express appreciation to Sam Gaertner, Ken Haas, and Carl Klockars for their helpful comments on an earlier draft.

REFERENCES

Adorno, T., Frenkel-Brunswick, E., Levinson, D., & Sanford, R. *The authoritarian personality.* New York: Harper, 1950.

Ajzen, I., & Fishbein, M. *Understanding attitudes and predicting social behavior.* Englewood Cliffs, New Jersey: Prentice-Hall, 1980.

Alker, H. R., Hosticka, C., & Mitchell, M. Jury selection as a biased social process. *Law and Society Review,* 1976, *11,* 9–41.

Andenaes, J. The moral or educative influence of criminal law. *Journal of Social Issues,* 1971, *27,* 17–32.

Arnold, S., & Gold, A. The use of a public opinion poll on a change of venue application. *Criminal Law Quarterly,* 1978–1979, *21,* 445–464.

Babcock, B. A. Voir dire: Preserving "its wonderful power." *Stanford Law Review,* 1975, *27,* 545–565.

Bailey, F. L., & Rothblatt, H. B. *Successful techniques for criminal trials.* New York: Lawyers Cooperative, 1971.

Balch, R. W., Griffiths, C. T., Hall, E. L., & Winfree, L. T. The socialization of jurors: The voir dire as a rite of passage. *Journal of Criminal Justice,* 1976, *4,* 271–283.

Ballard v. U.S. United States Reports, 1946, *329,* 173–179.

Bem, D., & Allen, A. On predicting some of the people some of the time. *Psychological Review,* 1974, *81,* 506–520.

Berg, K., & Vidmar, N. Authoritarianism and recall of evidence about criminal behavior. *Journal of Research in Personality,* 1975, *9,* 147–157.

Berk, R. Social science and jury selection: A case study of a civil suit. In G. Bermant, C. Nemeth, & N. Vidmar (Eds.), *Psychology and the law.* Lexington, Massachusetts: Lexington, 1976.

Berk, R. A., Hennessy, M., & Swan, J. The vagaries and vulgarities of "scientific" jury selection. *Evaluation Quarterly,* 1977, *1,* 143–158.

Berman, J., & Sales, B. A critical evaluation of the systematic approach to jury selection. *Criminal Justice & Behavior,* 1977, *4,* 219–240.

Bermant, G. Juries and justice: The notion of conspiracy is not tasty to Americans. *Psychology Today,* May 1975, pp. *13–15.*

Bermant, G. *Conduct of the voir dire examination: Practices and opinions of federal district judges.* Washington, D.C.: Federal Judicial Center, 1977.

Bermant, G., & Shapard, J. The voir dire examination, juror challenges and adversary advocacy. In B. D. Sales (Ed.), *Perspectives in law and psychology, Volume II: The trial process.* New York: Plenum, 1980.

Bigam, R. G. Who should conduct the voir dire? The attorneys. *Judicature,* 1977, *61* (2), 71; 76–78.

Blauner, R. The sociology of jury selection. In A. F. Ginger (Ed.), *Jury selection in criminal trials.* Tiburon, California: Law Press, 1975.

Blauner, R. The Huey Newton jury *voir dire.* In R. Blauner (Ed.), *Racial oppression in America.* New York: Harper, 1972.

Blunk, R., & Sales, B. Persuasion during the voir dire. In B. Sales (Ed.), *Psychology in the legal process*. New York: Spectrum, 1977.

Bray, R., & Noble, A. Authoritarianism and decisions of mock juries: Evidence of jury bias and group polarization. *Journal of Personality and Social Psychology*, 1978, *36*, 1424–1430.

Broeder, D. The University of Chicago jury project. *Nebraska Law Review*, 1959, *38*, 744–761.

Broeder, D. The Negro in court. *Duke Law Journal*, 1965, 19–31. (a)

Broeder, D. *Voir dire* examinations: An empirical study. *Southern California Law Review*, 1965, *38*, 503–528. (b)

Brooks, W. N., & Doob, A. Justice and the jury. *Journal of Social Issues*, 1975, *31*, 171–182.

Bryan, W. *The chosen ones: The psychology of jury selection*. New York: Vantage, 1971.

Cavoukian, A. *Eyewitness testimony: The ineffectiveness of discrediting information*. Paper presented at the meeting of the American Psychological Association, Montreal, September 1980.

Chevigny, P. G. The Attica cases: A successful jury challenge in a northern city. *Criminal Law Bulletin*, 1975, *11*, 157–171.

Christie, R. Probability v. precedence: The social psychology of jury selection. In G. Bermant, C. Nemeth, & N. Vidmar (Eds.), *Psychology and the law*. Lexington, Massachusetts: Lexington, 1976.

Clement, D. E., & Schiereck, J. J., Jr. Sex composition and group performance in a visual signal detection task. *Memory and Cognition*, 1973, *1*, 251–255.

Cook, S. W., & Selltiz, C. A multiple-indicator approach to attitude measurement. *Psychological Bulletin*, 1964, *62*, 36–55.

Constantini, E., & King, J. The partial juror: Correlates and causes of prejudgment. *Law and Society Review*, 1980–1981, *15*, 9–40.

Crosby, F., Bromley, S., & Saxe, L. Recent unobtrusive studies of black and white discrimination and prejudice: A literature review. *Psychological Bulletin*, 1980, *87*, 546–563.

Darr, J. E. *People v. Jones*—The jury must be drawn from the district of the crime. *Hastings Law Journal*, 1974, *25*, 547–574.

Daughtrey, M. C. Cross sectionalism in jury selection: Procedures after *Taylor v. Louisiana*. *Tennessee Law Review*, 1975, *43*, 1–107.

Davis, J. H., Bray, R. M., & Holt, R. W. The empirical study of decision processes in juries: A critical review. In J. L. Tapp & F. J. Levine (Eds.), *Law, justice, and the individual in society: Psychological and legal issues*. New York: Holt, 1977.

Doob, A. N. Public's view of the criminal jury trial. Report to the Law Reform Commission of Canada on the results of the public opinion poll conducted on matters related to the criminal jury in Canada. In *Studies on the jury*. Ottawa, Ontario: Law Reform Commission of Canada, 1979.

Doob, A. N., & Kirshenbaum, H. M. Some empirical evidence on the effect of s.12 of the Canada Evidence Act upon the accused. *Criminal Law Quarterly*, 1972, *15*, 88–96.

Ebbesen, E., & Konečni, V. J. Decision making and information integration in the courts: The setting of bail. *Journal of Personality and Social Psychology*, 1975, *32*, 805–821.

Epstein, S. The stability of behavior: On predicting most of the people much of the time. *Journal of Personality and Social Psychology*, 1979, *37*, 1097–1126.

Etzioni, A. Creating an imbalance. *Trial*, 1974, *10* (November/December), 28–30.

Faber, T. Change of venue in criminal cases: The defendant's right to specify the county of transfer. *Stanford Law Review*, 1973, *26*, 131–157.

Farmer, M. C. Jury composition challenges. *Law and Psychology Review*, 1976, *2*, 43–74.

Feild, H. S. Juror background characteristics and attitudes toward rape: Correlates of jurors' decisions in rape trials. *Law and Human Behavior*, 1978, *2*, 73–93.

Fenelon, J. R., & Megargee, E. I. Influence of race on the manifestation of leadership. *Journal of Applied Psychology*, 1971, *55*, 353–358.

Fiedler, F. E., & Meuwese, W. Leader's contribution to task performances in cohesive and uncohesive groups. *Journal of Abnormal and Social Psychology*, 1963, *67*, 83–87.

Finkelstein, M. O. *Quantitative methods in law*. New York: Free Press, 1978.

Fishbein, M., & Ajzen, I. *Belief, attitude, intention, and behavior*: An introduction to theory and research. Reading, Massachusetts: Addison-Wesley, 1975.

Foster, M. *Jury selection*. Unpublished manuscript, Simon Fraser University, British Columbia, 1979.

Fox, R. Survey evidence of community standards in obscenity prosecutions. *Canadian Bar Review*, 1972, *1*, 315–330.

Gaertner, S. L. Nonreactive measures in racial attitude research: A focus on "liberals." In P. Katz (Ed.), *Towards the elimination of racism*. Elmsford, New York: Pergamon, 1976.

Gerbasi, K., Zuckerman, M., & Reis, H. Justice needs a new blindfold: A review of mock jury research. *Psychological Bulletin*, 1977, *84*, 323–345.

Gillespie, M. What the Miami race riots mean to all of us. *Ms.*, April 1980, pp. 87.

Ginger, A. F. *Minimizing racism in jury trials*. Berkeley, California: National Lawyers Guild, 1969.

Ginger, A. F. (Ed.), *Jury selection in criminal trials*. Tiburon, California: Law Press, 1975.

Gough, H. Clinical versus statistical prediction in psychology. In L. Postman (Ed.), *Psychology in the making*. New York: Knopf, 1962.

Gutman, S. The attorney conducted *voir dire* of jurors. *Brooklyn Law Review*, 1972–1973, *39*, 290–329.

Hackman, R., & Vidmar, N. Effects of size and task type on group performance and member reactions. *Sociometry*, 1970, *33*, 37–54.

Ham v. South Carolina. United States Reports, 1973, *409*, 524–534.

Hamilton, V. L. Obedience and responsibility: A jury simulation. *Journal of Personality and Social Psychology*, 1978, *36*, 126–146.

Hans, V. P. Evaluating the jury: The uses of research in policy formation. In R. Roesch & R. Corrado (Eds.), *Evaluation and criminal justice policy*. Beverly Hills, California: Sage Publications, Inc., in press.

Hans, V. P., & Doob, A. N. Section 12 of the Canada Evidence Act and the deliberations of simulated juries. *Criminal Law Quarterly*, 1976, *18*, 235–253.

Hart, H. M., & McNaughton, J. T. Evidence and inference in the law. In D. Lerner (Ed.), *Evidence and inference*. Glencoe, Illinois: Free Press, 1959.

Hawrish, E., & Tate, E. Determinants of jury selection. *Saskatchewan Law Review*, 1974–1975, *39*, 285–292.

Hepburn, J. R. The objective reality of evidence and the utility of systematic jury selection. *Law and Human Behavior*, 1980, *4*, 89–102.

Hoffman, L. R. Group problem solving. In L. Berkowitz (Ed.), *Advances in experimental social psychology*. New York: Academic Press, 1965.

Holdsworth, W. *A history of English law XI*. Boston: Little, Brown, 1938.

Horowitz, I. A. Juror selection: A comparison of two methods in several criminal cases. *Journal of Applied Social Psychology*, 1980, *10*, 86–99.

Howe, M. de W. Juries as judges of criminal law. *Harvard Law Review*, 1939, *52*, 582–616.

Hyman, I. A. Psychology, education, and schooling: Social policy implications in the lives of children and youth. *American Psychologist*, 1979, *34*, 1024–1029.

Jury Selection and Service Act of 1968, 28 U.S.C., 1861–1869. Washington, D.C.: U.S. Government Printing Office.

Kadish, M. R., & Kadish, S. H. The institutionalization of conflict: Jury acquittals. *Journal of Social Issues*, 1971, *27*, 199–218.

Kairys, D., Kadane, B., & Lehoczky, P. Jury representativeness: A mandate for multiple source lists. *California Law Review*, 1977, *65*, 776–827.

Kairys, D., Schulman, J., & Harring, S. (Eds.). *The jury system: New methods for reducing prejudice*. Cambridge, Massachusetts: National Jury Project and National Lawyers Guild, 1975.

Kalven, H., & Zeisel, H. *The American jury*. Boston: Little, Brown, 1966.

Kassin, S. M., & Wrightsman, L. S. On the requirements of proof: The timing of judicial instruction and mock juror verdicts. *Journal of Personality and Social Psychology*, 1979, *37*, 1877–1887.

Kuhn, R. S. Jury discrimination: The next phase. *Southern California Law Review*, 1968, 41, 235−328.

Lamont, J. Public opinion polls and survey evidence in obscenity cases. *Criminal Law Quarterly*, 1972−1973, 15, 135−159.

Law Reform Commission of Canada. *The jury in criminal trials* (Working Paper 27, 1980). Ottawa, Ontario: Minister of Supply and Services Canada, 1980.

Lempert, R. Uncovering "nondiscernible" differences: Empirical research and the jury-size cases. *Michigan Law Review*, 1975, 73, 644−708.

Levit, W., Nelson, A., Ball, T., & Chernik, A. Expediting voir dire: An empirical study. *Southern California Law Review*, 1971, 44, 916−995.

McConahay, J., Mullin, C., & Frederick, J. The uses of social science in trials with political and racial overtones: The trial of Joan Little. *Law and Contemporary Problems*, 1977, 41, 205−229.

McElroy, B. T. Public surveys—The latest exception to the hearsay rule. *Baylor Law Review*, 1976, 28, 59−76.

Meehl, P. E. *Clinical vs. statistical prediction*. Minneapolis: University of Minnesota Press, 1954.

Mischel, W. *Personality and assessment*. New York: Wiley, 1968.

Mischel, W. On the interface of cognition and personality: Beyond the person−situation debate. *American Psychologist*, 1979, 34, 740−754.

Mitchell, H. *Authoritarian punitiveness in simulated juror decision-making: The good guys don't always wear white hats*. Presented at the meeting of the Midwestern Psychological Association, Chicago, May, 1972.

Nemeth, C. Jury trials: Psychology and law. In L. Berkowitz (Ed.), *Advances in experimental social psychology* (Vol. 13). New York: Academic Press, 1981.

Nisbett, R., & Ross, L. *Human inference: Strategies and shortcomings of social judgment*. Englewood Cliffs, New Jersey: Prentice-Hall, 1980.

Note: The case for black juries. *Yale Law Journal*, 1970, 79, 531−550.

Note: The changing role of the jury in the nineteenth century. *Yale Law Journal*, 1964, 74, 170−192.

Okun, J. Investigation of jurors by counsel: Its impact on the decisional process. *Georgetown Law Journal*, 1968, 56, 839−892.

Padawer-Singer, A. M., Singer, A., & Singer, B. Voir dire by two lawyers: An essential safeguard. *Judicature*, 1974, 57, 386−391.

Penrod, S. *Evaluating social scientific methods of jury selection*. Paper presented at the meeting of the Midwestern Psychological Association, St. Louis, May, 1980. (a)

Penrod, S. *Practicing attorneys' jury selection strategies*. Paper presented at the meeting of the American Psychological Association, Montreal, September, 1980. (b)

People v. Attica Brothers. Miscellaneous Reports, 2d series, 1974, 79, 492−510; *New York Supplement*, 2d Series, 1974, 359, 699−717 (Erie Co. Sup. Ct.).

Piel, E. J. Voir dire in state and federal practice. In E. Margolin (Ed.), *16th annual defending criminal cases: The rapidly changing practice of criminal law*, Vol. 2. New York: Practicing Law Institute, 1978.

Pollock, A. The use of public opinion polls to obtain changes of venue and continuances in criminal trials. *Criminal Justice Journal*, 1977, 1, 269−288.

Radzinowicz, L. *A history of English criminal law and its administration from 1750: The movement for reform*. New York: Macmillan, 1948.

Radzinowicz, L. *A history of English criminal law and its administration from 1750: The clash between private initiative and public interest in the enforcement of law*. New York: Macmillan, 1957.

Regina v. Hubbert. Criminal Reports New Series, 1975, 31, 27−47.

Rokeach, M., & Kliejunas, P. Behavior as a function of attitude-toward-object and attitude-toward-situation. *Journal of Personality and Social Psychology*, 1972, 22, 194−201.

Rokeach, M., & Vidmar, N. Testimony concerning possible jury bias in a Black Panther murder trial. *Journal of Applied Social Psychology*, 1973, 3, 19−29.

Ruhe, J. A. *The effects of varying racial compositions upon attitudes and behavior of supervisors and subordinates in simulated work groups.* Unpublished doctoral dissertation, University of Florida, 1972.

Sage, W. Psychology and the Angela Davis jury. *Human Behavior,* January 1973, pp. 56–61.

Saks, M. The limits of scientific jury selection: Ethical and empirical. *Jurimetrics Journal,* 1976, *17,* 3–22. (a)

Saks, M. Scientific jury selection. *Psychology Today,* January 1976, pp. 48–57. (b)

Saks, M., & Hastie, R. *Social psychology in court.* Princeton, New Jersey: Van Nostrand-Reinhold, 1978.

Schulman, J., Shaver, P., Colman, R., Emrick, B., & Christie, R. Recipe for a jury. *Psychology Today,* May 1973, pp. 37–44; 77; 79–84.

Shapley, D. Jury selection: Social scientists gamble in an already loaded game. *Science,* September 1974, pp. 1033–1034.

Shaw, M. *Group dynamics: The psychology of small group behavior* (2nd ed.). New York: McGraw-Hill, 1976.

Sheppard v. Maxwell. United States Reports, 1966, *384,* 333–342.

Simon, R. *The jury: Its role in American society.* Lexington, Massachusetts: Lexington, 1980.

Spector, P. Scientific jury selection warps justice. *Harvard Law Record,* 1974, *58,* 15.

Stanley, Jr., A. J. Who should conduct voir dire? The judge. *Judicature,* 1977, *61*(2), 70; 72–75.

State v. Kramer. Wisconsin Reports, 2d Series, 45, 20–38; *North Western Reporter,* 2d Series, 1969, *171,* 919–936.

Stroble v. California. United States Reports, 1952, *343,* 181–204.

Suggs, D. The use of psychological research by the judiciary: Do the courts adequately assess the validity of the research? *Law and Human Behavior,* 1979, *3,* 135–148.

Suggs, D., & Sales, B. D. The art and science of conducting the voir dire. *Professional Psychology,* 1978, *9,* 367–388.

Summer, F. Voter registration lists: Do they yield a jury representative of the community? *University of Michigan Journal of Law Reform,* 1972, *5,* 385–407.

Tapp, J. L., & Keniston, A. *Wounded Knee—Advocate or expert.* Paper presented at the meeting of the American Psychological Association, Washington, D.C., August, 1976.

Taylor v. Louisiana. United States Reports, 1975, *419,* 522–543.

Tribe, L. Trial by mathematics: Precision and ritual in the legal process. *Harvard Law Review,* 1971, *84,* 1329–1393.

United States v. Guzman. Federal Supplement, 1972, *337,* 140–156 (S.D.N.Y.).

United States v. Irvin. Southern Reporter, 2d Series, 1953, *66,* 288–311.

United States v. Wood. United States Reports, 1936, *299,* 123–151.

Van Dyke, J. *Jury selection procedures.* Cambridge, Massachusetts: Ballinger, 1977.

Vidmar, N. Social science and jury selection. In Law Society of Upper Canada (Ed.), *Psychology and the litigation process.* Toronto, Ontario: Law Society of Upper Canada, 1976.

Vidmar, N. The other issues in jury simulation research. *Law and Human Behavior,* 1979, *3,* 95–106.

Vidmar, N., & Judson, J. *The use of social science data in a change of venue application: A case study* (Research Bulletin #488). London, Ontario: University of Western Ontario, 1979.

Vidmar, N., & Judson, J. The use of social science in a change of venue application. *Canadian Bar Review,* 1981, *59,* 76–102.

Webb, E. J., Campbell, D. T., Schwartz, R. D., & Sechrest, L. *Unobtrusive measures: Nonreactive research in the social sciences.* Chicago, Illinois: Rand McNally, 1966.

Weiten, W., & Diamond, S. A critical review of the jury simulation paradigm: The case of defendant characteristics. *Law and Human Behavior,* 1979, *3,* 71–93.

Wicker, A. Attitudes vs. actions: The relationship of verbal and overt behavioral responses to attitude objects. *Journal of Social Issues,* 1969, *25,* 41–78.

Woodward, J. A scientific attempt to provide evidence for a decision on change of venue. *American Sociological Review*, 1952, *17*, 447–452.

Zeigler, D. D. Young adults as a cognizable group in jury selection. *Michigan Law Review*, 1978, *76*, 1045–1101.

Zeisel, H. . . . And then there were none: The diminution of the federal jury. *University of Chicago Law Review*, 1971, *38*, 710–724.

Zeisel, H., & Diamond, S. The jury selection in the Mitchell-Stans conspiracy trial. *American Bar Foundation Research Journal*, 1976, *1*, 151–174.

Zeisel, H., & Diamond, S. The effect of peremptory challenges on jury and verdict: An experiment in a federal district court. *Stanford Law Review*, 1978, *30*, 491–531.

chapter

4

Effects of Defendants' and Victims' Characteristics on Jurors' Verdicts

Francis C. Dane

Lawrence S. Wrightsman

83

THE PSYCHOLOGY
OF THE COURTROOM

It is popular lore that the jury is responsive to the variations among individual defendants, and it is generally assumed further that these variations make less, or even no, difference to the judge.

—Kalven & Zeisel, 1966, p. 193

The Chicago Jury Project (Kalven & Zeisel, 1966) collected evidence that many characteristics of defendants and victims were related to disagreements between a jury and a judge regarding guilt or innocence or the probability that the defendant committed the crime. Kalven and Zeisel interpreted the causes of those disagreements in keeping with the above assumption, although only judges' perceptions were assesed in the Project.

Our thorough review of the literature completely supports the premise that juries do react to defendant characteristics, but a number of scholars have questioned the assumption that defendants' and victims' characteristics have no effect on judges (see, e.g., Bell, 1973; Champagne & Nagel, Chapter 9, this volume; Howard, 1975). The purpose of this chapter is to review research on the various defendants' and victims' characteristics to which jurors have been found to be responsive. We also attempt to provide an integrative framework within which these characteristics and their effects may be more extensively examined in future research.

Most of the characteristics that have been studied are *extralegal* characteristics, in that they have no direct legal relevance to the guilt or innocence of the defendant. While a defendant's gender or race may be relevant to an eyewitness identification, such characteristics become extralegal when used directly in the jurors' decisions: for example, "I can't believe that a woman would stab someone," or "Black people are always pulling knives on each other." The distinction between legally relevant and extralegal characteristics should not be made on the basis of the characteristics themselves, but rather on the manner in which the jurors consider the characteristics in their decisions. (For more information about how extralegal factors may operate in the decision process, see Kaplan, Chapter 7, this volume.)

Whether a given characteristic is legally relevant or not also depends upon the type of decision being made by the jurors. In some jurisdictions, jurors may determine the sentence, and characteristics which may be extralegal for a verdict may be legally relevant to a sentencing decision. In the case of a statutory rape charge in which the victim consented, for example, the fact that the defendant assumed the victim was of legal age to consent is not a legitimate defense in most states. The victim's complicity would be an extralegal factor when jurors decide on a verdict, but would be legally relevant when they (or another jury or judge) assign sentence after conviction. The distinction between verdicts and sentences is important, for the range of factors relevant to sentencing is broader than that for verdicts.

We have grouped the characteristics of defendants and victims into six major categories: gender, socioeconomic status, moral character, general attractiveness, race, and attitude similarity. These categories are neither mutually exclusive nor independent; there may be some overlap among them. A few of the characteristics exhibit rather predictable effects; for example; a prior criminal record, as an indication of moral character, leads jurors toward guilt, if it influences them at all. But the effects of other characteristics—especially the physical attractiveness of the defendant—are less straightforward and predictable. Regardless of the consistency of findings, we have attempted to summarize as much of the relevant research as possible, although failure to mention a particular study is more likely to be due to a lack of space than any inadequacy inherent in that study.

Our review is, of course, not the first review of defendants' and victims' characteristics, and we fully expect that it will not be the last. Nagel (1969) provided an excellent review of the effects of defendants' and victims' characteristics upon all phases of the criminal justice system, but his work is now quite dated. In a more specific issue, Hagan (1974) collated archival research on extralegal characteristics and concluded that the available evidence was inadequate to either confirm or disconfirm the existence of bias in judicial sentencing. Hagan recommended that multivariate techniques be used in conjunction with data collected from sources other than official court records. Similarly, Stephan's (1975) review of litigants' characteristics included a call for more sophisticated research techniques. (It was from Stephan's article that the general categories in this chapter were obtained.) Their perception of a lack of methodological sophistication also led Gerbasi, Zuckerman, and Reis (1977) and Weiten and Diamond (1979) to call for additional research.

One theme common to the previously mentioned reviews and others is the variety of dependent measures used to examine the effects of defendants' and victims' characteristics. While we must defer to the above reviews for more thorough discussions of the issue, we will point out a few of the relative merits of the more frequently employed measures: verdicts, sentences, and guilt scales. A verdict is, of course, the outcome of most criminal jury trials, and therefore would appear to be the most ecologically valid measure. The verdict however, has often been omitted as a dependent measure in both archival and simulation research (see Bray & Kerry, Chapter 10, this volume). Historically, a dichotomous verdict was not sufficiently sensitive to measure the sometimes subtle effects of extralegal characteristics, although currently available statistical procedures, such as log-linear chi-square (cf. Feinberg, 1977) and discriminant (cf. Bock, 1975) analyses provide very adequate solutions to this problem. When the focus of research is on punishment, however, sentences are a more appropriate measure. Nonetheless, it is inappropriate to generalize from effects on sentencing to effects on verdicts. When considering actual sentences, and for simulations in which the case materials definitely lead to conclusions of guilt, the issue of a verdict is moot. But in simulations in which mock jurors are asked to *assume* guilt, asking them to impose sentences may be questionable even from the standpoint of examining punishment. Dane (1979), for example, reported that mock jurors who had voted not guilty and were then asked to assume guilt and assign sentence suggested considerably more lenient sentences than did those who had voted guilty and therefore did not have to assume guilt. But Bray and Noble (1978) found no such difference in sentences as a function of verdicts. More research is needed to determine the extent and conditions of this problem.

Finally, the use of rating scales of "guiltiness" appears to be most appropriate for instances in which the researcher does not necessarily wish to generalize to jurors' behaviors but is instead using a trial simulation as a vehicle for examining the effects of independent variables on decision making in general, impression formation, and so on. Again, however, attempts to generalize about jurors' decisions using "guiltiness" scales are tenuous at best, and are more likely to be entirely inappropriate. On the other hand, guilt scales may be used to suggest variables likely to affect jurors' decisions, and may be useful to either demonstrate the potential impact of a variable or more fully explore a particular theoretical explanation for an otherwise demonstrable effect on jurors' decisions.

Clearly, we have only begun to introduce the issue of different dependent measures, and have not even touched upon other methodological issues, such as the relative merits of simulation versus archival methods. These and other issues have been considered in previous reviews, and are also examined by Bray and Kerr (Chapter 10, this volume). Our purpose, instead, is to ensure that readers are aware of such issues, and also to warn readers to exercise caution when interpreting the effects noted in this chapter. Archival studies often include confounding variables such as race, socioeconomic status, and gender when examining other characteristics, while simulation studies usually control for extraneous variables but often lack the external validity of archival studies. All of the various methods may be used to contribute to an understanding of defendants' and victims' characteristics, but not all methods may be applied to the same problems.

While the reviewers mentioned previously concentrated on empirical findings or methodological issues, others have concentrated on applying psychological theories to an understanding of the effects of defendants' and victims' characteristics on juror verdicts. Austin, Walster, and Utne (1976) and Izzett and Sales (1979), for example, have persuasively argued that equity theory (cf. Berkowitz

& Walster, 1976) adequately explains many of the effects we are going to discuss in this chapter. In both those reviews, however, it was also acknowledged that equity theory could not be used to explain *all* of the relationships among the various characteristics and decisions made by jurors. Perlman (1977) and McGillis (1978) have each noted the degree to which legal philosophy and the principles of attribution theory (cf. Harvey, Ickes, & Kidd, 1976, 1979) are aligned. Both scholars proposed that attribution theory be used as a general framework for the psychological study of the justice system as well as an integrative framework within which extralegal characteristics may be studied. Furthermore, Kidd and Utne (1978) have not only pointed out the utility of attribution theory, but have also argued that equity theory falls within such an approach, as a subsystem of concepts rather than as an independent set of explanatory concepts.

Alternatively, Davis, Bray, and Holt (1977) advocated a two-stage application of theory to decisions by jurors and juries; in doing so they recognized that a theory explaining predeliberation decisions of jurors may have little relevance to the decision process that occurs during group deliberations. For example, the effects of extralegal characteristics upon an individual's decision process may best be explained by using a reinforcement model of attraction, such as that of Byrne and Clore (1970). In contrast, a social decision scheme like the one formulated by Davis (1973) may best be used to summarize the extent to which this individual juror's decision is maintained during the give and take with the rest of the jury.

A major point emphasized in this chapter is that the effects of defendants' and victims' characteristics are often quite complex. Extralegal characteristics may result in interactive effects among themselves, as well as interactions with jurors' characteristics. Barnett and Feild (1978), for example, reported that the effect on sentencing of a defendant's physical attractiveness may be influenced by the defendant's gender. Snyder (1971) reported an interaction between the moral character of a litigant and the male–female composition of the jury. Reflecting even more complexity, the conclusions of Kauffman and Ryckman (1979) were that a three-way interaction exists among mock jurors' locus-of-control scores, the degree of similarity between the defendant's attitudes and the jurors', and crime severity. The extent to which the mock jurors held the defendant responsible for an offense was found to be related to a combination of all three of the variables. Another kind of interaction was manifested in a study by Foley, Chamblin, and Fortenberry (1979), in which a male defendant's race affected jurors' perceptions of his socioeconomic status, which in turn was related to both the ratings of guilt that the jurors made and the punishments they suggested.

The search of a comprehensive theory continues; to date, no single theoretical approach has been successfully applied to the full range of effects of defendants' and victims' characteristics on verdicts. The lack of an integrative approach may well have contributed to the plethora of research findings. By having used a variety of theoretical and atheoretical approaches, we have avoided the constraints inherent in any one theory, and therefore have been better able to examine those extralegal factors beyond the purview of any particular theory. The disadvantage, of course, is a resulting lack of cohesion within the field, as well as a lack of integration with other psycho-legal and general psychological interests.

Convincing arguments exist for the applicability of several theories to extralegal characteristics and their effects. But each also reveals limits or shortcomings. We thus believe that what is needed is *not* another theory of the same magnitude, but instead a metatheoretical system into which a variety of currently applicable theories may be integrated. Such a system would also have to be sufficiently flexible to contend with new theoretical developments, as well as any results not adequately explained by existing theories. In the next section, we describe one such metatheoretical system.

SCRIPTS

One approach that may be used to attain the required cohesion and integration needed, without creating the undesirable constraints associated with yet another theory, is the "bundle of concepts coded by the term 'scripts' [Abelson, 1978, p.1]." *Script processing* is a conceptual approach containing the proposition that a variety of behaviors may be carried out or understood by virtue of a common sequence. This emphasis on *common sequence* is essential. The context, or social situation, in which the events occur is often considered to be the major determinant of whether or not the events are likely to be perceived as sequential. For example, consider the act of giving money to a stranger. In the context of doing so in a grocery store, the individual expects the sequence to include an exchange of material goods. But this is not so in the context of a religious service. More formally, a script is a *"coherent sequence of events expected by the individual, involving him* [or her] *either as a participant or an observer* [Abelson, 1976, p. 23, italics in original]." Script processing has been applied to international politics as well as to attitude formation and decision making (Abelson, 1973, 1976). Although script processing has yet to be applied specifically to the decision processes of jurors, the jury trial does fit the formal definition of a script insofar as a trial is a coherent sequence of events for which jurors all have expectations. In a criminal trial, these expectations may include presentation of incriminating evidence by the prosecution, presentation of exculpatory evidence by the defense, and deliberation to a unanimous verdict by members of the jury. Even at the gross level just described, different expectations among jurors concerning the sequencing or occurrence of the events may affect the "playing" of the script, and different cognitions of what should be in the script may alter the processing of events. One juror may expect the defendant to completely discredit the prosecution's evidence, while another juror's script may not include this event. If the defendant does not discredit the prosecution's evidence, these two jurors could hold different opinions about the defendant's guilt. If common expectations concerning the prosecution's portion of the script are not fulfilled (say, for example, that no incriminating evidence is presented), the outcome of the script will be different from that in which the expectations are met.

At more molecular levels of the trial script, each witness may be considered an event, or even each witness' response to a single question may be considered an event. As the level of consideration moves from the more molar to the more molecular, extralegal characteristics may become of increasingly greater importance with respect to the outcome of the script. Consider, for example, a brief, truncated response by a defendant to a penetrating question from the prosecuting attorney. If the defendant is black or of a lower socioeconomic status, this response may lead to different inferences than if the defendant were white or wealthy.

Events sequenced within the script are labelled *vignettes* (Abelson, 1976), that is, events of a relatively short duration encoded in memory. Vignettes may exist at three different cognitive levels: episodic, categorical, and hypothetical. *Episodic vignettes* are concrete, usually singular encodings: Mary once shoplifted a necklace or George once assaulted Ralph. A *categorical vignette* may be a generic conceptualization resulting from collections of episodic vignettes: Women I know commit nonviolent crimes while men I know commit violent crimes. A categorical vignette may also come about as a result of encoding generic information without episodic referents: I don't know anyone who has committed a crime, but I read in the newspaper that women commit nonviolent crimes while men commit violent crimes. In contrast, *hypothetical vignettes*, the most abstract level, involve not only the processing of episodic or categorical vignettes, but also the application of conditions, inferences, and abstract rules: Since the defendant is a woman charged with a violent crime, and since women in general commit nonviolent crimes, I believe her denial of the charge.

Returning once more to the definition of a script, we take note of something that has been implicit in the previous paragraphs: Expectations concerning the sequencing of events may result from either participation in the script or observation of a script being performed by others. That is, it is not necessary that an individual already have participated in the justice system in order to develop an expectation for a sequence of trial events. Observation is sufficient for the development of a script and, more importantly, it need not be either direct or realistic. It is possible that scripts or vignettes related to trials—and particularly the impact of extralegal characteristics—may result from sources other than real trials. For example, the person may "reason": On television they never prosecute the wrong person, so this real defendant must be the right (guilty) person. It is also not the case that an event, or vignette, must be the result of a cause–effect relationship. Simple coexistence of two phenomena may constitute a vignette, such as in the example of defendant's gender and the type of crime mentioned earlier. The defendant's being a woman or a man may not be an event in the same manner that shoplifting is an event; yet each may be an occurrence that is sequentially related in the cognitive structure of a trial participant. Similarly, while vignettes may be neatly classified as either episodic, categorical, or hypothetical, the same is not true for scripts. A script may contain any number of vignettes, as well as several different kinds of vignettes. A juror may have encoded an episodic vignette concerning the defendant's gender, a categorical vignette concerning the defendant's race, and an hypothetical vignette concerning the victim's attractiveness. Thus, it appears to be more reasonable to discuss defendants' and victims' characteristics in terms of vignettes rather than in terms of scripts, a point to which we shall return at the conclusion of the chapter.

RESEARCH ON SPECIFIC CHARACTERISTICS: GENDER

Defendants

The paucity of research on the effects of gender may stem from the fact that Green's (1961) initial examination of sentences in actual cases led him to conclude that no relationship existed between defendants' gender and sentences assigned them. While women did tend to receive shorter sentences, the relationship did not hold after type of crime was controlled. Kalven and Zeisel (1966), however, reported that men were five times more likely to be convicted of killing their spouses by juries, in those cases in which the judge also would have ruled a conviction. Nagel (1969) found sentences to be more lenient for women when the crimes were either grand larceny or burglary.

Researchers using simulations, in contrast to those using actual cases, have usually found more complex effects, a result more than likely due to the fact that the simulation researchers could examine a wider variety of variables in their studies. Stephan (1974), for example, reported that jurors deciding a homicide of spouse case were more likely to vote to convict a defendant of the same gender as themselves, although at the same time males were, overall, more likely to be perceived as victims of circumstance. Since the majority of jurors studied by Kalven and Zeisel were males, Stephan's results appear to be consistent with theirs. Barnett and Feild (1978), using a burglary charge, found the gender of the defendant to interact with the defendant's overall attractiveness. Specifically, women were assigned shorter sentences than men when they were portrayed as attractive, but men and women portrayed as unattractive received equivalent sentences. Similarly, Smith, and Carnahan (1979) found an interaction between the defendant's gender and socioeconomic status when jurors assigned responsibility in a manslaughter case. When the defendant was of higher status, male and female defendants were assigned equal responsibility, but when the defendant was of lower status, males were assigned greater responsibility. Despite the different ratings of responsibility, no differences were obtained on a measure of suggested sentences, and verdicts were not measured at all.

Victims

Apparently, no studies have been reported in which the gender of the victim served as a variable, except those studies on homicide of spouse.

Conclusions

The more recent research does not appear to alter the conclusion made by Green in 1961 that the role of the defendant's gender differs depending on the type of crime. In fact, Kalven and Zeisel (1966) went so far as to suggest that "the crimes committed by women are so different that a simple comparison . . . would reveal little [p. 202]." Simple comparisons have, however, revealed that the effects of the gender of the defendant—and presumably the victim—are somewhat more complicated than those reported in early studies. The variables considered in the simulations were not included in the early archival studies, so this result is hardly surprising. What is surprising, however, is that homicide of spouse is the only crime for which verdicts have been examined, and the only crime for which victims' gender has been examined. Given Green's (1961) conclusion that type of crime more adequately explains the sentencing differences resulting from defendants' gender, and Stephan's (1974) results concerning the interaction between the defendant's and jurors' gender, a considerable amount of additional research is required before general conclusions can be drawn. Perhaps a systematic series of simulations of the crimes included in Green's study would be in order.

Let us try to relate the above to the script processing approach. Within this approach, the relationship between type of crime and the effect of the defendant's gender becomes an important variable in determining how jurors may process information during the trial. Different effects may be expected for various levels of vignettes concerning gender. For example, a juror aware of the observation that fewer women are brought to trial for burglary (Kalven & Zeisel, 1966) may be likely to acquit when operating at a categorical level: Few women are burglars so this woman is not likely to be a burglar. On the other hand, a hypothetical vignette may result in a greater likelihood of conviction with the same information: Few women are brought to trial for burglary, but the prosecutor has charged this woman, so the prosecutor must be convinced of the woman's guilt. Of course, a script processing approach would be useful only to the extent that one is able to predict, or at least measure after the decision, jurors' levels of script processing. Insofar as this concern is relevant to all characteristics to be discussed, we will postpone our discussion of measurement and prediction until all characteristics have been reviewed.

SOCIOECONOMIC STATUS

The amount of research in which the socioeconomic status of either defendants or victims has been related to the verdicts of juries is only somewhat greater than that concerning gender. Kalven and Zeisel (1966) again provide us with a possible explanation: "the vast majority of serious criminals happen to be not well off [p. 196]." However, new research efforts as well as reanalyses of previous results have increased, perhaps as a result of increased concern over white-collar and politically motivated crimes.

Defendants

Kalven and Zeisel also indicated that average and well-to-do defendants were slightly more likely to have a defense counsel superior to the prosecutor, while the reverse held for poor defendants. Depending upon the extent to which the performance of counsel enters into the jurors' trial scripts, such differences may contribute to different conviction rates. Nagel (1969), however, did not find a statistically reliable relationship between socioeconomic status and conviction rates, although he did report that indigent defendants received longer prison sentences if convicted. Hagan's (1974) reanalyses of a variety of actual cases, including Nagel's, indicated that the socioeconomic status of the defendants was not related to actual sentences once relevant variables such as type of crime and prior record were controlled. Similarly, Chirocas and Waldo (1975) found no relationship between actual sentences and defendants' socioeconomic status.

In contrast to the studies of actual trial outcomes, simulation studies have exhibited a profusion of effects from manipulations of the defendant's socioeconomic status. Shaw (1972) found that a defendant described as an architect was trusted more than one described as a janitor, but he did not ask his subjects for either sentences or verdicts. Legent (1973) reasoned that a defendant's socioeconomic status was likely to be related to the length of pretrial detention, but found no effect for length of pretrial detention upon jurors' reactions to the defendant. Gleason and Harris (1976) manipulated the defendant's socioeconomic status with information about occupation and annual income; the difference had no effect upon ratings of guilt, but the defendant of lower socioeconomic status was perceived as more blameworthy. Using a different manipulation, Rumsey (1976) found that a defendant described as having a socioeconomically deprived background tended to receive longer sentences than did a defendant described as having a fortunate background. Perhaps the jurors in Rumsey's study viewed the deprived defendant as more blameworthy, or, as Sigall and Ostrove (1975) have suggested, the expected recidivism rate for more fortunate defendants may be lower, and a lesser punishment may be considered more effective for them. An expected high rate of recidivism for defendants of a deprived background could, on the other hand, be viewed as a condition of general blameworthiness; jurors may think that sooner or later these defendants are going to be guilty of something. Bray, Struckman-Johnson, Osborne, McFarlane, and Scott (1978), however, reported that a defendant of lower socioeconomic status received shorter sentences, despite the fact that defendant status did not affect either the individual or group verdicts. In both the Rumsey and the Bray *et al.* simulatious, the defendant was charged with homicide, but Rumsey used a negligent homicide charge while Bray *et al.* used murder. Thus, the type of crime may interact with the defendant's socioeconomic status even when the outcome (death) for different crimes is the same. However, such a result is not surprising in light of the archival research discussed earlier in this section.

Using a different approach, Foley *et al.* (1979) examined perceived socio-economic status rather than manipulating it. Within the context of the framework of this chapter, we might say that Foley *et al.* assessed the jurors' vignettes regarding socioeconomic status. Subjects who perceived the *defendant's* socioeconomic status to be relatively high rated the defendant as less guilty and gave him shorter sentences. On the other hand, the socioeconomic status of the *jurors* was directly related to their ratings of the defendant's guilt and suggested sentences. Foley *et al.* did not, however, examine the extent to which the two variables may have interacted. In contrast, Shepherd and Sloan (1979) did not find their defendant's socioeconomic status to be related to sentencing, although socioeconomic status and perceived attitude similarity did interact in affecting judged responsibility. When the defendant's socioeconomic status was low, attitude similarity did not produce any different ratings for responsibility for the crime. But when the defendant's socioeconomic status was relatively high, the defendant with attitudes similar to those of the jurors was perceived as less responsible for the crime. Perhaps similarity of the defendant's socioeconomic status to that of jurors, rather than the status per se, affects jurors' decisions.

Capitalizing on a very different type of operational definition, Fontaine and Kiger (1978) have provided indirect evidence for the effects of socioeconomic status on verdicts in their study on defendants' dress and supervision. If a defendant is dressed in prison clothing, a juror may interpret this as an indication that the defendant is either too poor to afford bail, or too dangerous to be allowed bail. By varying both the dress and the degree of supervision—while in the courtroom, defendants either had no supervision or an armed guard—Fontaine and Kiger attempted to separate the two possible interpretations. When the defendants were not supervised, the one in prison clothing was more likely to be convicted, which is consistent with other results. But when there was supervision, wearing prison clothing resulted in fewer convictions. If one assumes—perhaps tenuously—that when defendants were supervised, jurors saw the prison clothing as indicating lower socioeconomic status, a leniency effect is obtained.

Victims

It is interesting—in fact it is distressing—to note that no archival research has been reported on victims' socioeconomic status. Simulations are also somewhat scarce, as well as contradictory. Boor (1976) concluded that wealthier victims evoked less sympathy from jurors, but Shaw (1972) found just the opposite. While Shaw did not examine suggested sentences, Boor found that the greater sympathy for penurious victims did not mean that their defendants received longer sentences. Kerr and Kurtz (1977) found socioeconomic status of the victim to be unrelated to suggested sentences.

Conclusions

In general, Hagan's (1974) conclusion concerning archival studies may also be applied to simulation studies, especially regarding the victim's socioeconomic status, but the number of studies here is very limited. That is, there does not appear to be a consistent relationship between either defendants' or victims' socioeconomic status and jurors' decisions. The results, however, also lead us to conclude that some sort of relationship *ought* to exist. For example, Bray et al. (1978) reported no effect for socioeconomic status on mock jurors' verdicts, but there was a moderately high proportion of not guilty verdicts in their study (59%). Perhaps the case was too heavily weighted toward acquittal. Again, this points to the different uses to which simulation cases may be put. Cases which have a great deal of exonerating or incriminating evidence may be useful for examining sentencing effects, but are probably too heavily biased to allow for an examination of verdicts. Alternatively, Foley et al. (1979) reported an effect, but they used a rating scale rather than categorical verdicts. Perhaps socioeconomic status affects jurors' verdicts only when the amount of incriminating evidence is either small or close to the amount of exculpatory evidence. (See end of this chapter for a more extensive discussion of this point.)

Several researchers reported effects upon variables that may be related to either verdicts or sentences, for example, sympathy or responsibility, but either did not include verdict or sentence measures, or they examined sentences and found no concomitant effects. Again, however, we point to the methodological problems inherent in asking jurors to suggest sentences after assuming guilt. We found no studies on socioeconomic status in which jurors' verdicts served as a factor in analyses of sentences; use of such a factor is likely to alter the results of the analyses. Thus, we find three possible conclusions: socioeconomic status is directly related to leniency, is inversely related to leniency, or is not related to jurors' decisions.

To us, the inconsistencies in the results of the studies suggest that vignettes associating socioeconomic status and guilt (or punishment) may be hypothetical rather than episodic or categorical. The type of information accompanying socioeconomic status, such as prior record, perceived dangerousness, or type of crime, may either increase, decrease, or not affect the likelihood of conviction. That the effects of socioeconomic status may be complex, however, does not mean that socioeconomic status should be written off as having no influence on jurors' decisions about either guilt or punishment. Instead, a systematic examination of the relationships that may exist in the jurors' scripts may lead to a determination of the additional characteristics that serve as conditionals in the hypothetical vignettes.

MORAL CHARACTER

In this section on moral character of defendants and victims as it affects verdicts, we have separated our discussion into specific subcategories related to moral character. For defendants, these include additional offenses committed either before the current charge (prior record) or at the same time (multiple offenses) and the degree of remorse or suffering shown by the defendant. For victims, the subcategories include precipitation of the crime and the degree of the victim's suffering. As in the case of socioeconomic status, the extent to which any given researcher examined moral character per se was sometimes difficult to determine.

Defendants' Additional Offenses

Hagan's (1974) reanalyses of a variety of archival studies used the defendants' prior records as a controlling variable, a procedure that resulted in the statistical elimination of effects for such variables as socioeconomic status and gender. Since Hagan did not report analyses on prior record per se, it is not possible to determine the relative influence of prior record, although the data clearly reflect an influence upon the sentencing decisions of judges and, where appropriate, jurors. Kalven and Zeisel (1966) claimed that 10% of the cases in which the jury convicted when the judge would have acquitted were attributable to the jurors' knowledge or presumptions of defendants' prior records. Kalven and Zeisel did not, however, distinguish between those cases in which prior record was made known and those in which the defendant did not testify (presumably to avoid the introduction of a prior record into evidence). Shaffer and Sadowsky (1979), using simulations, have found that defendants' refusal to testify increases the likelihood of their being convicted, thus making it impossible to determine the relative influence of prior record upon jurors' decisions in Kalven and Zeisel's study.

As is the case with characteristics previously discussed, there is more simulation research than archival research on the effects of prior record, and the simulation studies are more difficult to interpret. Among the factors manipulated in the well-known study by Landy and Aronson (1969) was the defendant's prior conviction record. The condition in which the defendant was described as unattractive—the one that produced longer recommended sentences—also included information that the defendant "was a notorious hoodlum and ex-convict who had been convicted of assualt and extortion [p. 145]," crimes which were not related to the charge under consideration, negligent homicide (with an automobile). A replication by Nemeth and Sosis (1973) included a prior record of traffic offenses for both defendants, with the unattractive defendant also having been convicted of breaking and entering and a drug violation. The manipulation of the defendant's attractiveness had the same effect in their replication, but the prior records again contained unrelated offenses. Subsequent replications involving the Landy and Aronson case materials have cast doubt upon the reliability of their original effects. For example, Izzett and Leginski (1974) reported that the effect on sentence resulting from the manipulation of the attractiveness factor, which included prior record, did not persist after the jurors had an opportunity to discuss the case. In the unattractive defendant condition, jurors' sentences were significantly more lenient after discussion than before, while the suggested sentences for those defendants described as attractive were relatively unaffected by discussion. Similarly, Weiten (1979) reported no differences with respect to verdicts when judge's instructions were included in the materials, although Weiten did obtain the original sentencing effect.

Those readers familiar with the Landy and Aronson case materials are aware that characteristics other than prior record were used to create differences between the attractive and unattractive defendants. However, Hatton, Snortum, and Oskamp (1971) did vary only the prior record of the defendant, and found that a defendant with prior traffic violations and one conviction for assault was more likely to be convicted of reckless driving than a defendant with no prior record.

Insofar as Landy and Aronson's case involved defendant characteristics other than prior record, it is not reasonable to conclude that the harsher treatment of the defendant with the prior record was due solely to the existence of that record, although the results of the archival studies and of Hatton *et al.* suggest that prior record contributed in some way to the differential sentence assignments. It is also possible that the level of vignettes used by jurors exerts some influence on the effect of defendants' prior records. For example, jurors with categorical vignettes may not distinguish between related and unrelated prior convictions (they may think that a criminal is a criminal is a criminal), while those with hypothetical vignettes may be more likely to convict only when prior convictions relating to the crime under consideration exist.

The presence of an accomplice also affects jurors' decisions. Kalven and Zeisel (1966) and Feldman and Rosen (1979) reported that a defendant received more lenient treatment when an accomplice was involved in the crime. This effect has usually been interpreted in conjunction with a diffusion of responsibility for the crime, which suggests to us a hypothetical level of script processing. Feldman and Rosen were also able to demonstrate that mock jurors aware of the exis- tance of an accomplice assigned less responsibility for the crime to their defen- dant than did those jurors whose case involved no mention of an accomplice. In an earlier simulation study, DeJong, Morris, and Hastorf (1976) found that both responsibility for planning the crime and the accomplice's fate affected jurors' decisions. Defendants described as more responsible for the planning of a rob- bery were given longer sentences than those described as following the plans of someone else, and defendants whose accomplices had escaped were given shorter sentences than were those whose accomplices were captured. DeJong *et al.* did not examine verdict preferences, perhaps because the variables of inter- est were expected to have a greater impact on punishment than on judgments of guilt. Defendants whose accomplices escape justice may be seen as having already received, by comparison, some punishment for their crime. Kerr and Sawyers (1978) reported that the amount of evidence for one charge affected the likelihood that mock jurors would convict on the second charge in a two-charge case. When the strength of the evidence for the first charge was high, jurors were less likely to convict on the second charge, whereas weak evidence for the first charge tended to increase the likelihood of conviction for the second charge. Apparently, as long as the mock jurors could convict, the presumably ensure punishment for one charge, they were willing to be lenient on the other charge. Concern with punishment on the part of jurors is consistent with the results of studies in which the extent of the defendant's suffering or remorse was manipu- lated.

Defendants' Remorse or Suffering

The emotional tone of the defendant seems to have an effect on likelihood of conviction. Savitsky and Sim (1974) reported that mock jurors were least likely to recommend conviction for a juvenile displaying a sad or distressed expres- sion, but that conviction rates increased as the juvenile defendants showed neutral, happy, and finally angry expressions. Rumsey (1976) found that a defendant described as remorseful received shorter suggested sentences than one described as having no remorse. Thus, not only is remorse likely to evoke more sympathy than a neutral disposition, but showing of emotions other than those seen as appropriate for one who regrets a criminal act may lead to greater punishment. Other evidence supporting a punishment orientation has been presented by Austin, Walster, and Utne (1976), who found that severe defen- dant suffering (paralysis) reduced suggested sentences, although some sentence was given. Less severe suffering (broken bones) did not affect sentences when compared to a condition in which the defendant suffered no physical injury. Austin and Utne (1976) demonstrated that the suffering experienced by the defendant need not be the result of the criminal act in order to achieve the effect of moderating sentences. Defendants who suffered severe injuries while out on bail awaiting sentencing were treated in the same ways as those who incurred the injury while committing the offense.

With the exception of the work by Savitsky and Sim (1974), who also measured guilt on a continuous scale, studies on defendants' remorse or suffering have measured jurors' reactions only by looking at suggested sentences. Kerr (1978b), however, used jurors' verdicts to demonstrate that expectations of more severe sentences may reduce the likelihood of conviction. Thus, while it is not possible to determine the extent to which prior punishment or remorse affects jurors' verdicts, it does appear as though jurors' expectations for forthcoming punishment may decrease the chances for conviction. If punishment, rather than rehabilitation or compensation of the victim, is the primary concern within jurors' trial scripts, one might expect severely injured defendants to be less likely to be convicted. It is also apparent that the level of script processing may alter the effects of the defendant's remorse and/or suffering in a manner similar to that described for prior record. Those jurors whose vignettes concerning remorse or suffering are categorical may not distinguish between suffering related to the crime and unrelated to it, while those with hypothetical vignettes may consider only related suffering in their decisions.

Victims' Precipitation

The results of simulation studies concerning the moral character of the victim (there is only anecdotal archival research) are considerably more complicated than those for the moral character of the defendant. Hatton et al. (1971), for example, included a condition in which the victim of the traffic accident in which the defendant was criminally charged had unsuccessfully sued for damages from a previous accident. The likelihood of conviction, however, for that condition was found to be nearly identical to that in the control condition. Smith (1976), on the other hand, found that the degree of preventative action taken by a victim of a burglary affected judged responsibility for the loss. Those victims who had not taken preventative action, such as locking the door, were perceived as more responsible for the loss than were those who had locked their doors. Miller, Smith, Ferree, and Taylor (1976) have also demonstrated that the degree of responsibility assigned to the victim is directly related to perceived precipitation of the crime. A victim injured in an automobile accident was perceived as more responsible for her injuries when she was driving a car than when she was a pedestrian. In a third condition, the woman was the victim of forcible rape rather than a traffic accident—a situation that Miller et al. claimed to be ambiguous with respect to precipitation—and the amount of responsibility assigned to the rape victim was less than that for the driver, but greater than that for the pedestrian. The assumption by Miller et al. that forcible rape constitutes a criminal act in which jurors' attributions of the cause or fault are ambiguous may be disturbing to some readers, but the assumption is based on a relative abundance of research.

Kaplan and Miller (1978), for example, reported that a defendant accused of raping a woman in a dark alley received lower guilt ratings, and shorter sentences, than one accused of raping a woman in a public library. These main effects, however, appeared to be due to an interaction between the location where the rape occurred and the gender of the mock juror's only child. Jurors who were parents of females rated the defendant's guilt higher and suggested longer sentences when the rape occurred in the library, whereas the ratings for both guilt and punishment were highly similar among the other conditions in the experiment. Thus, not only may victims' potential precipitation of the crime affect jurors' decisions, but identification with the victim may also be influential.

Feild (1979), in an extremely ambitious design, reported that the effect of manipulation of potential precipitation—in one case the defendant forced his way into the victim's apartment; in the other he was allowed in to make a phone call—interacted with the strength of evidence presented, as well as with the victim's sexual experience. Defendants in the first case were assigned longer sentences than those in the second. The strength of the evidence against the defendant did not appear to affect recommended sentences when the defendant was invited into the apartment, although a strong case against the defendant resulted in significantly longer sentences than a weak case when the defendant forced his way in. Similarly, the difference between the sentences assigned in the precipitation and nonprecipitation conditions was significantly smaller for sexually experienced victims than for sexually inexperienced victims. That is, whether or not the rape had been potentially precipitated was more important when the victim was sexually inexperienced than in cases with experienced victims. (Feild also manipulated victim's attractiveness, defendant's race, and victim's race; the effects of these variables will be discussed when we consider those characteristics later in this chapter. For extensive discussions on attitudes toward rape, see Feild, 1978a, 1978b.)

Victims' Suffering

Jones and Aronson (1973) studied the effects of manipulations of the moral character of a rape victim in a study that has generated further research. Victims of a rape or attempted rape who were less "respectable" (divorced) were perceived to be *less* responsible for the crime than were more respectable victims, even though suggested sentences for the defendant were longer when the victim was respectable. Hoiberg and Stires (1973), however, reported that pretrial publicity focusing on the brutality of a rape–murder case did not affect guilt ratings when compared to a case in which the brutality was not mentioned. Of course, the outcome of the crime was the same, and jurors may have focused only on that. Additional replications and extensions of Jones and Aronson's case materials have produced the same effect for sentencing but not for responsibility (Kerr & Kurtz, 1977), as well as no effects whatsoever (Kahn *et al.*, 1977). Kahn *et al.* also suggested that methodological and statistical shortcomings in Jones and Aronson (1973) are also alternative explanations for the original effects.

Force used by the attacker and resistance by the victim are other variables related to the amount of suffering experienced by the victim, and may, in turn, affect jurors' decisions. Whether or not attackers' force and victims' resistance are extralegal characteristics depends on the specific definition in a particular legal code. When rape is defined as intercourse without voluntary consent, however, these variables may be considered extralegal. Krulewitz (1977) has shown that the amount of force used by a rapist is related to perceptions regarding the occurrence of the crime, while Emmert (1978) concluded that the amount of the victim's resistance affected decisions concerning whether or not the situation was one involving rape. Olah, Oros, Koss, and Emmert (1979) manipulated amounts of force and resistance, as well as delay in reporting the event, and found that only the delay factor affected jurors' verdicts. Defendants were perceived as less likely to be convicted as the delay in reporting increased. Amounts of force and resistance, however, did influence the extent to which the jurors perceived the situation as one involving rape. When the amount of force was high, amount of resistance had no effect upon interpretations of rape. When the amount of force was low, however, victims who offered greater resistance were more likely to be perceived as having been raped than those who offered less resistance. Sporer (1979) reported that when the victim was only 12 years old (and presumably could not have precipitated the rape), longer sentences were suggested than when the victim was 25 years old. Consistent with previous research, Sporer also noted that suggested sentences were longer in those conditions in which the victim's father or husband was killed trying to capture the rapist than in those in which he was only slightly injured. As with the previous characteristics concerning moral character, the amount of victims' suffering does appear to be a part of jurors' scripts, although the processing of this particular vignette appears to deal more with sentences than with verdicts.

Conclusions

It appears that jurors are more likely to convict, or suggest longer sentences for, defendants of lower moral character, and that defendants are treated more harshly when the victim is of high moral character. When defendants incur severe injury during the criminal act, jurors treat them more leniently. These trends indicate that jurors' primary concerns during the trial are related more to punishing the defendant than rehabilitation or compensating the victim. While moral character appears to be a factor in the script processing of jurors, the research also suggests that a higher order reason or purpose behind the script may also be present (i.e., retribution).

GENERAL ATTRACTIVENESS

We turn now to a category of defendants' and victims' characteristics that includes no specific trait, but contains instead a variety of characteristics that may combine to affect the general impressions jurors form regarding the defendant or victim. Studies for which general attractiveness is a factor are those in which a number of characteristics were simultaneously examined, making it impossible to determine which specific characteristic(s) among those examined was influential. The effects of physical attractiveness are also examined in this section.

Defendants

By combining a variety of defendants' and victims' characteristics, we were able to determine from Kalven and Zeisel's (1966) data that in about 14% of those cases in which the jury acquitted when the judge would have convicted, the acquittal was the result of either the defendant being attractive, the victim being unattractive, or both. A similar percentage of cases in which the jury convicted when the judge would have acquitted appeared to owe their outcomes to the unattractiveness of the defendants, attractiveness of the victims, or both. Similarly, Snyder (1971) examined a number of civil cases and found that attractive litigants won their cases more often than less attractive litigants, but only in cases with exclusively male juries.

Mitchell and Byrne (1972) varied the general attractiveness of a defendant through a report given by a court psychologist, combined with judge's instructions to either pay special attention to or disregard that testimony. A control condition was included in which the judge's instructions contained no mention of the psychologist's report; jurors' authoritarianism scores were also obtained. The less attractive defendant received longer sentences. General attractiveness did not affect guilt ratings or parole recommendations, probably because the case materials were highly incriminating. The effect of the judge's instructions was limited to nonauthoritarian jurors, who were better able to disregard the psychologist's testimony when told to do so than authoritarian jurors.

Using different case materials and a different measure of authoritarianism, Vidmar and Crinklaw (1973) replicated the results of Mitchell and Byrne (1972). They also examined the reasons given by jurors for sentences and concluded that retribution, rather than utility, better described the jurors' motivations for assigning punishment. That is, the jurors were more interested in punishing the defendant than in using sentence as a general deterrent to crime, especially when the defendant was unattractive. Others (Reynolds & Sanders, 1973; Rumsey & Castore, 1974) have replicated the phenomenon by which longer sentences are given to unattractive defendants. Berg and Vidmar (1975) reported that attractiveness of defendants contributed to ratings of their guilt (jurors were more certain of the guilt of an unattractive defendant); they also found the interaction between attractiveness and authoritarianism obtained by Mitchell and Byrne (1972).

Furthermore, Berg and Vidmar were able to clarify the nature of this interaction: highly authoritarian jurors remembered more facts about the defendant's character and fewer facts about the crime situation than did less authoritarian jurors. Thus, authoritarian jurors may be less able to disregard judges' instructions concerning general attractiveness (Mitchell & Byrne, 1972) because they pay more attention to attractiveness than their less authoritarian counterparts.

Given the research discussed thus far, it is not possible to determine whether generally unattractive defendants are at a disadvantage or generally attractive defendants have a special advantage compared to a defendant of average attractiveness. Kaplan and Kemmerick (1974) presented jurors with case materials containing postive traits, negative traits, both positive and negative traits ("neutral" condition), or no information about the defendant's attractiveness. As the descriptions decreased from positive through neutral to negative, ratings of guilt increased. Ratings in the no information control conditions were similar to those in the negative trait conditions, suggesting that jurors assumed unfavorable things about the defendant when given no information about character. Similar effects were obtained for sentences, further supporting a conclusion that attractive defendants are treated more leniently.

But there remain qualifications. Friend and Vinson (1974) reported that instructions to ignore information regarding the attractiveness of a defendant resulted in a reversal of the leniency effect. When no instructions were given, attractive defendants received shorter sentences than either average or unattractive defendants, but unattractive defendants received shorter sentences when instructions to disregard were included. Although Friend and Vinson also examined authoritarianism, they did not report the interaction between that factor and attractiveness first obtained by Mitchell and Byrne (1972). Izzett and Fishman (1976) found attractive defendants rated as more likely to be guilty than unattractive defendants. The jurors' sentences, however, were affected by both the attractiveness of the defendant and the amount of justification provided for the crime. When no justification was provided, the attractive defendant received longer sentences, but the opposite happened when the justification for the crime was high. Izzett and Fishman used embezzlement as the crime in their study, while the majority of others used negligent homicide. It may be that attractive defendants receive more lenient treatment only when the criminal activity is of a less voluntary nature, for example, negligence or theft based on dire need. This explanation, of course, requires that the jurors be operating at a hypothetical level of script processing, and we must ask ourselves if this assumption is warranted.

Additional evidence for the existence of hypothetical vignettes has been obtained from studies on the effects of defendants' physical attractiveness. Efran (1974) reported that female defendants of greater physical attractiveness received lower ratings of guilt and shorter sentences from male jurors, but that the attractiveness of male defendants did not affect female jurors' reactions. Bray's (in press) extension of Efran's study produced similar results for both male and female jurors' reactions to a female defendant—more attractive defendants received lower guilt ratings, more lenient punishments, and lower ratings for the likelihood of future cheating incidents. Sigall and Ostrove (1975), however, demonstrated that this effect must be qualified by whether or not physical attractiveness might have facilitated the crime. Physically attractive defendants received shorter sentences when the crime was not related to attractiveness (burglary), but sentences were equivalent when the crime was related to attractiveness (swindling). McFatter (1978) found a general leniency effect for physically attractive defendants in 10 different crimes, including burglary and swindling. McFatter's defendants, however, were males, while Sigall and Ostrove's were females. Of greater importance, however, is that McFatter presented his jurors with one-line statements specifically stating that the defendant committed the crime, while Sigall and Ostrove used longer summaries of the trial. Although Sigall and Ostrove's summaries were heavily weighted toward a guilty verdict, they did not state outright that the defendant committed the crime, as did McFatter's materials. Whether the explicit guilt statement, the gender of the defendant, or both may be responsible for the different results is a question that must await additional research for an answer.

Victims

The attractiveness of victims also seem to exert some influence on jurors' reactions toward the defendant. Thornton (1977) reported that the physical attractiveness of a rape victim did not affect jurors' ratings of guilt, although male jurors did assign longer sentences when the victim was attractive. Kerr (1978a) used an auto theft case and found that jurors were more likely to convict defendants only when the victim was attractive and had taken precautions, such as removing keys and locking doors. Kerr also determined that the conviction effect was due to a lower standard of proof rather than a difference in the subjective probability that the defendant had committed the crime. Kerr's results also support the existence of hypothetical vignettes concerning victims' attractiveness, although it is clear that considerably more research is required.

Conclusions

Overall, we can conclude that attractive defendants are more leniently treated, but this advantage may not hold when the defendant's attractiveness could have facilitated the crime. Similarly, there is a limited amount of evidence that defendants whose victims are attractive may receive harsher treatment than those whose victims are unattractive. As is true of the moral character factor, the effects of attractiveness appear to result from hypothetical vignettes, subject to conditionals such as type of crime and judge's instructions. Additional research might well be directed toward a more extensive examination of the use of such conditionals in jurors' scripts. Attractiveness may also function as a conditional for other hypothetical vignettes. Feild (1979), for example, found no overall effects for the physical attractiveness of a rape victim, but the victim's attractiveness did alter the effects of the defendant's and victim's race on sentences. Finally, we note that with the exception of Kerr (1978a), the simulation studies included ratings of guiltiness or suggested sentences. There exists no evidence for determining the effects of defendants' attractiveness on jurors' verdicts.

RACE

That racial differences have had an effect on the United States criminal justice system from its inception cannot be questioned (Bell, 1973). What has been questioned, however, is the extent to which race of the participant leads to a different kind of treatment or unfair treatment. Because much of the simulation research includes both defendants' and victims' race as factors, we will forego separate discussions for victims and defendants. Instead, we will separately review archival and simulation studies.

Archival Research

Early archival research indicated that black defendants received longer sentences than white defendants, but that the effect of the defendants' race was altered by the race of the victim. For example, Bullock (1961) found that black defendants received longer sentences when the victim was white, but received shorter sentences than whites when the victim was black. When nonracial factors (e.g., type of crime) were controlled by Bullock, the data did not provide as much support for racial discrimination, although nonracial factors were more likely to contribute to longer sentences when the defendant was black.

Broeder (1965) also concluded that race per se has less impact than other variables that vary with race, although he provided case study interviews demonstrating a high degree of prejudice against black defendants during jury deliberations. Likewise, Kalven and Zeisel (1966) reported black defendants as the only group for which jurors displayed more antipathy than sympathy, and provided anecdotal evidence suggesting that jurors were more lenient toward defendants whose crimes were against blacks. Nagel's (1969) examination of assault and grand larceny trials demonstrated that blacks were more likely to be convicted of these offenses than whites. For the assault cases, blacks were slightly more likely to receive a prison sentence than probation, and almost twice as many blacks as whites received prison sentences longer than a year. For the grand larceny cases, more blacks received prison sentences than probation, but whites were more likely to receive longer prison sentences. Hindelang

(1969) also concluded that black defendants, overall, received longer sentences than did white defendants.

Let us begin to summarize the archival findings. Hagan's (1974) reanalyses of a large number of archival studies indicated that when type of crime and prior record were controlled, the race of the defendant did not affect the length of sentences in noncapital cases; furthermore, the effect of race existed only in capital cases from Southern states. Hagan did, however, find support for the conclusion that crimes against white victims resulted in longer sentences, especially in those cases in which the defendant was black. In a similar vein, Howard (1975) provided data indicating that the greatest proportion of death penalties for rape involved those cases in which a black defendant was convicted of raping a white woman. The archival data indicate that black defendants are more harshly treated than white defendants, and that those whose victims are white are more harshly treated than those whose victims are black. Clear evidence for discrimination against black defendants is present only when the victims are white. As Bell (1973) points out, however, the effects of discriminatory practices may occur long before the defendant is sentenced.

Simulation Research

Simulation research has provided less consistent evidence for discrimination against blacks than archival research, perhaps as a result of less realistic settings. For example, Kaplan and Simon (1972) failed to find that defendants' race had an effect on mock jurors' verdicts in a case dealing with negligent homicide. But Ugwuegbu (1979), using a rape trial, found that the races of the defendant, victim, and jurors all interacted with the type of evidence presented during the simulation. White jurors judged a defendant as most culpable when the defendant was black and the victim was white, but only in those conditions in which approximately equal amounts of incriminating and exonerating evidence were presented. On the other hand, black jurors judged white defendants most culpable when the victim was black and the evidence was either balanced or strongly favored conviction. Overall, jurors were most lenient when the defendant was of the same race as themselves, but especially so when the evidence was balanced.

Feild (1979) reported that black defendants received longer sentences than whites in a rape case, but that the defendant's race interacted with a number of victims' characteristics. Black defendants received longer sentences when the victim was white than when the victim was black, but only in those conditions in which the victim was physically attractive. The victims' race and attractiveness did not affect sentences for white defendants. Black defendants received longer sentences than whites when the victim was both attractive and sexually inexperienced, but sentences for black and white defendants did not differ in the other combinations of victims' attractiveness and sexual experience. The relationship between the defendant's race and the victim's sexual experience was also affected by the extent to which the victim may have precipitated the crime. When the victim clearly did not precipitate the rape, black defendants received longer sentences than whites in cases with sexually inexperienced victims; but black and white defendants received equivalent sentences when the victim was sexually experienced. If the victim could have precipitated the rape, blacks received longer sentences in cases with sexually experienced victims, but not when the victim was sexually inexperienced.

Faranda and Gaertner (1979) found evidence for even more subtle forms of discrimination in a study on defendants' race, jurors' authoritarianism, and admissible evidence. When the defendant was black, incriminating but inadmissible evidence resulted in higher guilt ratings from those jurors who were relatively authoritarian, but did not affect the guilt ratings of less authoritarian jurors. Interestingly, when the defendant was white, the more authoritarian jurors were unaffected by incriminating but inadmissible evidence, while the less authoritarian jurors rated the defendant as *less* guilty when the incriminating evidence was labelled inadmissible. According to Faranda and Gaertner, discrimininatory practices of highly authoritarian white jurors are "against black defendants," while those for less authoritarian whites are of a "for white defendants" form. Oros and Elman (1979) did not find evidence for differential treatment of black and white defendants in a rape trial, but they reported that a number of the subjects receiving case materials in which the defendant was black were suspicious about the nature of the study. Foley *et al.* (1979) also failed to find any effect of the race of the defendant in a child molestation case, although their results did provide the support for Bullock's (1961) conclusion concerning nonracial factors: Foley *et al.* determined that black defendants were perceived as having a lower socioeconomic status than white defendants, and that those defendants of lower status received higher guilt ratings and longer sentences.

Conclusions

In response to the available evidence, we believe that the races of the defendant and the victim are used as events in categorical vignettes for verdicts, and perhaps in hypothetical vignettes for sentencing decisions. Defendants who are of the same race as jurors appear less likely to be convicted, whereas if victims are of the same race as jurors, there is a greater likelihood of conviction. For sentencing decisions, these categorical vignettes may be modified by such considerations as defendants' socioeconomic status, victims' attractiveness or moral character, and specific aspects of the crime. The interaction between race of the defendant and of the victim more likely results from an additive combination of the two factors such that cases involving defendants of a different race than the jurors and victims of the same race result in the most severe punishment of the defendant by the jurors. It may also be that jurors do not utilize vignettes involving defendants' race when the victim is of a race different from their own.

The effect of either factor alone upon the outcome (verdict or sentence) of the script may be limited to those cases in which the evidence does not strongly favor either the prosecution or the defense. One of the most glaring deficits in this body of research is the total disregard for races other than black or white. The question that remains unanswered, therefore, is whether the effects of race really are racial, or are a minority-majority distinction in the jurors' scripts.

ATTITUDE SIMILARITY

The similarity of attitudes between jurors and defendants or victims is the most subtle of the characteristics considered in this chapter. It is a "special" characteristic in that it is the only one that cannot be considered independently of the individuals seated in the jury box. Attitude similarity is the only characteristic for which archival studies are not available, since identifying the attitudes of defendants, victims, and jurors from transcripts is usually not possible; it is also the only characteristic for which simulation studies on victims are not available. Yet attitude similarity may be an important factor in jurors' decisions. Indeed, Bell (1973) has argued that the lack of similarity between the attitudes of defendants and those of other participants in the criminal justice system may be the most influential factor in the treatment of black defendants.

Does attitude similarity carry any weight? Yes, concluded Griffitt and Jackson (1973), in a study using a negligent homicide trial. They reported that mock jurors whose attitudes on a variety of issues were dissimilar to those ascribed to the defendant rated him as more guilty of the offense and suggested longer sentences than did those who believed the defendant's attitudes were similar to theirs. Mitchell and Byrne (1973) obtained a similar result, but it was limited to relatively authoritarian jurors. Kerr and Anderson (1978) reported that religious similarity resulted in fewer guilty votes in a child molestation case, but did not find that attitude similarity affected sentencing decisions.

In the Griffitt and Jackson, Mitchell and Byrne, and Kerr and Anderson studies, the attitudes manipulated were not relevant to the criminal charge. In contrast, Laughlin and Izzett (1973) did use attitudes related to a charge of euthanasia, and reported only a trend for jurors whose attitudes were similar to the defendant's to suggest shorter sentences. When jurors were given an opportunity to discuss the evidence, jurors with attitudes similar to the defendant's suggested shorter sentences while dissimilar jurors were unaffected by the discussions. Bray (1974, 1976) used a 45-min audiotape in his simulation and found leniency effects with a scale of guiltiness; jurors whose attitudes were similar to the defendant's attitudes rated the defendant as less guilty. Jurors' predeliberation and postdeliberation verdicts, however, were unaffected by the attitude similarity manipulation. Bray's use of an audiotape, as opposed to a short, written summary, may account for the differences between his results and those of Kerr and Anderson (1978). Gerbasi and Zuckerman (1975) used summaries of trials for a variety of crimes, and consistently found that those jurors whose attitudes were similar to the defendants' rated guilt lower and suggested shorter sentences.

More recently, Shepherd and Sloan (1979) have suggested that the leniency effect may be more accurately conceptualized as a shift toward harshness for defendants whose attitudes are dissimilar to those of jurors. Using attitudes toward the punishment of criminals, Shepherd and Sloan found that dissimilar attitudes resulted in longer sentences than either similar attitudes or a control condition in which no information about attitudes was given to the jurors. Kauffman and Ryckman (1979) reported that severity of the crime, jurors' beliefs about the locus of control, and similarity of attitudes all interacted to affect the jurors' judgments of responsibility. Those jurors who believed themselves responsible for their own actions treated a defendant more harshly if the defendant's attitudes were similar to their own. Jurors who did not accept as much responsibility for their actions reacted just the opposite way. This difference was greatest when the severity of the crime was perceived as being rather high. The conclusion would seem to be that the extent to which jurors perceive themselves as similar to the defendant may influence reactions to the defendant, but that the influence is likely to be moderated or reversed by a number of other situational constraints.

We have not, of course, covered all the effects attributable to similarity in attitudes, but we have attempted to represent its use in research on jurors' decisions. Given the inconsistencies within the area, it hardly seems necessary to state that more research will be required before any conclusions can be drawn with confidence. Perhaps subsequent research ought to focus on determining which of the salient characteristics of defendants and especially of victims contribute to jurors' perceptions of similarity in attitudes. Since it is highly unlikely that formal declarations of attitudinal positions will be made in court, it would be helpful to determine what cues jurors use in assessing attitude similarity before they incorporate it into the trial script.

PARTING SHOTS

It is not enough to state that extralegal characteristics have an impact upon jurors' decisions. One must also attempt to assess the extent of that impact. How much do these characteristics affect jurors? Unfortunately, the question is considerably easier to ask than to answer. Kalven and Zeisel (1966) estimated that about 22% of the disagreements in verdict between judges and jurors were the result of extralegal characteristics. But this 22% constituted only 4% of the 3576 trials in their survey. The latter percentage, however, is probably misleading; Kalven and Zeisel did not identify the percentage of cases in which extralegal characteristics resulted in judge–jury agreements.

Hagan (1974) made a comprehensive attempt to answer the "how much" question. For the archival studies that he reanalyzed, Hagan also derived an estimate of the amount of variation in sentencing for which a particular characteristic accounted. Race of the defendant accounted for only 1.5% of sentence variation, while the combination of defendants' and victims' race accounted for 22% of the variance in capital rape trials. The socioeconomic status of defendants accounted for less than 1% of the variance in noncapital cases, but about 4% in capital cases. Defendants' gender accounted for a negligible portion of the variance. Thus, except for the combination of defendants' and victims' race with respect to the death penalty for rape, archival research leads us to conclude that the answer to the "how much" question is "not much."

Simulation studies, on the other hand, provide larger estimates of the impact of extralegal characteristics, probably because other factors that may affect jurors' reactions have been eliminated from most simulations. Savitsky and Sim (1974) reported that the emotional state of the defendant accounted for approximately 33% of the variance in jurors' reactions, while Foley *et al.* (1979) found 33% of the variance in sentencing to be attributable to extralegal characteristics. Feild (1979) found that a total of 61% of the variance in sentencing was accounted for by all of the effects produced by his numerous variables (precipitation, race, physical attractiveness, and sexual experience of the victim; race of the defendant; and strength of evidence), although the largest single percentage was 11% (for victims' precipitation). These estimates should be cautiously interpreted, however, in that variance is limited at the start of a simulation through the control of other variables.

Ugwuegbu (1979), for example, found the pervasive opposite-race defendant/same-race victim effect to be confined mainly to those conditions in which the evidence was balanced, that is, in a "close case." Close cases are more likely to come before a jury, yet it remains difficult to state that extralegal characteristics are of sufficient strength to override the legal evidence presented during a trial. That extralegal characteristics do not account for a great proportion of variation in any given measure, however, should not detract from the perception of the importance of such effects.

NEW DIRECTIONS

Defendants' and victims' characteristics do, however slightly, influence jurors' reactions to the defendant, making it all the more important to consider the rather complex manner in which these reactions take place. Many of the studies reviewed included interactions among various characteristics, reflecting the difficulty of evaluating the impact of any one characteristic in isolation. Feild (1979) found several three-way interactions in his study, and he included only one characteristic of the defendant. To consider 9 or 10 factors in a single factorial design is an invitation to excessive costs in terms of both time and money. Multiple regression and discriminant analysis techniques appear to be more applicable for research on such effects.

Rose and Prell (1955) concluded that jurors' conceptual definitions of crimes did not fit those espoused in formal law, a position echoed by Sherman and Dowdle (1974). The latter reported that individual juror's ratings of the severity of a crime and the appropriate punishment of it did not correspond with those inferred from the local criminal law. To what extent has research provided the legal system with the information necessary to counteract such conclusions? According to Weiten and Diamond (1979), very little. Simulation research is too often not generalizable to the courtroom, while archival research too seldom allows one to measure the appropriate variables. Previous reviewers have called for more realistic simulations of the trial experience, and we are not to be the exception. Rather than dwell on this point, however, what we would suggest is that a script processing approach may provide more useful information to those involved in the justice system.

We have stated that the cognitive level of jurors' vignettes may contribute to the impact on their decisions of defendants' or victims' characteristics. Knowing that a characteristic is incorporated into the script as a categorical or hypothetical vignette may allow one to determine the extent or direction of the characteristic's influence. But how does one go about determining the level of vignettes? The first logical step may be to assess jurors' scripts, perhaps by having individuals provide descriptions of various crimes, which may then be examined for consistently mentioned characteristics. One explanation for the effects of some characteristics may be that the characteristics manipulated in simulations may be different from what jurors expect. That is, women may receive preferential treatment from jurors because crime scripts involve only male criminals. Such scripts could then be altered to examine the cognitive level of vignettes within the script. If changing the defendant's gender alters only the jurors' verdicts, then one could conclude that the vignette is categorical. If, on the other hand, changing the gender of the defendant results in different perceptions of other characteristics (e.g., socioeconomic status, attractiveness, etc.), then a hypothetical level may be operating. In addition to using more realistic simulations, we all need to examine the relationships among characteristics as they are encoded in the jurors' scripts.

Although we have discussed the effects of defendants' and victims' characteristics in terms of vignettes, it is necessary to point out that a single vignette does not operate in isolation. All vignettes are incorporated into the jurors' scripts, and it is important to examine each vignette as it relates to the overall trial script. For example, a categorical vignette, such as that for prior record, may increase the likelihood of conviction in isolation, yet that same vignette may be overshadowed by other vignettes in the script, such as that for race of the defendant and victim. If this is true, then there is a greater chance that such effects will be demonstrated in more comprehensive and realistic simulations than in those that include only brief summaries of the case.

Perhaps a more important direction for research involves determining *which* reactions of the juror are influenced by a given characteristic or group of characteristics. Often, for a variety of reasons, researchers have measured sentences or a continuous scale of guilt. While these may provide the dependent measures suitable for a desired type of statistical analysis, or information concerning punishment, jurors rarely sentence defendants or provide a *rating* of guilt. Archival research also appears to suffer from this shortcoming, in that a high proportion of such studies have included sentences rather than verdicts. Comprehensive studies on verdicts, such as those of Kalven and Zeisel (1966) and Nagel (1969), are exceptions, although archival studies examining *interactions* among characteristics are also required.

Finally, the script processing approach may lead to an ethical question: What happens when we are able to simulate a courtroom trial accurately? Prior to considering this question, we should first question whether or not a script simulation of a trial is possible. The answer would have to be "possibly yes, probably no." Abelson's (1973) simulation of a right-wing ideologist is not sufficiently complex to be immediately applicable to the myriad of vignettes that occur in a jury trial script, but that technique is certainly available. What we have proposed, however, is not that a computer simulation of a jury trial be constructed, but rather that use be made of the advantages that may exist with the use of the script processing approach. We believe that it can serve as a general framework for continued research. Existing research indicates that extralegal characteristics do have some effects; application of the script processing approach may provide us with better information concerning how and how much the characteristics influence decisions during actual trials.

REFERENCES

Abelson, R. P. The structure of belief systems. In K. Colby & R. Schank (Eds.), *Computer simulation of thought and language*. San Francisco, California: Freeman, 1973.

Abelson, R. P. Script processing in attitude formation and decision making. In J. S. Carroll & J. W. Payne (Eds.), *Cognition and social behavior*. Hillsdale, New Jersey: Erlbaum, 1976.

Abelson, R. P. *Scripts*. Invited address to the meetings of the Midwestern Psychological Association, Chicago, May 1978.

Austin, W., & Utne, M. K. *The differential impact of an offender's suffering on simulated jurors' convictions and sentencing behavior*. Unpublished manuscript, University of Virginia, 1976.

Austin, W., Walster, E., & Utne, M. K. Equity and the law: The effect of a harmdoer's "suffering in the act" on liking and assigned punishment. In L. Berkowitz & E. Walster (Eds.), *Advances in experimental social psychology* (Vol. 9). New York: Academic Press, 1976.

Barnett, M. J., & Feild, H. S. Character of the defendant and length of sentence in rape and burglary crimes. *Journal of Social Psychology*, 1978, *104*, 271–277.

Bell, D. A., Jr. Racism in American courts: Cause for black disruption or despair? *California Law Review*, 1973, *61*, 165–203.

Berg, K. S., & Vidmar, N. Authoritarianism and recall of evidence about criminal behavior. *Journal of Research in Personality*, 1975, *9*, 147–157.

Berkowitz, L., & Walster, E. (Eds.). *Advances in experimental social psychology* (Vol. 9). New York: Academic Press, 1976.

Bock, R. D. *Multivariate statistical methods in behavioral research*. New York: McGraw-Hill, 1975.

Boor, M. Effects of victim injury, victim competence, and defendant opportunism in the decisions of simulated jurors. *Journal of Social Psychology*, 1976, *100*, 315–316.

Bray, R. M. *Decision rules, attitude similarity, and jury decision making*. Unpublished doctoral dissertation, University of Illinois, 1974.

Bray, R. M. *The effects of attitude similarity, assigned decision rule, and jury sex on the decisions of simulated jurors*. Paper presented at the meetings of the Southeastern Psychological Association, New Orleans, March 1976.

Bray, R. M. Defendant attractiveness and mock juror judgments. *Replications in Social Psychology*, in press.

Bray, R. M., Struckman-Johnson, C., Osborne, M. D., McFarlane, J. B., & Scott, J. The effects of defendant status on the decisions of student and community juries. *Social Psychology*, 1978, *41*, 256–260.

Broeder, D. W. The Negro in court. *Duke Law Journal*, 1965, *19*(1), 19–31.

Bullock, H. A. Significance of the racial factor in the length of prison sentences. *Journal of Criminal Law, Criminology, and Police Science*, 1961, *52*, 411–417.

Byrne, D., & Clore, G. L. A reinforcement model of evaluative responses. *Personality: An International Journal*, 1970, *1*, 103–128.

Chirocas, T. L., & Waldo, G. P. Socioeconomic status and criminal sentencing: An empirical assessment of a conflict proposition. *American Sociological Review*, 1975, *40*, 753–772.

Dane, F. C. *Quantifying reasonable doubt: An examination of empirical and theoretical approaches*. Unpublished doctoral dissertation, University of Kansas, 1979.

Davis, J. H. Group decisions and social interaction: A theory of social decision schemes. *Psychological Review*, 1973, *80*, 97–125.

Davis, J. H., Bray, R. M., & Holt, R. W. The empirical study of decision processes in juries: A critical review. In J. L. Tapp & F. J. Levine (Eds.), *Law, justice, and the individual in society: Psychological and legal issues*. New York: Holt, 1977.

DeJong, W., Morris, W. N., & Hastorf, A. H. Effect of an escaped accomplice on the punishment assigned to a criminal defendant. *Journal of Personality and Social Psychology*, 1976, *33*, 192–198.

Efran, M. G. The effect of physical appearance on the judgment of guilt, interpersonal attraction, and severity of recommended punishment on a simulated jury task. *Journal of Research in Personality*, 1974, *8*, 45–54.

Emmert, D. *Effect of victim-offender relationship and victim resistance on attributions of rape*. Unpublished masters thesis, Kent State University, Kent, Ohio, 1978.

Faranda, J. A., & Gaertner, S. L. *The effect of inadmissible evidence introduced by the prosecution and the defense, and the defendant's race on the verdicts of high and low authoritarians*. Paper presented at the meetings of the Eastern Psychological Association, Philadelphia, April 1979.

Feild, H. S. Attitudes toward rape: A comparative analysis of police, rapists, crisis counselors, and citizens. *Journal of Personality and Social Psychology*, 1978, *36*, 156–179. (a)

Feild, H. S. Juror background characteristics and attitudes toward rape: Correlates of jurors' decisions in rape trials. *Law and Human Behavior*, 1978, *2*, 73–93. (b)

Feild, H. S. Rape trials and jurors' decisions: A psycholegal analysis of the effects of victim, defendant, and case characteristics. *Law and Human Behavior*, 1979, *3*, 261–284.

Feldman, R., & Rosen, F. Diffusion of responsibility in crime, punishment, and other adversity. *Law and Human Behavior*, 1979, *4*, 313–322.

Fienberg, S. E. *The analysis of cross-classified categorical data*. Cambridge, Massachusetts: MIT Press, 1977.

Foley, L. A., Chamblin, M. H., & Fortenberry, J. H. *The effects of race, socioeconomic status, and personality variables on jury decisions*. Paper presented at the meetings of the American Psychological Association, New York City, September 1979.

Fontaine, G., & Kiger, R. The effects of defendant dress and supervision on judgments of simulated jurors: An exploratory study. *Law and Human Behavior*, 1978, 2, 63–71.

Friend, R., & Vinson, M. Leaning over backwards—Jurors' responses to defendants' attractiveness. *Journal of Communcation*, 1974, 24, 124–129.

Gerbasi, K. C., & Zuckerman, M. *An experimental investigation of jury biasing factors*. Paper presented at the meetings of the Eastern Psychological Association, New York City, April 1975.

Gerbasi, K. C., Zuckerman, M., & Reis, H. T. Justice needs a new blindfold: A review of mock jury research. *Psychological Bulletin*, 1977, 84, 323–345.

Gleason, J. M., & Harris, V. A. Group discussion and defendant's socioeconomic status as determinants of judgments by simulated jurors. *Journal of Applied Social Psychology*, 1976, 6, 186–191.

Green, E. *Judicial attitudes in sentencing*. New York: Macmillan, 1961.

Griffitt, W., & Jackson, T. Simulated jury decisions: The influence of jury-defendant attitude similarity–dissimilarity. *Social Behavior and Personality*, 1973, 1, 1–7.

Hagan, J. Extra-legal attributes and criminal sentencing: An assessment of a sociological viewpoint. *Law and Society Review*, 1974, 8, 357–383.

Harvey, J. H., Ickes, W. J., & Kidd, R. F. (Eds.). *New directions in attribution research* (Vol. 1). Hillsdale, New Jersey: Erlbaum, 1976.

Harvey, J. H., Ickes, W. J., & Kidd, R. F. (Eds.). *New directions in attribution research* (Vol. II). Hillsdale, New Jersey: Erlbaum, 1979.

Hatton, D. E., Snortum, J. R., & Oskamp, S. The effects of biasing information and dogmatism upon witness testimony. *Psychonomic Science*, 1971, 23, 425–427.

Hindelang, M. E. Equality under the law. *Journal of Criminal Law, Criminology, and Police Science*, 1969, 60, 306–313.

Hoiberg, B. C., & Stires, L. K. The effect of several types of pretrial publicity on the guilt attributions of simulated jurors. *Journal of Applied Social Psychology*, 1973, 3, 267–275.

Howard, J. C. Racial discrimination in sentencing. *Judicature*, 1975, 59, 120–125.

Izzett, R. R. & Fishman, L. Defendant sentences as a function of attractiveness and justification for actions. *Journal of Social Psychology*, 1976, 100, 285–290.

Izzett, R. R., & Leginski, W. Group discussion and the influence of defendant characteristics in a simulated jury setting. *Journal of Social Psychology*, 1974, 93, 271–279.

Izzett, R. R., & Sales, B. D. Person perception and juror's reactions to defendants: An equity theory interpretation. In B. D. Sales (Ed.), *Perspectives in law and psychology* (Vo. 2): *The jury, judicial and trial processes*. New York: Plenum, 1979.

Jones, C., & Aronson, E. Attributions of fault to a rape victim as a function of respectability of the victim. *Journal of Personality and Social Psychology*, 1973, 26, 415–419.

Kahn, A., Gilbert, L. A., Latta, R. M., Deutsch, C., Hagen, R., Hill, M., McGaughey, T., Ryen, A. H., & Wilson, D. W. Attributions of fault to a rape victim as a function of respectability of the victim: A failure to replicate or extend. *Representative Research in Social Psychology*, 1977, 8, 98–107.

Kalven, H., Jr., & Zeisel, H. *The American jury*. Boston: Little, Brown, 1966.

Kaplan, K. J., & Simon, R. J. Latitude and severity of sentencing options, race of the victim, and decisions of simulated jurors: Some issues arising from the "Algiers Motel" trial. *Law and Society Review*, 1972, 7, 87–98.

Kaplan, M. F., & Kemmerick, G. Juror judgment as information integration: Combining evidential and non-evidential information. *Journal of Personality and Social Psychology*, 1974, 30, 493–499.

Kaplan, M. F., & Miller, L. E. Effects of jurors' identification with the victim depend on likelihood of victimization. *Law and Human Behavior*, 1978, 2, 353–361.

Kauffman, R. A., & Ryckman, R. M. Effects of locus-of-control, outcome severity, and attitudinal similarity of defendant on attributions of criminal responsibilities. *Personality and Social Psychology Bulletin*, 1979, 5, 340–343.

Kerr, N. L. Beautiful and blameless: Effects of victim attractiveness and responsibility on mock jurors' verdicts. *Personality and Social Psychology Bulletin,* 1978, *4,* 479–482. (a)

Kerr, N. L. Severity of prescribed penalty and mock jurors' verdicts. *Journal of Personality and Social Psychology,* 1978, *36,* 1431–1442. (b)

Kerr, N. L., & Anderson, A. B. *Defendant-juror religious similarity and mock jurors' judgments.* Paper presented at the meeting of the American Psychological Association, Toronto, August 1978.

Kerr, N. L., & Kurtz, S. T. Effects of a victim's suffering and respectability on mock juror judgments: Further evidence on the just world theory. *Representative Research in Social Psychology,* 1977, *8,* 42–56.

Kerr, N. L., & Sawyers, G. W. *Independence of multiple verdicts within a trial by mock jurors.* Unpublished manuscript, University of California, San Diego, 1978.

Kidd, R. F., & Utne, M. K. Reactions to equity: A perspective on the role of attributions. *Law and Human Behavior,* 1978, *2,* 301–312.

Krulewitz, J. *Sex differences in rape attributions.* Paper presented at the meetings of the Midwestern Psychological Association, Chicago, May 1977.

Landy, D., & Aronson, E. The influence of the character of the criminal and his victim on the decisions of simulated jurors. *Journal of Experimental Social Psychology,* 1969, *5,* 141–152.

Laughlin, E. R., & Izzett, R. R. *Deliberation and sentencing by attitudinally homogeneous juries.* Paper presented at the meetings of the Midwestern Psychological Association, Chicago, May 1973.

Legent, P. *The deserving victim: Effects of length of pretrial detention, crime severity, and juror attitudes on simulated jury decisions.* Unpublished doctoral dissertation, Yale University, Connecticut, 1973.

McFatter, R. M. Sentencing strategies and justice: Effects of punishment philosophy on sentencing decisions. *Journal of Personality and Social Psychology,* 1978, *36,* 1490–1500.

McGillis, D. Attribution and the law: Convergences between legal and psychological concepts. *Law and Human Behavior,* 1978, *2,* 289–300.

Miller, F. M., Smith, E. R., Ferree, M. M., & Taylor, S. E. Predicting perceptions of victimization. *Journal of Applied Social Pscyhology,* 1976, *6,* 352–359.

Mitchell, H. E., & Byrne, D. *Minimizing the influence of irrelevant factors in the courtroom: The defendant's character, judge's instructions, and authoritarianism.* Paper presented at the meetings of the Midwestern Psychological Association, Cleveland, May 1972.

Mitchell, H. E., & Byrne, D. The defendant's dilemma: Effect of jurors' attitudes and authoritarianism on judicial decisions. *Journal of Personality and Social Psychology,* 1973, *25,* 123–129.

Nagel, S. S. *The legal process from a behavioral perspective.* Homewood, Illinois: Dorsey, 1969.

Nemeth, C., & Sosis, R. H. A simulated jury study: Characteristics of the defendant and the jurors. *Journal of Social Psychology,* 1973, *90,* 221–229.

Olah, R. J., Oros, C. J., Koss, M. P., & Emmert, D. *Effects of assailant force, victim resistance, and victim post-rape behaviors on attributions of rape.* Paper presented at the meetings of the Midwestern Psychological Association, Chicago, May 1979.

Oros, C. J., & Elman, D. *The effects of judge's instructions on the decisions of mock jurors.* Paper presented at the meetings of the Eastern Psychological Association, Philadelphia, April 1979.

Perlman, D. *Attributions in the criminal justice process: Concepts and empirical illustrations.* Paper presented at the meetings of the American Psychology-Law Society, Snowmass, Colorado, June 1977.

Reynolds, D., & Sanders, M. *The effects of defendant attractiveness, age, and injury on severity of sentence given by simulated jurors.* Paper presented at the meetings of the Western Psychological Association, Anaheim, California, April 1973.

Rose, A. M., & Prell, A. E. Does the punishment fit the crime? A study in social valuation. *American Journal of Sociology,* 1955, *61,* 247–259.

Rumsey, M. Effects of defendant background and remorse on sentencing judgments. *Journal of Applied Social Psychology,* 1976, *6,* 64–68.

Rumsey, M., & Castore, C. *The effects of defendant description and group discussion on individual sentencing.* Paper presented at the meetings of the Midwestern Psychological Association, Chicago, May 1974.

Savitsky, J., & Sim, M. Trading emotions: Equity theory of reward and punishment. *Journal of Communication,* 1974, *24,* 140–147.

Shaffer, D. R., & Sadowski, C. Effects of withheld evidence on juridic decisions, II: Locus of withholding strategy. *Personality and Social Psychology Bulletin,* 1979, *5,* 40–43.

Shaw, J. I. Reactions to victims and defendants of varying degrees of attractiveness. *Psychonomic Science,* 1972, *27,* 329–330.

Shepherd, D. H., & Sloan, L. R. Similarity of legal attitudes, defendant social class, and crime intentionality as determinants of legal decisions. *Personality and Social Psychology Bulletin,* 1979, *5,* 245–248.

Sherman, R. C., & Dowdle, M. D. The perception of crime and punishment: A multidimensional scaling analysis. *Social Science Research,* 1974, *3,* 109–126.

Sigall, H., & Ostrove, N. Beautiful but dangerous: Effects of offender attractiveness and nature of crime on juridic judgments. *Journal of Personality and Social Psychology,* 1975, *31,* 410–414.

Smith, S. H. *The effects of preventative action, severity of consequences, and order of dependent measures on the attribution of responsibility.* Unpublished masters thesis, University of Kansas, 1976.

Smith, S. H., & Carnahan, R. *The assignment of blame as a function of the sex, physical attractiveness and respectability of the defendant.* Unpublished manuscript, Indiana University Northwest, 1979.

Snyder, E. C. Sex role differential and juror decisions. *Sociology and Social Research,* 1971, *55,* 442–448.

Sporer, S. L. *Legal and extra-legal factors in judicial sentencing.* Paper presented at the meetings of the Eastern Psychological Association, Philadelphia, April 1979.

Stephan, C. Sex prejudice in jury simulation. *Journal of Psychology,* 1974, *88,* 305–312.

Stephan, C. Selective characteristics of jurors and litigants: Their influences on juries' verdicts. In R. J. Simon (Ed.), *The jury system in America: A critical overview.* Beverly Hills, California: Sage, 1975.

Thornton, B. Effect of rape victim's attractiveness in a jury simulation. *Personality and Social Psychology Bulletin,* 1977, *3,* 666–669.

Ugwuegbu, D. C. E. Racial and evidential factors in juror attributions of legal responsibility. *Journal of Experimental Social Psychology,* 1979, *15,* 133–146.

Vidmar, N., & Crinklaw, L. D. *Retribution and utility as motives in sentencing behavior.* Paper presented at the meetings of the Midwestern Psychological Association, Chicago, May 1973.

Weiten, W. *Methodological problems in jury simulation research on attraction.* Paper presented at the meetings of the American Psychological Association, New York City, September 1979.

Weiten, W., & Diamond, S. S. A critical review of the jury simulation paradigm: The case of defendant characteristics. *Law and Human Behavior,* 1979, *3,* 71–93.

PART II

TESTIMONY

chapter

The Reliability of Eyewitness Testimony: A Psychological Perspective

Steven Penrod
Elizabeth Loftus
John Winkler

The recent publication of three volumes on the psychological aspects of eyewitness testimony (Clifford & Bull, 1978; E. F. Loftus, 1979; Yarmey, 1979b)

119

THE PSYCHOLOGY
OF THE COURTROOM

represents a significant milestone both for psychology and for the legal system. For the first time, the growing mass of psychological research on the eyewitness has been assembled in a form easily accessible to psychologists as well as to legal practitioners and the interested public. Nonetheless, the publication of these volumes should not be interpreted as a sign that all the major questions concerning eyewitness testimony and its reliability have been answered. In this chapter, we review and summarize the most recent research and the most reliable classic research findings, but at the same time we call attention to unanswered questions and research opportunities.

Research on the psychological aspects of eyewitness reliability has a long history. Among such early theorists and researchers as Cattell (1895) and Watson (1913) was Münsterberg in his volume *On the Witness Stand* (1908). Münsterberg roundly criticized the legal profession for its ignorance of research in disciplines other than law and was answered most effectively by the legal scholar Wigmore (1909). Wigmore framed his reply brilliantly; it took the form of a description of an imaginary trial that occurred on April 1, 1909 in the Superior Court of Wundt County, with a Mr. X. Perry Ment assisting with the defense. This satirical article contains many elements of the legal profession's reaction to Münsterberg's *On the Witness Stand*.

Various other notable contributions appeared during the first few decades of the century: Stern (1910, 1939); the German psychologist Gross (1911); and Whipple (1909–1915, 1917–1918). Psychological research was also reported in law journals at a fairly early date. Marston (1924) reported empirical research in a law journal; a psychologist and a lawyer—Hutchins and Slesinger (1928)—collaborated on research also reported in a law journal. During the same period, psychologists McCarty (1929) and Burtt (1931) published books reporting empirical research on the reliability of eyewitness testimony and a lawyer, Gardner (1933), published a useful review in a law journal.

Despite these promising early starts, the 1940s and 1950s proved rather fallow. Marshall's research (1966, 1979) marked the beginning of vigorous activity again. In 1973, Levine and Tapp published a law review article that comprehensively surveyed both the psychological and legal aspects of eyewitness testimony. Ellis (1975) reviewed the growing body of psychological research on facial recognition, while Goldstein (1977) surveyed the literature more generally and adduced the need for safeguards designed to minimize false identifications. Woocher (1977) also reviewed the psychological research and United States Supreme Court rulings regarding the unreliability of eyewitness testimony and suggested several safeguards designed to reduce the possibility of mistaken identifications. Almost simultaneously, in Britain, the Devlin Report (1976) on identification evidence had reached many of the same conclusions—although often without benefit of the research evidence (Bull & Clifford, 1976). And in 1980, a conference on "The Psychology of Eyewitness Testimony" was held at the University of Alberta—the first conference devoted solely to research on this topic.

We view the accelerating rate of publications on topics related to eyewitness testimony as a promising sign; the quality, breadth and pace of research have improved markedly in the past decade and show no signs of slackening. In this chapter we report on more than 60 research articles and papers that appeared in 1979 and 1980.

As the title of this chapter implies, our review focuses on the question of eyewitness reliability. In fact, it might be more appropriate to say that we are interested in the sources and extent of eyewitness unreliability as evidenced by psychological research on human perception and memory. Although the term *eyewitness* may imply that we are concerned only with visual witnessing, we are, in fact, dealing with any type of information that might be registered by a witness to an event. While many of the studies we review are laboratory experiments concerning human memory rather than witness reliability per se, we believe that this research is highly relevant to the problems of witness reliability that are encountered every day in legal settings.

This chapter is organized around three general topics: first, the basic processes in human memory and their relationships to eyewitness reliability; second, facial recognition; and finally, the role of the eyewitness in the legal system. In each of the three areas we highlight research which underscores the sources and magnitude of eyewitness unreliability.

THE IDEAL EYEWITNESS

Before discussing the literature on eyewitnesses, it seems useful to specify a model of the characteristics and behaviors desired in the "ideal" eyewitness. A study by Lavrakas and Bickman (1975) is instructive in this regard. These investigators asked 54 prosecutors to rate the importance of 32 witness and case characteristics in terms of their impact on decision making in four phases of prosecution (initial review by the prosecutor, preliminary hearings, plea bargaining and trial). Some of the highest rated factors were: Is the witness available? How good is the witness's memory for the defendant's face? Is there a witness available in addition to the victim? Does the victim recall the incident clearly? Was the victim intoxicated? Was the victim harmed? The fact that these questions were considered to be most important suggests that a major concern of prosecutors is the *quality* of the eyewitness accounts. Other characteristics of the witness, such as intelligence and demographics, for example, received much lower ratings.

If the quality of eyewitness testimony is taken as the fundamental criterion, the ideal eyewitness might be described as a person who (at least with respect to some target event): (a) perceived all that transpired during the event, (b) accurately encoded these perceptions, (c) exhaustively stored the encoded perceptions in memory, and (d) fully and accurately retrieved the encodings from memory in the form of later report(s). This view of the ideal eyewitness highlights the four stages of information processing that are routinely examined by researchers of human perception and memory. But what do we know about how well actual eyewitnesses generally match the ideal? It is to this question that we now turn.

EYEWITNESSING: BASIC PROCESSES IN HUMAN MEMORY

In this section we examine the four stages of information processing, briefly describe the theories relevant to each, and then review the research evidence concerning their limitations and shortcomings. The picture that emerges demonstrates that eyewitness performance is far from ideal, and indicates that eyewitness unreliability is a problem that is systematic in nature. Further documentation of the systematic nature of imperfections in perception and memory may be of great value to decision makers who must rely on eyewitness reports.

Perception

Before any event can be stored in memory for later retrieval, it must first be within a perceiver's range. We know that there are certain physical limitations on our senses; despite these, however, our sensory systems are quite responsive—perhaps moreso than most people imagine. Galanter (1962) provides sensory threshold values for vision (a candle flame at 30 mi on a dark and clear night); taste (1 tsp of sugar in 2 gal of water); hearing (a watch tick at 20 ft with quiet background); smell (1 drop of perfume diffused into a six-room apartment); and touch (the wing of a fly falling from a distance of 1 cm onto your cheek).

It should be emphasized that perception is now generally regarded as a constructive process (Lindsay & Norman, 1977) involving such subprocesses as figure-ground discrimination, feature detection and analysis, grouping, patterning, and pattern recognition. Neisser (1976) has emphasized the role of hypothesis testing and analysis by synthesis. One implication of the constructive process view is that perception does not produce records of events that are as direct or complete as some lay persons are inclined to believe.

Of course, our sensory systems do have to be properly deployed before an event will be perceived. We cannot see behind us, nor can we perceive everything that goes on around us (Norman, 1976). Even when events are perceived, they may not be perceived accurately. And although sensory organs may be in proper working order and properly adapted to the prevailing sensory conditions (e.g., rod receptors in the eye that require an hour to achieve complete adaptation to darkness [Wist, 1976] have had that hour to adjust), distortions in perceptual judgments are common. Gardner (1933) noted the tendency to overestimate vertical distances and the duration of events but to underestimate the size of filled spaces such as furnished rooms. Similarly, Grether and Baker (1972) have noted that estimates of distances, speed, size and acceleration are particularly difficult when the observed objects or context are unfamiliar. Cattell (1895) was one of the first researchers to demonstrate such biases. He found that his students underestimated the weight of their textbooks by nearly 30%, overestimated the distance between two campus buildings by 15%, and overestimated the walking time from one part of a building to another by 90%.

Examples of erroneous estimates of stimuli are also common in the eyewitness research literature that uses "staged" crimes (a method first described by Münsterberg, 1908). Gardner, for instance, reported great variation in estimates of a supposed criminal's height (with a mean overestimate of 8 in.); Marshall's (1966) subjects overestimated the length of a film clip by a factor of 3; Buckhout (1974) reported overestimates of the duration of witnessed events by a factor of 2½; Johnson and Scott (1976) found even more distorted duration estimates (males overestimated by 75% and females by 600%). These distortions are consistent with Schiffman and Bobko's (1974) finding that overestimates of duration are related to the complexity of the event being reported.

In a study highly relevant to eyewitness perception, Tickner and Poulton (1975) demonstrated that an observer's ability to detect certain types of stimuli varies as a function of the stimuli. In their study, subjects viewing a videotaped street scene more often detected criminal actions (stealing) than they detected target persons whose pictures were available to them prior to and throughout the videotape. Clifford and Scott (1978) have obtained similar results: Their subjects provided more complete information about the *actions* in a 1-min film than they provided about the *persons* in the film. It may be argued that some of the difficulties in perception arise at different stages of information processing.

Encoding: The Acquisition of Information

Modern theories of memory are nearly unanimous in their treatment of memory as a three-stage process (a) encoding or acquisition, (b) storage or retention, and (c) retrieval (Bourne, Dominowski & Loftus, 1979; Crowder, 1976). In the study of eyewitness reliability, we are mainly concerned with long-term memory and can examine sources of eyewitness unreliability within the context of encoding, storage, and retrieval stages.

Memory encoding is the stage in which information enters the memory system. Encoded information reflects the operations performed on input during perception, comprehension, and decision making (Craik & Jacoby, 1979). Although memory researchers are concerned with a number of theoretical issues that relate in varying degrees to eyewitness reliability—for instance, short-term memory capacity and chunking of information (Miller, 1956), encoding specificity (Tulving & Thompson, 1973), semantic versus episodic memory (Tulving, 1972), visual versus verbal encoding (Kosslyn, 1975), and "depth" of processing (Craik & Lockhart, 1972)—much of the research on eyewitness performance can be conveniently organized under event and witness factors, two general headings that are probably more meaningful to the lay person than the awkward psychological terminology.

STIMULUS EVENT FACTORS AFFECTING EYEWITNESS PERFORMANCE

The first group of factors that affect encoding of information are factors associated with the event being witnessed, and include frequency, exposure time, event complexity, organization and type of facts, event stressfulness, and seriousness of the offense.

Frequency

The classic studies conducted by Ebbinghaus (1885/1964) using nonsense syllables compellingly demonstrated that memory improves with practice or repeated exposure to stimuli, an effect that has been demonstrated in a variety of contexts (Waugh, 1963). In the eyewitness realm, Gardner (1933) noted that a witness's memory for an event was a function both of the number of times it was observed and the number of times it was reported by the witness. McCarty (1929) and Burtt (1948) also noted the effects of frequency of exposure. Sanders and Warnick (1979) recently demonstrated the effect of repeated exposures to a target mock criminal. In their study, subjects were either exposed or not exposed to a 3-min. videotaped interview with the target person before viewing a 20-sec purse snatching "incident" tape. Witnesses with prior exposure to the target were nearly twice as likely as those without prior exposure to correctly identify the target (60% versus 33%) from a six-person lineup. However, as we note later in this chapter, in the section labeled Unconscious Transference, there are several studies that demonstrate that prior exposures can lead to increases in the likelihood of incorrect identifications.

Exposure time

In 1909, Whipple observed that witness accuracy should improve as the duration of the target event increased. Waugh (1967) and Roberts (1972) have demonstrated this effect with word recall and Hintzman (1976) found a positive linear relationship between exposure time and recall. Bricker and Pruzansky (1966) obtained similar results with voice recognition, and much the same effects have been demonstrated with picture recognition (Hintzman, Summers, & Block, 1975; Intraub, 1979; Weaver & Stanny, 1978). Laughery, Alexander, and Lane (1971) and Hall (1980) have shown the same results with slides of faces. Ellis, Davies, and Shepherd (1977) reported a logarithmic relationship between facial recognition and exposure time; G. R. Loftus and Kallman (1979) obtained similar results in memory for pictures. Read (1979) has shown that longer rehearsal periods following exposure to photographs of faces (subjects were instructed to form verbal descriptions or mental images of the faces) also improves recognition performance. And Graefe and Watkins (1980) have obtained similar rehearsal effects with faces, scenic views, random shapes, and line drawings.

Event complexity

We have already noted that event complexity seems to contribute to errors in estimates of event duration (Schiffman & Bobko, 1974). On the other hand, stimulus complexity appears to enhance recognition of stimuli. Franken and Davis (1975) report that recognition of previously seen photographs was better when the images were more complex. Similar effects have been demonstrated by Shepard (1967), G. R. Loftus (1972), and J. E. Wells (1972). Recently, Carr, Deffenbacher, and Leu (1979) have found that recognition of faces and land-scapes is better sustained than recognition of objects and words. These results should be qualified by two considerations. First, Goldstein and Chance (1971) have shown that even prolonged study of complex but meaningless stimuli is not associated with good recognition performance. Second, there may be substantial differences between recall of complex stimuli (generating information about a previously seen stimulus) and recognition (judgment of whether a stimulus has been seen before) of complex stimuli. As complexity increases, the probability that portions of the stimuli will be misrecollected may increase while the probability of recognition may increase. In a recent discussion of recognition memory, Mandler (1980) suggests that this may occur because the additional structural information in a complex stimulus may enhance the likelihood that it will match some stored internal representation.

Organization and type of facts

Research by G. Mandler (Mandler, 1972, 1980; Mandler, Pearlstone, & Koopmans, 1969) has demonstrated that the organization or meaningfulness of stimuli is related to memory for the stimuli. Mandler argues, for instance, that our knowledge of when or where events occurred (context) diminishes more rapidly than our knowledge about the organization or structure of events. J. M. Mandler has conducted a series of studies (Mandler & Johnson, 1976; Mandler & Parker, 1976; Mandler & Ritchey, 1977; Mandler & Stein, 1974) more directly relevant to eyewitness reliability. Her method was to expose subjects to a series of scenes composed of natural objects that were either realistically organized or disorganized. After a delay (ranging from a few minutes to 4 months), subjects were presented with a series of scenes including the originals and new versions of the old scenes containing various types of transformations.

Mandler and Ritchey (1977) found, for example, that subjects' recognition performance was best (in terms of signal detection) for scenes in which new objects were added and worst for scenes in which the sizes of objects were manipulated. Manipulations producing intermediate performances (in descending order) included: deletions of objects, changes in types of objects, rearrangements, changes in orientation, changes in the details of an object, and movements in the horizontal plane. To date no eyewitness research has examined differential recall so systematically, but a similar cataloging of effects using realistic stimulus material would clearly be useful.

Some early investigations do illustrate the effects of differential recall. For example, Cattell's (1895) research demonstrated that memory for mundane events and details was quite poor (e.g., details about the building where the class met, comments made 1 week earlier by the lecturer, and the weather conditions 1 week earlier).

Early research by Myers (1913) also demonstrated that insignificant characteristics of familiar objects, such as sizes and markings of currency, border details, and stimuli to which laboratory subjects have not attended, are poorly remembered (but see Craik & Lockhart, 1972 on "incidental learning"). Gardner (1933) suggested that interesting, colorful and unusual scences were more likely to attract attention and be remembered. Research by Lewis (1975) confirms these hypotheses in part—subjects viewing films (real and animated cartoon sequences) were more likely to report large and moving stimuli than small and and stationery stimuli.

An interesting eyewitness study by Marshall, Marquis, and Oskamp (1971) also demonstrates that certain characteristics of stimulus events are more memorable or readily available (Tversky & Kahneman, 1973) to observers than are other characteristics and that this availability is strongly related to recall accuracy. Marshall *et al.* showed a 2-min film of an accident between an automobile and a pedestrian and a resulting scuffle to two groups of subjects. The first group generated lists of events they had seen in the film; these were tabulated for frequency of mention. The events most frequently mentioned by the first group were the events that were most completely and accurately described by the second group. Unfortunately, the Marshall *et al.* report does not indicate which specific types of information were more frequently mentioned and recalled except to note a slight advantage of objects over sounds and actions.

An interesting archival study of assailant descriptions given to Seattle police by 100 victims of street-type crimes showed that the frequency with which particular assailant features were mentioned varied substantially: 93% mentioned sex but progressively fewer mentioned age, height, build, race, weight, complexion, and hair color, and only 22% mentioned eye color. These findings should be viewed cautiously since they are based on archival data and, of course, do not assess the accuracy of the descriptions.

The relationship between particular stimulus characteristics and accurate memory is also illustrated by the research on facial recognition reviewed later in this chapter. We merely note here that when Carr, Deffenbacher, and Leu (1979) compared the effects of "interference" (exposure to new nontarget stimuli at the time of the original exposure session) on memory for faces, landscapes, objects, and nouns, they found less forgetting of faces over a 2-week period.

Event stressfulness

Events clearly vary in the extent to which they are arousing or stressful (e.g., compare the stressfulness of reading this chapter to that of being the victim of a late-night mugging in which the robber is armed with a knife). Since event stressfulness is clearly a by-product of the event stimulus conditions and the witness's or participant's reaction to those conditions, stress must be both an event and a witness factor. Some researchers have resolved this by separating the two factors and speaking of the violence of the event, and the stress experienced by the witness. In theory the two can be separated (e.g., a bloody murder might be witnessed by someone who was simply not very upset by it), but in practice it is probably very hard to do. We do not propose to resolve this point. The psychological research on the influence of arousal and stress on human performance often refers to the stress performance relationships specified in a "law" formulated by Yerkes and Dodson (1908). The *Yerkes-Dodson Law* postulates a curvilinear relationship between arousal and performance such that performance is facilitated by increasing arousal up to a point, but progressively undermined after that point. Studies which clearly demonstrate arousal on both the functional and dysfunctional sides of the arousal curve are difficult to obtain—a point to keep in mind when considering the following studies.

There are strong anecdotal illustrations of the effects of stress (e.g., Baddeley, 1972, notes the effects of stress on the performance of soldiers in combat). Kuehn's (1974) archival study of crime victims' descriptions of their assailants suggests that completeness of the descriptions varied as a function of the level of violence in the crime and the extent to which the victim was injured.

A number of eyewitness studies have attempted to manipulate event stressfulness in an effort to assess the impact of stress on eyewitness performance. Johnson and Scott (1976) exposed subjects to either a low arousal condition (the target person was overheard in a discussion and viewed briefly) or a high arousal condition (the target person was overheard in a violent argument and viewed briefly holding a bloodstained letter opener). Males' recall and recognition were more accurate under high arousal, while females' memory for setting and actions was superior under high arousal but their recognition was poorer. Overall performance on recognition (picking the target person out of 50 photographs) was poorer under high arousal (33% correct) than low arousal conditions (49% correct). In general the results are inconclusive with respect to arousal. It is likely that subjects were not *extremely* aroused by the high arousal incident (as was confirmed by subjects' self-assessment of arousal).

Clifford and Scott (1978) showed subjects one of two versions of a 1-min filmed scenario in which two policemen question a third person about a criminal they are seeking. In the mild version, the third person is weakly restrained; in the more violent (arousing) version one of the policemen assaults the third person. Clifford and Scott found that recall for the violent film (particularly for the females) was significantly poorer and that recall of the actions in the film was particularly reduced in the violent version. Sanders and Warnick (1979) used a similar procedure in which subjects viewed either a nonviolent episode in which the target person in a 20-sec film picked up and handed a dropped satchel to the woman carrying it or a violent version in which the target person pulled the satchel from the woman's arm and began running. They obtained only a marginally significant difference (albeit with a low power design) between low arousal recognition accuracy (57% correct identifications from a six-person lineup) and high arousal accuracy (37%).

Using a different paradigm in which subjects were led to believe they had been victims of 11 thefts, Greenberg, Wilson, Ruback, and Mills (1979) found that male subjects who reported high levels of anger were more likely to accurately identify the target in a six-person lineup (high anger = 71% accurate, moderate anger = 50% accurate and low anger = 17% accurate). Accuracy was unrelated to anger for females (accuracy ratings for high, moderate, and low levels of anger were 58%, 57% and 55%, respectively). And in an even more recent study, Witt (1980) showed all subjects a 3-min film of an armed robbery of a supermarket (the film contents were not manipulated) that had been immediately preceded either by 10 min of tense and gory scenes from the killer shark movie *Jaws* (aroused condition) or 10 min of a dull travelogue (no arousal condition). With one exception (better free recall of events early in the target segment for subjects who had not been aroused), there were no arousal effects across a series of free recall, yes/no, multiple-choice, short answer, and photo-spread dependent variables.

On the whole, the eyewitness arousal/stress research suggests that eyewitness performance *is* adversely affected by observation of or participation in episodes which are highly arousing. The conflicting gender differences reported in these studies merit further study.

Seriousness of the offense

Leippe, Wells, and Ostrom (1978) staged a brief theft incident before subjects who were then asked to pick the thief out of a six-person photo-spread. Identification accuracy was affected by the value of the stolen object when the value was known in advance (when the object stolen was a calculator, the accuracy rate was 56%; when it was a cigarette, the accuracy rate was 19%), but not when the value was conveyed to subjects only after the theft (with calculator, 13%, with cigarettes, 35%). These results suggest that the seriousness of events influences observers at the encoding rather than retrieval stage of processing, but other research suggests that event seriousness can also affect processing at retrieval.

In a study in which subjects were led to believe that a thief had stolen $3 or $20 from *them*, Greenberg, Wilson, and Mills (in press) found that 2 months after the event a marginally greater proportion of the victims who had lost $20 correctly picked the thief from a photo lineup (76% versus 54% for the victims who had lost $3). On the other hand, Malpass, Devine, and Bergen (1980) collected data from a staged vandalism incident using a very realistic lineup situation that indicate that subjects who learn, after the incident, that the offender may be treated severely (made to pay damages and serve jail time on a felony conviction) are much more likely to make an identification of someone in the lineup than those who learn the offender may be treated mildly (a lecture from the dean)—83% versus 46%. Although witnesses who believed severe treatment would follow had a higher rate of correct identification (hit rate) than the second group (75% versus 59%), the first group was much more likely to pick a suspect even when the perpetrator was not in the lineup (73% error rate versus 22%). Mild treatment condition subjects appeared to be far less eager to "nail" the criminal; their caution is reflected in the rate at which they declined to make identification even when the perpetrator was present (41% failure to identify rate versus 8% for severe treatment condition subjects). As an aside, we might note that Wells and Lindsay (1980) have used Bayesian analysis of empirical data obtained in another lineup study (E. F. Loftus, 1976) to demonstrate that failure to identify can be more diagnostic (with respect to the probability that a suspect is the criminal) than identification.

WITNESS FACTORS AFFECTING EYEWITNESS PERFORMANCE

In this section we discuss two general types of witness-related factors that affect the ways in which experiences are encoded. (The distinction between the two sets of factors is somewhat crude.) The first group of factors concerns the effect of observers' *expectations* about the events they encounter on their perception and encoding of information about those events, and the impact of these encodings on subsequent performance of memory tasks. The principal question is: *What gets encoded?* The second group of factors is closely related to expectations, but concerns the ways in which the encoded information is *processed* before entering long-term memory. The principal question with respect to the second set of factors is: *How well is the information processed?*

Expectations

As early as 1918, Whipple noted that "observation is peculiarly influenced by expectation, . . . we tend to see and hear what we expect to see and hear [p. 228]." The litany of possible (and often overlapping) categories of expectations is quite long—for example, stereotypes (Hamilton, 1979), cultural biases (Allport & Postman, 1945), personal prejudices (Hastorf & Cantril, 1954), temporarily induced biases (Biederman, Glass, & Stacy, 1973; Siipola, 1935), attributional biases (Ross, 1977), expectations induced by motivational states (Buckhout, 1968; Marshall, 1969), prior information about events (Dooling & Christiaansen, 1977), effects of training (Postman, Bruner, & McGinnies, 1948). Extended discussion of the role of expectations in eyewitness reliability can be found in Clifford and Bull (1978) and Yarmey (1979b), both of which emphasize the influence of stereotypes concerning "criminal" appearance and personality characteristics, and in E. F. Loftus (1979), who additionally considers cultural and personal expectations.

Among the more compelling demonstrations that expectations can affect eyewitness reports is Allport and Postman's (1945) finding that subjects who verbally transmitted a description of a scene (in which a black man was interacting with a white man holding a razor) more often than not produced terminal reports in which the black man was holding the razor. The regularity with which human beings are shot by hunters who "misperceived" powerfully illustrates the tendency to see what we want to see. The classic Bruner and Postman study (1949) in which subjects showed a marked inability to detect objects such as red aces of spades conveys an impression of how difficult it is to overcome expectations, as does the Hastorf and Cantril (1954) study of observers' recollections of a particularly nasty Dartmouth-Princeton game. In this latter study, fans characteristically portrayed the other team as the one that "played dirty." Indeed, many avid sports fans would probably acknowledge such biases.

Shoemaker, South, and Lowe (1973) provided evidence that people hold stereotypes of criminal appearances and these stereotypes can affect judgments of the likelihood that someone has committed a crime. The influence of defendant characteristics such as attractiveness has been demonstrated in jury simulation studies (see Dane & Wrightsman, Chapter 4, this volume). Finally, Clifford and Bull (1978) report a staged-incident study by Hollin which indicates that people use stereotype information (such as "blue eyes go with blond hair") to make inferences about a target person's characteristics.

Processing encoded information

A number of recent experimental studies have examined the relationship between the ways in which information is initially processed and the accuracy of subsequent recognition. In this section we summarize the results from a selected number of those studies. Citations are provided for articles of theoretical interest, but we concentrate on studies which use (a) manipulations that are analogous to many actual eyewitness situations and (b) stimuli such as faces and pictured scenes which generalize more readily to typical eyewitness stimuli.

Several studies dovetail nicely with the expectation results already discussed for they manipulate the *preexposure instructions* given to subjects and thereby presumably affect the ways in which stimuli are encoded and processed. For example, studies by Newtson (Newtson, 1973; Newtson & Engquist, 1976; Newtson, Engquist, & Bois, 1977) have shown that subjects can vary their encoding of stimulus sequences such as filmed interactions between individuals from a fine-grained analysis (in which sequences are broken into very small but meaningful chunks) to a coarse-grained analysis (in which meaningful chunks encompass longer series of small chunks). As an illustration, Massad, Hubbard, and Newtson (1979) obtained chunking differences in the perceptual organization and impression of characters of a simple cartoon by varying the way they characterized the cartoon to the subjects before the subjects viewed it. Interestingly, the initials impressions could be modified only when subjects viewed the cartoon a second time. (See also Cohen & Ebbesen, 1979 for a related study.) In another study more relevant to eyewitnessing, Thorson and Hochhaus (1977) showed subjects an 8-sec videotape of an auto accident. Subjects who were told the content of the film in advance and were informed about recall questions they would be asked provided under estimated the speed of cars but were better able to identify the cars afterwards.

Several groups of researchers have shown subjects pictures of faces and asked the subjects to attend to, remember, or make differentiating judgments about the faces. Blaney and Winograd (1978) report that children who judged how "nice" a face was better performed a subsequent recognition task than children who judged the size of target noses or were merely instructed to remember the faces. On the other hand, Read (1979) found no difference in recognition accuracy between subjects who made visual similarity judgments of faces and subjects who rated faces on a series of 34 adjective scales; Yarmey (1979c) found no difference in recognition performance between subjects who were instructed to remember a series of photographs of themselves and subjects who were tested for incidental recognition without getting any prior instruction.

The Read and Yarmey findings are somewhat surprising in light of facial recognition studies which have manipulated subjects' *depth of processing* (Craik & Lockhart, 1972) of faces. Bower and Karlin's (1974) study illustrates the depth of processing approach. These researchers instructed subjects to make one of three judgments about photographs from a college yearbook: target's gender, likeableness, or honesty. It was hypothesized that the simple gender judgments could be made with a form of information processing that might be characterized as shallow, rapid, or lower level, while more complex processing would be required for likeableness and honesty judgments. In simple terms, the Craik and Lockhart argument is that deeper processing extracts more information from the stimulus and therefore aids later recognition. Bower and Karlin's hypothesis was confirmed; faces about whom the more complex judgments were made were better recognized than faces whose gender was judged, even when the subjects asked to give gender were also instructed to remember the faces for a later recognition task. Similarly, Patterson and Baddeley (1977) report better recognition of faces rated for personality characteristics than of faces rated for physical features, and Nowicki, Winograd, and Millard (1979) indicated similar findings. Mueller, Carlomusto, and Goldstein (1978) also found poorer recognition of faces judged for facial characteristics when compared to recognition of faces judged for personality or general body characteristics (e.g., where subjects were asked to rate posture from face photographs). Recognition performance for subjects asked to judge body and personality characteristics did not vary. Courtois and Mueller (1979) report that multiple feature judgments of faces produced better recognition than single feature judgments but that requests for a judgment of whether the face of the person to be observed "looks like you" produced the most accurate performance. Similar results are reported by Mueller and Wherry (in press) and by Mueller, Bailis, and Goldstein (1979).

Another series of studies has examined the influence of *verbal labels* on recognition performance for visual stimuli. Numerous experiments have shown that picture memory performance is better than memory for object labels and words (e.g., Davies, Milne, & Glennie, 1973; Standing, 1973; and Nelson, Metzler, & Reed, 1974) and the typical explanation for this is that pictures generate a dual code (visual and verbal) in contrast to the single verbal code for labels. (See Clifford & Bull, 1978 for an extended discussion of the dual coding research.) G. R. Loftus (1972) and Rowe and Rogers (1975) have found some support for this hypothesis, but Intraub (1979) has not. Taken together, the research supporting enhanced performance for pictures plus labels further indicates that the type of label given to a picture can also have effects on recognition accuracy.

In extensions of earlier research by Daniel (1972) and Pezdek (1977), Jörg and Hörmann (1978) found that when subjects were presented with pictures with printed labels that were specific versus general versus not labeled (e.g., "flounder," "fish," or no label), their performance in a subsequent recognition test which included alterations of the original picture was affected. For example, subjects who had seen general labels were better able to distinguish highly dissimilar pictures while subjects who had seen specific labels were more successful with highly similar pictures. In a similar study, Gentner and Loftus (1979) presented subjects with a series of 16 pictures (some depicting a specific activity and some depicting a general activity) that subjects matched with 1 of 16 sentences containing either a general or a specific verb (e.g., eat versus picnic, talk versus argue) that could appropriately label the picture. Only one sentence was supplied for each picture, either a sentence with a general verb or one with a specific verb. Thus, subjects were sometimes supplied sentences with verbs describing specific activities (e.g. picnic), but the pictures that these sentences described depicted a general activity (e.g. eating). Sometimes general verbs were supplied for specific-act pictures. In other instances the verb and the picture matched. In a forced-choice recognition test administered 1 week later, subjects were presented with the pairs of specific activity and general activity pictures (one old and one new) to indicate the pictures they had viewed a week earlier. Both the type of picture and the type of verb in the sentence given subjects affected their recognition accuracy (e.g., subjects were more likely to select a specific picture in the recognition task if they had originally viewed a picture with a specific activity or had been supplied with a sentence with a specific verb). In another recent study, G. R. Loftus and Kallmann (1979) showed subjects 160 pictures of complex natural scenes presented for various lengths of time on a slide projector (between .05 and 1 sec each). Some subjects were instructed to write down some detail from each picture that they thought would help them recognize the picture later. Except when the pictures were shown at very rapid speeds, the subjects who named a detail scored significantly higher on a subsequent recognition task. Picture details have also been found to aid in recognition in the work of Weaver and Stanney (1978).

A final set of studies relevant to the initial encoding of stimuli are those that have examined the improvement in memory that results from *rehearsal of stimuli*. The improvement in memory for rehearsed (mentally repeated) words is well acknowledged in the memory research literature and recent research also suggests that rehearsal of visual stimuli can improve memory. For instance, Weaver and Stanney found that subjects who were presented with a series of pictures of natural settings performed better when the off-time between pictures was 6 sec rather than 2. In a study using faces, Read (1979) also manipulated off-time and gave subjects an auditory detection task or one of two types of explicit rehearsal instructions: "Try to continue 'seeing' the last face" versus "Try to rehearse a verbal description of the face." Both types of rehearsal improved recognition (but did not, themselves, yield different results) and increased off-time improved performance. In several studies, Graefe and Watkins (1980) presented subjects a series of pictures containing two similar stimuli and cued them to visually rehearse ("imagine," "visualize," etc.) one of two stimuli. For all types of stimuli, the rehearsed stimuli were more accurately recognized. Uncued stimuli did not benefit at all from the rehearsal period.

Eugenio, Buckhout, Kostes, and Ellison (1979) have used a rehearsal-like manipulation in a study that used a slide and tape presentation of a staged assault. Subjects viewed the presentation, immediately gave an "initial" eyewitness report of the incident, then were assigned either to a 5-min rehearsal condition (they were told to imagine seeing the incident again) or a 5-min psychomotor game designed to block rehearsal. Subjects then gave a second report, repeated the treatment, and gave a third report. Eugenio *et al.* did not obtain a difference between the imagination and game conditions, but there was a significant improvement in hit rates over trials for both groups. It may be argued that the immediate report constituted an equivalent "rehearsal" for both groups (i.e., the interpolated game either did not destroy the rehearsal-like benefits of the immediate reports or these benefits were not enhanced by the subsequent rehearsal). It would be interesting to know whether an immediate report/rehearsal of the incident would yield better memory performance than a delayed report/no rehearsal condition.

We can most succinctly summarize the research on the relationship between eyewitness reliability and eyewitness encoding by highlighting event and eyewitness characteristics that are most likely to promote eyewitness accuracy. With respect to event characteristics, the research suggests that accuracy is likely to be enhanced when eyewitnesses have had repeated opportunities to make observations and/or have had an opportunity to observe events or persons over an extended period of time; when events are meaningful and the target events or persons are a central aspect of the events; when the events are arousing or stressful, but not so arousing or stressful that they impair eyewitness performance; and when the events are of sufficient severity that they attract attention without also motivating eyewitnesses to make excessive numbers of false identifications.

With respect to witness characteristics, the research suggests that eyewitness reliability is likely to be enhanced when eyewitnesses have advance information that allows them to anticipate events or stimulus persons (although, on the other hand, eyewitness testimony should be scrutinized to determine whether the advance "knowledge" is of a variety—such as a stereotype—that might bias the witness's response). The eyewitness's account is also likely to be more reliable if the stimulus information has been processed in some "deep" or meaningful way that is appropriate to the events. Inappropriate initial assessments of events are less likely to result in processing or extraction of relevant event features and details that would aid later recognition and recall. Finally, there is some evidence that an immediate rehearsal of events (perhaps a prompt reporting of events to the police) will improve subsequent witness performance.

Although it would clearly be desirable to possess indices of the comparative impact these various factors have on eyewitness reliability, to date the research allows neither absolute nor relative assessments of the magnitude of their influence on eyewitness reliability. Although such assessments are possible, the complexity of the experimental designs and stimulus materials required for such assessments clearly place the necessary research beyond the resources of most active investigators.

Storage of Information

As we have seen, a variety of factors can affect which stimuli are perceived and the degree to which they are encoded. Given the number of influences on perception and encoding, it should be no surprise to suggest that the representation of an event that enters a witness's memory is unlikely to be an accurate rendering. Unfortunately, the problem of inaccurate representation is further compounded by the fact that changes in the memorial representation can take place during the interval between the original encoding and the subsequent eyewitness report. In this section we discuss this "retention interval" and factors that influence memory during this period of time.

Ebbinghaus's (1885/1964) classic research on learning clearly demonstrated that learned materials are forgotten during the retention interval. Initially the loss is quite rapid but it slows over time (thus describing a negatively accelerated "forgetting curve"). Although these results have been replicated many times, the explanation of forgetting is still an open question (Bourne, Dominowski, & Loftus, 1979). Current popular theories emphasize interference (distortions in memory produced by information learned before or after an event) and the availability of cues at the time of retrieval (Tulving & Thompson, 1973), a topic we discuss in the next major section of this chapter, Retrieval of Information. For now, we briefly review research on the relationship between the retention interval and forgetting by examining some of the many studies using different stimuli and retention intervals.

THE LENGTH OF THE RETENTION INTERVAL

Dallenbach (1913) had students view a picture and later, after varying time periods, answer 60 questions about it and indicate their willingness to take an oath about the accuracy of their answers. The average number of incorrect answers for the immediate test was 9, but increased to 13 after a 45-day delay. The number of incorrect answers "sworn to" increased from 3 to 7 over the same period. Over 50 years later, Shepard (1967) presented subjects with 600 pictures of everyday objects and scenes. Recognition performance of subjects shown 60 sets of old and new pictures 2 hours after the viewing was 100%; but after a 4-month delay, performance had dropped to near-chance levels of 57% correct. The Mandler and Ritchey (1977) study which transformed various picture characteristics in recognition tests showed that recognition memory for target objects did not drop in a 24-hour period, but did drop over a 1-week period and even more over 4 months. As already noted, subjects differentially recalled certain aspects of the stimuli (recognition was better for pictures in which additions and deletions were made than for pictures in which objects changed size or moved).

Shepherd and Ellis (1973) conducted a study that assessed recognition of facial photographs immediately and after 6 and 35 days. They found that the decrease in recognition accuracy was due almost entirely to poorer recognition of average (not unusual) faces at 35 days. Laughery, Fessler, Lenorovitz, and Yoblick (1974) used both facial slides and a 1-min clip and found no reduction in facial recognition accuracy after a 1-week retention interval. Finally, Carr, Deffenbacher, and Leu (1979) showed subjects equal numbers of nouns, objects, landscapes, and faces and tested recognition at 2 min and 2 weeks. Although statistical tests were not reported, performance on all four types of stimuli appear worse after 2 weeks, with recognition of faces and landscapes apparently more durable.

Saslove and Yarmey (1980) compared immediate and 24-hour recognition of voices and obtained no differences, but McGehee (1937) found that voice recognition fell from 83% accuracy at 1 day, to 81%, 69%, 57%, 35%, and 13% after delays of 1 week, 2 weeks, 1 month, 3 months, and 5 months. The results are more remarkable in light of the fact that chance performance would have been 20%.

Davis and Sinha (1950) had subjects read a 750-word story and tested recall of the story over various lengths of time up to 1 year later. The length of the retention interval dramatically affected recall. In an even more relevant study, Marshall (1969) asked subjects about a 42-sec film clip and found significantly better performance with immediate tests than with tests administered 1 week later. Egan, Pittner, and Goldstein (1977) had subjects who were informed in advance that they were to play eyewitnesses view a 15-sec "robbery." Subjects were then given photo-spread or live lineup recognition tests 2, 21, and 51 days after the robbery. Correct identification rates were 98% for lineups and 85% for photo-spreads (averaged across retention intervals). The correct identification rates were not affected by length of retention interval (although given the high accuracy rates, there may have been ceiling effects). The percentage of subjects making false identifications did increase significantly from 48% to 62% to 93% for 2, 21, and 56 days, and the percentage of subjects making no errors declined from 45% to 29% to 7% for each delay period. The high false identification rate arose because subjects were not advised that only one of the two robbers was in the lineup/photo-spread.

In a study in which subjects were shown a film of an armed robbery and shooting without prior knowledge that they would serve as eyewitnesses, Lipton (1977) found that subjects questioned after 1 week generated 18% fewer recall items than subjects questioned immediately. The 1-week subjects were also 4% less accurate in their recall. And, compared to immediate recall subjects, Sanders and Warnick (1979) obtained a significant reduction in recall of their perpetrator's physical features with only a 4-min delay after the incident. In sum, the research on the length of the retention interval supports Ebbinghaus's (1885/1964) original finding that the longer the interval, the worse the performance. Of course, unless one knows a great deal about the specific conditions under which the incident was viewed (e.g., what happened? how long did it take?), it is impossible to predict the precise forgetting curve.

INTERFERENCE WITH STORED INFORMATION

There is mounting evidence that information learned by eyewitnesses subsequent to observing an event can alter their memory of the original event. Bird (1927) observed this effect when he found that students taking an exam mistakenly accepted inaccurate newspaper accounts of Bird's introductory psychology lectures. Somewhat later, Belbin (1950) showed that subjects who attempted to recall the details of a poster they had seen were less able to recognize it later than a group who did not attempt recall. Apparently the subjects inserted erroneous details into their recall, and these importations were the cause of the subsequent recognition failure.

More recently, Fischhoff (1977) has demonstrated the impact of postevent activities on memory. Subjects who were given answers to general knowledge questions overestimated how much they would have known and actually *did* know about the answers to the questions before being given the answers. Efforts to undo this "knew-it-all-along" effect failed.

In a series of studies by E. F. Loftus and her associates, a variety of memory interference effects have been obtained. In one study (Loftus, 1975) subjects who viewed a 1-min film of an automobile accident were asked a series of questions about the incident in which the form of the first question varied. Of the subjects who were asked in the first question how fast the car was going "when it ran the stop sign," 53% reported in the last question that they had seen the stop sign. This compared to 35% of subjects who in the first question were asked how fast the car was going "when it turned right" reporting they had seen the stop sign. In a second study, 17% of subjects initially asked about the speed of a car passing a nonexistent barn reported having seen the barn when questioned 1 week later. Fewer than 3% of subjects who were asked a question that did not mention the barn later recalled having seen a barn. Using a similar procedure E. F. Loftus, Miller, and Burns (1978) presented subjects with a series of slides depicting an accident and asked questions containing either consistent, misleading, or irrelevant "information." Some subjects received the information immediately after viewing the film and others received the information just prior to a later recognition test (retention intervals were immediate, 20 min, 1 day, 2 days, and 1 week). Proportions of correct responses dropped from over 80% for consistent information, given immediately or delayed, to 46% for immediate misleading information and less than 20% for delayed misleading information. (See the later discussion of Retrieval of Information for further discussion of "delayed question" and other retrieval effects.)

E. F. Loftus, Altman, and Geballe (1975) were able to alter subjects' assessments of the noisiness, violence, belligerence, and antagonism shown in a 3-min videotpaed segment of a classroom demonstration/disruption simply by manipulating the emotional connotations of a 25-item questionnaire given immediately after the videotape (1 week before the final assessments).

E. F. Loftus (1977) also obtained false information effects in a study that used a postevent question to supply false information about the color of a car shown in a slide series depicting an accident between an automobile and a pedestrian. Powers, Andriks, and Loftus (1979) have obtained similar results with questions presupposing an object's existence, and Cole and Loftus (1979) have used a reaction time method to demonstrate that the effects of misleading information apparently occur prior to the time of retrieval and therefore reflect altered underlying memories.

Related memory interference effects have been reported by Dooling and Christiaansen (1977). In a somewhat complex study designed to explore Tulving's (1972) distinction between semantic and episodic memory, Dooling and Christiaansen had subjects read a prose passage. The finding of interest was that within 1 week after reading the passage, subjects who had been told that the passage concerned a famous person (Adolph Hitler or Helen Keller) were more likely than subjects told they were reading about a fictitious character to falsely recognize thematic material related to but not identical to the stimulus materials. The authors interpret the results by suggesting that subjects relied on their semantic (general knowledge) memory of the famous persons rather than their episodic memory of the reading session. (See also the Davis and Sinha [1950] study discussed earlier.)

Hastie, Landsman, and Loftus (1978) have also induced interference by urging subjects who viewed a series of slides depicting a mugging to guess at answers on an initial test. On a final test given 10 min later, guessing subjects generated more false answers. A second study using a filmed accident showed that subjects who "guessed" about the color of a nonexistent car were significantly more confident about their answer 2 days later (an increase from 2.6 to 3.4 on a 5-point scale). Nonguessers' confidence decreased significantly (from 2.4 to 1.9).

Although the definitive theory of forgetting has yet to appear, there is clear evidence that not everything we process remains permanently available to us. While the mechanisms of forgetting are poorly understood, research has identified several factors which have relatively predictable relationships to the availability of stored information. Every lay person knows from personal experience that extended retention intervals are associated with poor memory. This effect has been confirmed by empirical research dating back to the nineteenth century. Recent research indicates that some stimuli (particularly faces) are more memorable than other stimuli, but precise forgetting curves have not been developed even for general categories of stimuli.

We have also noted that memories appear rather susceptible to interference during the storage interval. Interference effects have been obtained using misleading questions, inconsistent information, postevent information, and even guessing.

Retrieval of Information

Several early eyewitness studies indicated that eyewitness reports could be biased or distorted at the retrieval stage—that is, at the time when the eyewitness was called upon to recall information or recognize previously seen stimuli. In this section, we discuss a series of factors that have been shown to influence eyewitness reports at the time of retrieval.

TYPES OF QUESTIONS

Some of the earliest research examined memories elicited by different types of questions (Burtt, 1931; Gardner, 1933; Whipple, 1909, 1912). In one suggestive (but somewhat flawed) study, Muscio (1915) used different question forms (the "indefinite" did you see *a* dog? versus the "definite" did you see *the* dog? versus the "conjecture" was there a dog? etc.). Among his results, Muscio reported that definite articles (*the* versus *a*) produced higher false rates.

Cady (1924) had subjects view a short live event and then tested the recall of the event produced by several forms of questions (e.g., "free narrative"—what happened? versus "controlled narrative"—describe X, versus multiple choice questions and lineup recognition). Marquis, Marshall, and Oskamp (1972) completed a similar study using a film of an automobile accident. Both Cady and Marquis *et al.* found that subjects who gave free narratives were most accurate but that their narrations were also least complete. Direct questions yielded less accurate but more complete responses. Snee and Lush (1941) also found that controlled narratives were more complete than free narratives. In addition, they found that an initial controlled narrative resulted in more complete subsequent free reports (without increasing errors of commission).

In a study discussed earlier, Lipton (1977) had subjects view a short filmed murder sequence and then assessed the percentage *accuracy* and *completeness* for unstructured testimony (91%, 21%), open-ended questions (83%, 32%), leading questions (72%, 79%), and multiple-choice questions (56%, 75%). Clifford and Scott (1978), on the other hand, failed to obtain a difference in accuracy for free narrative versus structured questions; however, Dent (1978) did.

On balance, the results of these studies seem to weigh somewhat in favor of an investigatory method that initially uses free or controlled narrative and is then followed by structured questions. This method has the best chance of eliciting an initial highly accurate rendering of facts that can then be elaborated on with the structured questions.

QUESTION BIAS

Muscio's (1915) finding that questions containing definite articles (*the* versus *a*) elicited higher false answer rates has been replicated by E. F. Loftus and Zanni (1975). In two studies, the false answer rates using *the* were 15% and 20%, whereas for *a* they were 7% and 6%, respectively. Loftus and Zanni also found that subjects responding to the definite article gave fewer uncertain or "I don't know" responses. But see also Zanni and Offermann (1978) who failed to obtain a significant effect using a smaller sample of subjects. In a similar study, E. F. Loftus and Palmer (1974) found that they could even manipulate subjects' estimates of the speed of an automobile in several accident films. Subjects asked how fast the cars were going when they smashed into each other estimated an average of 40.8 mph. When other words were substituted for *smashed*, the estimates varied significantly: *collided* yielded 39.3 mph, *bumped*, 38.1 mph, *hit*, 34 mph, and *contacted*, 31.8 mph. In a second study, speed estimates and verbs were both related to the probability that subjects reported having seen broken glass in an accident film. The *yes* response rate for subjects presented the word *smash* was 32%, *hit* yielded 14%, and the control condition got 12% yes responses.

Other studies have demonstrated similar question-induced biases. In his study, Lipton (1977) made use of multiple-choice questions which either contained the correct answer (positive bias) or did not contain a correct answer (negative bias) and compared the performance on open-ended questions (neutral). There were highly significant effects for both *accuracy* and *completeness*. The respective percentages were: neutral, 83%, 32%; positive bias, 76%, 78%, and negative bias, 52%, 73%. Clifford and Scott (1978) indicate that 5% of their subjects were able to avoid being misled (on a final report) after being exposed to negatively biased questions in an initial report. Most recently, Dodd and Bradshaw (1980) showed that the person asking the questions made a difference. Leading questions asked by a biased person did not have the same impact as leading questions asked by a neutral person, reflecting the influence of pragmatic conditions on normal language processing.

In a final biasing study somewhat reminiscent of that of Dooling and Christiaansen (1977), Snyder and Uranowitz (1978) obtained rather provocative retrieval effects using a story-recalling methodology (Bartlett, 1932/1957) quite relevant to many eyewitness situations. They had subjects read a 746-word life history of "Betty K." One week later, the subjects returned to recall factual details about Betty K. and answer 36 multiple-choice questions. Subjects learned, either immediately after reading the story or immediately before completing the questionnaires, something that made no difference to the life history—that Betty was heterosexual, or homosexual, or got no additional information. Snyder and Uranowitz found that subjects reconstructed the events of Betty K.'s life in a manner that supported and reinforced their induced perceptions of Betty's sexual preferences. Subjects' errors reflected the biasing information and there was some evidence that they tended to remember facts about Betty K. that supported their induced biases. One wonders whether similar distortions in memory would be obtained with eyewitnesses who later learn that what they thought they witnessed was "in fact" something else entirely!

LINEUP INSTRUCTION BIASES

Several researchers have compellingly demonstrated that eyewitness performance in lineup situations can be significantly affected by the retrieval of memory information instructions the eyewitnesses receive. Ellis, Davies, and Shepherd (1977) showed 10 faces to 60 subjects who were then asked to identify any "old" faces in a new group of 24 faces that did not contain any "old" faces. Subjects given lax instructions ("don't worry too much about making mistakes") made twice as many false identifications as subjects given strict instructions telling them to be certain about their identifications. Egan and Smith (1979) found that subjects given lax instructions accurately responded 88% of the time that a target was in a five-person lineup (hit rate), and were accurate 21% of the time in stating that the target was absent (correct rejection rate). Strict instruction subjects had a hit rate of 92% and a correct rejection rate of 63%. Malpass and Devine (1980) either led witnesses of a staged act of vandalism to think that the perpetrator was believed to be in a five-person lineup (biased instructions) or that the perpetrator only might be in the lineup (unbiased instructions). Using lineups with and without the target, the subjects getting unbiased instructions had a hit rate of 83% and a correct rejection rate of 67%. For subjects getting the biased instructions, the hit rate was 75% and the correct rejection rate was 22%. In their lineup study, Warnick and Sanders (1980) explicitly provided some of their eyewitnesses an "I don't know" category for responding, while others received an "I don't know" category plus written instructions not to guess. A third group also received the explicit "I don't know" option, plus written *and* oral instructions about not guessing. A fourth group given no special instructions served as controls. The target was always present. Briefly, the results showed that the control group produced more false identifications than the other three groups (43% versus a mean of 23%), more "not presents" (33% versus 11%) but far fewer "I don't knows" (00% versus 35%).

The results from these lineup studies illustrate the fact that relatively subtle differences in instructions can have rather striking effects on eyewitness performance. The situation is compounded when one considers the study by Malpass, Devine, and Bergen (1980) discussed earlier that demonstrated that more severe crimes might lead to higher false identification rates.

DISGUISES

Several studies have shown the rather obvious finding that recognition of disguised faces is more difficult than recognition of undisguised faces. Laughery and Fowler (1977) report, for example, that correct recognition of a face initially viewed with a beard decreased from 92% to 50% when viewed clean-shaven. Patterson and Baddeley (1977) also found that they could undermine facial recognition with a variety of changes in the appearance of targets. From a high of 98% hits with identical targets viewed with dissimilar distractor faces, the rate dropped to 91% for targets viewed with similar distractors faces, 82% for changed-pose targets with similar distractors and 45% for disguised faces (beards, glasses, changed hair style, etc.) viewed with dissimilar distractors. In a second study, subjects were presented with 80 faces including those of 10 men subjected to eight systematic disguises. Five of the 10 men's faces had been studied in advance by subjects. Patterson and Baddeley found that for three-quarter facial views with heads turned slightly, the rates of correct identification ranged from 89% for no changes in features to 89% when glasses only, were added, 64% wig only, added, 67% glasses and wig added, 67% beard only, added, 56% beard and glasses added, 52% beard and wig added, and 39% when beard, wig, and glasses were added. Profile views were identified an average of 50% of the time compared to 65% for three-quarter views.

Saslove and Yarmey (1980) report that subjects found it very difficult to correctly identify voices (initially heard for 11 sec) when there was a change in voice tone from conversational to hostile or vice versa. A complementary false alarm-correct rejection effect was obtained. Patterson and Baddeley particularly noted that the hit rate for subjects who made their identifications after a 24-hour delay, were initially uninformed about the object of the study, were presented disguised voices, was 13%, actually below the chance rate, which would have been expected by 20%. They noted that this condition is probably the one that most closely approximates actual earwitness identification situations.

UNCONSCIOUS TRANSFERENCE

Buckhout (1974) staged a mock assault before a group of 141 students. Seven weeks later, when the students were asked to pick the assailant from a group of six photographs, 40% were able to select the assailant. Of the 60% who failed to make a correct identification, two-thirds selected a person who had been at the scene as an innocent bystander (this was more than double the rate expected by chance). E. F. Loftus (1976) obtained similar results in a study using an audiotape and photograph presentation of an assault story. Three days after the presentation, subjects were shown a five-person photo-spread. When the criminal's photo was present, 84% chose correctly. When the photo-spread included a picture of an innocent, incidental character from the original story, 60% selected the bystander, 16% selected another person, but only 24% correctly refused to make an identification.

The systematic nature of the intrusions obtained in these studies suggests that the subjects are confusing their contexts and placing a somewhat familiar face in the wrong context (See Wall, 1965, for an illustrative anecdote).

Deffenbacher, Leu, and Brown (1979) showed subjects two sets of photographs in two separate rooms and tested subjects' memory for the viewing "context" 1 week later. Although facial recognition was high (ranging from 87% to 99% across experimental conditions), recall of the context (the room) was at chance levels (51.3%). Only 9 of 72 subjects discriminated context at better than chance levels.

There is a suggestion in a recent theoretical piece by Mandler (1980) that familiarity judgments are independent of retrieval processes. Following Tulving's (1972) distinction between semantic and episodic memory, Craik and Jacoby (1979) speculated that semantic, general knowledge information (such as facial familiarity) may be easier to retrieve than specific contextual, episodic information (such as the place where the face was seen). Both these theoretical observations could help to explain the unconscious transference effects.

MULTIPLE RETRIEVALS

In his classic memory research, Bartlett (1932/1957) demonstrated that retelling of stories produced systematic distortions in those stories. Wall (1965) provides an example of a witness in a court case whose testimony, repeated over a number of retrials, grew clearer with each retelling. Mandler and Parker (1976) have demonstrated this "multiple retreval" effect in their study assessing memory for pictures. Using two recognition tests separated by a week, they found, for instance, that 78% of the recognitions on the second tests were the same as the recognitions on the first test and that this rate was higher than the accuracy scores on either test (which ranged from 78% to 58%). Mandler and Parker interpret these results as indicating that in addition to remembering information from the pictures they originally viewed, subjects on the second test also tended to remember their *answers* on the first test. Further studies using realistic eyewitness stimuli and repeated retrievals are clearly justified.

CONTEXT EFFECTS

Research on context effects has shown that a person's ability to remember information is heavily influenced by the relation between the storage of that information and the retrieval context. With a different context, retrieval can suffer; with the same context, retrieval is enhanced. Context has been studied in a variety of forms. For example, Carr (1925), in one of the earliest demonstrations of the importance of context, found that changes in the level of maze illumination disrupted maze learning performance in rats. Somewhat later, Burri (1931) found changes due to the presence or absence of an audience; Gartman and Johnson (1972) found changes due to the nearby list words; Eich, Weingartner, Stillman, and Gillin (1975) found changes due to the presence or absence of drugs; and Smith, Glenberg, and Bjork (1978) found changes due to environmental context. In short, the conceptual garbage can of "context" has been alleged to be responsible for enhancing recall in a variety of situations.

In a situation that more closely resembles the one to which an eyewitness is exposed, two investigations have been conducted in which event context is reinstated at the time the witness is tested (Malpass & Devine, 1980; Shaul, 1978). In both cases superior performance was obtained in the reinstated context.

HYPNOTIC AIDS TO MEMORY

The popular press is fond of touting the use of hypnosis to aid retrieval of information in criminal investigations (Brody, 1980). There are also accounts in professional journals of "successful" uses of hypnosis in investigation—that is, apparently successful inductions of hypnotic hypermnesia. On the whole, however, evidence about the effectiveness of hypnosis is rather mixed, if not negative. In a laboratory study, Stalnaker and Riddle (1932) demonstrated modest increases in recall with hypnosis but also found a tendency for subjects to confabulate or invent details they could not remember. Dorcus (1960) found that for eight cases using hypnosis, only three yielded improved memory for events, but even these instances were not spectacular. White, Fox, and Harris (1940) and Dhanens and Lundy (1975) also found some improvement in recall, but in the Dhanens and Lundy study unhypnotized subjects given instructions similar to those used with hypnotized subjects also produced similar improvements. A report by Salzberg (1977) confirms that hypnosis is not necessarily helpful in investigations. A recent review of the memory and hypnosis literature by Hilgard and Loftus (1979) makes the point that there is no evidence that the mechanisms of hypnotic recall are any different from ordinary mechanisms of memory.

Orne (1979) has made a number of significant points in an excellent review of the use and misuse of hypnosis in court. Orne notes first of all that hypnosis cannot assure the veracity of information and points out that even subjects in deep hypnosis can willfully fabricate. Indeed, the veracity of such often cannot be evaluated even by the subject. This problem is compounded by the fact that hypnosis in investigatory settings may prompt subjects to fabricate more than is the case in laboratory settings. While Orne concedes that hypnosis may help refresh memories, he feels that hypnosis should not be undertaken if the witness, police, or hypnotist have preconceptions about the identity of the criminal, for such preconceptions may result in hypnotic fabrications that "confirm" the preconceptions. Furthermore, such fabrications may be accepted by the eyewitness as true, and the eyewitness's confidence in the veracity of the "memories" may increase (as in the multiple retrieval effect previously discussed). Without proper safeguards, the net effect of the hypnotic procedures may, as Orne observes, be to create a convincing and apparently honest eyewitness who would be testifying about fabricated memories. Orne suggests a number of safeguards designed to minimize these possibilities. An interesting discussion of these ideas appears in Holden (1980). After interviewing Orne, Holden was led to conclude: "In fact, memory is a shifty thing to begin with, and easily altered by suggestions. . . . people are prone to accepting information that can then be incorporated into a fixed new version of the event [p. 1444]." Given these dangers, determining the proper role of hypnosis will not be easy.

THE POLYGRAPH

Ancient methods of lie detection such as trial by ordeal (e.g., holding or licking hot irons) have given way to more modern methods of lie detection such as the polygraph. The polygraph monitors changes in a variety of physiological responses (e.g., respiration, skin conductance, blood pressure, and blood volume) which serve as the basis for deciding whether a suspect is telling the truth. The polygraph was developed for police work (Smith, 1967) but it is now widely used in government and industry. With certified polygraph "experts" now numbering in the thousands, polygraph tests have become big business and the courts are less reluctant to admit polygraph testimony as evidence (Lykken, 1975). In general this practice appears reasonable as the research literature provides some scientific support for the validity and reliability of polygraph evidence.

Two general types of questioning techniques are used in polygraph tests. The control question technique (Barland & Raskin, 1973; Reid & Inbau, 1966) uses questions designed to carry emotional implications calculated to provoke feelings of anxiety or guilt (e.g., "Have you beaten your children?"). Relative to these control questions, truthful subjects presumably show less autonomic reaction to questions critical to the investigation while deceptive subjects show greater reaction. The second type of question is the information or guilty-knowledge technique (Lykken, 1960, 1974, 1975) in which an investigator poses questions about details of the crime that only the criminal would know and then examines the subject's physiological responses when exposed to various possible answers. The expectation is that a guilty person will show a greater reaction to the "correct" answer.

Advocates of polygraph techniques claim that the polygraph is a quite valid tool. There is a claim of 100% accuracy by Kubis (1950), and some laboratory support exists for claims of 85–90% accuracy (Podlesny & Raskin, 1977). Horvath and Reid (1971) gave 10 polygraph experts a set of 40 polygraph records for analysis (20 from known guilty and 20 from known innocent suspects). The average hit rate was 85%; the false answer rate, 10%. A recent series of studies reported by Raskin, Barland, and Podlesny (1978) support a 90% accuracy rate (with guilty-knowledge technique eliciting results superior to those that the control question technique yields). Raskin *et al.* found that the standard objective physical measures provide reliable data but that behavioral cues observed by the polygraph operator were not diagnostic. They found no evidence that psychopathy or any of a number of other individual difference factors (e.g., age, sex, previous arrests, experience with polygraphs, type of crime, MMPI profiles) were related to accuracy scores—that is, no evidence that some people can "beat the lie detector" (but see Barland & Raskin, 1973). They also found no evidence of higher rates of false negatives from "friendly polygraphers" (such as polygraphers hired by defense attorneys). Finally, Raskin *et al.* note that the overwhelming majority of errors are false positives and they suggest methods for further evaluating positive responses strongly disputed by the subjects who provided the positive responses.

Despite this rather glowing picture of polygraph success, it is important to remember that many of these studies have been conducted under optimal circumstances with well-trained polygraphers and may not generalize to the less pristine circumstances under which many polygraph examinations are conducted. Secondly, the false positive rates may cause us to be hesitant about accepting polygraph information in business settings. At the same time, the low false negative rate may reduce doubts about using the polygraph as an exculpatory tool in criminal investigations.

As we have emphasized throughout this chapter, each stage of human memory process is susceptible to its own unique forms of failure and bias. Even if information has been accurately and completely encoded and somehow protected from the vicissitudes of storage, there is no guarantee that the information can be fully or accurately retrieved. Research demonstrates that certain types of questions are more likely to yield accurate information (free recall) while other types of questions are likely to yield more complete recall (structured questions). On the other hand, information contained in a question or even variations in instructions concerning the degree of confidence expected for eyewitness identifications can produce biased responses. Multiple retrievals and retrievals under hypnosis may produce erroneous "intrusions" which are reported with great confidence by eyewitnesses. The instrusion effect together with the unconscious transference of information from one "episode" to another may cast doubt on even the most confident of eyewitnesses.

FACIAL RECOGNITION

One of the most widely studied aspects of eyewitness performance is facial recognition. In addition to the studies conducted by researchers interested in eyewitness reliability, there are cognitive psychologists who have either a specialized interest in the processes underlying facial memory and recognition or who have chosen to use faces as stimuli in their memory studies. We have already discussed some of the facial recognition research in other contexts, and excellent reviews of the literature are available (Clifford & Bull, 1978; Yarmey, 1979b). Rather than recapitulate material, we will focus here on recent research and underscore the most reliable findings and emerging issues.

The Influence of Facial Characteristics on Facial Recognition

A variety of facial features have been found to influence recognition accuracy. We have already seen some evidence of this in the encoding studies discussed earlier (e.g., Mueller, Carlomusto, & Goldstein, 1978). An early and interesting speculation about facial memory by Galton (1883) was that people who were poor at forming mental images were better able to imagine the face of an acquaintance than the face of a loved one. However, Yarmey (1975) and Read and Peterson (1975) found just the opposite.

As one illustration of the variations in facial memorability, Goldstein, Stephenson, and Chance (1977) reviewed the results from a number of studies and found that some faces were never falsely recognized and some faces were frequently falsely recognized. But which facial features "count most"? We have already noted that certain types of disguises affect recognition more than others (Patterson & Baddeley, 1977). McKelvie (1976) reports that masked eyes reduce recognition more than masked mouths (see also Seamon, Stolz, Bass, & Chatinover, 1978; van Santen & Jonides, 1978). Ellis, Davies, and Shepherd (1977) found that written descriptions of faces most frequently mentioned hair, followed by eyes, nose, mouth, eyebrows, chin, ears, forehead, and cheek. In a multidimensional scaling analysis of similarity ratings produced from groupings of 100 faces, Ellis *et al.* found that hair length and style, face shape, age, eyebrows, lips, and mouth were the best predictors of similarity ratings. A comparable study by Milord (1978) also found support for age and hair, but even stronger support for facial expression characteristics such as lighthearted-ness, friendliness, and warmth. A study by Sorce and Campos (1974) provides additional support for the proposition that facial expression affects recog-nizability.

Fleishman, Buckley, Klosinsky, Smith, and Tuck (1976) found better memory for faces rated high and low in attractiveness than for neutral faces. Going and Read (1974) obtained better recognition of faces previously rated "unique." Cohen and Carr (1975); Davies, Shepherd, and Ellis (1979b); and Light, Kayra-Stuart, and Hollander (1979) have obtained similar results. The Light *et al.* series of studies are notable in that they consider and test a variety of theoretical predictions about the bases of better recognition of atypical faces. Light *et al.* rule out the possibility that atypical faces receive greater attention and process-ing, find no evidence of more elaborate encoding (Craik & Tulving, 1975); but find some support for the proposition that more typical (and therefore similar) faces have greater "interitem similarity" (Rosch & Mervis, 1975) and are there-fore more difficult to distinguish from one another. Yarmey (1979a) reports that likeability and attractiveness affected facial memory.

Recognition of faces even after the passage of many years is well documented. Bahrick, Bahrick, and Wittlinger (1975) found that people out of high school as long as 35 years still accurately recognized 90% of their classmates' high school photographs. The rate was 75% for a group out of school over 40 years. Recall of names was poorer—recent graduates generated 47 names but individuals out of school for 40 years recalled only 19 names.

Two other recent facial recognition studies reported in Seamon (1980) dem-onstrate good recognition of photographs taken at different times. In the first study, subjects who saw facial photographs that were recently taken were able to recognize targets in photographs taken 10 years earlier at better than chance levels of accuracy. The second study examined recognition of photographs cov-ering time spans from infancy to young adulthood. Subjects were given com-plete sets of photographs on eight individuals that covered infancy, childhood, early teens, and young adulthood. Correct pairing rates were: teen−young adult, 95%; child−young adult, 85%; and infancy−young adult, 55%. Research by Pittenger, Shaw, and Mark (1979) identifies some human cognitive models of growth and topological change that could account for this type of performance.

Cross-Racial Identification

A series of well-designed studies have demonstrated that cross-racial identifi-cation of faces is generally more difficult than same-race identifications. Mal-pass and Kravitz (1969), who initiated this research, found among other things that whites had more difficulty than blacks in identifying black faces (58% versus 68% correct). Cross, Cross, and Daly (1971), in an interesting and complex study, found white targets were more difficult for blacks to recognize (white subjects got 45% correct versus blacks who scored 27% correct), but blacks and whites performed equally well in recognizing black targets (39% and 40%, respectively). Shepherd, Deregowski, and Ellis (1974) reported that both blacks and whites had trouble recognizing faces of the other race and Luce (1974) reports that whites were poor at recognizing black faces, Orientals were poor with white faces, and blacks were poor with both. Subsequent studies to be discussed have supported these results and have attempted to account for them by testing several theoretical accounts of the phenomenon.

Probably the most widely tested theoretical position on the cross-racial effects is the *racial attitude hypothesis* which holds that facial processing is dominated by attention to stereotypical features. If this notion is correct, then cross-racial identification should improve with training in recognition cues. Several studies testing this notion succeeded in improving white recognition of black faces by training white subjects to identify relevant features of black faces (Elliott, Wills, & Goldstein, 1973; Lavrakas, Buri, & Mayzner, 1976; Malpass, Lavigueur, & Weldon, 1973). The training results are also consistent with alternative cross-racial identification hypotheses. For example, Ellis (1975) theorized and Ellis, Deregowski, and Shepherd (1975) demonstrated that blacks and whites characteristically attend to different features in faces; there were some indications that whites tended to use features (such as hair and eye color) that would be diagnostic of white faces. It was not clear that the features frequently mentioned by black subjects (ears, chin, face outline) would be more diagnostic of black faces. Goldstein and Chance (1976) assessed the "study time" devoted to white and Japanese faces in an effort to assess the structural similarity of faces within the two classes. The study showed no differences in study time. In a second experiment Goldstein and Chance (1979) found less variability in white subjects' similarity ratings of Japanese and female faces than in white and male faces. However, the better recognition by whites of white faces (both male· *and female*) argues against the simple hypothesis that perceived similarity makes recognition more difficult.

In a related vein, Sorce (1979) tested preschool children for racial awareness and found evidence that physiognomic features were more salient racial discrimination cues than skin color, that white children particularly attended to hair features, and that children in a segregated community attained racial awareness earlier than children in an integrated neighborhood. One may speculate that parental attitudes underlie the last finding. Although the racial attitude hypothesis suggests that attitudes should be related to cross-racial identification, Brigham and Barkowitz (1978) found neither a relationship between attitude and facial recognition accuracy nor a relationship between interracial experience and facial recognition accuracy (replicating earlier findings by Malpass & Kravitz, 1969; and Luce, 1974). However, the hypothesis that differential experience with members of another race affects ability to recognize members of that race has received some research support (Chance, Goldstein, & McBride,

1975; Feinman & Entwisle, 1976; Lavrakas *et al.*, 1976). Thus, the findings are at best inconsistent and inconclusive.

We conclude the section on cross-racial identification with a somewhat provocative study by Lindsay, Wells, and Rumpel (1980), who examined eyewitness accuracy both with the criminal present in and the criminal absent from the lineup. In terms of standard signal detection terms (d'), Lindsay *et al.*'s subjects' cross-racial identifications were superior to their same race identifications. With a Caucasian target, Oriental witnesses made significantly fewer false alarms than did Caucasian witnesses, while hit rates did not differ.

In summary, it is clear that a variety of facial characteristics can affect memory for faces. Judgments of faces appear to be affected by features such as hairstyle and age, and by personality traits associated with the faces as well. Unusual faces also appear to be more memorable. Generally the evidence indicates that cross-racial identification of faces is less accurate than within-race identifications, although the precise basis of this effect is still unclear. In the future it might be possible to construct indices of facial memorability that reflect the influences of facial characteristics. Unfortunately, we do not yet possess the necessary data.

THE EYEWITNESS IN THE LEGAL SYSTEM

Eyewitnesses are typically called upon to make identifications at two points in the legal process—first, during the investigation of suspects (often in the police station), they may be called upon to (*a*) help compose a facial composite using a "photo-kit," (*b*) examine mug shots, (*c*) pick a suspect out of a photo-spread, or (*d*) make an identification from a live lineup. Second, the eyewitness may be called upon during the prosecution of defendants to make an identification in a courtroom trial. In this section we briefly review the research on eyewitness accuracy in the investigative settings and recent research on the impact of eyewitness testimony in courtroom settings. For a review of the legal aspects of eyewitness testimony in the United States, see Woocher (1977); for the complementary British picture, Clifford and Bull (1978).

Lineups and Photo-Spreads

There is now an extensive body of research on eyewitness performance in lineup and photo-spread situations where the witness is asked if he or she recognizes one of a small number of persons (usually 5 to 12) presented live or in photographs. For example, a report sponsored by the Police Foundation (Model Rules, 1974) recommends that: "whenever a photograph depicting a definite suspect is displayed to a victim or eyewitness, it should be arranged at random with seven or more photographs of different persons [p. 8]." For live lineups, the recommendation was that: "all lineups should consist of at least four persons in addition to the suspect [p. 12]." Buckhout and his colleagues have simulated the procedure. For example, Buckhout (1974) staged a mock assault before students and 7 weeks later presented them with six photographs that included the assailant. Forty percent made correct identifications, but 25% (including the assault "victim") incorrectly picked an innocent bystander to the event (see our earlier discussion of Unconscious Transference). A second study (Buckhout, Alper, Chern, Silverberg, & Slomovitz, 1974) used a staged purse snatching. After 3 weeks, subjects viewed two lineups: one with the criminal and one without. Of 52 eyewitnesses, only 13.5% made a correct identification on the first lineup and rejected all the members of the second lineup; 13.5% impeached their initially correct identification on the first lineup with a false alarm on the second. Another 13.5% picked a target who looked like the criminal from both line-ups, 36.5% erroneously picked yet another person from the first line-up, 3.8% picked wrong persons on both line-ups, and 19.2% made no identifications. In a third study, Buckhout (1975) convinced a New York television station to show a 12-sec mugging on their news program. Viewers were then shown a six-person lineup and asked to telephone in their identification. Over 2100 calls were recorded and only 14.1% picked the correct person. A total of 25.9% said the criminal was not in the lineup. If the nonidentifications are ignored, 19.8% made correct identifications versus the 16.7% expected by chance. The false alarm rate was 60%.

Brown, Deffenbacher, and Sturgill (1977, Study 2) examined identification accuracy for the faces of "suspects" who had been previously viewed under one of four different conditions (all subjects saw some faces from all conditions in a final live lineup): (a) live viewing in an initial "criminal" lineup plus viewing in mug shots, (b) live viewing in the initial "criminal" lineup only, (c) viewing of mug shots only, or (d) new faces viewed for the first time in a final live lineup. Rates of identification of suspects (no data was supplied on accuracy or false alarms) for viewing condition groups were 65%, 51%, 20%, and 8%, respectively. The rates in a similar, previously unreported study were 68%, 54%, 27%, and 10%; the rates in yet another similar study (study 3) were 45%, 24%, 29%, and 18%. Gorenstein and Ellsworth (1980) replicated and extended this result, asking whether the mug shot shown after the live viewing in the initial lineup had to actually be selected by the subject, or whether merely presenting the mug shot to the subject was sufficient to enhance the chances of its later being recognized. Their results indicate that it is the prior choice of the mug shot by the subject, not mere familiarity with it, that contributes to subsequent increases in its false recognition. If the subject chooses the mug shot after the initial lineup viewing, the subject is likely to choose that very same incorrect face once again at a later time, even though the correct face is also available for choosing. Egan, Pittner, and Goldstein (1977) had subjects view a mock robbery for 15 sec and then tested identification accuracy using either live lineups or photo-spreads after delays of 2, 21, and 56 days. The percentage of subjects making no errors decreased from 45% to 29% to 7% over the same time spans.

Leippe, Wells, and Ostrom (1978) staged a theft incident and had subjects make an immediate identification from a photo-spread. They obtained an average correct identification rate of 30.8%, but did not report the false alarm rate. Egan and Smith (1979) had subjects view a mock robbery for 20 sec and then, after 2- or 35-day delays, the subjects were presented with a live, five-person lineup. The hit rate at 2 days was 75% and at 35 days was 56%. The overall false-alarm rate when the criminal was present was 10%, but it was 58% when the criminal was absent. In another staged-theft study similar to Leippe *et al.* Wells, Lindsay, and Ferguson (1979) obtained a hit rate of 58% and a false alarm rate of 20% using a photo-spread. Finally, Warnick and Sanders (1980) reported a 38% and a 24% false alarm rate using a photo-spread method.

In Lindsay, Wells, and Rumpel's (1981a) staged-theft study, subjects who were shown a photo-spread had a hit rate of 81%, a miss/false identification rate of 16% when the criminal was present, and a false alarm rate of 78% when the criminal was absent.

In order to roughly assess the relationship between exposure times, retention intervals, and eyewitness accuracy, Penrod (1980) has used the data from these studies and several others to test simple regression models for hit rates and false alarms. These models use encoding exposure durations ranging from 12 to 120 sec and retention intervals ranging from immediate to 8 weeks as predictors. The resulting expressions for percentage of hits = 51.4% (intercept) − .07 (exposure duration in seconds) − 3.30 (retention interval in weeks). The percentage of false alarms equation for instances when the criminal was present in the lineup = 33.8% (intercept) − .16 (exposure duration in seconds) + 4.98 (retention interval in weeks). Because there were only four data points, no false alarm model (where the criminal was not in the lineup) was tested. The first model accounts for 14% of the variance in hit rates (which had a mean of 39% in 19 studies). The second model accounts for 38% of the variance in the criminal-present false alarms (which had a mean of 32.8% in 17 studies). The simple correlations were .00 for hit rate and exposure time, − .34 for hit rate and retention interval, − .36 for false alarm rate and exposure time and .55 for false alarm rate and retention interval.

Because of the great variation in methods used in these studies and the many other plausible models that might be tested with the data, the results are offered very cautiously. Systematic manipulation of these variables in a well-designed experimental study would clearly provide better insight into the effect of these estimator and system variables (Wells, 1978) on recognition and false answer performance.

We would like to call attention to two recent articles which tackle significant practical problems with lineups. In the first, Wells, Leippe, and Ostrom (1979) provide a much needed, empirically based method for assessing the fairness of a lineup which computes the functional size of a lineup. The *functional size* of a lineup takes into account the fact that many lineups contain individuals who can be easily ruled out as suspects. These individuals may contribute to the nominal size of a lineup, but if they would very rarely or never be selected, they do not contribute to its functional size.

Finally, Lindsay and Wells (1980) report a study in which they manipulated the similarity of the lineup target to the other members of the lineup. They found that fair lineups (those whose members were high in similarity) did result in fewer identifications. The reduction of identifications was greatest for innocent suspects (i.e., reduced false identifications) and Lindsay and Wells concluded that the cost of fair lineups (in terms of notidentifying guilty suspects) is rather small.

Because lineups are a relatively common vehicle for eyewitness identifications in the criminal justice system, it is an area meriting additional research attention. Better studies will help to disentangle the influences of factors such as prior exposure and exposure times, retention intervals, lineup size, and other variables on recognition performance.

Mug Shot Studies

We have already briefly described the Brown *et al.* (1977) studies in which subjects were presented with live lineups that were composed of suspects of four types: those who had previously been viewed in a live "criminal" lineup *and* in mug shots, those seen in the lineup only, those seen in mug shots only and those who had not been viewed before. In one of these studies, the subjects correctly identified 72% of the lineup targets in the mug shots after 1 week; in the second study where eyewitnesses were *not* aware on the initial viewing that they would be asked to recognize the targets several days later, the hit rate was 28%. These two studies provide some idea as to the range of accuracy that might be expected using mug shots. More important, perhaps, were the inflated rates of false identification induced by viewing individuals in mug shots. Compared to the false alarm rates for faces never seen, individuals who had been viewed in mug shots only were significantly more likely to be misidentified as members of the original "criminal" lineups. False alarm rates for new faces were 8%, 10%, and 18% in the three studies, while the false alarm rates for faces seen only in mug shots were 20%, 27%, and 29%, respectively. Subjects clearly demonstrated an inability to completely distinguish the contexts (lineup versus mug shot) in which the faces had originally been viewed—yet another demonstration of the unconscious transference effect discussed earlier. Using rather different procedures, Laughery *et al.* (1971) had obtained similar results. The Laughery *et al.* findings prompted a study by Davies, Shepherd, and Ellis (1979a) that also demonstrated that exposure to mug shots can distort eyewitness memory.

Davies *et al.* showed subjects a 90-sec videotape of a three-person card game and then placed subjects in one of four treatment conditions. In two of these conditions, subjects searched 100 mug shots trying to identify targets, who were not present in the mug shots. Half of these subjects who searched mug shots were informed before the final recognition task that none of the targets had been present in the group of 100 but would definitely be present in the final group; half of the subjects who searched were not so informed. In the third condition, subjects saw the 100 photographs but were asked to rate them for pleasantness. The control subjects spent an equivalent amount of time listening to a comedy recording. The final recognition task consisted of 36 photographs including the original three targets. The average hit rate was 34%. The control group and group rating faces for pleasantness had a higher hit rate (47%) than either the informed search subjects (30%) or the uninformed search subjects (11%). The false alarm data were most interesting—they ranged from 3.4% for subjects rating faces, to 2.4% for the control group, 1.3% for the informed search subjects and 0% for the uninformed search subjects. Thus, the subjects in the two search conditions (subjects who searched for faces not included in the set of 100 mug shots were least likely to make false identifications. The false alarm rates may be somewhat deflated because Davies *et al.* used a 5-point rating scale as their dependent measure rather than a dichotomous (old/new) variable. Only ratings at the extreme end of the scale were scored as identifications. Because the Davies *et al.* final set of mug shots did not include any of the photographs contained in the set of 100 mug shots, the results of this study are not directly comparable to those of Brown *et al.* (1977). In any event, Davies *et al.* do not discuss the earlier study. They couch the discussion of their results in terms of a change in recognition criterion induced by the search subjects' exposure to large numbers of nontarget mug shots—that is, the continued failure to successfully locate the target faces caused subjects to adopt increasingly conservative strategies. The authors support this interpretation by noting that the false alarm rate for the 100 mug shots viewed in the two search conditions dropped significantly from the first 50 to the second 50 mug shots. Unfortunately this rationale clearly cannot explain the Brown *et al.* findings. Pending further research on biases induced by mug shots, we will probably have to be content with the two separate and perhaps countervailing effects of the Brown *et al.* and Davies *et al.* studies.

Facial Composites

The use of drawings, facial composites and "photo-kits" to construct "faces" of criminals is a widespread practice both in the United States and Great Britain (Darnbrough, 1977). Several studies assessing the accuracy of these methods have appeared in recent years (see Baddeley, 1979 for a recent review). In one study, Harmon (1973) had police artists prepare drawings of individuals based upon descriptions of other artists who served as subjects in the study. These artists gave verbal descriptions of close friends, from memory, to the police artist. Harmon found that subjects were very poor at identifying the resulting drawings. However, when the drawings were made from photographs of the target individuals, identification accuracy was quite high. Ellis, Shepherd, and Davies (1975) evaluated the Photo-kit system by having subjects attempt to reproduce photographs using the kit. Performance was quite poor even when the subjects had the photograph available for comparison (on average, only two out of five features were correctly selected). Constructions from memory were even worse (one of five features correct). On the whole, the photo-kit method has yet to demonstrate its value as an aid to identification.

More recent studies have used the facial composite systems to explore standard facial recognition. For example, Davies, Ellis, and Shepherd (1977) showed subjects a photo-kit face then systematically varied features in the face to determine which feature changes were most likely to be detected. Forehead/hair changes were most easily detected, followed by eyes, nose, and mouth. Sensitivity to changes in the chin depended on the similarity of distractors and the presence of the target face for comparisons. The same researchers (1978) have shown that with familiar faces (those of celebrities) and unknown faces, photographs yield significantly better recognition than do line drawings, which yielded approximately one-half as many recognitions as photographs or outlines of features, which resulted in approximately one-fourth as many correct recognitions as the photographs. Finally, Matthews (1978) has also assessed the importance (to facial recognition) of various facial features by measuring the reaction times on judgments of whether pairs of comparison faces (constructed with a kit) were the same or different. Between zero and six features were varied for 20 basic faces. Reaction time and errors for judgments that faces were different decreased systematically as additional features were added. Matthews concluded that priority is given to assessments of hairline, eyes, and chin, which are processed rapidly. Subjects showed evidence of a secondary and slower analysis of eyebrows, nose, and mouth.

Although subjects in studies of composites demonstrate some sensitivity to changes in those composites, it is not clear that composites are helpful for eyewitness identification.

The Impact of Courtroom Eyewitness Testimony

There are ample demonstrations in the research literature that a variety of subtle factors can significantly affect courtroom judgments (see Dane & Wrightsman, Chapter 4, this volume). Garcia and Griffitt (1978) have shown that subtle factors can also affect the perception of witnesses (see Miller & Burgoon, Chapter 6, this volume). What then is the impact of eyewitness testimony? A study by E. F. Loftus (1974) offers a partial answer to this question. She provided subjects with a description of an armed robbery that resulted in two deaths. Of subjects who heard a version of the case that contained only circumstantial evidence, 18% convicted. For subjects who received the same evidence plus an eyewitness identification, the conviction rate was 72%. Startlingly, the conviction rate of a third group of subjects, who received the circumstantial evidence plus an identification from a witness who had very poor vision and was not wearing eyeglasses the day of the crime, was only slightly lower at 68%. At least three other groups of investigators have taken this result as a point of departure for further research on the impact of eyewitness testimony, and particularly the effects of discrediting that testimony. For example, Cavoukian (1980) asked subjects to read a case summary containing either: (*a*) no eyewitness testimony, (*b*) eyewitness testimony, (*c*) eyewitness testimony which was later discredited, or (*d*) forewarning of the subsequent discrediting. Discrediting the eyewitness testimony had no significant influence; that is, the eyewitness had the same effect regardless of whether or not his testimony had been discredited, replicating the results of E. F. Loftus (1974). Forewarning subjects, however, was very effective and significantly increased the impact of the discrediting. But two studies by Weinberg and Baron (1980) and by Hatvany and Strack (in press) failed to replicate the unsuccessful discrediting of the eyewitness. The reason why discrediting sometimes works and sometimes does not seems to depend on the type of discrediting. For example, in E. F. Loftus (1974) the testimony seemed to have been only partially discredited so that jurors could still believe it if they chose to. In the Hatvany and Strack study, on the other hand, not only did the witness recast the testimony and apologize for even having taken the stand, but proof was actually provided that the original testimony could not possibly have been correct.

Wells, Lindsay, and Ferguson (1979) have conducted the most compelling (and, in some ways, disturbing) study of "juror" assessments of eyewitness testimony. Wells *et al.* presented subjects with eyewitnesses, some of whom had previously made correct eyewitness identifications and some of whom had made incorrect identifications. Subjects viewed the eyewitnesses being cross-examined (with either leading or nonleading questions). Subjects were asked to assess witnesses' accuracy and confidence, and the likelihood that witnesses could have made an accurate identification considering the circumstances surrounding their original observations. Based on these ratings, the jurors believed 80% of the eyewitnesses (although only 57% of the eyewitnesses had made correct identifications and jurors expected only 58% accuracy). Jurors were no more likely to believe accurate than inaccurate eyewitnesses, although they were more likely to believe accurate witnesses who were cross-examined with leading questions. Jurors' impressions of witness confidence were unrelated to actual witness accuracy, but these impressions of witness confidence accounted for 50% of the variance in jurors' decisions to believe eyewitnesses' testimony! Jurors who viewed leading question cross-examinations were less confident that they could generally detect eyewitness accuracy and expected lower rates of accuracy. In sum, jurors' reliance on their assessments of witness confidence is quite problematic. Not only do jurors rely heavily on their assessments of eyewitness confidence, but there is strong evidence that eyewitness confidence and eyewitness accuracy are only weakly related. Penrod (1980) has examined 16 eyewitness studies in which confidence and accuracy relationships were reported and has found an average correlation (weighted for degrees of freedom) of only .231 between them. (See Miller & Burgoon, Chapter 6, this volume, for a related consideration of the relationship between perceived confidence and perceived credibility of witnesses).

Deffenbacher (in press) attempted to determine the conditions under which eyewitness accuracy and confidence are related to one another and the conditions under which they are not. Deffenbacher surveyed 25 empirical studies containing 43 reports on the eyewitness accuracy-confidence relationship. He found support for a relationship in 77% of these studies, but even more importantly, he found a relationship between the strength of the accuracy-confidence correlation and the quality of eyewitnessing circumstances. The accuracy-confidence correlation was higher in those circumstances where eyewitnesses made their initial observations and reports under optimal conditions (e.g., warnings, moderate stress, long exposure time, familiarity with targets, unbiased testing instructions). Deffenbacher's results suggest the need to construct reliable indices of witnessing conditions, as such indices may be useful in determining whether jurors can reasonably assume that a witnesses' confidence is related to their accuracy.

In a study similar to Wells, Lindsay, and Ferguson (1979), Lindsay, Wells, and Rumpel (1981) confirmed the lack of juror ability to discriminate between accurate and inaccurate eyewitnesses. Lindsay et al. found some evidence that jurors were sentitive to eyewitnessing conditions and could adjust the base-line rates at which they would believe the testimony of eyewitnesses who had superior or inferior viewing conditions. Unfortunately, the jurors still overestimated the base-rates of witness accuracy—particularly in conditions where the eyewitnesses were least accurate. Hastie (1980) has offered evidence that jurors are relatively sensitive to the factors that might affect eyewitness performance. He examined the deliberations of 11 six-person mock juries (composed of jurors on jury duty at the time) for the frequency with which the jurors addressed issues raised in the psychological literature on eyewitness performance. Hastie reports four basic weaknesses in the jurors' deliberation:

1. Jurors were insensitive to possible biases introduced by police procedures.
2. Little consideration was given to interference effects during retention.
3. Jurors showed a lack of sophistication in evaluating police procedures for testing recognition.
4. Jurors overrelied on witnesses' statements about the confidence of their identifications when assessing the accuracy of those identifications.

Given the influence of eyewitness testimony—and particularly eyewitness confidence—on jury decision making, further research on the interplay of eyewitnessing conditions, eyewitness accuracy and confidence, and jury use of eyewitness testimony is needed. Ideally, this research might yield procedures which would minimize the number of errors introduced throughout the eyewitness assessment process.

Expert Psychological Testimony about the Eyewitness

A number of recent articles have addressed the question of the courtroom role of the psychologist as an expert on eyewitness reliability. Woocher (1977) has an extended discussion of the legal aspects of such expert testimony, as does Addison (1978). Fishman and Loftus (1978) and E. F. Loftus (1979) consider some case law and anecdotal experiences. Lower (1978) discusses his experiences as a (thwarted) expert witness on eyewitness reliability.

A very different approach to the issue of expert testimony is a recent empirical study by E. F. Loftus (1980) in which she presented student jurors with one of two trial summaries—one about a mild assault and one about a murder. In both cases, eyewitness testimony was an important part of the evidence. Some subjects read standard versions of the trials, while other subjects read versions in which an expert witness testified for the defense about factors known to reduce eyewitness reliability (stress, presence of a weapon, intoxication). The expert testimony reduced the conviction rates of individual jurors from 68% to 43% in the murder case and from 47% to 35% in the mild assault. A second study using six-person juries provided confirmation of these results using group judgments.

We would like to emphasize the findings concerning: (a) the impact of eyewitness testimony on juror judgments, (b) jurors' inability to discriminate between accurate and inaccurate eyewitnesses, and (c) jurors' inability to accurately calibrate for the extent to which poor observing conditions (e.g., exposure time, long retention intervals) may have undermined eyewitness accuracy. In light of these findings, the E. F. Loftus (1980) results suggest that further empirical research on the impact of expert testimony (or judicial admonitions) concerning eyewitness reliability is clearly merited. There is a distinct possibility that the expert testimony serves to help jurors properly evaluate eyewitness testimony and minimize the other difficulties reported by Hastie (1980).

CONCLUSIONS

This review of recent eyewitness research has ranged rather widely and thus a summary of its major points may be in order. As we tried to emphasize at the outset of the chapter, the fact that eyewitness testimony is relatively unreliable should not surprise members of the psychological community. Anyone familiar with the basic perception and memory processes is aware that eyewitness performance can be undermined at many steps along the way from information encoding to information retrieval. *Features of the stimulus situation* such as viewing conditions, length of exposure, event complexity and novelty, event stressfulness, and seriousness of the viewed event have all been shown to affect encoding of information and later eyewitness performance.

Similarly, *charateristics of the eyewitness* may profoundly affect performance:

Prior expectations may affect memory for an event in a variety of ways as may an eyewitness's interpretations of an event at the time of its occurrence. Perhaps less well known is the fact that even stored memories are subject to *change and distortion over time.* Although forgetting is a problem with long retention intervals, new, postevent information can systematically bias previously stored information. Such interference effects may be particularly problematic in legal settings where information received subsequent to an event may significantly change the interpretations of the prior event.

Also problematic in the legal domain is the fact that eyewitness performance is affected by a variety of *factors at the time of retrieval.* For example, the types of questions employed at retrieval may bias verbal reports, lineup formats may bias visual identifications, and multiple retrievals may introduce biasing information into memory. Hypnotic aids to memory have come under attack because they may introduce fabrications unless carefully controlled. On the other hand, the research on polygraphs indicates that with careful controls, polygraph techniques may achieve reasonably high levels of accuracy. In addition, research on *facial recognition* has begun to identify facial characteristics that affect recognition accuracy above and beyond the well-known cross-racial effects.

In areas most relevant to the legal system, new and provocative findings are appearing at a rapid rate. Recent *lineup and mug shot studies* have tackled problems such as eyewitnesses' overall performance, the relationship between personal and situational factors and eyewitness accuracy, the relationship between accuracy and confidence of eyewitnesses, juror use of eyewitness testimony, and the impact of lineup fairness on eyewitness performance. All of these studies have rather direct implications for the legal system.

If we have done nothing else in this chapter, we hope we have effectively underscored first of all that eyewitness unreliability is a real phenomenon of significant magnitude. Secondly, we hope we have demonstrated that existing psychological research can explain—in a systematic way—the bases of eyewitness unreliability. Finally, we trust that we have fostered the conviction that our knowledge about the systematic bases of eyewitness unreliability can be used to reduced that unreliability and improve the quality of judgments that must inevitably be based upon eyewitness testimony. This, surely, is the challenge of the future.

REFERENCES

Addison, B. M. Expert testimony on eyewitness perception. *Dickinson Law Review*, 1978, *82*, 465–485.

Allport, G. W., & Postman, L. J. The basic psychology of rumor. *Transactions of the New York Academy of Sciences*, Series II, 1945, *8*, 61–81.

Baddeley, A. D. Selective attention and performance in dangerous environments. *British Journal of Psychology*, 1972, *63*, 537–546.

Baddeley, A. D. Applied cognitive and cognitive applied psychology: The case of face recognition. In L.-G. Nilsson (Ed.), *Perspectives on memory research: Essays in honor of Uppsala University's 500th anniversary*. Hillsdale, New Jersey: Erlbaum, 1979.

Bahrick, H. P., Bahrick, P. O., & Wittlinger, R. P. Fifty years of memory for names and faces: A cross-sectional approach. *Journal of Experimental Psychology: General*, 1975, *104*, 54–75.

Barland, G. H., & Raskin, D. C. Detection of deception. In W. F. Prokasy & D. C. Raskin (Eds.), *Electrodermal activity in psychological research*. New York: Academic Press, 1973.

Bartlett, F. C. *Remembering: A study in experimental and social psychology*. London and New York: Cambridge Unive. Press, 1957. (Originally published, 1932.)

Belbin, E. The influence of interpolated recall upon recognition. *Quarterly Journal of Educational Psychology*, 1950, *2*, 163–169.

Biederman, I., Glass, A. L., & Stacy, E. W. Searching for objects in real-world scenes. *Journal of Experimental Psychology*, 1973, *97*, 22–27.

Bird, C. The influences of press upon the accuracy of report. *Journal of Abnormal and Social Psychology*, 1927, *22*, 123–129.

Blaney, R. L., & Winograd, E. Developmental differences in children's recognition memory for faces. *Developmental Psychology*, 1978, *14*, 441–442.

Bourne, L. E., Dominowski, R. L., & Loftus, E. F. *Cognitive processes*. Englewood Cliffs, New Jersey: Prentice-Hall, 1979.

Bower, G. H., & Karlin, M. B. Depth and processing pictures of faces and recognition memory. *Journal of Experimental Psychology*, 1974, *103*, 751–757.

Bricker, P. D., & Pruzansky, S. Effects of stimulus content and duration on talker identification. *The Journal of the Acoustical Society of America*, 1966, *40*, 1441–1449.

Brigham, J. C., & Barkowitz, P. Do "they all look alike?" The effect of race, sex, experience, and attitudes on the ability to recognize faces. *Journal of Applied Psychology*, 1978, *8*, 306–318.

Brody, J. E. Hypnotism is a powerful but vulnerable weapon in fight against crime. *New York Times*, October 14, 1980, pp. 15, 17.

Brown, E., Deffenbacher, K., & Sturgill, W. Memory for faces and the circumstances of encounter. *Journal of Applied Psychology*, 1977, *62*, 311–318.

Bruner, J. S., & Postman, L. J. On the perception of incongruity: A paradigm. *Journal of Personality*, 1949, *18*, 206–223.

Buckhout, R. Through a bag, darkly. *American Psychologist*, 1968, *23*, 832–833.

Buckhout, R. Eyewitness testimony. *Scientific American*, 1974, *231* (6), 23–31.

Buckhout, R. Nearly 2000 witnesses can be wrong. *Social Action and the Law*, 1975, *2*, 7.

Buckhout, R., Alper, A., Chern, S., Silverberg, G., & Slomovits, M. Determinants of eyewitness performance on a line-up. *Bulletin of the Psychonomic Society*, 1974, *4*, 191–192.

Bull, R., & Clifford, B. Identification: The Devlin report. *New Scientist*, 1976, *70*, 307–308.

Burri, C. The influence of an audience upon recall. *Journal of Educational Psychology*, 1931, *22*, 683–690.

Burtt, M. E. *Legal psychology*. Englewood Cliffs, New Jersey: Prentice-Hall, 1931.

Burtt, M. E. *Applied psychology*. Englewood Cliffs, New Jersey: Prentice-Hall, 1948.

Cady, H. M. On the psychology of testimony. *American Journal of Psychology*, 1924, *35*, 110–112.

Carr, T. H., Deffenbacher, K. A., & Leu, J. R. *Is there less interference in memory for faces?* Paper presented at the meeting of the Psychonomic Society, Phoenix, Arizona, 1979.

Cattell, J. M. Measurements of the accuracy of recollection. *Science*, 1895, *2* 761–766.

Cavoukian, A. Eyewitness testimony: The ineffectiveness of discrediting information. Paper presented at the meeting of the American Psychological Association, Montreal, September, 1980.

Chance, J., Goldstein, A. G., & McBride, L. Differential experience and recognition memory for faces. *Journal of Social Psychology*, 1975, *97*, 243–253.

Clifford, B. R., & Bull, R. *The psychology of person identification*. London: Routledge & Kegan Paul, 1978.

Clifford, B. R., & Scott, J. Individual and situational factors in eyewitness testimony. *Journal of Applied Psychology*, 1978, *63*, 352−359.

Cohen, C. E., & Ebbesen, E. B. Observational goals and schema activation: A theoretical framework for behavioral perception. *Journal of Experimental Social Psychology*, 1979, *15*, 305−329.

Cohen, M. E., & Carr, W. J. Facial recognition and the von Restorff effect. *Bulletin of the Psychonomic Society*, 1975, *6*, 383−384.

Cole, W. G., & Loftus, E. F. Incorporating new information into memory. *American Journal of Psychology*, 1979, *92*, 413−425.

Courtois, M. R., & Mueller, J. H. Processing multiple physical features in facial recognition. *Bulletin of the Psychonomic Society*, 1979, *14*, 74−76.

Craik, F. I. M., & Jacoby, L. J. Elaboration and distinctiveness in episodic memory. In L.-G. Nilsson (Ed.), *Perspectives on memory research: Essays in honor of Uppsala University's 500th anniversary*. Hillsdale, New Jersey: Erlbaum, 1979.

Craik, F. I. M., & Lockhart, R. S. Levels of processing: A framework for memory research. *Journal of Verbal Learning and Verbal Behavior*, 1972, *11*, 671−684.

Craik, F. I. M., & Tulving, E. Depth of processing and the retention of words in episodic memory. *Journal of Experimental Psychology: General*, 1975, *104*, 268−294.

Cross, J. F., Cross, J., & Daly, J. Sex, race, age, and beauty as factors in recognition of faces. *Perception and Psychophysics*, 1971, *10*, 393−396.

Crowder, R. G. *Principles of Learning and Memory*. Hillsdale, New Jersey: Erlbaum, 1976.

Dallenbach, K. M. The relation of memory error to time-interval. *Psychological Review*, 1913, *20*, 323−337.

Daniel, T. C. Nature of the effect of verbal labels on recognition memory for form. *Journal of Experimental Psychology*, 1972, *96*, 152−157.

Darnbrough, M. A. *A survey on the use of Photo-fit in England and Wales*. Home Office, Crown Copyright, 1977.

Davies, G., Ellis, H., & Shepherd, J. Cue saliency in faces as assessed by the Photo-fit technique. *Perception*, 1977, *6*, 263−269.

Davies, G., Ellis, H., & Shepherd, J. Face recognition accuracy as a function of mode of representation. *Journal of Applied Psychology*, 1978, *63*, 180−187.

Davies, G., Milne, J. E., & Glennie, B. J. On the significance of "double encoding" for superior recall of pictures to names. *Quarterly Journal of Experimental Psychology*, 1973, *25*, 413−423.

Davies, G. M., Shepherd, J. W., & Ellis, H. D. Effects of interpolated mugshot exposure on accuracy of eyewitness identification. *Journal of Applied Psychology*, 1979, *64*, 232−237. (*a*)

Davies, G. M., Shepherd, J. W., & Ellis, H. D. Similarity effects in face recognition. *American Journal of Psychology*, 1979, *92*, 507−523. (*b*)

Davis, R. D., & Sinha, D. The effect of one experience upon the recall of another. *Quarterly Journal of Experimental Psychology*, 1950, *2*, 43−52.

Deffenbacher, K. Eyewitness accuracy and confidence: Can we infer anything about their relationship? *Law and Human Behavior*, in press.

Deffenbacher, K. A., Leu, J. R., & Brown, E. L. *Remembering faces and their immediate context*. Paper presented at the meeting of the Psychonomic Society, Phoenix, 1979.

Dent, H. R. Interviewing child witnesses. In M. M. Gruneberg, P. E. Morris, & R. N. Sykes (Eds.), *Practical aspects of memory*. New York: Academic Press, 1978.

Devlin, Rt. Hon. Lord Patrick (Chair). *Report to the Secretary of state for the home Department of the departmental committee on evidence of identification in criminal cases*. London: H. M. Stationery Office, 1976.

Dhanens, T. P., & Lundy, R. M. Hypnotic and waking suggestions and recall. *International Journal of Clinical and Experimental Hypnosis*, 1975, *23*, 68−79.

Dodd, D. H., & Bradshaw X. Leading questions and memory: Pragmatic constraints. *Journal of Verbal Learning and Verbal Behavior*, 1980, *19*, 695−704.

Dooling, D. J., & Christiaansen, R. E. Episodic and semantic aspects of memory of prose. *Journal of Experimental Psychology: Human Learning and Memory*, 1977, *3*, 428—436.

Dorcus, R. M. Recall under hypnosis of amnesic events. *International Journal of Clinical and Experimental Hypnosis*, 1960, *8*, 57—61.

Ebbinghaus, H. E. *Memory: A contribution to experimental psychology*. New York: Dover, 1964. (Originally published, 1885).

Egan, D., Pittner, M., & Goldstein, A. G. Eyewitness identification: Photographs vs. live models. *Law and Human Behavior*, 1977, *1*, 199—206.

Egan, D. M., & Smith, K. H. *Improving eyewitness identification: An experimental analysis*. Paper presented at the meeting of the American Psychology-Law Society, Baltimore, October 1979.

Eich, J. E., Weingartner, H., Stillman, R. C., & Gillin, J. C. State-dependent accessibility of retrieval cues in the retention of a categorized list. *Journal of Verbal Learning and Verbal Behavior*, 1975, *14*, 408—417.

Elliott, E. S., Wills, E. J., & Goldstein, A. G. The effects of discrimination training of the recognition of white and oriental faces. *Bulletin of the Psychonomic Society*, 1973, *2*, 71—73.

Ellis, H. D. Recognizing faces. *British Journal of Psychology*, 1975, *66*, 409—426.

Ellis, H. D., Davies, G. M., & Shepherd, J. W. Experimental studies of face identification. *Journal of Criminal Defense*, 1977, *3*, 219—234.

Ellis, H. D., Deregowski, J. B., & Shepherd, J. W. Descriptions of white and black faces by white and black subjects. *International Journal of Psychology*, 1975, *10*, 119—123.

Ellis, H. D., Shepherd, J., & Davies, G. An investigation of the use of the Photofit technique for recalling faces. *British Journal of Psychology*, 1975, *66*, 29—37.

Eugenio, P., Buckhout, R., Kostes, S., & Ellison, K. W. *Hypermnesia in the eyewitness to a crime*. Paper presented at the meeting of the American Psychological Association, New York City, September 1979.

Feinman, S., & Entwisle, D. R. Children's ability to recognize other children's faces. *Child Development*, 1976, *47*, 506—510.

Fischhoff, B. Perceived informativeness of facts. *Journal of Experimental Psychology: Human Perception and Performance*, 1977, *3*, 349—358.

Fishman, D. B., & Loftus, E. F. Expert psychological testimony on eyewitness identification. *Law and Psychology Review*, 1978, *4*, 87—103.

Fleishman, J. J., Buckley, M. L., Klosinsky, M. J., Smith, N., & Tuck, B. Judged attractiveness in recognition memory of women's faces. *Perceptual and Motor Skills*, 1976, *43*, 709—710.

Franken, R. E. & Davis, J. Predicting memory for pictures from rankings of interestingness, pleasingness, complexity, figure-ground and clarity. *Perceptual and Motor Skills*, 1975, *41*, 243—247.

Galanter, E. Contemporary psychophysics. In R. Brown, E. Galanter, E. H. Hess & G. Mandler (Eds.), *New Directions in Psychology*. New York: Holt, 1962.

Galton, F. *Inquiries into human faculty*. London: Dent, 1883.

Garcia, L. T., & Griffitt, W. Impact of testimonial evidence as a function of witness characteristics. *Bulletin of the Psychonomic Society*, 1978, *11*, 37—40.

Gardner, D. S. The perception and memory of witnesses. *Cornell Law Quarterly*, 1933, *18*, 391—409.

Gartman, L. M., & Johnson, N. F. Massed versus distributed repetitions of homographs: A test of the differential encoding hypothesis. *Journal of Verbal Learning and Verbal Behavior*, 1972, *11*, 801—808.

Gentner, D., & Loftus, E. F. Integration of verbal and visual information as evidenced by distoritons in picture memory. *American Journal of Psychology*, 1979, *92*, 363—375.

Going, M., & Read, J. D. Effects of uniqueness, sex of subject, and sex of photograph on facial recognition. *Perceptual and Motor Skills*, 1974, *39*, 109—110.

Goldstein, A. G. The fallibility of the eyewitness: Psychological evidence. In B. D. Sales (Ed.), *Psychology in the legal process*. New York: Spectrum, 1977.

Goldstein, A. G., & Chance, J. E. Visual recognition memory for complex configurations. *Perception and Psychophysics*, 1971, *9*, 237—241.

Goldstein, A. G., & Chance, J. Measuring psychological similarity of faces. *Bulletin of the Psychonomic Society*, 1976, *7*, 407–408.

Goldstein, A. G., & Chance, J. Do "foreign" faces really look alike? *Bulletin of the Psychonomic Society*, 1979, *13*, 111–113.

Goldstein, A. G., Stephenson, B., & Chance, J. Face recognition memory: Distribution of false alarms. *Bulletin of the Psychonomic Society*, 1977, *9*, 416–418.

Gorenstein, G. W., & Ellsworth, P. Effect of choosing an incorrect photograph on a later identification by an eyewitness. *Journal of Applied Psychology*, 1980, *65*, 616–622.

Graefe, T. M., & Watkins, M. J. Picture rehearsal: An effect of selectivity attending to pictures no longer in view. *Journal of Experimental Psychology*, 1980, *6*, 156–162.

Greenberg, M. S., Wilson, C. E., & Mills, M. K. An experimental approach to victim decision making. In V. J. Konečni & E. B. Ebbesen (Eds.), *Social Psychological Analysis of Legal Processes*. San Francisco, California: W. H. Freeman, in press.

Greenberg, M. S., Wilson, C. E., Ruback, R. B., & Mills, M. K. Social and emotional determinants of victim crime reporting. *Social Psychology Quarterly*, 1979, *42*, 364–372.

Grether, W. F., & Baker, C. A. Visual presentation of information. In H. P. Van Cott & R. G. Kinkade (Eds.), *Human engineering guide to equipment design*. Washington, D.C.: U.S. Government. Printing Office, 1972.

Gross, H. [*Criminal Psychology* (4th ed.)] (M. Kallen, Trans.). Mount Claire, New Jersey: Paterson Smith, 1911.

Hall, D. F. *Memory for faces and words: Effects of stimulus presentation interval and depth of processing*. Paper presented at the meeting of the Midwestern Psychological Association, St. Louis, May 1980.

Hamilton, D. L. A cognitive-attributional analysis of stereotyping. In L. Berkowitz (Ed.), *Advances in Experimental Social Psychology* (Vol 12). New York: Academic Press, 1979.

Harmon, L. D. The recognition of faces. *Scientific American*, 1973, *229*, 71–83.

Hastie, R. *From eyewitness accuracy to beyond reasonable doubt*. Paper presented at the meeting of the Law and Society Association and the Research Committee on the Sociology of Law of the International Sociological Association, Madison, June 1980.

Hastie, R., Landsman, R., & Loftus, E. F. Eyewitness testimony: The dangers of guessing. *Jurimetrics Journal*, 1978, *19*, 1–8.

Hastorf, A. H., & Cantril H. They saw a game: A case study. *Journal of Abnormal and Social Psychology*, 1954, *49*, 129–134.

Hatvany, N., & Strack, F. The impact of a discredited key witness. *Journal of Applied Social Psychology*, in press.

Hilgard, E. R., & Loftus, E. F. Effective interrogation of the eyewitness. *International Journal of Clinical and Experimental Hypnosis*, 1979, *27*, 342–357.

Hintzman, D. L. Repetition and memory. In G. H. Bower (Ed.), *The psychology of learning and motivation* (Vol. 10). New York: Academic Press, 1976.

Hintzman, D. L., Summers, J. J., & Block, R. A. What causes the spacing effect? Some effects of repetition, duration, and spacing on memory for pictures. *Memory and Cognition*, 1975, *3*, 287–294.

Holden, C. Forensic use of hypnosis on the increase. *Science*, 1980, *209*, 1443–1444.

Horvath, F. S., & Reid, J. E. The reliability of polygraph examiner diagnosis of truth and deception. *Journal of Criminal Law*, 1971, *62*, 276–281.

Hutchins, R., & Slesinger, H. Some observations of the law of evidence—memory. *Harvard Law Review*, 1928, *41*, 860–873.

Intraub, H. The role of implicit naming in pictorial encoding. *Journal of Experimental Psychology: Human Learning and Memory*, 1979, *5*, 78–87.

Johnson, C., & Scott, B. *Eyewitness testimony and suspect identification as a function of arousal, sex of witness, and scheduling of interrogation*. Paper presented at the meeting of the American Psychological Association, Washington, D. C., September 1976.

Jörg, S., & Hörmann, H. The influence of general and specific verbal labels on the recognition of labeled and unlabeled parts of pictures. *Journal of Verbal Learning and Verbal Behavior*, 1978, 17, 445−454.

Kosslyn, S. M. Information representation in visual images. *Cognitive Psychology*, 1975, 7, 341−370.

Kubis, J. F. Experimental and statistical factors in the diagnosis of consciously suppressed affective experience. *Journal of Clinical Psychology*, 1950, 6, 12−16.

Kuehn, L. L. Looking down a gun barrel: Person perception and violent crime. *Perceptual and Motor Skills*, 1974, 39, 1159−1164.

Laughery, K. R., Alexander, J. L., & Lane, A. B. Recognition of human faces: Effects of target exposure time, target position, pose position, and type of photograph. *Journal of Applied Psychology*, 1971, 55, 477−483.

Laughery, K. R., Fessler, P. K., Lenorovitz, D. R., & Yoblick, D. A. Time delay and similarity effects in face recognition. *Journal of Applied Psychology*, 1974, 59, 490−496.

Laughery, K. R., & Fowler, R. H. *Factors affecting facial recognition.* University of Houston Mug File Project (Report No. UHMUG-2) 1977.

Lavrakas, P. J., & Bickman, L. *What makes a good witness?* Paper presented at the meeting of the American Psychological Association, Chicago, August−September 1975.

Lavrakas, P. J., Buri, J. R., & Mayzner, M. S. A perspective of the recognition of other-race faces. *Perception and Psychophysics*, 1976, 20, 475−481.

Leippe, M. R., Wells, G. L., & Ostrom, T. M. Crime seriousness as a determinant of accuracy in eyewitness identification. *Journal of Applied Psychology*, 1978, 63, 345−351.

Levine, F. J., & Tapp, J. The psychology of criminal identification: The gap from *Wade* to *Kirby*. *University of Pennsylvania Law Review*, 1973, 121, 1079−1131.

Lewis, M. S. Determinants of visual attention in real-world scenes. *Perceptual and Motor Skills*, 1975, 41, 411−416.

Light, L., Kayra-Stuart, F., & Hollander, S. Recognition memory for typical and unusual faces. *Journal of Experimental Psychology*, 1979, 5, 212−228.

Lindsay, P. H., & Norman, D. A. *Human information processing: An introduction to psychology* (2d ed.). New York: Academic Press, 1977.

Lindsay, R. C. L., & Wells, G. L. *What price justice? Exploring the relationship of lineup fairness to identification accuracy.* Unpublished manuscript, University of Manitoba, 1980.

Lindsay, R. C. L., Wells, G. L., & Rumpel, C. M. *Cross-racial eyewitness identifications: It may be better if they all look alike.* Unpublished manuscript, University of Manitoba, 1980.

Lindsay, R. C. L., Wells, G. L., & Rumpel, C. M. Can people detect eyewitness-identification accuracy within and across situations? *Journal of Applied Psychology*, 1981, 66, 79−89.

Lipton, J. P. On the psychology of eyewitness testimony. *Journal of Applied Psychology*, 1977, 62, 90−93.

Loftus, E. F. Reconstructing memory: The incredible eyewitness. *Psychology Today*, December 1974, pp. 116−119.

Loftus, E. F. Eyewitness. *Puget Soundings*, October 1975, pp. 32−37.

Loftus, E. F. Unconscious transference in eyewitness identification. *Law and Psychology Review*, 1976, 2, 93−98.

Loftus, E. F. Shifting human color memory. *Memory and Cognition*, 1977, 5, 696−699.

Loftus, E. F. *Eyewitness testimony.* Cambridge, Massachusetts: Harvard Univ. Press, 1979.

Loftus, E. F. Impact of expert psychological testimony on the unreliability of eyewitness identification. *Journal of Applied Psychology*, 1980, 65, 9−15.

Loftus, E. F., Altman, D., & Geballe, R. Effects of questioning upon a witness' later recollections. *Journal of Police Science and Administration*, 1975, 3, 162−165.

Loftus, E. F., Miller, D. G., & Burns, H. J. Sematic integration of verbal information into a visual memory. *Journal of Experimental Psychology: Human Learning and Memory*, 1978, 4, 19−31.

Loftus, E. F., & Palmer, J. P. Reconstruction of automobile destruction: An example of the interaction between language and memory. *Journal of Verbal Learning and Verbal Behavior*, 1974, *13*, 585–589.

Loftus, E. F., & Zanni, G. Eyewitness testimony: The influence of the wording of a question. *Bulletin of the Psychonomic Society*, 1975, *5*, 86–88.

Loftus, G. R. Eye fixations and recognition memory for pictures. *Cognitive Psychology*, 1972, *3*, 525–551.

Loftus, G. R., & Kallman, H. J. Encoding and use of detail information in picture recognition. *Journal of Experimental Psychology: Human Learning and Memory*, 1979, *5*, 197–211.

Lower, J. S. Psychologists as expert witnesses. *Law and Psychology Review*, 1978, *4*, 127–139.

Luce, T. S. Blacks, whites, and yellows: They all look alike to me. *Psychology Today*, November 1974, pp. 105–108.

Lykken, D. T. The validity of the guilty knowledge technique: The effect of faking. *Journal of Applied Psychology*, 1960, *44*, 258–262.

Lykken, D. T. Psychology and the lie detector industry. *American Psychologist*, 1974, *29*, 725–739.

Lykken, D. T. The right way to use a lie detector. *Psychology Today*, March 1975, pp. 56–60.

McCarty, D. G. *Psychology for the lawyer*. Englewood Cliffs, New Jersey: Prentice-Hall, 1929.

McCarty, D. G. *Psychology and the law*. Englewood Cliffs, New Jersey: Prentice-Hall, 1960.

McGehee, F. The reliability of identification of the human voice. *Journal of General Psychology*, 1937, *17*, 249–271.

McKelvie, S. J. The role of eyes and mouth in the memory of a face. *American Journal of Psychology*, 1976, *89*, 311–323.

Malpass, R. S., & Devine, P. G. *Eyewitness identification: Line-up instructions and the absence of the offender*. Unpublished manuscript, State University of New York at Plattsburgh, 1980.

Malpass, R. S., Devine, P. G., & Bergen, G. T. *Realism vs. the laboratory*. Unpublished manuscript, State University of New York at Plattsburgh, 1980.

Malpass, R. S., & Kravitz, J. Recognition for faces of own and other race. *Journal of Personality and Social Psychology*, 1969, *13*, 330–334.

Malpass, R. S., Lavigueur, H., & Weldon, D. E. Verbal and visual training in face recognition. *Perception and Psychophysics*, 1973, *14*, 285–292.

Mandler, G. Organization and recognition. In E. Tulving & W. Donaldson (Eds.), *Organization of memory*. New York: Academic Press, 1972.

Mandler, G. Recognizing: The judgment of previous occurrence. *Psychological Review*, 1980, *87*, 252–271.

Mandler, G., Pearlstone, Z., & Koopmans, H. J. Effects of organization and semantic similarity on recall and recognition. *Journal of Verbal Learning and Verbal Behavior*, 1969, *8*, 410–423.

Mandler, J. M., & Johnson, N. S. Some of the thousand words a picture is worth. *Journal of Experimental Psychology: Human Learning and Memory*, 1976, *2*, 529–540.

Mandler, J. M., & Parker, R. E. Memory for descriptive and spatial information in complex pictures. *Journal of Experimental Psychology: Human Learning and Memory*, 1976, *2*, 38–48.

Mandler, J. M., & Ritchey, G. H. Long-term memory for pictures. *Journal of Experimental Psychology: Human Learning and Memory*, 1977, *3*, 397–405.

Mandler, J. M., & Stein, N. L. Recall and recognition of pictures by children as a function of organization and distractor similarity. *Journal of Experimental Psychology*, 1974, *102*, 657–669.

Marquis, K. H., Marshall, J., & Oskamp, S. Testimony validity as a function of question form, atmosphere, and item difficulty. *Journal of Applied Social Psychology*, 1972, *2*, 167–186.

Marshall, J. *Law and psychology in conflict*. Indianapolis, Indiana: Bobbs, 1966.

Marshall, J. The evidence: Do we see and hear what is? Or do our senses lie? *Psychology Today*, February 1969, pp. 48–52.

Marshall, J. *Law and Psychology in conflict* (2nd ed.) Indianapolis, Indiana: Bobbs, 1979. (Originally published, 1966).

Marshall, J., Marquis, K. H., & Oskamp, S. Effects on a kind of question and atmosphere of interrogation on accuracy and completeness of testimony. *Harvard Law Review*, 1971, *84*, 1620–1643.

Marston, W. M. Studies in testimony. *Journal of Criminal Law and Criminolgy*, 1924, *15*, 5−31.

Massad, C. M., Hubbard, M., & Newtson, D. Selective perception of events. *Journal of Experimental Social Psychology*, 1979, *15*, 513−532.

Matthews, M. L. Discrimination of identikit constructions of faces: Evidence for a dual-processing strategy. *Perception and Psychophysics*, 1978, *23*, 153−161.

Miller, G. A. The magical number seven plus or minus two: Some limits on our capacity for processing information. *Psychological Review*, 1956, *63*, 81−97.

Milord, J. T. Aspects of faces: A (somewhat) phenomenological analysis using multidimensional scaling methods. *Journal of Personality and Social Psychology*, 1978, *36*, 205−216.

Project on Law Enforcement Policy and Rulemaking, J. A. LaSota (Director) and G. W. Bromley (Deputy Director). *Model Rules: Eyewitness Identification.* Washington, D.C.: Police Foundation, 1974.

Mueller, J. H., Bailis, K. L., & Goldstein, A. G. Depth of processing and anxiety in facial recognition. *British Journal of Psychology*, 1979, *70*, 511−515.

Mueller, J. H., Carlomusto, M., & Goldstein, A. G. Orienting task and study time in facial recognition. *Bulletin of the Psychonomic Society*, 1978, *11*, 313−316.

Mueller, J. H., & Wherry, K. L. Orienting strategies at study and test in facial recognition. *American Journal of Psychology*, in press.

Münsterberg, H. *On the witness stand: Essays on psychology and crime.* New York: Clark, Boardman, 1908.

Münsterberg, H. *Psychology and social sanity.* Garden City, New York: Doubleday, 1914.

Muscio, B. The influence of the form of a question. *British Journal of Psychology*, 1915, *8*, 351−389.

Myers, C. G. A study of incidental memory. *Archives of Psychology*, 1913, *26*, 1−108.

Neisser, U. *Cognition and reality: Principles and implications of cognitive psychology.* San Francisco, California: W. H. Freeman, 1976.

Nelson, T. O., Metzler, J., & Reed, D. A. Role of details in the long-term recognition of pictures and verbal descriptions. *Journal of Experimental Psychology*, 1974, *102*, 184−186.

Newtson, D. Attribution and the unit of perception of ongoing behavior. *Journal of Personality and Social Psychology*, 1973, *28*, 28−38.

Newtson, D., & Engquist, G. The perceptual organization of ongoing behavior. *Journal of Experimental Social Psychology*, 1976, *12*, 847−862.

Newtson, D., Engquist, G., & Bois, J. The objective basis of behavior units. *Journal of Personality and Social Psychology*, 1977, *12*, 847−862.

Norman, D. A. *Memory and attention: An introduction to human information processing* (2d ed.). New York: Wiley, 1976.

Norman, D. A. Perception, memory, and mental processes. In L.-G. Nilsson (Ed.), *Perspectives on memory research: Essays in honor of Uppsala University's 500th anniversary.* Hillsdale, New Jersey: Erlbaum, 1979.

Nowicki, S., Jr., Winograd, E., & Millard, B. A. Memory for faces: A social learning approach. *Journal of Research in Personality*, 1979, *13*, 460−468.

Orne, M. T. The use and misuse of hypnosis in court. *The International Journal of Clinical and Experimental Hypnosis*, 1979, *27*, 311−341.

Patterson, K. E., & Baddeley, A. D. When face recognition fails. *Journal of Experimental Psychology: Human Learning and Memory*, 1977, *3*, 406−407.

Penrod, S. *Confidence, accuracy, and the eyewitness.* Unpublished manuscript, University of Wisconsin, 1980.

Pezdek, K. Cross-modality semantic integration of sentence and picture memory. *Journal of Experimental Psychology: Human Learning and Memory*, 1977, *3*, 515−524.

Pittenger, J. B., Shaw, R. E., & Mark, L. S. Perceptual information for the age level of faces as a higher-order invariant of growth. *Journal of Experimental Psychology: Human Perception and Performance*, 1979, *5*, 478−493.

Podlesny, J. A., & Raskin, D. C. Physiological measures and the detection of deception. *Psychological Bulletin*, 1977, *84*, 782–799.

Postman, L. J., Bruner, J. S., & McGinnies, E. Personal values as selective factors in perception. *Journal of Abnormal and Social Psychology*, 1948, *43*, 142–154.

Powers, P. A., Andriks, J. L., & Loftus, E. F. The eyewitness accounts of females and males. *Journal of Applied Psychology*, 1979, *64*, 339–347.

Raskin, D. C., Barland, G. H., & Podlesny, J. A. *Validity and reliability of detection of deception* (U.S. Government 19780-0267-969). June 1978, U.S. Department of Justice.

Read, J. D. Rehearsal and recognition of human faces. *American Journal of Psychology*, 1979, *92*, 71–85.

Read, J. D., & Peterson, R. H. Individual differences in the ease of imagining the faces of others. *Bulletin of the Psychonomic Society*, 1975, *5*, 347–349.

Reid, J. E., & Inbau, F. E. *Truth and deception: The polygraph ("lie detector") technique*. Baltimore, Maryland: Williams & Wilkins, 1966.

Roberts, W. A. Free recall of word lists varying in length and rate of presentation: A test of the total-time hypothesis. *Journal of Experimental Psychology*, 1972, *92*, 365–372.

Rosch, E., & Mervis, C. B. Family resemblances: Studies in the internal structures of categories. *Cognitive Psychology*, 1975, *7*, 573–605.

Ross, L. The intuitive psychologist and his shortcomings: Distortion in the attribution process. In L. Berkowitz (Ed.), *Advances in Experimental Social Psychology* (Vol. 10). New York: Academic Press, 1977.

Rowe, E. J., & Rogers, T. B. Effects of concurrent auditory shadowing on free recall and recognition of pictures and words. *Journal of Experimental Psychology: Human Learning and Memory*, 1975, *1*, 415–422.

Salzberg, H. C. The hypnotic interview in crime detection. *The American Journal of Clinical Hypnosis*, 1977, *19*, 255–258.

Sanders, G. S., & Warnick, D. *Some conditions maximizing eyewitness accuracy: A learning/memory model*. Unpublished manuscript, State University of New York at Albany, 1979.

Sanders, G. S., & Warnick, D. H. *Truth and consequences: The effect of responsibility on eyewitness behavior*. Unpublished manuscript, State University of New York at Albany, 1980.

Saslove, H., & Yarmey, A. D. Long-term auditory memory: Speaker identification. *Journal of Applied Psychology*, 1980, *65*, 111–116.

Schiffman, H. R., & Bobko, D. J. Effects of stimulus complexity of the perception of brief temporal intervals. *Journal of Experimental Psychology*, 1974, *103*, 156–159.

Seamon, J. G. *Memory and Cognition*. London and New York: Oxford Univ. Press, 1980.

Seamon, J. G., Stolz, J. A., Bass, D. H., & Chatinover, A. I. Recognition of facial features in immediate memory. *Bulletin of the Psychonomic Society*, 1978, *12*, 231–234.

Shaul, R. D. *Hypnotic hypermnesia, cognitive strategy, and eyewitness testimony*. Unpublished doctoral dissertation, Brigham Young University, Utah, 1978.

Shepard, R. N. Recognition memory for words, sentences, and pictures. *Journal of Verbal Learning and Verbal Behavior*, 1967, *6*, 156–163.

Shepherd, J. W., Deregowski, J. B., & Ellis, H. D. A cross-cultural study of recognition memory for faces. *International Journal of Psychology*, 1974, *9*, 205–211.

Shepherd, J. W., & Ellis, H. D. The effect of attractiveness on recognition memory for faces. *American Journal of Psychology*, 1973, *86*, 627–633.

Shoemaker, D., South, D., & Lowe, J. Facial stereotypes of deviants and judgments of guilt or innocence. *Social Forces*, 1973, *51*, 427–433.

Siipola, E. M. A group study of some effects of preparatory set. *Psychological Monographs*, 1935, *46*, 27–38.

Smith, B. M. The polygraph. *Scientific American*, 1967, *216* (1), 25–30.

Smith, S. M., Glenberg, A. M., & Bjork, R. A. Environmental context and human memory. *Memory and Cognition*, 1978, *6*, 342–353.

Snee, T. S., & Lush, D. E. Interaction of narrative and interrogatory methods of obtaining testimony. *Journal of Psychology*, 1941, *11*, 229–236.

Snyder, M., & Uranowitz, S. W. Reconstructing the past: Some cognitive consequences of person perception. *Journal of Personality and Social Psychology*, 1978, *36*, 941–950.

Sorce, J. F. The role of physiognomy in the development of racial awareness. *The ;Journal of Genetic Psychology*, 1979, *134*, 33–41.

Sorce, J. F., & Campos, J. J. The role of expression in the recognition of a face. *American Journal of Psychology*, 1974, *87*, 71–82.

Stalnaker, J. M., & Riddle, E. E. The effect of hypnosis on long-delayed recall. *Journal of General Psychology*, 1932, *6*, 429–440.

Standing, L. Learning 10,000 pictures. *Quarterly Journal of Experimental Psychology*, 1973, *25*, 207–222.

Stern, L. W. Abstracts of lectures in the psychology of testimony and on the study of individuality. *American Journal of Psychology*, 1910, *21*, 270–282.

Stern, L. W. The psychology of testimony. *Journal of Abnormal and Social Psychology*, 1939, *34*, 3–20.

Thorson, G., & Hochhaus, L. The trained observer: Effects of prior information on eyewitness reports. *Bulletin of the Psychonomic Society*, 1977, *10*, 454–456.

Tickner, A. H., & Poulton, E. C. Watching for people and actions. *Ergonomics*, 1975, *18*, 35–51.

Tulving, E. Episodic and semantic memory. In E. Tulving and W. Donaldson (Eds.), *Organization of memory*. New York: Academic Press, 1972.

Tulving, E., & Thompson, D. M. Encoding specificity and retrieval processes in episodic memory. *Psychological Review*, 1973, *80*, 352–373.

Tversky, A., & Kahneman, D. Availability: A heuristic for judging frequency and probability. *Cognitive Psychology*, 1973, *5*, 207–232.

van Santen, J. P. H., & Jonides, J. A. A replication of the face-superiority effect. *Bulletin of the Psychonomic Society*, 1978, *12*, 378–380.

Wall, P. M. *Eyewitness identification in criminal cases*. Springfield, Illinois: Thomas, 1965.

Warnick, D. H., & Sanders, G. S. *False identifications and the line-up setting*. Paper presented at the meeting of the Eastern Psychological Association, April 1980.

Watson, J. B. Psychology as the behaviorist views it. *Psychological Review*, 1913, *20*, 158–177.

Waugh, N. C. Immediate memory as a function of repetition. *Journal of Verbal Learning and Verbal Behavior*, 1963, *2*, 107–112.

Waugh, N. C. Presentation time and free recall. *Journal of Experimental Psychology*, 1967, *73*, 39–44.

Weaver, G. E., & Stanny, C. J. Short-term retention of pictorial stimuli as assessed by a probe recognition technique. *Journal of Experimental Psychology: Human Learning and Memory*, 1978, *4*, 55–65.

Weinberg, H. I., & Baron, R. S. *The discredible eyewitness*. Paper presented at the meeting of the Midwestern Psychological Association, St. Louis, May 1980.

Wells, G. L. Applied eyewitness-testimony-research: System variables and estimator variables. *Journal of Personality and Social Psychology*, 1978, *36*, 1546–1557.

Wells, G. L., Leippe, M. R., & Ostrom, T. M. Guidelines for empirically assessing the fairness of a lineup. *Law and Human Behavior*, 1979, *3*, 285–293.

Wells, G. L., & Lindsay, R. C. L. On estimating the diagnosticity of eyewitness nonidentifications. *Psychological Bulletin*, 1980, *88*, 776–786.

Wells, G. L., Lindsay, R. C. L., & Ferguson, T. J. Accuracy, confidence, and juror perceptions in eyewitness identification. *Journal of Applied Psychology*, 1979, *64*, 440–448.

Wells, J. E. Encoding and memory for verbal and pictorial stimuli. *Quarterly Journal of Experimental Psychology*, 1972, *24*, 242–252.

Whipple, G. M. The observer as reporter: A survey of the "psychology of testimony." *Psychological Bulletin*, 1909, *6*, 153–170.

Whipple, G. M. Recent literature on the psychology of testimony. *Psychological Bulletin*, 1910, 7, 365–368.

Whipple, G. M. The psychology of testimony. *Psychological Bulletin*, 1911, 8, 307–309.

Whipple, G. M. Psychology of testimony and report. *Psychological Bulletin*, 1912, 9, 264–269.

Whipple, G. M. Psychology of testimony and report. *Psychological Bulletin*, 1913, 10, 264–268.

Whipple, G. M. Psychology of testimony and report. *Psychological Bulletin*, 1914, 11, 245–250.

Whipple, G. M. Psychology of testimony. *Psychological Report*, 1915, 12, 221–224.

Whipple, G. M. Psychology of testimony. *Psychological Bulletin*, 1917, 14, 234–236.

Whipple, G. M. The obtaining of information: Psychology of observation and report. *Psychological Bulletin*, 1918, 15, 217–248.

White, R. W., Fox, G. F., & Harris, W. W. Hypnotic hypermnesia for recently learned material. *Journal of Abnormal and Social Psychology*, 1940, 35, 88–103.

Wigmore, J. H. Professor Münsterberg and the psychology of evidence. *Illinois Law Review*, 1909, 3, 399–445.

Wist, R. E. Dark adaptation and the Hermann grid illusion. *Perception and Psychophysics*, 1976, 20, 10–12.

Witt, K. S. *Arousal, sex of witness, and memory for a filmed crime.* Unpublished honors thesis, Harvard College, 1980.

Woocher, F. D. Did your eyes deceive you? Expert Psychological testimony on the unreliability of eyewitness identification. *Stanford Law Review*, 1977, 29, 969–1030.

Yarmey, A. D. *Social-emotional factors in recall and recognition of human faces.* Paper presented at the meeting of the Midwestern Psychological Association, Chicago, May 1975.

Yarmey, A. D. The effects of attractiveness, feature saliency, and liking on memory for faces. In M. Cook and G. Wilson (Eds.), *Love and attraction: An international conference.* Elmsford, New York: Pergamon, 1979 (a).

Yarmey, A. D. *The psychology of eyewitness testimony.* New York: Free Press, 1979 (b).

Yarmey, A. D. Through the looking glass: Sex differences in memory for self-facial poses. *Journal of Research in Personality*, 1979, 13, 450–459 (c).

Yerkes, R. M., & Dodson, J. D. The relation of strength of stimulus to rapidity of habit-formation. *Journal of Comparative and Neurological Psychology*, 1908, 18, 459–482.

Zanni, G. R., & Offermann, J. T. Eyewitness testimony: An exploration of question wording upon recall as a function of neuroticism. *Perceptual and Motor Skills*, 1978, 46, 163–166.

Factors Affecting Assessments of Witness Credibility

Gerald R. Miller
Judee K. Burgoon

Judgments of the demeanor of witnesses are central to the trial process. Since trial outcomes usually hinge on assessing the relative likelihood and/or veracity of conflicting information claims, legal decision makers—whether they be the judges and jury members of the traditional trial or the hearing officers and mediators of some of the newer, less formal modes of dispute resolution— cannot escape the responsibility of evaluating witness credibility. Miller and Boster (1977) mention the notion of the trial as a test of credibility as one of three important ways of conceptualizing the trial process, characterizing this

THE PSYCHOLOGY
OF THE COURTROOM

perspective as demanding attention "not only to the factual information presented, but also to the way in which it is presented, the apparent qualifications of witnesses, and numerous other relevant factors [pp. 28−29]."

In the assessment of witness demeanor, the issue of intent to deceive, or deliberate falsehood, may or may not enter into the judgment. For instance, assume a judge or a juror is skeptical about testimony because a witness seems confused and hesitant when responding to questions. Under such circumstances, the judge or juror may absolve the witness of any duplicity: for example, "I feel this witness is trying to testify accurately but seems uncertain of what happened." Or the judge or juror may mentally indict the witness for lying: for example, "I feel this witness is a perjurer."

This distinction between honest error and outright deception fits nicely with the results of several studies investigating the major dimensions of communicator credibility (Berlo, Lemert, & Mertz, 1969−1970; Cronkhite & Liska, 1976; McCroskey, 1966; Whitehead, 1968). Despite some minor variations in these factor analytic studies, two major dimensions of credibility that emerge consistently are *competence* and *trustworthiness*. The former is most germane to assessments of witness credibility when intent to deceive seems unlikely, whereas the latter relates primarily to situations where the judge or juror believes the witness may be offering untruthful testimony.[1] Other frequently identified dimensions such as *dynamism, composure,* and *sociability,* while emerging as orthogonal components in some of the investigations, probably act as antecedents that influence perceptions of competence and trustworthiness. For example, if a witness lacks dynamism and composure, as reflected by a barely audible voice, high incidence of vocal disruptions such as nonfluency, and numerous nonverbal adaptors such as self-touching and fidgeting with clothing (Ekman & Friesen, 1969); he or she is likely to be perceived as relatively incompetent and/or untrustworthy.

The preceding example anticipates one of our two major objectives in this chapter: identifying variables that should and do influence judges' and jurors' assessments of witness credibility. Our second major objective is to examine the findings of studies concerned with the ability of observers to detect deception perpetrated by relative strangers, both to ascertain how skillful persons are at this task and to isolate variables that facilitate or inhibit accurate detection of deception.[2]

[1]Competence and trustworthiness also correspond to the most common legal reasons for seeking to impeach witnesses. In most cases, impeachment can be based on the witness's incompetence to testify about issues (competence) or possible self-interest and bias on the part of the witness (trustworthiness).

[2]Several recent studies have examined the influence of degree of familiarity on the ability of observers to detect deception (Bauchner, n.d.; Brandt, Miller, & Hocking, 1980 a,b). As would be expected, these studies indicate that if observers know something about a communicator/deceiver's truthful communication style, they are more accurate in detecting deception. Since jurors who were familiar with witnesses would normally be excused from jury duty, studies dealing with attempts to detect deception on the part of relative strangers are most relevant to the trial setting.

Actually our efforts regarding the first objective are more modest than initially implied, since our discussion focuses on nonverbal and verbal characteristics associated with the actual presentation of testimony—characteristics that can be considered *intrinsic determinants* of credibility (Miller, Bauchner, Hocking, Fontes, Kaminski, & Brandt, 1981). Obviously, there are also numerous *extrinsic determinants* of credibility—attributes and characteristics witnesses bring with them to the courtroom setting. Some of the more obvious include education, occupational status, socioeconomic status, general reputation, race, sex, and physical appearance. Furthermore, extrinsic and intrinsic determinants often interact to shape overall perceptions of credibility. Thus, a hesitant, nonfluent witness of acknowledged impeccable character is likely to be perceived as nervous or uncertain, but a witness of shady reputation who manifests the same behaviors probably will be viewed as an unconvincing liar.

Unfortunately, space limitations prevent us from surveying all of these areas thoroughly. In the following sections, we first examine nonverbal communication behaviors associated with judgments of credibility; we next consider some verbal characteristics of testimony proper that relate to credibility assessments; and finally, we examine the question of observers' accuracy in detecting deception. Although the final product falls short of a comprehensive, holistic picture of the perceptual process of evaluating witnesses, it does provide useful clues regarding some of the important presentational variables impinging on this process and also supplies a tentative answer to the question of how well courtroom decision makers can identify deceptive testimony.

NONVERBAL CUES ASSOCIATED WITH CREDIBILITY

Nonverbal cues that may be used by witnesses to establish their credibility or by jurors to evaluate credibility are of utmost importance. Hocking, Miller, and Fontes (1978) report that observers, asked to make judgments of the truthfulness of strangers, indicated a subjective estimate of about 58% confidence in their judgments when they viewed the strangers responding with no accompanying audio—that is, when their judgments were based entirely on the strangers' nonverbal behaviors. Adding the audio portion yielded only a modest increase in subjective judgments of confidence to about 64%. This result is consistent with much other research showing that people rely more heavily on nonverbal than verbal cues in interpreting social meaning, especially when the cues are spontaneously presented or inconsistent (Argyle, Alkema, & Gilmour, 1971; Bugental, 1974; Mehrabian & Wiener, 1967).

Diverse bodies of literature offer insights into the nonverbal cues associated with witness credibility and truthfulness, though little of the research has been conducted in the courtroom. In general, the research can be divided into that which takes the perspective of an *encoder* and that which takes the perspective of a *decoder.* In the former category are studies exploring nonverbal behaviors manifested by persons attempting to present themselves favorably, to be persuasive, or to deceive others; in the latter are studies centering on the cues perceived by observers as credible, persuasive, or deceptive.

Credible and Deceptive Encoding Behaviors

Several studies have examined the behaviors exhibited by individuals intent on enhancing their credibility and persuasiveness. For example, Timney and London (1973) had people roleplay jurors whose task was to convince another juror of the correctness of their own decision. In their study as well as others (Maslow, Yoselson, & London, 1971; Mehrabian & Williams, 1969), cues that correlated with intention to persuade and appearance of confidence included those indicating more *extroversion and involvement,* such as forceful, rhythmic gestures, more eye contact, higher vocal volume, and faster speaking rate; moderate *relaxation,* such as a somewhat relaxed posture, fewer anxiety revealing behaviors, and fluent speech; and more *positivity,* such as more affirmative head nods, more facial activity, and greater intonation. These cues are summarized by nonverbal code in Table 6.1.

Other studies focusing on the negative end of the credibility continuum have examined the behaviors manifested by communicators engaged in lying to or misleading others. Ekman and Friesen (1969, 1975) identify four general strategies for managing emotional expressions, all of which are relevant to courtroom deceit by witnesses. First, a witness may *qualify* a given expression by adding another expression that comments about the first, as when a person smiles at his or her own foolish statement. Though the qualifying expression is typically not used to distort the meaning of the original one, it can be used effectively to introduce ambiguity, and hence, deception. Second, a witness may *curtail* a response, providing an abbreviated version of a normal performance, in the hope that less opportunity will be provided for deception detection. A third strategy involves *modulation*—the over- or under-intensification of emotions—as when a witness chooses to exaggerate or minimize the emotions expressed. Finally, a witness may *falsify* an emotional expression by simulating a feeling not actually experienced, neutralizing the expression to show nothing of what is felt, or masking the true feeling through substitution of another expression.

As another general guide to deceptive practices, Ekman and Friesen (1969) contend that the body regions providing the best deception clues are the hands and the feet because they are less carefully monitored by persons engaged in deception. The trunk may also reveal intensity, though not evaluative valence. By contrast, the face is most carefully controlled and therefore may present less valid information, the exception being micromomentary facial cues (fleeting facial expressions such as a grimace), which are not easily detected by the naked eye. Translated to the courtroom, this means that the most valuable cues are typically not available, while those that are most easily misinterpreted constitute the primary fund of available visual information. In a later section of this chapter, we discuss the accuracy of observers in detecting deception when viewing each of the body regions.

While the physical arrangement of many courtrooms poses some practical problems for jurors in discerning witness deception, many cues are still available to the skilled observer. It must be stressed, however, that these behaviors do not stem exclusively from deception. Similar communication patterns may appear under conditions of stress, negative affect, or disinterest. Consequently, accurate determination of when such cues signal dissembling is difficult and interpretations must be made cautiously. Single cues may be particularly misleading; reasonable judgments are possible only when a consistent pattern of cues presents itself.

In a review of early deception research, Knapp, Hart, and Dennis (1974) proposed a number of functions of deception cues that provide a useful classification scheme. Six of these functions are relevant to nonverbal cues. The first, most obvious configuration of cues shows *underlying anxiety or nervousness*. A host of physiological indicators—blushing, perspiring, increased blood pressure, altered breathing cycle, shaking, altered latency, rate of blinking, and increased Galvanic Skin Response—may be present when a person is lying (Cutrow, Parks, Lucas, & Thomas, 1972). Unfortunately, many of these signs are detectable only with the aid of sophisticated equipment. One autonomic response available to the unaided observer is pupil size: prevaricators typically show pupil dilation (often a slow dilation followed by rapid constriction) or pupil instability (Berrien & Huntington, 1943; Clark, 1975; Heilveil, 1976). Other bodily activity indicative of anxiety and tension includes random body and limb movements, such as abortive, restless flight movements; frequent shifts of leg or body positions; frequent leg crossing by males (Ekman & Friesen, 1969, 1972, 1974; Feldman, Devin-Sheehan, & Allen, 1978; Knapp *et al.*, 1974; McClintock & Hunt, 1975) and excessive use of adaptor behaviors (behaviors that relieve physiological or psychological needs), particularly self-adaptors such as tearing at fingernails, holding knees, digging into palms; face-play adaptors such as scratching the nose or chin; and object adaptors such as playing with a pencil or smoking a cigarette (Knapp *et al.*, McClintock & Hunt). These latter behaviors, however, do not appear consistently, as evidenced by their failure to arise in some investigations (Ekman & Friesen, 1974). It is likely that well-rehearsed witnesses would display few self-adaptors, although inadvertent touching of face and hair might still be observed. Finally, at the vocal level, lying has commonly been accompanied by a higher fundamental frequency, or pitch (Ekman & Friesen, 1974; Ekman, Friesen, & Scherer, 1976; Streeter, Krauss, Geller, Olson, & Apple, 1977) and occasionally, though not consistently, by increased nonfluencies (supported by Mehrabian, 1971; not supported by Knapp *et al.*, 1974).

A second configuration of cues shows *underlying reticence or withdrawal.* Such behaviors as fewer illustrative gestures, postural body blocks, orienting the body to face others less directly, less forward body lean, and increased interpersonal distance may be exhibited (Ekman & Friesen, 1972; Ekman et al., 1976; Knapp et al., 1974; Mehrabian, 1971). These cues all translate into reduced *immediacy*, a global term for the degree of closeness and desire for approach that exists between people. Eye contact may also be reduced (Knapp et al., 1974; Mehrabian, 1971), although some studies have shown that people who greatly value manipulative skills (high Machiavellians) and people with time to plan their performances may carefully control their eye contact to keep it as normal as possible (Exline, Thibaut, Hickey, & Gumpert, 1970; McClintock & Hunt, 1975; Matarazzo, Wiens, Jackson, & Manaugh, 1970). In terms of vocal cues, research results have been mixed. Although a majority of studies have found more pauses and openings for questioner probes when communicators are lying (Feldman et al., 1978; Knapp et al., 1974), longer delays in responding (response latencies) (Baskett & Freedle, 1974, Cutrow et al., 1972; Goldstein, 1923; Krauss, Geller, & Olson, 1976; Kraut, 1978; Matarazzo et al., 1970), shorter word duration and a trend toward shorter speaking time (Knapp et al., 1974; Mehrabian, 1971; Motley, 1974); other studies have either found shorter response latencies for some communicators who are lying (English, 1926; Marston, 1920) or have not supported differences in speaking duration (Matarazzo et al., 1970). Even though Goldstein (1923) found support for a methodological explanation of latency differences, the conflicting results still point to variability in the conditions under which certain vocal cues will be exhibited.

A third category of cues involves *excessive behaviors that deviate from a communicator's normal response patterns.* These behaviors generally express more extreme feelings than are actually felt, such as more outward composure than is experienced inwardly or feigned favorable reactions. In addition to the reduction in immediacy behaviors mentioned earlier, these cues include fewer head nods, fewer gestures, less leg and foot movement, more pleasant facial expressions, and either a faster or slower speaking rate (Mehrabian, 1971, 1972). Increases in pleasant facial expressions seem attributable to the deceiver trying to placate the observer and are likely to occur only among highly anxious communicators. More skillful communicators experience less anxiety and consequently display less of the negative affect that characterizes this type of "pleasant" expression. As for speaking rate changes, it appears that they are also mediated by stress level: Under conditions of minimal discomfort (presumably when telling the truth) or extreme discomfort (induced by certain deception circumstances), speaking rate is usually faster; under moderate discomfort (that may accompany other deceptive circumstances), the rate of speech is usually slower than normal. In generalizing to the courtroom, then, it would be necessary to estimate the level of stress involved before predicting the speaking rate that would signal deception.

While superficially the face may reveal some pleasantness, a fourth category of behaviors generally shows *underlying negative affect* (Mehrabian, 1971; Zuckerman, DeFrank, Hall, Larrance, & Rosenthal, 1979). Specific cues that have often been observed include reduced immediacy, briefer glances, a trend toward fewer mutual glances, less frequent smiling, and displeased mouth movements (Feldman *et al.*, 1978; Knapp *et al.*, 1974; McClintock & Hunt, 1975). Feldman *et al.*, as well as Zuckerman *et al.*, also found that persons engaged in deception showed less general happiness and facial pleasantness, as judged by observers.

The fifth configuration of cues, originally classified by Knapp *et al.* (1974) as indirect responses, shows *underlying vagueness or uncertainty*. Many vagueness and uncertainty cues are linguistic and will be discussed later, but a few nonverbal cues are relevant. One such cue, the hand shrug, a show of helplessness involving turning out of the palms, is an unmonitored behavior that frequently accompanies deceit (Ekman & Friesen, 1972, 1974). Other nonverbal correlates include a less direct body orientation (Exline *et al.*, 1970; Mehrabian, 1971) and the previously mentioned increases in silence and hesitations before speaking. Tangentially related is the Zuckerman *et al.* (1979) finding that observers rate deceptive voices less dominant and assertive than honest voices.

The final category involves incongruous responses, or cues that show *external behavior to be in contradiction with actual feelings*. The few empirically validated cues in this category include momentary facial expressions of negative emotions that may occur with generally pleasant faces (Haggard & Isaacs, 1966) and other simultaneously occurring, contradictory nonverbal cues, such as greater eye contact coupled with increased self-touching or pleasant faces coupled with reticence and anxiety cues (Knapp *et al.*, 1974; McClintock & Hunt, 1975). Cues that have been the subject of conjecture include failure to emphasize remarks with naturally occurring gestures, nonverbal behaviors that are not synchronized with vocal rhythm, and nonverbal messages that are inconsistent with verbal ones.

All of the correlates of deception discussed above are summarized in Table 6.1, where they can be compared to those cues accompanying encoding that are intended to be persuasive and credible.

Behaviors Decoded as Credible or Deceptive

A number of studies have sought to identify nonverbal cues that are interpreted by observers as credible or persuasive. These cues are likely to be used by jurors or judges in assessing credibility of witnesses. Of particular interest is the degree to which the cues match those that are encoded by communicators attempting to be credible and the extent to which they differ from cues accompanying deception.

Most studies show that communicators who are extroverted, involved, positive, and moderately relaxed are perceived as more credible and persuasive, which is the same pattern encoded by communicators seeking to increase their believability. Three studies by Mehrabian and Williams (1969) that required observers to rate the persuasiveness of speakers found higher ratings associated

TABLE 6.1
Nonverbal Correlates of Credibility and Deception

Nonverbal code	Cues encoded as		Cues decoded as	
	Persuasive/credible	Deceptive	Persuasive/credible	Deceptive
Kinesics	More or continuous eye contact	Reduced eye contact (fewer, briefer glances)	More eye contact	Less eye contact
	More affirmative head nods	Fewer head nods		
	More facial activity	Less smiling; less happiness; displeased mouth movements; micromomentary expressions; but more pleasant faces by highly anxious	More facial activity; more involvement	Less seriousness; less empathy; more smiling
	More gestures by women; more rhythmic, forceful gestures	Fewer gestures; fewer illustrators; more hand shrugs	More gestures; more illustrators	Excessive gestures
	Moderate levels of postural relaxation; less trunk swivel by women	Frequent shifts in leg/body position; tense leg and foot positions; less leg and foot movement; leg crossing by males; body blocks; abortive, restless flight movements	Moderate relaxation	More tension and anxiety; more postural shifts
		Physiological indicators: blushing, blinking, shaking, perspiring, dilated or instable pupils		

Proxemics	Smaller reclining angle	Body less directly facing audience Less forward lean Greater distances	Body less directly facing audience for males Closer distances	
Haptics	Fewer adaptor behaviors and self-manipulations; but more self-manipulations with receptive audience	More self-, face-play and object adaptors; longer adaptors	Less self-manipulations and adaptors	Less self-grooming
Vocalics	Higher volume Faster speaking rate More fluency More intonation	Slower or faster speaking rate than normal More nonfluencies Higher pitch More pauses or probe openings More response latency Shorter word duration; shorter speaking time	Higher volume Moderate to slightly faster speaking rate More fluency More intonation and pitch variety Lower pitch More vocal involvement Conversational delivery style	More nonfluencies More response latency
Overall		Contradictions or inconsistencies among nonverbal cues More information from hands and feet than face	Use of General American Dialect Positive violations of expectations (e.g., dressing unappealingly but conveying effective verbal message)	Greater reliance on voice than face and on face than body

with more eye contact, more gestures, more facial activity, less self-touching, moderate relaxation, less direct body orientation for males (facing the audience less squarely), closer distances, higher vocal volume, more intonation, and faster speaking rate. Ekman *et al.* (1976) similarly found more positive evaluations assigned to speakers using fewer long adaptors, more illustrative gestures, and lower pitch; and Zuckerman *et al.* (1979) reported that greater vocal variety and facial activity increased perceptions of honesty.

Regarding vocal cues alone, the majority of studies have reported that greater credibility in general, and specifically, greater honesty, is associated with a conversational delivery, minimal nonfluency, a moderate to slightly rapid speaking rate, lower pitch, and more variety in pitch and intonation (Addington, 1971; Apple, Streeter, & Krauss, 1979; Brown, Strong, & Rencher, 1973, 1974; Lay & Burron, 1968; Miller & Hewgill, 1964; Pearce & Brommel, 1972; Pearce & Conklin, 1971; Sereno & Hawkins, 1967). Faster and slower speaking rates were found to produce gains on some dimensions of credibility but to result in losses on others; higher volume also produced mixed reactions. In general, this research indicates that an animated but not overly intense, anxiety-free presentation generates more positive perceptions of the communicator. In addition, General American Dialect has been found to produce more positive evaluations than regional or foreign dialects (Buck, 1968; Delia, 1972; Giles, 1973; Giles & Powesland, 1975; Mulac, Hanley, & Prigge, 1974; Toomb, Quiggins, Moore, MacNeil, & Liddell, 1972). These findings are also summarized in Table 6.1.

Another area of import to the courtroom concerns the degree to which nonverbal cues create expectations that are violated by other verbal or nonverbal messages. Burgoon (1978; Burgoon, Stacks, & Woodall, 1979) has demonstrated that communicators who are attractive, highly credible, or of high status may actually increase their credibility by violating expectations. In her studies, the distances that people normally adopt were violated by a confederate who sat much closer or much further than the distance another interactant had established. This created messages that were at odds with those being communicated verbally and through other nonverbal channels. In the case of those who moved closer, for instance, the deviation may have communicated greater affection and interest, thereby serving as a positive violation of expectations.

Although manipulation of distance is rarely an available option for witnesses, other nonverbal cues can be varied. One such cue is appearance. For instance, a witness might dress unconventionally, which would probably produce low initial credibility, and then positively violate the expectations of the judge and jurors by offering very coherent, rational testimony. The possible effectiveness of such an unorthodox approach is supported by two studies on the effects of dress on persuasiveness. In the first study (Cooper, Darley, & Henderson, 1974), householders were more convinced about a tax issue by an advocate dressed in hippie garb than by a conventionally dressed advocate. In the second study (McPeek & Edwards, 1975), a long-haired speaker and a seminarian presented the same pro- and antimarijuana speeches to various audiences. The antimarijuana audiences were more persuaded by the unconventional-looking speaker than by the clean-cut seminarian. A plausible interpretation of these effects is that the long-haired speaker's original appearance created negative expectations that were then positively violated by presenting a rational, out-of-character speech. While such a tactic would be risky in a trial setting, the strategic possibilities merit further investigation. Also of interest would be the possibilities for negative violations; for example, an attractive, supposedly competent witness presenting testimony in a halting fashion.

A final area of nonverbal research has focused on those cues observers rely on in making attributions of deceit. Before considering specific cues, we would like to comment on code and region dominance. As noted earlier, most persons place greater trust in nonverbal than verbal cues when the two modes are inconsistent. Among the various nonverbal behaviors, however, the literature suggests contradictory preferences among receivers. On the one hand, most people questioned said they thought the face was more important than the body, and that if they were trying to deceive, they would need to exercise more control over the face (Ekman & Friesen, 1969, 1974). Moreover, under normal circumstances, people are more influenced by facial cues than by vocal ones (Bugental, Kaswan, & Love, 1970; DePaulo, Rosenthal, Eisenstat, Rogers, & Finkelstein, 1978; Mehrabian & Ferris, 1967). But when people are specifically asked to make judgments of truthfulness, they tend to rely more heavily on vocal cues, especially as the discrepancy among the vocal, facial, and verbal messages increases (DePaulo & Rosenthal, cited in Rosenthal & DePaulo, 1979; DePaulo et al., 1978; Krauss et al., 1976; Zuckerman et al., 1979). Thus, while people claim they are more attentive to the face, they actually depend more on the voice to make judgments of veracity. One reasonable explanation for this discrepancy is that when truthfulness is not at issue, the face is more informative and thus more dominant. When deception is a possibility, observers who are aware of their own efforts to monitor and control facial expressions may become more distrustful of facial expressions by others, and shift their focus to auditory cues. Rosenthal and DePaulo (1979) also note that facial cues seem more relevant to judgments of positivity, while vocal cues seem to influence judgments of dominance. Perhaps detection of deception requires going beyond judgments of pleasantness or unpleasantness to evaluate other facets of expression, such as apparent confidence and assertiveness, which are gleaned from vocal patterns. The fact that deceptive faces are seen as less pleasant and deceptive voices as less dominant (Zuckerman et al., 1979) suggests that judges of deception do differentiate between the nonverbal codes on the kind of information conveyed and perceive differences between honest and deceptive presentations.

As for specific cues believed to signal deception, observers are quite stereotypical in their perceptions. When asked what behaviors they look for to ascertain whether someone is lying, a sample of adults said they thought liars would display less eye contact, more tension and nervousness, slower responses to questions, excessive gesturing and swallowing, increased nonfluencies, greater "stiffness," unnatural smiles or "tight" faces, squinting, and adaptor behaviors such as scratching the head (Hocking et al., 1978). Other, more systematic investigations have found that the following cues are perceived as deceptive: less fluency, more hesitations, too rapid or too slow responses, higher pitch levels, less seriousness, less empathy, more nervousness, more smiling, more postural shifts, and less self-grooming (Baskett & Freedle, 1974; Krauss et al., 1976; Kraut, 1978; Streeter et al., 1977).

When these cues, summarized in Table 6.1, are compared to those encoded as deceptive, it becomes evident that observers are looking for indications of anxiety, withdrawal, excess (or deviations from normality), negative affect, uncertainty, and contradictions among cues; in other words, they are generally looking for many of the same cues that are typically encoded by liars. The relatively low levels of accuracy achieved by most observers assessing truthfulness, discussed later in this chapter, are therefore somewhat surprising. In no instances are observers' attributions totally at odds with what is actually encoded. There do appear to be cues, however, that are ignored or possibly misinterpreted by observers. For example, observers seem not to be attentive to the communicative value of head nods; at least, no research has yet uncovered their use of such cues. Nor do they seem to be aware of reduced gesturing, particularly the use of illustrative gestures accompanying speech, as indicating deception. Instead, they expect exaggerated gestures, which may be confused with the more forceful, rhythmic gestures accompanying intended persuasion. Conversely, a relative lack of gestures may be misinterpreted as signaling composure. Facial expressions may also be easily misinterpreted, since only those who are highly anxious exhibit the increased smiling expected by observers and since fleeting expressions of negative affect may go unnoticed by the human eye. As for important vocal cues, observers apparently fail to make use of deviations in speaking rate, increased pitch (fundamental frequency) level, and reduced speaking time as indicators of deception. Finally, the uncertainty introduced by contradictory cues may heighten distraction and ambiguity, leading to inaccurate judgments. Some of these same discrepancies become apparent when considering verbal behaviors that accompany deceit and comparing them to the behaviors attended to by observers seeking to make veracity judgments.

THE CREDIBILITY OF ACTUAL TESTIMONY

Research on language associated with credibility and deceit is not extensive. Fortunately, most of the findings come from investigations already cited so that parallels between verbal and nonverbal cues can be drawn.

In terms of encoding, the dimensions outlined by Knapp et al. (1974) serve as a useful organizing framework. Regarding *anxiety or nervousness*, Knapp et al.

predicted an increase in word and phrase repetitions when people are lying but failed to observe such an increase. Regarding *reticence*, they predicted and confirmed fewer total words, more openings for probes by an interviewer, and a trend toward shorter messages. Kraut (1978) and Mehrabian (1971) also report increased brevity when communicators are engaged in unrehearsed deception. Moreover, Bradac, Bowers, and Courtright (1979), in their review of language immediacy, concluded that immediacy decreases when the communicator is under stress and increases when the communicator likes the person being addressed. In other words, language reflects more remoteness and less involvement with the other when the communicator is under stress. Taken collectively, these findings suggest that immediacy should be reduced when lying.

As far as *vagueness or uncertainty* is concerned, many verbal indicators of lying have been identified: inability to find words to fill time, a more restricted code (such as fewer different words, fewer factual statements, fewer references to the communicator's own personal experiences, fewer references to verifiable past experiences) and more sweeping, leveling, "allness" terms that produce broad generalities (Knapp *et al.*, 1974; Mehrabian, 1971). Meerloo (1978) has also suggested that liars often employ verbal ambiguity and double entendre. The fact that speakers use more verbal reinforcers (e.g., *uh-huh, Right!*) when intending to persuade (Mehrabian & Williams, 1969) suggests that under conditions of low confidence, as would often be the case when there is an attempt to perpetrate deception, fewer such reinforcers might be expected.

In the area of *negative affect*, two indicators of deception have been reported: fewer group references (e.g., *we, our, us*) and more disparaging remarks (Knapp *et al.*, 1974; Todd, 1976). One final dimension relevant to verbal behavior is *dependency*, which refers to communicators' tendencies to disassociate or distance themselves from their own remarks. It includes the following confirmed indices of deceit: more "other" references (e.g., *them, they*), fewer self-interest statements, and a trend toward fewer self-references (Kanpp *et al.*, 1974).

In terms of decoding, Kraut (1978) found that observers judged implausible, inconsistent, and nonconcrete statements to be less truthful. Baskett and Freedle (1974) report that agreeing to socially desirable descriptions of oneself or rejecting highly negative ones was interpreted as evidence of lying. The shortage of research on verbal behaviors judged by observers to be deceptive clearly underscores a need for more activity in this area.

Translating the research on verbal correlates of deception and credibility to the courtroom context, it is evident that lying manifests itself in alterations of witnesses' normal language patterns. Moreover, it would seem that a reasonably attentive juror might become aware of some of these deviations over the course of a trial. Nevertheless, there is little empirical evidence that observers are aware of these behaviors, much less that they use them in attempting to detect deception. Consequently, it is unlikely that these indicators are used effectively by jurors, especially given jurors' lack of familiarity with the typical language patterns of witnesses. This pessimistic conclusion is further substantiated by the research concerning observers' accuracy in detecting deception.

OBSERVER ACCURACY IN DETECTING DECEPTION

Having examined some of the nonverbal, paralinguistic, and verbal behaviors associated with deception, we next consider the question of observer accuracy in detecting deceptive communication. This section centers on two major issues: first, how accurate observers are in detecting deception perpetrated by relative strangers; second, how certain variables, such as the types of cues available to the observer, facilitate or inhibit accurate detection.

Although a substantial literature has accumulated in this area, no available studies correspond closely with the circumstances existing between jurors and witnesses in actual trial settings—thus the term *observer accuracy* rather than *juror accuracy* is used advisedly. Ekman and Friesen (1969) distinguish three varying dimensions of deceptive situations: (*a*) the magnitude of *saliency* of the deception, (*b*) the pattern of adoption of deceptive and detective *roles*, and (*c*) the degree of *antagonism or collaboration* between the parties regarding discovery or maintenance of deception. They argue that convincing deceptive performances should be most difficult to carry off when high saliency exists for both communicator and observer, role asymmetry pertains such that the communicator is cast in the twin roles of deceiving and attempting to determine deceptive success while the observer is cast primarily in the detector role, and an antagonistic relationship exists with the communicator seeking to maintain successful deception and the observer striving to detect it.

The preceding conditions typically hold for instances of deceptive courtroom communication. Salience is high for both witnesses and jurors, since all parties realize that deception is a definite possibility and that high stakes are involved: If witnesses fail to deceive, they may suffer severe legal penalties; if the jury fails to detect deception, its verdict may subvert the goal of justice by conferring unwarranted rewards or punishments on the litigants. While witnesses are cast largely in the deceiver role, they also try to assess the jury's belief in the untruthful testimony. Conversely, the jury primarily plays the detective role, but it may also seek to deceive witnesses regarding its evaluation of the testimony; for example, jurors may minimize or mask their nonverbal responses. Finally, the situation is clearly antagonistic; witnesses try to mislead the jury and the jury tries to spot witnesses' misleading testimony.

By contrast, most studies of detecting deception do not approximate Ekman and Friesen's (1969) maximally challenging conditions for successful falsehood. In particular, the degree of salience is often relatively low for communicator, observer, or both. Several studies have not even required the communicators to lie, but merely to roleplay liars (Maier, 1966; Maier & Janzen, 1967; Maier & Thurber, 1968). Strategies aimed at heightening salience for the communicator/deceiver include stressing the professional advantages of being able to lie successfully, as in the case of nurses (Ekman & Friesen, 1974) and criminal justice students (Hocking, Bauchner, Kaminski, & Miller, 1979; Miller *et al.*, 1981) and stating that ability to deceive is an indicator of social skill and intelligence (Bauchner, Kaplan, & Miller, 1980; Brandt *et al.*, 1980b; Exline *et al.*, 1970; Miller *et al.*, 1981; Shulman, 1973; Streeter *et al.*, 1977). These strategies undoubtedly produce higher salience than roleplaying, but they probably fail to achieve the level of ego involvement generated by lying from the witness stand.

The same reservation can be lodged regarding the observers who have participated in prior studies. Most have been undergraduate students who were told their success in detecting deception would provide evidence of their degree of "interpersonal sensitivity" (Brandt *et al.*, 1980b). In several instances (Bauchner, n.d.; Kraut, 1978), observers have been promised cash rewards for successful deception detection, a procedure calculated to increase salience somewhat while still falling short of the stakes jurors perceive they are playing for in courtroom decision making.

Other procedural details also detract from the courtroom verisimilitude of the typical research setting. Several studies have required communicator/deceivers to lie entirely (Ekman & Friesen, 1974) or partially (Hocking *et al.*, 1979) about their feelings about themselves rather than about factual matters relating to some disputed issue. Not only do attempts to mislead jurors about witnesses' self-feelings occur infrequently—witnesses are seldom asked how they "feel" about something but are instead queried about facts involved in the disputed issue—but, as we shall note shortly, some evidence indicates that optimal conditions for detecting self-feeling deception and factual deception may not coincide.

In addition to low salience, a second limitation in research studies' attempts to simulate the courtroom situation stems from the fact that in striving to eliminate potentially contaminating factors so as to test unambiguously hypotheses dealing with nonverbal behavior, investigators have sometimes relied on observational conditions that depart radically from actual courtroom interaction. For example, some studies have edited the audio portion from deceptive messages (Ekman & Friesen, 1974; Hocking *et al.*, 1978, 1979) thus providing observers with only the nonverbal behaviors of communicator/deceivers, while others have used shots of the body only (Ekman & Friesen, 1974; Hocking *et al.*, 1979; Littlepage & Pineault, 1979) to permit accuracy comparisons with observers given access to the facial cues of deceivers. While all things are possible, it is doubtful that in the foreseeable future jurors will be able to study the nonverbal behaviors of witnesses without also being privy to their spoken words or to observe the testimony of a decapitated witness even though such improbable circumstances might enhance detection of witness deception.

Finally, several studies have involved a different relationship between observers and deceiver/communicators than the one which ordinarily holds between jurors and witnesses in the courtroom. In particular, the previously mentioned roleplaying investigations (Maier, 1966; Maier & Janzen, 1967; Maier & Thurber, 1968) required observers to roleplay a college professor interacting with another person who roleplayed either an honest or a dishonest student. Since the observers engaged in interrogative dialogue with the deceivers, their activities more closely approximated those of an attorney and witness in the trial setting. By contrast, jurors typically function as third parties in the courtroom, observing the communicative give-and-take between witness and attorney and arriving at judgments about the former's veracity on the basis of these observations.

Despite possible threats to validity posed by the kinds of procedural departures from courtroom settings discussed above, research on detecting deceptive communication still yields several cautious generalizations of instructive utility to the trial process. Having underscored the value of a cautious interpretative posture, we now consider these studies in greater detail.

General Degree of Accuracy in Detecting Deception

Most studies dealing with accuracy have scored single judgments of deception dichotomously and then combined scores for a number of observers and/or multiple scores for a single observer to derive a mean accuracy score that can range from .00 (no accurate responses) to 1.00 (all accurate responses). Table 6.2 summarizes the mean accuracy scores for seven studies permitting this kind of analysis of accuracy. For five of the studies, the overall mean accuracy scores tend to group around .50, or about 50% accuracy. In only two studies does overall mean accuracy exceed .60; observers attained a mean accuracy of .64 in the Littlepage and Pineault (1979) study and a mean of .71 in the Maier and Thurber (1968) investigation.

In addition, several studies have used other types of indices to score judgments of veracity. Maier and Janzen (1967) permitted observers to record an uncertain response. In only one of their four conditions do the accuracy scores substantially exceed .50 when the uncertain responses are discarded and only the correct and incorrect ones compared. In a study concerned with pitch changes during attempted deception, Streeter et al. (1977) had observers rate the truthfulness of each response by communicator/deceivers on a scale ranging from one ("not at all truthful") to seven ("completely truthful") and computed a detectability index by subtracting the truthful responses. Inspection of mean detectability indices reveals a reasonably substantial mean in only one of four treatments, indicating that in the other three conditions true and false statements were rated about equally truthful. Finally, while not reporting accuracy scores, Kraut (1978) indicates his observers were moderately accurate in judging whether a communicator/deceiver was lying.

Two other points about accuracy deserve mention. First, in those studies

TABLE 6.2
Mean Accuracy Scores in Detecting Deception for Seven Studies[a]

Study	Major variable(s)	Highest accuracy condition	Lowest accuracy condition	Overall mean accuracy
Bauchner et al., 1977	Mode of presentation (live, video, audio, transcript)	.57	.32	.46
Brandt et al., 1980b	Familiarity with deceiver	.59	.38	.48
Ekman & Friesen, 1974	Shot (head vs. body); Familiarity with deceiver	.63	.42	.49
Fay & Middleton, 1941	Vocal cues	.63	.51	.56
Hocking et al., 1979	Mode of presentation (video, audio, transcript); Shot (head and body vs. head vs. body)	.64	.43	.53[b]
Littlepage & Pineault, 1979	Shot (head vs. body)	.54	.43	.50[c]
		.85	.35	.64
Maier & Thurber, 1968	Mode of presentation (live, audio, transcript)	.77	.58	.71

[a]Single judgments were scored dichotomously (Correct or incorrect) and then summed to derive a mean that could range from .00 to 1.00.
[b]Factual deception.
[c]Self-feeling deception.

where accuracy in judging truthful versus untruthful responses has been compared (Ekman & Friesen, 1974; Littlepage & Pineault, 1979; Maier & Janzen, 1967), observers identify lies somewhat better than truthful behavior. While this may suggest that nonverbal "clues" are more readily spotted when deceptive messages are being sent, the possibility of a lying bias cannot be dismissed; that is, since observers are cued to expect deception, they may lean toward overestimating the number of lies communicated. Such a bias would, of course, inflate the accuracy scores for untruthful messages and suppress the scores for truthful ones.

Second, as would be expected, there are marked individual differences in ability to deceive (Hocking et al., 1979; Kraut, 1978). Some communicators are good liars—almost all their messages, both truthful statements and lies, are judged as truthful. Others are poor liars—almost all their messages, regardless of veracity, are judged as untruthful. These differences underscore the need for careful control of the samples of statements presented to observers in deception studies. At least two approaches to this problem are possible: Researchers can use equal numbers of truthful and untruthful statements for each communicator/deceiver (Hocking et al., 1979), on the assumption that the number of good and poor liars will balance out, or researchers can use previously tested samples for communicator/deceivers that fall near the midpoint of the accuracy range (Brandt, Miller, & Hocking, 1980a).

Notwithstanding possible procedural problems, one particularly crucial conclusion emerges from the studies thus far conducted: *Observers are not very successful in detecting deception perpetrated by relative strangers.* It is not wholly justified to treat dichotomous judgments of truth or falsity as if they conform to a binomial probability distribution, for it is unlikely that persons approach their daily communicative transactions with the assumption that lying and telling the truth are equally probable events. Nevertheless, the fact remains that observers in most prior studies would probably have done as well had they flipped a coin to determine if the communicator/deceivers were lying, particularly since lying and telling the truth occurred with equal frequency in a majority of the studies. To the extent that these findings are generalizable to situations involving assessment of witness veracity, they paint a discouraging picture concerning jurors' ability to make accurate assessments.

Moreover, this picture is further clouded by the propensity of observers to express considerable confidence in their judgment even when they are wrong. Hocking (1976) and Littlepage and Pineault (1979) report that observers were quite confident of most of their veracity judgments even though many were erroneous. Translated to the courtroom environment, this finding raises the specter of jurors evaluating a witness's veracity inaccurately while remaining very certain of the correctness of their evaluations.

Given the substantial body of folklore and conventional wisdom regarding the ways liars reveal themselves by their nonverbal behaviors, what accounts for the apparent lack of observer success in detecting deceptive messages? One possible explanation lies in the view of motivation, or drive, expressed in drive-reduction learning theories (Brown, 1961). This view holds that drive is a generalized energizer which increases the vigor of all competing response tendencies. For complex activities, such as communicating, high drive inhibits task performance; more specifically, it produces the kinds of verbal and nonverbal disruptions stereotypically associated with lying. Increased drive can be triggered by various antecedents, only one of which is knowledge of intent to deceive another. Thus, as mentioned earlier, many behavioral displays that are taken as evidence of lying may actually result from drive-producing factors associated with the person (e.g., communication apprehension or manifest anxiety) or with the situation (e.g., publicly testifying in court about an extremely stressful experience such as a rape). Stated differently, many behaviors thought to signal deceit are precisely those expected of an anxious or strongly motivated witness, and this behavioral correspondence probably results in numerous faulty inferences, or misattributions, of lying.

Effects of Available Facial and Body Cues on Detecting Deception

Ekman and Friesen's (1969, 1974) *leakage hypothesis* posits that the body provides a richer source of useful nonverbal cues for detecting deception than does the face. These theorists reason that people are aware of the necessity to control nonverbal behavior to deceive successfully, but that in seeking to exert such control, they are more conscious of the face than the body. Consequently, in deceptive transactions, the body "leaks" more valuable nonverbal information than the face.

To test this hypothesis Ekman and Friesen (1974) had student nurses either lie or tell the truth about their self-feelings while viewing a segmentalized film stimulus. This stimulus contained pictures of pleasant landscapes and badly disfigured burn victims. Since the nurses always said they were feeling pleasant and relaxed, they consistently told the truth when viewing the landscapes and consistently lied when viewing the burn victims.

Results indicated that observers who saw the nurses' bodies only were more accurate in detecting deception than their counterparts who saw the faces only, but only when observers had first viewed a sample of the deceivers' truthful communication (familiarization manipulation). While differing significantly, the degree of successful detection was not particularly high for observers in either condition: observers in the face/familiar condition had a mean accuracy of .45 as compared with a mean of .56 for those subjected to the body/familiar treatment.

Several limitations of this study prevent generalizing of its findings confidently to the courtroom setting. We have already mentioned that procedures such as eliminating the verbal behavior of communicator/deceivers and showing observers shots of only the body depart markedly from the realm of everyday social transactions. Even more troublesome is the fact that nurses consistently told the truth while viewing pleasant landscapes and lied consistently while viewing burn victims. In terms of the drive-reduction interpretation previously outlined, stressful pictures of burn victims would be likely to trigger anxiety and to culminate in behaviors stereotypically associated with lying. Consequently, the cards seem to be stacked in favor of lying judgments, but it is hard to ascertain whether the nonverbal cues used by observers were occasioned by the communicator/deceivers' knowledge of intent to deceive or by the anxiety they experienced when viewing the unpleasant pictures of burn victims. This interpretative ambiguity is further illustrated by the fact that, when compared to honest conditions, mean accuracy is consistently higher in all the deception conditions employed in the study.

In a study designed to investigate the effects of several variables on detecting deception, Hocking *et al.* (1979) replicated Ekman and Friesen's (1974) findings for self-feeling deception: Observers who viewed only the body of communicator/deceivers were significantly more accurate in detecting deception than observers who viewed the head only or the head and body. For factual lying, however, the outcome was reversed: observers who viewed the head only and the head and body were more accurate than observers who saw the body only. In addition, the analyses for factual lying revealed that observers who also heard the communicator/deceivers' verbal responses were more accurate than those who did not, a finding that bodes well for the actual trial setting. Interestingly, this difference in accuracy ratings for audio and visual as opposed to video only was not observed for self-feeling deception.

To further confuse matters, Littlepage and Pineault (1979) have reported an extended replication of Ekman and Friesen's (1974) results using factual deception and permitting observers to hear the accompanying verbal behavior. Their results showed that the superiority of body cues held only for untruthful statements: Facial cues yielded an accuracy mean of only .35 as compared to a mean of .85 for body shots; for honest statements, the mean was .70 for facial shots and .66 for shots of the body. Littlepage and Pineault also interpret their results to show that prior exposure to the deceivers' truthful behavior is unnecessary for confirmation of the leakage hypothesis, because their observers were not provided with an extensive sample of truthful responses. It should be noted, however, that all communicator/deceivers were first required to state their names truthfully, and while admittedly limited, this procedure ensured observers of an initial sample of truthful behavior.

What conclusions germane to juror assessment of witness veracity can be drawn from these conflicting findings? Encouragingly, the results of both the Hocking et al. (1979) and Littlepage and Pineault (1979) studies regarding factual lying suggest that accuracy of detection is not adversely affected, and may in fact be enhanced, by including the verbal responses of witnesses. Concerning the possible superiority of nonverbal body cues as helpful indicators of deception, the findings, though mixed, lend some credence to the leakage hypothesis. If this hypothesis is tenable, it underscores two pragmatic issues associated with the trial setting: First, it may be difficult for jurors to focus on the body at the expense of the face, even if instructed to do so; second, the design and construction of many witness stands prevents jurors from observing those body cues considered essential for accurate assessment of witness veracity.

Effects of Mode of Presentation on Detecting Deception

The question of possible influences of the mode of presenting testimony on detection accuracy also concerns the kinds of cues available to jurors. Conceivably, testimony can be presented live, on color or monochromatic videotape, by means of audiotape, or via written transcript. When moving along the continuum from live testimony to written transcript, an increasing amount of nonverbal and paralinguistic (i.e., vocalic) information is filtered from the message. Research dealing with the mode of presentation seeks to determine whether this filtering process systematically affects the success of observers in detecting deceptive communication.

In one of the earliest studies dealing with this issue, Fay and Middleton (1941) examined how well observers could detect deception in messages presented over a public address system. As Table 6.2 indicates, observers were only moderately successful, with mean accuracy ranging from .51 to .63. Unfortunately, this study provides limited information, since the public address system was not compared with other presentational alternatives.

Maier and Thurber (1968) report higher mean detection accuracy when observers listened to (.77) or read (.77) an interview containing deceptive responses rather than watching it live (.58). They concluded that visual cues supplied by communicator/deceivers are distractors, not helpful aids. In addition, their discussion ends with the following observation which pertains directly to the trial setting.

> Juries are composed of untrained observers and often must make judgments about the integrity of a witness. The witness is always present and, as these results suggest, may serve as a distractor. It is therefore not surprising that decisions of higher courts, in which the testimony is read, might well reverse decisions of a lower court. . . . It is also interesting to note that the symbol of justice stands with a sword in her right hand, a pair of balance scales in her left, and a blindfold over her eyes—she can only hear [p. 30]!

To date, the most extensive investigation of the effects of mode of presentation on detection accuracy has occurred in the context of a larger research project dealing with the impact of videotaped trials and depositions on juror information processing and decision making (Miller & Fontes, 1979). Hocking et al. (1979) found no evidence that mode of presentation affected observers' abilities to detect deceptive testimony. Indeed, though not differing significantly, mean accuracy in detecting factual deception was as high or higher for those modes providing limited nonverbal and paralinguistic information (transcript = .62; audio = .61) than for modes providing richer configurations of nonverbal cues (monochromatic videotape = .57; color videotape = .61). In a second study comparing live, video, audio, and transcript modes; Bauchner et al. (1977) observed no significant differences in detection accuracy, although the mean for the live mode (.57) was the highest of the four modes. For both these studies, the power associated with all tests exceeded .80, suggesting that the likelihood of Type II error was low.

Finally, Bauchner et al. (1980) examined the effects of the availability and use of nonverbal information on detection of deception. As anticipated, trained coders estimated the amount of nonverbal and total information available in various modes in the following descending order: live, video, audio, and transcript. Untrained observers were then exposed to one of the four modes, made judgments of veracity, and estimated the amount of nonverbal and total information used in making these judgments. Path analysis revealed that available and used information were both inadequate predictors of judgmental accuracy:

The paths from available/used nonverbal and total information were not significant, and the variance explained was negligible ($R^2 = .01$; $R^2 = .04$). Analysis of variance also produced no significant differences in detection accuracy among the four presentational modes.

In general, then, it appears that the greater access to nonverbal cues afforded by some presentational modes does not enhance detection accuracy; in fact, some evidence suggests that elimination of such cues actually leads to greater accuracy. This conclusion should be interpreted in light of the finding that success at detecting falsehoods is only moderate regardless of the presentational mode employed. Indeed, it appears that much of the conventional wisdom about the skill of observers in detecting deception on the part of relative strangers, as well as the strongly held assumptions about the vital role of nonverbal communication in this process, should be viewed cautiously, if not with outright skepticism.

Two additional points concerning deception detection in courtroom trials impose additional limitations on the studies reviewed. First, almost all studies to date have examined veracity judgments rendered independently by individuals. During jury deliberation, jurors have an opportunity to exchange opinions about the veracity of witnesses. It is interesting to note that Maier and Lavrakas (1976) found that group judgments tended to be more suspicious than individual evaluations. Second, few of the studies have allowed communicator/deceivers to rehearse deceptive messages. Since it is doubtful that much perjured testimony occurs on the spur of the moment, future research might well examine the influence of rehearsal on observers' ability to detect deception.

SUMMARY

The research reviewed in this chapter has suggested several potentially useful generalizations about factors influencing perceptions of witness credibility:

1. *Certain patterns of nonverbal and vocal cues are somewhat systematically associated with deceptive communication.* Included among these cues are behaviors symptomatic of underlying anxiety and of reticence or withdrawal, excessive behaviors that deviate from a communicator's normal response patterns, behaviors signaling negative affect, behaviors indicative of vagueness or uncertainty, and incongruous responses suggesting that external behavior contradicts actual feelings.
2. *When asked to report those nonverbal cues that signal deceptive messages, observers mention many of the actual behaviors associated with deceptive encoding.* This finding suggests that observer difficulty in detecting deception stems primarily from inability to detect or to interpret nonverbal cues, rather than from ignorance of or misinformation about the cues themselves.

3. *Despite knowledge of relevant cues, observers are not notably successful in detecting deception perpetrated by relative strangers.* In attempting to determine whether a communicator was lying or telling the truth, observers in most studies were right about half the time. Furthermore, when messages were presented via different modes that transmit varying amounts of nonverbal and vocalic behavior, there was no evidence to indicate that success in detecting deception was positively related to the amount of available nonverbal information. Indeed, there was some indication that observers were most successful when nonverbal information was minimal, as when they were asked to base veracity judgments on examination of a written transcript.

We offer these generalizations cautiously for two reasons: First, because little extant research has occurred in the confines of actual courtrooms; second, because most available research focuses on one or two strands of the complex fabric of social perceptions that constitute jurors' and judges' evaluations of witnesses. To tread cautiously is not to negate the value of present findings; some empirical evidence is certainly better than none. Still, many unanswered questions remain; indeed, the scientific jury will be required to remain out for some time to come if it hopes to return a confident verdict on the issue of factors affecting the assessment of witness credibility.

REFERENCES

Addington, D. W. The effect of vocal variations on ratings of source credibility. *Speech Monographs,* 1971, *38,* 242–247.

Apple, W., Streeter, L. A., & Krauss, R. M. Effects of pitch and speech rate on personal attributions. *Journal of Personality and Social Psychology,* 1979, 37, 715–727.

Argyle, M., Alkema, F., & Gilmour, R. The communication of friendly and hostile attitudes by verbal and non-verbal signals. *European Journal of Social Psychology,* 1971, *1,* 385–402.

Baskett, G., & Freedle, R. O. Aspects of language pragmatics and the social perception of lying. *Journal of Psycholinguistic Research,* 1974, 3, 112–131.

Bauchner, J. E. *The effects of familiarity on observers' abilities to detect deception.* Unpublished doctoral dissertation in progress, Michigan State University, (n.d.).

Bauchner, J. E., Brandt, D. R., & Miller, G. R. The truth-deception attribution: Effects of varying levels of information availability. In B. D. Ruben (Ed.), *Communication yearbook I.* New Brunswick, New Jersey: Transaction Books, 1977.

Bauchner, J. E., Kaplan, E. P., & Miller, G. R. Detecting deception: The relationship of available information to judgmental accuracy in initial encounters. *Human Communication Research,* 1980, *6,* 251–264.

Berlo, D. K., Lemert, J. B., & Mertz, R. J. Dimensions for evaluating the acceptability of message sources. *Public Opinion Quarterly,* 1969–1970, *33,* 563–576.

Berrien, F., & Huntington, G. An exploratory study of pupillary responses during deception. *Journal of Experimental Psychology,* 1943, *32,* 443–449.

Bradac, J. J., Bowers, J. W., & Courtright, J. A. Three language variables in communication research: Intensity, immediacy, and diversity. *Human Communication Research,* 1979, *5,* 257–269.

Brandt, D. R., Miller, G. R., & Hocking, J. E. Effects of self-monitoring and familiarity on deception detection. *Communication Quarterly*, 1980, *28*, 3−10. (a)

Brandt, D. R., Miller, G. R., & Hocking, J. E. The truth-deception attribution: Effects of familiarity on the ability of observers to detect deception. *Human Communication Research*, 1980, *6*, 99−110. (b)

Brown, B. L., Strong, W. J., & Rencher, A. C. Perceptions of personality from speech: Effects of manipulations of acoustical parameters. *Journal of the Acoustical Society of America*, 1973, *54*, 29−33.

Brown, B. L., Strong, W. J., & Rencher, A. C. Fifty-four voices from two: The effects of simultaneous manipulations of rate, mean fundamental frequency and variance of fundamental frequency on ratings of personality from speech. *Journal of the Acoustical Society of America*, 1974, *55*, 313−318.

Brown, J. S. *The motivation of behavior.* New York: McGraw-Hill, 1961.

Buck, J. F. The effects of negro and white dialectical variations upon attitudes of college students. *Speech Monographs*, 1968, *35*, 181−186.

Bugental, D. E. Interpretations of naturally occurring discrepancies between words and intonation: Modes of inconsistency resolution. *Journal of Personality and Social Psychology*, 1974, *30*, 125−133.

Bugental, D. E., Kaswan, J. W., & Love, L. R. Perception of contradictory meanings conveyed by verbal and nonverbal channels. *Journal of Personality and Social Psychology*, 1970, *16*, 647−655.

Burgoon, J. K. A communication model of personal space violations: Explication and an initial test. *Human Communication Research*, 1978, *4*, 129−142.

Burgoon, J. K., Stacks, D. W., & Woodall, W. G. A communicative model of violations of distancing expectations. *Western Journal of Speech Communication*, 1979, *43*, 153−167.

Clark, W. R. *A comparison of pupillary response, heart rate, and GSR during deception.* Paper presented at the meeting of the Midwestern Psychological Association, Chicago, April 1975.

Cooper, J., Darley, J. M., & Henderson, J. E. On the effectiveness of deviant- and conventional-appearing communicators. *Journal of Personality and Social Psychology*, 1974, *29*, 752−757.

Cronkhite, G., & Liska, J. A critique of factor analytic approaches to the study of credibility. *Communication Monographs*, 1976, *43*, 91−107.

Cutrow, R. J., Parks, A., Lucas, N., & Thomas, K. The objective use of multiple physiological indices in the detection of deception. *Psychophysiology*, 1972, *9*, 578−588.

Delia, J. G. Dialects and the effects of stereotypes on impression formation. *Quarterly Journal of Speech*, 1972, *58*, 285−297.

DePaulo, B. M., Rosenthal, R., Eisenstat, R. A., Rogers, P. L., & Finkelstein, S. Decoding discrepant nonverbal cues. *Journal of Personality and Social Psychology*, 1978, *36*, 313−323.

Ekman, P., & Friesen, W. V. Nonverbal leakage and clues to deception. *Psychiatry*, 1969, *32*, 88−106.

Ekman, P., & Friesen, W. V. Hand movements and deception. *Journal of Communication*, 1972, *22*, 353−374.

Ekman, P., & Friesen, W. V. Detecting deception from the body or face. *Journal of Personality and Social Psychology*, 1974, *29*, 288−298.

Ekman, P., & Friesen, W. V. *Unmasking the face.* Englewood Cliffs, New Jersey: Prentice-Hall, 1975.

Ekman, P., Friesen, W. V., & Scherer, K. R. Body movement and voice pitch in deceptive interaction. *Semiotica*, 1976, *16*, 23−27.

English, H. Reaction-time symptoms of deception. *American Journal of Psychology*, 1926, *37*, 428−429.

Exline, R., Thibaut, J., Hickey, C., & Gumpert, P. Visual interaction in relation to Machiavellianism and an unethical act. In R. Christie and F. L. Geis (Eds.), *Studies in Machiavellianism.* New York: Academic Press, 1970.

Fay, P. J., & Middleton, W. C. The ability to judge truthtelling or lying from the voice as transmitted over a public address system. *Journal of General Psychology*, 1941, *24*, 211−215.

Feldman, R. S., Devin-Sheehan, L., & Allen, V. L. Nonverbal cues as indicators of verbal dissembling. *American Educational Research Journal*, 1978, *15*, 217−231.

Giles, H. Communication effectiveness as a function of accented speech. *Speech Monographs*, 1973, *40*, 330−331.

Giles, H., & Powesland, P. F. *Speech style and social evaluation*. New York: Academic Press, 1975.

Goldstein, E. Reaction times and the consciousness of deception. *American Journal of Psychology*, 1923, *34*, 562−581.

Haggard, E., & Isaacs, K. Micromomentary facial expressions as indicators of ego mechanisms in psychotherapy. In L. Gottschalk and A. Auerbach (Eds.), *Methods of research in psychotherapy*. New York: Appleton, 1966.

Heilveil, I. Deception and pupil size. *Journal of Clinical Psychology*, 1976, *32*, 675−676.

Hocking, J. E. *Detecting deceptive communication from verbal, visual, and paralinguistic cues: An exploratory experiment*. Unpublished doctoral dissertation, Michigan State University, 1976.

Hocking, J. E., Bauchner, J. E., Kaminski, E. P., & Miller, G. R. Detecting deceptive communication from verbal, visual, and paralinguistic cues. *Human Communication Research*, 1979, *6*, 33−46.

Hocking J. E., Miller, G. R., & Fontes, N. E. Videotape in the courtroom: Witness deception. *Trial*, 1978, *14*, 52−55.

Knapp, M. L., Hart, R. P, & Dennis, H. S. An exploration of deception as a communication construct. *Human Communication Research*, 1974, *1*, 15−29.

Krauss, R. M., Geller, V., & Olson, C. *Modalities and cues in the detection of deception*. Paper presented at the meeting of the American Psychological Association, Washington, D.C., August 1976.

Kraut, R. E. Verbal and nonverbal cues in the perception of lying. *Journal of Personality and Social Psychology*, 1978, *36*, 380−391.

Lay, C. H., & Burron, B. F. Perception of the personality of the distant speaker. *Perceptual and Motor Skills*, 1968, *26*, 951−956.

Littlepage, G. E., & Pineault, M. A. Detection of deceptive factual statements from the body and the face. *Personality and Social Psychology Bulletin*, 1979, *5*, 325−328.

McClintock, C., & Hunt, R. Nonverbal indicators of affect and deception in an interview setting. *Journal of Applied Social Psychology*, 1975, *5*, 54−67.

McCroskey, J. C. Scales for the measurement of *ethos*. *Speech Monographs*, 1966, *33*, 65−72.

McPeek, R. W., & Edwards, J. D. Expectancy disconfirmation and attitude change. *Journal of Social Psychology*, 1975, *96*, 193−208.

Maier, N. R. F. Sensitivity to attempts at deception in an interview situation. *Personnel Psychology*, 1966, *19*, 55−65.

Maier, N. R. F., & Janzen, J. The reliability of persons making judgments of honesty and dishonesty. *Perceptual and Motor Skills*, 1967, *25*, 141−151.

Maier, N. R. F., & Thurber, J. A. Accuracy of judgments of deception when an interview is watched, heard, and read. *Personnel Psychology*, 1968, *21*, 23−30.

Maier, R. A., & Lavrakas, P. J. Lying behavior and evaluation of lies. *Perceptual and Motor Skills*, 1976, *42*, 575−581.

Marston, W. M. Reaction-time symptoms of deception. *Journal of Experimental Psychology*, 1920, *3*, 72−87.

Maslow, C., Yoselson, K., & London, H. Persuasiveness of confidence expressed via language and body language. *British Journal of Social and Clinical Psychology*, 1971, *10*, 234−240.

Matarazzo, J., Wiens, A., Jackson, R., & Manaugh, T. Interviewer speech behavior under conditions of endogenously present and exogenously-induced motivational states. *Journal of Clinical Psychology*, 1970, *26*, 141−148.

Meerloo, J. A. Camouflage versus communication: In the beginning was the lie. *Communication*, 1978, *3*, 45.

Mehrabian, A. Nonverbal betrayal of feeling. *Journal of Experimental Research in Personality*, 1971, *5*, 64−73.

Mehrabian, A. *Nonverbal communication.* Chicago: Aldine-Atherton, 1972.

Mehrabian, A., & Ferris, S. L. Inference of attitudes from nonverbal communication in two channels. *Journal of Consulting Psychology,* 1967, *31,* 248–252.

Mehrabian, A., & Wiener, M. Decoding of inconsistent communications. *Journal of Personality and Social Psychology,* 1967, *6,* 108–114.

Mehrabian, A., & Williams, M. Nonverbal concomitants of perceived and intended persuasiveness. *Journal of Personality and Social Psychology,* 1969, *13,* 37–58.

Miller, G. R., Bauchner, J. E., Hocking, J. E., Fontes, N. E., Kaminski, E. P., & Brandt, D. R. ". . . And nothing but the truth": How well can observers detect deceptive testimony? In B. D. Sales (Ed.), *The trial process.* New York: Plenum, 1981.

Miller, G. R., & Boster, F. J. Three images of the trial: Their implications for psychological research. In B. D. Sales (Ed.), *Psychology in the legal process.* New York: Spectrum, 1977.

Miller, G. R., & Fontes, N. E. *Videotape on trial: A view from the jury box.* Beverly Hills, California: Sage Publications, 1979.

Miller, G. R., & Hewgill, M. A. The effect of variations in nonfluency on audience ratings of source credibility. *Quarterly Journal of Speech,* 1964, *50,* 36–44.

Motley, M. Acoustic correlates of lies. *Western Speech,* 1974, *38,* 81–87.

Mulac, A., Hanley, T. D., & Prigge, D. Y. Effects of phonological speech foreignness upon three dimensions of attitude of selected American speakers. *Quarterly Journal of Speech,* 1974, *60,* 411–420.

Pearce, W. B., & Brommel, B. J. The effect of vocal variations on ratings of source credibility. *Quarterly Journal of Speech,* 1972, *58,* 298–306.

Pearce, W. B., & Conklin, F. Nonverbal vocalic communication and the perception of a speaker. *Speech Monographs,* 1971, *38,* 235–241.

Rosenthal, R., & DePaulo, B. M. Expectancies, discrepancies, and courtesies in nonverbal communication. *Western Journal of Speech Communication,* 1979, *43,* 76–95.

Sereno, K. K., & Hawkins, G. J. The effects of variations in speakers' nonfluency upon audience ratings of attitude change toward the speech topic and speakers' credibility. *Speech Monographs,* 1967, *34,* 58–64.

Shulman, G. *An experimental study of the effects of receiver sex, communicator sex, and warning on the ability of receivers to detect deception.* Unpublished masters thesis, Purdue University, Indiana, 1973.

Streeter, L. A., Krauss, R. M., Geller, V., Olson, C., & Apple, W. Pitch changes during attempted deception. *Journal of Personality and Social Psychology,* 1977, *35,* 345–350.

Timney, B., & London, H. Body language concomitants of persuasiveness and persuasibility in dyadic interaction. *International Journal of Group Tensions,* 1973, *3–4,* 48–67.

Todd, W. B. *Linguistic indices of deception as manifested by women: A content analytic study.* Unpublished doctoral dissertation, Florida State University, 1976.

Toomb, J. K., Quiggins, J. G., Moore, D. L., MacNeil, L. B., & Liddell, C. M. *The effects of regional dialects on initial source credibility.* Paper presented at the meeting of the International Communication Association, Atlanta, April 1972.

Whitehead, J. L. Factors of source credibility. *Quarterly Journal of Speech,* 1968, *54,* 59–63.

Zuckerman, M., DeFrank, R. S., Hall, J. A., Larrance, D. T., & Rosenthal, R. Facial and vocal cues of deception and honesty. *Journal of Experimental Social Psychology,* 1979, *15,* 378–396.

COURTROOM DECISION MAKERS

chapter

Cognitive Processes in the Individual Juror

Martin F. Kaplan

Reference to the cognitive functioning of the individual juror encompasses a broad spectrum of jury phenomena. Questions of cognitive processes leading to the formation of a judgment are not easily separable from any question or issue relating to the jury. Indeed, almost every chapter in this volume can be considered a different look at the various influences on the juror's cognitive processes.

197

THE PSYCHOLOGY
OF THE COURTROOM

Copyright © 1982 by Academic Press, Inc.
All rights of reproduction in any form reserved.
ISBN: 0-12-404920-6

Moreover, treating juries as groups does not evade the question of the individual's cognitive activity. Whatever the group input, pressures, or interactions, the individual must ultimately reach a personal verdict. The jury, in the last analysis, is a collection of individuals, and the "group decision" is a compilation of individual votes.

Naturally, no single treatment of the juror can hope to address all theoretical and empirical issues, nor discuss all influences on the juror's cognition. This chapter will be limited to two general themes. First, an account of the cognitive processes involved in judgment formation will be described, with the aim of providing a unitary and inclusive model of judgment. Second, some of the major influences on juror judgment will be discussed and, where reasonable, related to the judgment model. To avoid repetition of other chapters in this volume, and in keeping with the traditional treatment of individual juror factors, empirical discussion will be limited to those personal and situational factors that promote individual differences between jurors, or more specifically, that result in juror bias.

To view the juror's judgment as a cognitive activity does not preclude looking at emotional considerations (see, for example, emotion as a product of drive reduction [Mitchell & Byrne, 1973]). But the verdict is a cognitive response: belief in guilt or innocence, or in civil responsibility. And the major source of the response is cognitive information: testimonial evidence. Evidential and nonevidential information is apprehended by the juror in the courtroom, in the jury room, and (unfortunate, but true) prior to the trial. The juror must evaluate the information with respect to the merits of the case (e.g., what a given piece of testimony tells about the defendant's guilt), determine the contribution each piece should make to the judgment, and then put the pieces together into a unitary judgment. This process of information evaluation, weighing, and integration is central to understanding the juror's cognition, and will serve here as the framework for organizing discussion of the factors that influence judgment.

Why this concern with cognitive processes? Why not simply enumerate the various influences on courtroom decisions along with suggestions for avoiding undesirable influences? Because if social psychologists are to contribute to the legal area uniquely as psychologists, the contribution should be made through both their methodological expertise and, more importantly, their knowledge of psychological processes. It is not enough to show how a case is helped or hurt by given events or juror characteristics. Instead, the social psychologist should be capable of relating courtroom behavior to broader aspects of judgmental functioning. In this chapter, an effort will be made to understand the individual juror's cognition in terms of more general models of judgment.

Information integration theory (Anderson, 1974) is a model of human judgment that may conceptually unite the various elements involved in the juror's evaluation, weighing, and combining of evidential and nonevidential information (Kaplan, 1977b; Kaplan & Scherching, 1980, 1981; Kaplan, Steindorf, & Iervolino, 1978). Before considering the elements which affect the individual juror, a brief account of the information integration theory approach to judgment is in order.

THE PROCESS OF JUDGMENT FORMATION

A judgment is an evaluation of some object with regard to some criterion dimension. For example, a defendant may be judged with regard to guilt, or culpability for some proscribed act. Any judgment may be based on some set of belief's about the object which are experientially relevant to the criterion dimension, and which are salient at the time of judgment. For example, a juror may hold beliefs about the defendant's motives, opportunities, or capabilities for the act in question. In turn, each belief, or piece of information, has itself an evaluative aspect, which represents its evaluation on the dimension. This evaluative component is termed the *scale value* of the belief—its quantitative position on the judgment dimension. Accordingly, the belief that the defendant hated the victim of a shooting may have a high scale value for guiltiness, while the belief that his lack of knowledge about, and access to guns may have a low scale value. In courtroom proceedings, scale values would be provided by testimony and evidence content.

All beliefs do not contribute equally to judgment. Knowledge about a driver's carelessness and neglect, for example, contributes more to judgments of traffic felony charges than does information about the driver's personal characteristics (Kaplan & Kemmerick, 1974). The extent to which any piece of information will affect the ultimate judgment is measured by the information's weight. As is true in forming any judgment from a number of bits of evidence, the weight of any given information would be a function of its reliability and validity. Reliability in courtroom proceedings would be affected by such factors as witness credibility, likelihood of events, and logical consistency of evidence, while validity would rely on the relevance of a particular bit of knowledge to the judgment to be made.

Judgment of an object requires *integration* of the weighted scale values of the various pieces of information by means of some combinational rule. The algebraic function of the rule is an empirical question, and may differ from one sort of judgment to another. For example, choosing between conflicting goals should necessitate subtraction of conflicting elements, predicting achievement should require multiplication of motivation and ability, and reconciling discrepancies in the same person may evoke averaging (see Anderson, 1974, for further examples). In most cases, however, where several informational stimuli are present and a single response must be given (as in the juror's task), an averaging rule seems to best describe the combination of weighted scale values. We will later see that the averaging rule has important implications for juror bias and for determining effects of deliberation.

One more element requires attention: the *initial impression.* Formally, this refers to the evaluative response to the object prior to, and aside from, presentation of stimulus information. For those interested in jury phenomena, the initial impression is easily recognizable as those juror biases that may arise before, and exist apart from, presentation of evidence in court. Such bias has a scale value and weight, and is averaged with the weighted scale values of the evidence-induced beliefs.

To illustrate the initial impression and its role in judgment, consider the following analogue. Suppose you are asked to mechanically reach a judgment by averaging a series of numbers, each representing the scale value for guilt appearance of a single piece of evidence. For ease of calculation, assume the values have equal weight. With paper and pencil you calculate the average to be 6.3 on a 10-point scale, but now you check your calculations with a desk calculator. After correctly entering the figures, adding and then dividing by n, you find the calculator mean to be 5.8. Why is the mean "judgment" different from that predicted by the incorporated scale values? A good bet is that you will find, upon questioning previous users of the calculator, that some value, in this case one that is lower than the mean of the entered series, was left in the register and was averaged with the evidence scale value. In your enthusiasm to reach a "judgment," you neglected to clear the machine.

Philosophical and anthropomorphic implications aside, people are like uncleared calculators. We may ask them to clear their registers (as in admonishments to lay biases aside) but, unlike calculators, there is no sure way with human beings, short of lobotomy, to totally clear the memory of past experience and prejudgments. This residue of past experience, or predisposition, is the initial impression, and is averaged into the final judgment product. One goal of the "fair and impartial trial," or more generally, "objective" judgment, is to minimize the weight or contribution of this residue.

This brief account of judgment formation can be summarized as follows: The person apprehends knowledge or information about the object in the form of beliefs about events. These beliefs are each evaluated with reference to the necessary judgment (scale value assignment) and are compared for relative importance for that judgment (weighting). The separate evaluations are then averaged, each weighted by its' importance, into a unitary judgment, which also includes an initial impression value with some degree of importance.

In the remaining sections of this chapter, we shall examine some elements of judicial proceedings (admissible and inadmissible evidence, juror bias, deliberation, legal norms) as they relate to cognitive processes in the juror. Some elements (e.g., witness credibility) will not be addressed at great length since they receive extended coverage elsewhere in this volume.

THE JUROR'S CONTRIBUTION TO THE JUDGMENT

Few would assert that the juror's mind is a tabula rasa, merely registering and reflecting courtroom evidence. Rather, jurors integrate into their judgment elements aside from the implications of the evidence for the verdict. These elements typically represent *bias* in the juror in that they contribute extralegal influences beyond the weight of evidence fairly presented in court. A number of sources of biasing have been noted in the literature; here we shall consider personal biases, biases induced by trial conditions, biases induced prior to the trial (i.e., pretrial publicity), effects of inadmissible evidence, and bias due to defendant characteristics. In each instance, it is abundantly clear that each source affects judgment to some degree; what is less clear is the *extent* to which bias contributes to the ultimate verdict when integrated with legally admissible evidence. Each source shall now be considered in turn.

Personal Biases

Unless jurors have been raised in a barrel they have some general conception regarding the likelihood of guilt of any accused, or of responsibility of plaintiff and defendant in civil proceedings. In other words, the juror brings to the trial a presumption of guilt or innocence, or of responsibility. Preexisting biases of two sorts have been generally investigated. The first consists of biases specific to the issue, as for example, a bias against ethnic minorities, or large corporations. The second is a more general outlook or philosophy, such as a bias in favor of injured parties, or a presumption of guilt of any indicted defendant. Since the second sort of bias exists as a general and internal disposition, it may be considered a personality trait.

Personality biases have been well documented, both in judges and jurors. Extensive differences between judges have been documented, both in acquittal rate and sentencing tendencies (see Simon & Oster, 1973, for a striking demonstration) but surprisingly, studies have failed to relate these differences to traditional personality variables (Saks & Hastie, 1978). One of the earliest systematic observations of consistent differences among judges in their leniency or stringency is credited to Gaudet (1938), who failed to uncover any relationship between sentencing and length of experience, local economic conditions, and other demographic variables. Subsequent studies, however, have produced some sporadic evidence for effects of background on judge performance. Pritchett (1948) observed consistent patterns of voting in the Roosevelt Supreme Court in civil and labor cases. Unfortunately, due to the narrow range in the backgrounds of the justices, no attempt was made to relate voting patterns to personal background. Instead, Pritchett invested each judge with a philosophy of "political jurisprudence" to account for consistencies in adopted positions. Similarly, Grossman and Tanenhaus (1969), based on informal data, observed that judges' decisions are affected by political and social backgrounds, and by their role expectations. More solid data is reported in Nagel's (1962) classic study of state and federal supreme court justices. As did Pritchett, Nagel found that length of experience was unrelated to tendencies to favor one side or another in appellate reviews. But, in criminal, injury, and business regulation cases, liberal tendencies (i.e., tendency to side more with the defense in criminal cases, with the injured party in civil cases, or against the business in regulation cases) were associated with political, religious, ethnic, and other variables. More liberal voting could be expected from judges who were from low-income backgrounds, or were Democrats, Catholics, non-American Bar Association members, persons who had not previously served as prosecutors, and attitudinal liberals than from judges who were not. Stecher (1977) replicated the effect of political differences in a study of the New York State Supreme Court. On the other side of the ledger, however, Steinberg (1977), in a study of the tendency of the judges of the New York Court of Appeals to vote with or against "disadvantaged" parties, could find no effects for party affiliation, religion, age, or law school attended (See Champagne and Nagel, Chapter 9, this volume for a more extensive review.)

In sum, background and personal factors probably do exert some sort of philosophical effect on judges' decisions (it would seriously jar our intuition were this not the case), but evidence of specific effects is thus far limited to demographic and group membership factors and is not found for personality variables. Moreover, the manifestation of a judge's propensities may be limited to specific types of cases, and to cases which are less clear-cut.

With respect to jurors, general personality variables have been observed to relate systematically to prejudgmental biases. Survey evidence has linked personal dispositions toward stringency with willingness to be on capital trial juries and favorable attitudes toward the death penalty. For example, persons willing to serve on juries trying capital cases are more conservative, compared to liberal (Crosson, 1968); more authoritarian, compared to egalitarian (Boehm, 1968); and are more stringent in attitudes toward punishing criminals and toward law enforcement (Thayer, 1970). Moreover, persons favoring capital punishment are more prone to convict, besides being politically conservative and authoritarian (Jurow, 1971). This "syndrome" of authoritarianism, punitiveness, and greater tendency to convict carries over to experimental work with simulated juries. Authoritarians in studies are more conviction-prone (Bray & Noble, 1978), are found to be more punitive (Bray & Noble, 1978; Mitchell & Byrne, 1973) and more attentive to extralegal factors (Mitchell & Byrne, 1973). Similarly, conservatives (Nemeth & Sosis, 1973) and dogmatics (Hatton, Snortum, & Oskamp, 1971; Rokeach & McLellan, 1969–1970) appear harsher in sentencing than do their opposites. Finally, jurors with stern attitudes toward punishment of criminals report both greater certainty of guilt and harsher sentences in simulated cases (Kaplan, 1977b; Kaplan & Schersching, 1980; Kaplan & Miller, 1978).

Research on personality determinants of bias has centered on the related variables of authoritarianism, conservatism, and dogmatism, probably because the intuitive connection to juridical decisions is so strong. It would be interesting for future research to investigate other cognitive personality variables with less obvious bearing on jury proceedings. For example, tolerance for ambiguity might interact with clarity of trial evidence in determining the effect of extralegal information (e.g., pretrial publicity, inadmissible evidence). A person who is intolerant of ambiguity may be more likely to turn to proscribed information to reach a decision rather than using the ambiguous legally relevant evidence. Those personality variables which act to bias judgment may be largely exerting their effect by determining the value of the initial impression described earlier in this chapter. Recognizing that judgment is a joint function of the initial impression and the information at hand, it is a serious shortcoming that few studies have sought to investigate the interaction of personality-based bias and characteristics of the trial information. If initial impression and trial information are averaged, with each contributing according to its relative weight, then a necessary step is to determine the weighting or informational conditions under which bias will *not* contribute to the judgment. That is, we should not be left with the idea that any source of bias (e.g., authoritarianism) contributes to judgment equally across the board. In principle, the contribution of a bias should not be evident in all cases, but should vary with the contribution of trial evidence.

We have seen evidence bearing on two forms of biases: specific and general. Both have in common that they are internal predispositions and are, presumably, relatively stable over time, although their stability across stiuations and cases is open to question. The qualities of internality, temporal stability, and generality across measures qualifies these biases as *traits*, or stable predispositions to respond in certain ways. Personality research often identifies another sort of predisposition, namely, *states*. These are transient predispositions, instilled by strong situational demands. For example, we can speak of anxiety as a trait produced by personal history that is at relatively constant levels over time, or as a state produced by a strong current threat (Spielberger, 1972).

An illustration of a juror state familiar to many may be found in the Patty Hearst trial (1976), where jurors reported great displeasure with the dramatic and overbearing deportment of her attorney, F. Lee Bailey; in the end, Patty Hearst did not fare well in their verdicts. On the other hand, jurors in the Chicago 7 conspiracy trial (1969) also reported negative states as a consequence of trial conditions, but here the discomfort may have been due, in part, to the trial judge. The defendants here fared a bit better than did Patty Hearst. Of course, these are informal observations, and it cannot be determined whether the outcomes were due to state dispositions and their association or lack of association with the defendant, or to strength of prosecution evidence.

A more controlled demonstration of state dispositional effects is available in Kaplan and Miller (1978, Experiment 3). Here, mock jurors participated in one of eight enacted trials of attempted manslaughter, in half of which the evidence gave a low appearance of defendant guilt; half gave a high appearance of guilt. Each type of case was tried in one of four manners. In the first, the trial was conducted in a straightforward manner, with attorneys and witnesses giving prompt and direct questions and answers. In the second, the judge introduced a number of annoyances, including unnecessary and irrelevant remarks and conferences, obnoxious lectures about courtroom decorum and rules, and similarly annoying interruptions. Care was taken to equally distribute his episodes of bad manners between defense and prosecution portions of the trial. The experimenter contributed to annoyance with frequent breakdowns of audiotaping equipment. In the remaining two presentation conditions, either the defense attorney or the prosecutor created annoyances by unnecessary and repetitious questions, extraneous remarks and objections, and generally obnoxious histrionics.

Compared to the straightforward control trial, trials made annoying by either the judge or the defense attorney led to juror ratings of greater defendant guilt. Thus, negative internal states, produced by unsettling trial conditions, produced negative judgments of the defendants. These effects were present in both the case with a predominant appearance of defendant guilt and the case with an appearance of innocence. The negative state was not automatically transferred to the judgment of the defendant, however. When the source of annoyance was the prosecutor (that is, a source that was neither neutral—the judge—nor associated with the defendant—his attorney) judgment was unaffected by state. This suggests several conclusions. First, temporary conditions can produce state dispositions which may affect defendant judgment. Second, this effect appears limited to states induced by neutral or defendant-associated parties. Third, these effects are independent of the strength of the evidence for incrimination. A fourth conclusion may be drawn from another finding: The biasing effect of annoyances was eliminated in a second vote taken after a 10-min deliberation period. Consequently, discussion of the facts of the case appears to reduce or even remove the manifestation of state disposition in judgment. These data have implications for the information integration model of juror cognition which will be discussed shortly.

Personal Biases and the Judgment Process

We will now consider the manifestation of trait (both general and specific) and state biases from the vantage of a general model of juror cognition. In this model, two broad determinants of judgment are identified: initial impression (preexisting disposition) and stimulus information. Both have scale values, reflecting their evaluations with respect to the criterion judgment (e.g., guilt appearance), and weights, reflecting effective importance. If the scale values are averaged, the weights are inversely related, so that increasing the importance of one element (e.g., information) decreases the importance of the other (e.g., initial impression). Trait and state biases, being internal characteristics produced by events other than stimulus information, and existing apart from the information contained in the trial, compose the initial impression. Consequently, the model has implications for the effect of biases as a function of trial content. Most importantly, the model predicts that bias will not always have the same effect, but that the relative presence of bias in judgment depends on the amount and weight of evidence in the case. Several experiments are informative (Kaplan & Miller, 1978).

In the Kaplan and Miller (1978) experiment discussed in the preceding section, state biases were produced by trial conduct, but were given weight in judgment of the defendant only when the annoying conditions were cognitively associated with the defendant. Thus, negative states alone will not affect judgment unless given some nonzero weight in integration. In two further experiments, general trait biases were measured by the Attitude-Toward-Punishment-of-Criminals scale (Wang & Thurstone, cited in Shaw & Wright, 1967), and subjects with lenient and stringent attitudes were identified. In the first experiment, subjects read six summaries of a variety of traffic felonies, indicated extent of belief in guilt, and recommended punishment, assuming guilt. Half the cases were constructed to give a moderately high appearance of guilt, and half gave a moderately low guilt appearance. Some subjects were told that the summaries were provided by an unreliable source (an inept clerk). Others were told that a reliable and accurate judge had written the summary, and the remainder were told nothing about the source. For both guilt and punishment responses, lenient and stringent subjects differed considerably when the facts were portrayed as unreliable, or when nothing was said about the reliability. When facts were characterized as reliable, however, the responses of the two subject groups converged to show no difference. This observation was true for both types of case summaries (high and low guilt appearance). Thus, the initial bias of subjects exerted an effect only when subjects were not impressed with the reliability of the evidence.

In the second experiment, stringent and lenient subjects judged guilt and punishment of defendants in two traffic felony cases, both designed to give a mixed appearance of guilt (i.e., some facts were incriminating, some exonerating). Half the subjects were told that the inconsistency in guilt appearance was natural since different witnesses were acquainted with different aspects of the case, and therefore all facts should be considered equally accurate and reliable. The remainder of the subjects were told that some of the facts might be inaccurate and might merit less credence than other facts. Once again, when led to believe that the evidence was questionable, stringent subjects assessed greater guilt and gave harsher sentences than lenient subjects; these differences between subjects' judgments vanished when evidence was cast as trustworthy. These data suggest that the effects of bias diminish with increased reliance on case information due to increased reliability. On the other hand, the effect of bias is not dependent on the incrimination value of the evidence; effects were symmetrical in the high and low guilt appearance cases. These conclusions, congruent with the information averaging model, furnish an important limitation to research that reports robust effects for various personality variables (e.g., authoritarianism). Most studies do not take care to provide a variety of cases, nor to vary either strength of evidence (in the form of weight) or incrimination value. Preexisting bias is not as robust as it might appear; it will have little effect in cases providing a reasonable amount of reliable evidence. Extrapolating, too, from the study of induced states, deliberation may also limit the extent of differences in judgment due to bias (but see Bray & Noble, 1978, for contrary evidence). The fact that the effect of bias depends on strength of evidence probably explains why studies of judges' backgrounds have not produced uniform results.

EXTRALEGAL AND LEGAL SOURCES OF BIAS

The preceding section considered trait and state aspects of personal dispositions as sources of bias, and embedded these in a general framework of juror cognition. Such dispositions, since they contribute a value over and above the value provided by evidence presented in court, may generally be considered extralegal variables. Other extralegal factors have received attention, and these will be briefly considered. However, this will by no means be a complete review since these factors are considered in more depth elsewhere in this volume. It will be instructive, though, to relate extralegal influences to the general model of cognition. Note that the factors being considered (defendant characteristics, pretrial publicity, and inadmissible evidence) all provide information about the case, in distinction to dispositional biases, which are preinformational. The only difference between these forms of information and admissible evidence lies in legal proscription; both give information, with scale value and weight, about the defendant's culpability.

Defendant Characteristics

Research has abundantly demonstrated that leniency or harshness of guilt and punishment judgments can be affected by defendant characteristics (see Dane & Wrightsman, Chapter 4, this volume; or Weiten & Diamond, 1979, for a review). In fact, the sheer popularity of defendant characteristics research has made it grow to epidemic proportions. Defendant attractiveness has been manipulated by ascription of personality traits (Kaplan & Kemmerick, 1974), social desirability of behavior (Landy & Aronson, 1969; Nemeth & Sosis, 1973), physical appearance (Efran, 1974; Sigall & Ostrove, 1975) and attitude similarity to jurors (Griffitt & Jackson, 1973; Mitchell & Byrne, 1973). In all cases, as in many uncited instances, the defendant portrayed more attractively received the more lenient sentence, and where included as a measure, was judged less likely to be guilty.

Before abandoning ourselves to a chorus of clucking tongues and gnashing teeth over the seducibility of jurors, we have to look further at the role of defendant characteristics in trial judgments. Weiten and Diamond (1979) and Vidmar (1979) have made blanket methodological criticisms of most studies which need not be repeated here. Instead, a conceptual question or two will be raised, based on the preceding discussion of dispositional bias. How do jurors integrate information about the defendant with information about the deed (i.e., the evidence)? What factors or conditions enhance or reduce the weight of defendant characteristics relative to trial evidence? Most studies are set on simply demonstrating an effect due to defendant characteristics, but fail to vary characteristics of the trial so that we may gauge the relative contribution of the trial or the manner in which the trial and defendant are combined. As an exception, Kaplan and Kemmerick (1974) found that characteristics of the evidence (e.g. whether it lent itself to an appearance of moderate guilt or seemed to call for moderate innocence) had a far greater effect on judgments than did defendant characteristics. Moreover, the two factors appeared to be combined linearly; that is, the contribution of defendant characteristics was the same both for cases where there was an appearance of innocence and for those with an appearance of guilt.

Most studies also fail to ask what factors will alter the relative weights of defendant and evidentiary information. Two studies tried to reduce the weight of the former by direct instructions to disregard (Mitchell & Byrne, 1973) or to consider the information useless (Kaplan & Kemmerick, 1974) but both were generally unsuccessful. Consequently, the interesting questions regarding integration of defendant and evidentiary information remain unanswered. The model would suggest that defendant information would be used to the extent that reliable and valid legal evidence is lacking. Studies might do well to vary the amount and/or credibility of testimony (see Baumeister & Darley, 1980, for an example). Conversely, it would be expected that the more informative the defendant characteristics were for the alleged crime, the more weight they would have. Some evidence appears to support this contention (Michelini & Snodgrass, 1978).

Pretrial Publicity

Pretrial publicity raises some important constitutional questions because it seemingly puts into conflict the constitutional provision for a fair trial guaranteed in the Sixth Amendment and the provisions for a public trial, also guaranteed in the Sixth Amendment, and for a free press, expressed in the First Amendment. The ramifications of this conflict are still being considered in Supreme Court rulings. We have striking examples of extraordinary pretrial publicity in such celebrated cases as the Lindbergh kidnapping (1934) and the Dr. Sam Sheppard murder case (1966), publicity that may have contributed to the convictions. Indeed, in *Sheppard* v. *Maxwell* the Supreme Court concluded that failure to control prejudicial pretrial publicity is evidence enough for reversal, even if no harmful effects on verdicts are proven. The assumption apparently was that pretrial publicity may affect verdicts.

The experimental evidence on the effectiveness and danger of pretrial publicity is mixed and does little to ease the predicament, nor to directly answer Justice Frankfurter's question (*Stroble* v. *California*, 1952) whether science can determine "when the impact of such newspaper exploitations has spent itself or whether the powerful impression . . . can be dissipated in the mind of the average juror by the tame and often pedestrian proceedings in court." By some coincidence, Justice Frankfurter asked the same question that has been asked ι ˍpeatedly here: How do jurors integrate pretrial publicity and trial evidence? What will enhance or reduce the weight of the pretrial publicity?

It is easy to show that persons reading about a defendant prior to trial will form judgments about guiltiness (e.g., Simon, 1968; Zanzola, 1977). But the judgments that count are the ones made after the trial is conducted. When verdicts are taken after simulated trials, they are not significantly affected by either favorable (Zanzola) or unfavorable (Simon) pretrial publicity, or the effects are limited (Hoiberg & Stires, 1973; Sue, Smith, & Gilbert, 1974). In the high school student sample used in the Hoiberg and Stires experiment, pretrial publicity consisting of heinous descriptions of the crime and a reported confession had effects on judgment only among females of low intelligence. Moreover, unlike the practice in real trials, jurors in the simulated trials were not instructed to disregard the pretrial publicity. Finally, Hoiberg and Stires provide no indication of how strong the trial evidence was in appearance. Consequently, the publicity may have been partially effective because

1. The remaining trial evidence was weak or ambiguous.
2. The pretrial publicity was quite relevant to the case (a confession).
3. The jurors affected were those least likely to be confident in their judgment.

If the information contained in the publicity is combined with trial information in a weighted average, the former should have an effect largely when the weight of the legal evidence is low (e.g., valid and reliable evidence is lacking during the trial), when the information conveyed by the pretrial publicity is highly relevant and useful for the charge (as in a confession), and when precautions to reduce the weight of the publicity (e.g., judicial instructions to ignore it) are lacking. Where trial evidence is complete and strong, and the information given in the publicity does not bear directly on the charge, its prejudicial effects should theoretically vanish.

This analysis can also account for Sue, Smith, and Gilbert's (1974) finding of a significant effect for pretrial publicity. Their newspaper account contained reference to discovery of the murder weapon in the defendant's possession— information that is highly relevant to the charge. In other words, the publicity contained evidence that was not given in court. Moreover, jurors did not deliberate, and were perhaps less accountable to others in their use of the publicity information. Where deliberation is included in the experiment as in Simon (1968) and Zanzola (1977), inadmissible evidence does not affect judgment. That the judicial instruction to disregard pretrial publicity was itself ignored may be due to an absence of strong legal evidence in the trial. As with juror predispositions, the antidote to prejudicial pretrial publicity is a strong case— evidence that its reliability and validity outweighs the inadmissible information. Judicial admonitions to ignore such information are not enough.

Inadmissible Evidence

Very similar remarks to those made about pretrial publicity may be made for inadmissible evidence. Both prejudicial publicity and inadmissible evidence are external sources of bias. As informational factors, they carry scale value for the judgment. It would be expected that the incriminating value of the extralegal information would interact with the value of trial evidence so that when the weight of the latter is low, or when the former is informative for the verdict, we should see effects for extralegal information. This expectation may be confirmed in Sue, Smith and Caldwell (1973), where jurors were influenced by relevant inadmissible evidence when trial evidence was weak, but not when the latter was strong. When jurors were confident of their decisions, they did not resort to the inadmissible evidence. This conclusion is weakened by a possible confound, in that "weak" evidence in this experiment was both conflicting (and therefore unreliable) and, of necessity, lower in incrimination value. The latter would also lead to a greater effect for incriminating pretrial publicity since it provides a more distant scale value than "strong" evidence to be integrated with the publicity.

Judicial instructions to disregard prejudicial inadmissible information add an interesting wrinkle. It is suggested that such instructions will be ignored (i.e., will not reduce the value given to inadmissible information) when the weight of admissible evidence is low. Weight of evidence aside, some studies have reported a "boomerang" effect for instructions. That is, when strong admonishments against considering the evidence are made, jurors will actually *increase* the weight attached to inadmissible evidence in their decisions. Thus, depending on the strength of judicial admonishment, jurors may either follow instructions and decrease weight (if inadmissibility is merely ruled upon—see Wolf & Montgomery, 1977) or may do the reverse of what instructions say and increase weight (if the admonishment is strong—see Broeder, 1959; Wolf & Montgomery, 1977). The latter effect is alternately explained in terms of focusing attention on the material (Broeder, 1959; Hans & Doob, 1976) or reactions to threats on freedom of judgment (Wolf & Montgomery, 1977).

Legal Bias

Placing decisions in the hands of private citizens results in a two-track system of justice: the rule of law and the order of custom (Diamond, 1971). The latter, which historically predates the former by centuries, refers to the application of moral principles (as distinct from a legal code) to the disposition of a case. As such, the jury brings to bear the existing mores of the day, or "conscience of the community," which can take on different values in different eras or even different communities in the same era. Witness the changing societal values reflected in the Supreme Court view of "separate but equal" in 1896 (*Plessy* v. *Ferguson*) and "separate but equal [is] inherently unequal" in 1954 (*Brown* v. *Board of Education*) and the different standards for pornography violations in different communities sanctioned by the Supreme Court (*Roth* v. *United States*). Historically, it has been ordained that jurors be selected from the community in which the crime was committed so that the decision could be made in the context of local customs. Thus, the jury has shifted its role from trier of facts (and applier of the law in a strict sense) to representative of the community conscience. The proper definition of the jury's role is still a matter of contention (Brooks & Doob, 1975).

In American jurisprudence, this evolution of jury role and authority is clearly evident. As recently as 1895 the jury was expected to follow the strict letter of the law as interpreted by the judge, and was given discretion only in deciding on the truth of facts (*Sparf and Hansen* v. *United States*, 1895). Today, however, the jury is permitted greater discretion, and may, in fact, override the letter of the law in applying the current values of the community to each individual case (see Brooks & Doob, 1975, for a fine discussion of this point). The *order of custom* role of the jury, which introduces discretionary factors into decisions, has been defended as a means of allowing for flexibility in administering the law to individual circumstances (Curtis, 1952), and enabling the law to keep pace with changes in societal views and tastes (Howe, 1939; Wigmore, 1929). In other words, allowing jurors to reflect the conscience of the community in their decisions allows the private citizen direct access to making laws and customs.

Clearly this view of jurors departs from the notion that they are to come to the trial with a "blank mind" and an impartial attitude. In other words, the door is opened to the use of extralegal and prejudicial factors in decision making. Whether the gains to be made by including current moral values in jurors' decision making outweigh the dangers is a matter with which legal philosophy has to grapple.

Yet another source of prescribed bias lies in the presumption of innocence which is supposed to guide the jury. Jurors are explicitly instructed that, until proven otherwise, they are to consider the defendant innocent—not to have a neutral attitude, not to say "I don't know," but to take the defendant as innocent. This is a prescribed value for the initial impression. Thus, in the mind of discerning jurors, mixed signals are being given. They are told to be impartial and open-minded (i.e., *neutral* on the question of appearance of guilt), but should presume innocence (i.e., *negative* on the same question) before hearing the evidence. Moreover, the juror is not discouraged from averaging into the conceptual equation some nonneutral variables reflecting the community's moral tone. Consequently, not all biases are proscribed. The bias which is explicitly encouraged—presumption of innocence—may, ironically, be the most fragile. In the experiments where lenient and stringent jurors converged in their judgments when evidence was characterized as valid and reliable (Kaplan & Miller, 1978), it was mostly the *lenient* subjects who overrode their initial bias and became more stringent.

REDUCTION OF BIAS

As reviewed earlier, studies in which there is an attempt to reduce bias by judicial instruction meet with only mixed success. For example, instructions to disregard defendant attitudes were successful for only low authoritarians (Mitchell & Byrne, 1973), and inadmissible evidence was disregarded only when the judge merely ruled on its inadmissibility without offering specific instructions to disregard (Wolf & Montgomery, 1977). On the other hand, it is more common to find judicial instructions themselves ignored, or worse, to even have a deleterious effect (Broeder, 1959; Wolf & Montgomery, 1977). Thus, attempts to directly reduce the weight of bias or of extralegal factors by judicial caveat are not very successful.

Another means of directly altering the weight of biasing factors is to reduce their reliability and/or relevance. As seen earlier, pretrial publicity, inadmissible evidence, and defendant characteristics may not weigh as heavily on juror judgments when they are not directly informative about the particular charge. However, convincing jurors that their initial impression is irrelevant or unreliable is easier said than done. Since predispositions are trait characteristics of relatively long standing, it is hard to imagine conditions in a single trial that will cause jurors to doubt their conception of criminals, human nature, or even specific subgroups of people. Only in motion picture or television dramatizations are traits so pliable. It may be possible, however, to alert people to the existence of potential prejudices in the course of voir dire so that they may exert some control over weighting. Such alerting may be more possible with short-term, or state dispositions, due to their greater lability. Extrapolating from Wolf and Montgomery (1977), simply mentioning that bias due to traits or to state conditions might exist ought to be more effective in reducing bias weight than strong admonishments to disregard bias.

Traditionally, the voir dire is the first line of defense against preexisting dispositions. Each side in a dispute is allowed a certain number of jury challenges, varying among jurisdictions, both peremptory and for demonstrated cause. Lately, in a number of celebrated cases, the voir dire has been used for offensive purposes, so that an attempt may be made to systematically select jurors for biases favorable for one side of the case (see, e.g., Hans & Vidmar, Chapter 2, this volume; Kairys, Schulman, & Harring, 1975; Schulman, Shaver, Colman, Emrich, & Christie, 1973). But systematic selection of jurors has its flaws, ranging from inadequate evaluation of effectiveness, to application of "pop" psychology rationales, to potential subversion of the fairness doctrine (see

Berk, Hennessy, & Swan, 1977; and Saks, 1976 for critiques). Demographic data, the major source of information prior to the voir dire, is gross and misleading and has been shown to be poorly related to verdicts (see previous discussion in this chapter; see also a survey of sitting jurors by Mills & Bohannon, 1980). Questioning during voir dire may not uncover biases, due either to lack of insight or evasiveness in the juror. Consequently, while obvious cases of bias or inability to lay bias aside may be detected and eliminated in voir dire, some bias is unavoidable. Few people totally lack preconceptions about civil or criminal matters; those who are completely without opinions or values are probably incapable of understanding evidence in any event and would make poor jurors. For those jurors with preconceptions who do wind up on the jury, the question remains: How can the weight of bias produced by dispositions and extralegal factors be minimized?

The likely solution lies in the studies reviewed here and within the information integration model. Simply put, the weight of a given element (e.g., disposition) is reduced by increasing the weight of another element (e.g., admissible evidence). If the evidential presentation is complete, is presented in an understandable and memorable fashion, is relevant and informative for the required judgment, and has a reasonable degree of credibility, the role of bias will probably be minimized. In studies both of dispositional bias and extralegal information, the effects of biasing agents were reduced when strong and reliable evidence was given. Trials that supply minimal or weak evidence, and in which the facts are highly contested, are good candidates for juror bias. This conclusion suggests the need for restraint on contentiousness in our adversarial system of justice, a point discussed in detail elsewhere (Kaplan & Schersching, 1980).

One additional safeguard is present in our current system: The requirement of deliberation by jurors. In Kaplan and Miller (1978, Experiment 3), predeliberation decision differences between juries due to their varying state dispositions vanished following deliberation. The predeliberation judgment (or any judgment for that matter) is based on an integration of trial evidence with the preexisting disposition and with extralegal information. In many cases, all trial evidence will not be represented in that integration since some information may have been initially overlooked, disbelieved, misunderstood, or forgotten. Moreover, additional information, while apprehended, understood, believed, and remembered, may still not be included in the judgment due to limitations in the capacity to process information. In short, the predeliberation judgment may be based on a narrow subset of all possible evidence. If the incrimination scale value of trial evidence is different from the value of the preexisting disposition or extralegal information (and if it is not, it makes little sense to speak of biasing effects), then the less evidence represented in the judgment, the more it will be colored by the biasing factors. That is, the predeliberation judgment, to the extent that it does not include trial evidence, will be closer to the preexisting bias value than to the trial evidence value.

During deliberation, jurors share trial information. Examination of the content of deliberation in studies of extralegal information (e.g., Hans & Doob, 1976; Wolf & Montgomery, 1977) and juror predisposition (Kaplan & Miller, 1978) show little discussion of the biasing factors relative to trial evidence. Some of the information being shared may not have been included in forming the predeliberation judgment. Consequently, later judgments will incorporate this information into the judgment equation, drawing the judgment away from the scale value of the preexisting disposition and/or extralegal information and toward the value of the trial evidence. While the biasing factors (e.g., extralegal information) may be implicit in judgment, even though not explicit in the discussion, the opportunity remains for additional legal information to be incorporated and thus affect the response. Even in those instances where biases or extralegal factors *are* mentioned, other jurors may discourage or serve as a corrective for expressed biases and thus reduce their weight. Postdeliberation judgments, then, represent an integration of more legal evidence than predeliberation judgments, producing less reliance on nonevidential factors (see Kaplan & Scherching, 1980, for a more detailed analysis).

There are several testable implications of this analysis. First, biasing effects of predispositions should diminish following deliberations and juries with different dispositions before deliberation should converge afterwards. They do (Kaplan & Miller, 1978). Second, in juries with more or less neutral dispositions, responses to evidence that is either moderately incriminating or moderately exonerating should polarize after deliberation, compared to predeliberation responses. Once again, they do (Kaplan, 1977a; Myers & Kaplan, 1976). Third, if juries are constrained to share only one type of evidence (e.g., either exonerating or incriminating) through contrived feedback, even when the evidence shared is opposite in value to the majority of trial evidence, jurors should shift in the direction of the shared evidence after deliberation. This they do, also (Kaplan, 1977a). Fourth, the extent to which jurors move away from preexisting dispositions toward the value of the evidence following deliberation should depend on the variety and nonredundancy of the shared information. That is, jurors will not be changed upon hearing facts that they have already incorporated into their thinking. If other jurors present facts that one juror has not taken into account, and each juror mentions different facts, there is more to be incorporated, and therefore more change likely from the predeliberation judgment. Juries whose members represent among them a wider pool of remembered facts, and who subsequently bring these into discussion, will show a larger shift from the predeliberation judgment, and by implication, less reliance on the preexisting disposition (Kaplan, 1977a; Kaplan & Miller, 1977).

One advantage of a deliberating jury over a single juror then, is that among the jurors more legal facts are noticed, remembered, and taken into account. If these facts are then shared in deliberation, more facts will be available to the single juror to counteract the preexisting disposition and/or extralegal information. It remains to be seen whether recent developments in the composition of juries (i.e., 6- versus 12-person juries) or in jury decision rules (unanimous versus nonunanimous) facilitate or hinder the sharing of reasonable and varied trial evidence. The amount and sort of information discussed and its effect on lessening the weight of bias should be an important consideration in evaluating these recent changes.

FROM JUDGMENT TO VERDICTS

We have examined the cognitive processes involved in forming subjective judgments of jurors, with a particular eye towards individual differences. To facilitate cohesion, we have built this examination around a model in which jurors evaluate and weigh information psychologically pertinent to the required judgment, and then integrate the separate evaluations into a single judgment. Now we consider how this subjective judgment of certainty of guilt is transformed into the response requirement of a dichotomous verdict.

Three decision-making traditions converge in this matter: Signal detection theory, Bayesian Probability, and Decision Theory (DT) (see Pennington & Hastie, 1981, for a general discussion and review of models of juror decision making.) All share the notion that the juror's evaluation of guilt must surpass a certain *criterion* in order to reach a guilt verdict, although the theories differ with respect to how the appearance of guilt and the criterion threshold are determined.

Thomas & Hogue (1976) offer a Signal Detection Theory analogue in which "apparent weight" of evidence (in our terms, the integrated scale values) is applied against a decision criterion. One may separate, for analytic purposes, the detectability of guilt in the evidence from the criterion, and then ask whether individual differences reside in one or the other. That is, two jurors may perceive similar apparent guilt in the case, but apply either lenient or stringent criteria (see Marshall & Wise, 1975, for such evidence). Another prime concern in this tradition is confidence in one's verdict, which is a function of the absolute difference between detectability and criterion.

The Bayesian Probability tradition is a mathematical-logical model of how people should think, constructed in terms of relations among probablistic opinions. It is a prescriptive, and not descriptive model; indeed, departures from optimal predictions are often the rule (see, e.g., Slovic & Lichtenstein, 1971). Subjective judgment is represented by a probability of guilt estimate, which is a function of an a priori probability of guilt regardless of the evidence (analogous to the initial impression discussed earlier in this chapter) and the probability of guilt given by the evidence (analogous to the concept of scale value employed earlier). Probabilities are expressed as likelihood ratios; for example, the probability of guilt given by the evidence is the ratio of the probability of the evidence that the defendant is guilty to the probability of given evidence that he or she is not guilty. The prior estimation of guilt relative to innocence combines *multi-*

plicatively (contrast this with the averaging rule pursued earlier) with the likelihood ratio for each piece of information to produce the overall probability. To more clearly explicate the evidence ratio, it can be stated as the ratio of the likelihood that the evidence would occur if the defendant were guilty to the likelihood of its occurrence if the defendant were innocent (Marshall & Wise, 1975). Bayesian theory typically assumes that each piece of evidence has an impact independent of the others, but Schum (1977) has lately suggested that conditional probability should be considered. That is, one must take into account the contingency of the probability of any given piece of evidence on the probabilities of prior evidence. This allows inclusion of the effects of discounting, inconsistency, source credibility, and redundancy, which have already been documented in this chapter. Since little empirical work within this model has been reported, and individual differences in prior probabilities, aggregation rule, or likelihood ratios have not been explored, further discussion of the Bayesian approach in this chapter would be premature.

Decision theory focuses on the utilities associated with the potential outcomes of a decision (Nagel & Neef, 1979). In the juror's case, these are the costs and benefits to acquit or to convict. Since costs or benefits depend also on whether the defendant is truly guilty or innocent, the expected value (utility) of a given verdict derives from a payoff matrix of the four possible outcomes: acquit when defendant is innocent, acquit when defendant is guilty, convict when defendant is innocent, and convict when defendant is guilty. For each outcome, the juror has some utility, representing the degree of satisfaction or dissatisfaction with that outcome. Some examples of factors which could affect utilities include:

1. Liking for the defendant
2. Motivation for vengeance
3. Expectancy for rehabilitation
4. Setting of an example for others
5. Danger to the community in releasing the defendant
6. Hardship for the defendant's family
7. Severity of the penalty
8. "Reasonable doubt" instructions

The reasonable doubt factor is interesting since it relates to Blackstone's (1769/1962) commentary that it is better that 10 guilty go free than that one innocent suffer. If this is the juror's belief, or if this is the thought conveyed by "Reasonable doubt" instructions, then the utility of acquitting when guilty should be higher than that of convicting when innocent.

The expected value of a conviction verdict (EVC) is an additive function of the utility of convicting when guilty (UCG), weighted by the probability of guilt (p_g), and the utility of convicting when innocent (UCI), weighted by $1 - p$. Similarly, the expected value of an acquittal verdict is an additive function of the utility of acquitting when guilty (UAG), weighted by the probability of innocence (p_i), and the utility of acquitting when innocent (UAI), weighted by $1 - p$

(J. Kaplan, 1967). The juror will vote for conviction when the first expected value is greater than the second, or when the probability of guilt exceeds the criterion: UAI − UCI/UCG − UAG.

Note that the Decision Theory analysis is primarily concerned with the effects of consequences of "true" and erroneous verdicts on criteria. It does not ask where the probability values for guilt and innocence came from, which has been the prime focus of the integration analysis that has been discussed in the bulk of this chapter. Consequently the two traditions—information integration and Decision Theory—may be considered complementary in scope. Given the Decision Theory analysis, it is possible to reconstruct a juror's criterion, given knowledge of probability values, so that differences among jurors can be determined. For example, Nagel and Neef (1979) report higher criteria (less stringency) in males compared to females in rape cases, and in liberals compared to conservatives, and business students compared to liberal arts students in consumer fraud cases. Similarly, Marshall and Wise (1975) report criterion differences between subjects differentiated by a priori measures of harshness. It is also possible to observe the effects of differing judicial instructions on the criteria. For example, if a judge explicitly instructs jurors using Blackstone's rule, conviction should—and does—require a probability of guilt threshold of .91. Conversely, changes in judicial instructions to emphasize protection of society, or to suggest that decisions should be based on a preponderance of evidence rather than the reasonable doubt standard should reduce the criterion (Kerr, Atkin, Stasser, Meek, Holt, & Davis, 1976; Nagel & Neef, 1979).

The reference to criterion inherent in decision theory approaches helps us to understand several discrepancies between judgments of a case and final verdict, that is, between what jurors think about the case and what they do in the jury room. In most treatments of deliberation effects, two potential influence processes are delineated: informational and normative (Myers & Lamm, 1976). Informational influences refer to any influence due to the information that is shared about the decision alternatives, and can include persuasive arguments; normative influence refers to pressure to conform to the judgments and decisions of other participants. It has been suggested that only the former affects judged appearance of guilt; that is, information shared by other jurors shifts an individual juror's judgment of defendant guilt, while normative or conformity pressures do not (see Kaplan & Schersching, 1981 for a detailed analysis). However, it remains possible that normative pressures affect the criterion adopted by a juror for conviction. Jurors may accept a lower or a higher value of subjective probability of guilt as necessary for a conviction vote in order to conform to group pressures for, respectively, conviction or acquittal, just as they may shift the criterion to conform to judicial standards.

Jurors may also shift criterion in response to variations in severity of punishment. If potential punishment is seen as very severe, jurors may require a very certain appearance of guilt before voting to convict; that is, the cost or dissatisfaction with a vote to convict when the defendant might be innocent (UCI) is too steep. Indeed, Kerr (1978) reports that as severity of prescribed penalty increases, more evidence is needed for conviction, and holding evidence constant, less conviction votes are obtained. In a thesis study conducted by Krupa (1979), this finding was further developed. Some students were led to believe that their decisions would have real consequences for a real defendant, while others believed the case was simulated. While "real" jurors were generally more conviction-prone, they turned in less convictions than simulated jurors when (*a*) the evidence was weakly incriminating, *and* (*b*) the prescribed punishment was severe, *and* (*c*) an external authority, rather than they, controlled the eventual punishment. Thus, "real" jurors substantially decreased convictions based on weak evidence when an overly severe punishment (in this case, expulsion from school for copying on an exam) that they could not influence would befall the defendant. When evidence was strong, and/or they would have the power to ameliorate punishment, conviction rate was unaffected by potential punishment severity.

The lesson here is that more is involved in a verdict than the question of how guilty the defendant appears. Many other considerations, including legal norms, costs and benefits, social pressures within the jury, and the justice value of prescribed punishment, can influence the criterion that must be surpassed before declaring another person guilty of an act. At the risk of ending a chapter with a worn and trite expression, it seems appropriate to say that future research needs to take cognizance of criteria and their vicissitudes in mediating the transformation of guilt assessment to verdict.

REFERENCES

Anderson, N. H. Cognitive algebra: Integration theory applied to social attribution. In L. Berkowitz (Ed.), *Advances in experimental social psychology* (Vol. 7). New York: Academic Press, 1974.

Baumeister, R. G., & Darley, J. M. *Reducing the biasing effect of perpetrator attractiveness in jury simulation studies.* Unpublished manuscript, Princeton University, New Jersey, 1980.

Berk, R. A., Hennessy, M., & Swan, J. The vagaries and vulgarities of "scientific" jury selection: A methodological evaluation. *Evaluation Quarterly*, 1977, *1*, 143−158.

Blackstone, W. *Commentaries on the laws of England of public wrongs.* Boston: Beacon, 1962. (Originally published, 1769.)

Boehm, V. R. Mr. Prejudice, Miss Sympathy, and the authoritarian personality: An application of psychological measuring techniques to the problem of jury bias. *Wisconsin Law Review*, 1968, 734−750.

Bray, R. M., & Noble, A. M. Authoritarianism and decisions of mock juries: Evidence of jury bias and group polarization. *Journal of Personality and Social Psychology*, 1978, *36*, 1424−1430.

Broeder, D. The University of Chicago jury project. *Nebraska Law Review*, 1959, *38*, 744−760.

Brooks, W. N., & Doob, A. N. Justice and the jury. *Journal of Social Issues*, 1975, *31*, 171−182.

Brown v. *Board of Education, United States Reports*, 1954, *347*, 483−496.

Crosson, R. F. An investigation into certain personality variables among capital trial jurors. *Proceedings of the 76th Annual Convention of the American Psychological Association*, 1968, *3*, 371−372.

Curtis, C. P. The trial judge and the jury. *Vanderbilt Law Review*, 1952, *5*, 150−166.

Diamond, S. The rule of law versus the order of custom. *Social Research*, 1971, *38*, 42−72.

Efran, M. G. The effect of physical appearance on the judgment of guilt, interpersonal attraction, and severity of recommended punishment in a simulated jury task. *Journal of Research in Personality*, 1974, *8*, 45–54.

Gaudet, F. G. Individual differences in the sentencing tendencies of judges. *Archives of Psychology*, 1938, *32*, 5; 9–26; 29–42; 55.

Griffitt, W., & Jackson, T. Simulated jury decisions: The influence of jury–defendant attitude similarity–dissimilarity. *Social Behavior and Personality*, 1973, *1*, 1–7.

Grossman, J. B., & Tanenhaus, J. *Frontiers of judicial research*. New York: Wiley, 1969.

Hans, V. P., & Doob, A. N. Section 12 of the Canada Evidence Act and the deliberations of simulated juries. *Criminal Law Quarterly*, 1976, *18*, 235–253.

Hatton, D. E. Snortum, J. R., & Oskamp, S. The effects of biasing information and dogmatism upon witness testimony. *Psychonomic Science*, 1971, *23*, 425–427.

Hoiberg, B., & Stires, L. The effect of several types of pre-trial publicity on the guilt attributions of simulated jurors. *Journal of Applied Social Psychology*, 1973, *3*, 267–275.

Howe, M. de W. Juries as judges in criminal cases. *Harvard Law Review*, 1939, *52*, 582–616.

Jurow, G. New data on the effect of a "death qualified" jury on the guilt determination process. *Harvard Law Review*, 1971, *84*, 567–611.

Kairys, D., Schulman, J., & Harring, S. (Eds.). The jury system: New methods for reducing prejudice. Philadelphia: National Jury Project and National Lawyers Guild, 1975.

Kaplan, J. Decision theory and the fact-finding process. *Stanford Law Review*, 1967, *20*, 1065–1092.

Kaplan, M. F. Discussion polarization effects in a modified jury decision paradigm: Informational influences. *Sociometry*, 1977, *40*, 262–271. (a)

Kaplan, M. F. Judgments by juries. In M. Kaplan & S. Schwartz (Eds.), *Human Judgment and decision processes in applied settings*. New York: Academic Press, 1977. (b)

Kaplan, M. F., & Kemmerick, G. Juror judgment as information integration: Combining evidential and nonevidential information. *Journal of Personality and Social Psychology*, 1974, *30*, 493–499.

Kaplan, M. F., & Miller, C. E. Judgments and group discussion: Effect of presentation and memory factors on polarization. *Sociometry*, 1977, *40*, 337–343.

Kaplan, M. F., & Miller, L. E. Reducing the effects of juror bias. *Journal of Personality and Social Psychology*, 1978, *36*, 1443–1455.

Kaplan, M. F., & Schersching, C. Reducing juror bias: An experimental approach. In P. Lipsitt & B. Sales (Eds.), *New directions in psycholegal research*. New York: Van Nostrand-Reinhold, 1980.

Kaplan, M. F., & Schersching, C. Juror deliberation: An information integration analysis. In B. Sales (Ed.), *Perspectives in law and psychology, Volume II: The trial process*. New York: Plenum, 1981.

Kaplan, M. F., Steindorf, J., & Iervolino, A. Courtrooms, politics, and morality: Toward a theoretical integration. *Personality and Social Psychology Bulletin*, 1978, *4*, 155–160.

Kerr, N. L. Severity of prescribed penalty and mock jurors' verdicts. *Journal of Personality and Social Psychology*, 1978, *36*, 1431–1442.

Kerr, N. L., Atkin, R., Stasser, G., Meek, D., Holt, R., & Davis, J. H. Guilt beyond a reasonable doubt: Effects of concept definition and assigned decision rule on the judgments of mock jurors. *Journal of Personality and Social Psychology*, 1976, *34*, 282–294.

Krupa, S. *Effects of control and severity of punishment alternatives on jury decision-making*. Unpublished master's thesis, Northern Illinois University, 1979.

Landy, D., & Aronson, E. The influence of the character of the criminal and his victim on the decisions of simulated jurors. *Journal of Experimental Social Psychology*, 1969, *5*, 141–152.

Marshall, C. R., & Wise, J. A. Juror decisions and the determination of guilt in capital punishment cases: A Bayesian perspective. In D. Wendt & C. Vlek (Eds.), *Utility, probability, and human decision making*. Dordrecht, Holland: Reidel, 1975.

Michelini, R. L., & Snodgrass, S. R. *Defendant characteristics and juridic decisions*. Unpublished manuscript, University of Minnesota at Duluth, 1978.

Mills, C. J., & Bohannon, W. E. Juror characteristics: To what extent are they related to jury verdicts? *Judicature*, 1980, *64*, 23–31.

Mitchell, H. E., & Byrne, D. The defendant's dilemma: Effects of jurors' attitudes and authoritarianism on judicial decisions. *Journal of Personality and Social Psychology*, 1973, *25*, 123−129.

Myers, D. G., & Kaplan, M. F. Group-induced polarization in simulated juries. *Personality and Social Psychology Bulletin*, 1976, *2*, 63−66.

Nagel, S. S. Judicial backgrounds and criminal cases. *Journal of Criminal Law, Criminology, and Police Science*, 1962, *53*, 333−339.

Nagel, S. S., & Neef, M. G. *Decision theory and the legal process.* Lexington, Mass.: Lexington, 1979.

Nemeth, C., & Sosis, R. A simulated jury study: Characteristics of the defendant and the jurors. *Journal of Social Psychology*, 1973, *90*, 221−229.

Pennington, N., & Hastie, R., Juror decision making models: The generalization gap. *Psychological Bulletin*, 1981, *89*, 246−287.

Plessy v. Ferguson, United States Reports, 1896, *163*, 537−563.

Pritchett, C. H. *The Roosevelt court.* New York: Macmillan, 1948.

Rokeach, M., & McLellan, D. D. Dogmatism and the death penalty: A reinterpretation of the Duquesne poll data. *Duquesne Law Review*, 1969−1970, *8*, 125−129.

Roth v. United States, United States Reports, 1957, *354*, 476−514.

Saks, M. The limits of scientific jury selection: Ethical and empirical. *Jurimetrics Journal*, 1976, *17*, 3−22.

Saks, M., & Hastie, R. *Social psychology in court.* New York: Van Nostrand-Reinhold, 1978.

Schulman, J., Shaver, P., Colman, R., Emrich, P., & Christie, R. Recipe for for a jury. *Psychology Today*, May 1973, pp. 37−44; 77−84.

Schum, D. Contrast affects in inference: On the conditioning of current evidence of prior evidence. *Organizational Behavior and Human Performance*, 1977, *18*, 217−253.

Shaw, M. E., & Wright, J. M. *Scales for the measurement of attitudes.* New York: McGraw-Hill, 1967.

Sheppard v. Maxwell, United States Reports, 1966, *384*, 333−363.

Sigall, H., & Ostrove, N. Beautiful but dangerous: Effects of offender attractiveness and nature of the crime on juridic judgment. *Journal of Personality and Social Psychology*, 1975, *31*, 410−414.

Simon, R. J. The effects of newspapers on the verdicts of potential jurors. In R. Simon (Ed.), *The sociology of law.* San Francisco, California: Chandler, 1968.

Simon, R., & Oster, P. R. Inside justice. *Chicago Sun-Times*, September 23, 1973, pp. 4; 20.

Slovic, P., & Lichtenstein, S. Comparison of Bayesian and regression approaches to the study of information processing in judgment. *Organizational Behavior and Human Performance*, 1971, *6*, 649−744.

Sparf and Hansen v. United States, United States Reports, 1895, *156*, 51−182.

Spielberger, C. D. Anxiety as an emotional state. In C. D. Spielberger (Ed.), *Anxiety: Current trends in theory and research* (Vol. 1). New York: Academic Press, 1972.

Stecher, J. Democratic and Republican justice: Judicial decision-making on five state supreme courts. *Columbia Journal of Law and Social Problems*, 1977, *13*, 137−181.

Steinberg, R. Sympathetic voting dimensions on the New York Court of Appeals. *Albany Law Review*, 1977, *41*.

Stroble v. California, United States Reports, 1952, *343*, 181−204.

Sue, S., Smith, R. E., & Caldwell, C. Effects of inadmissible evidence on the decisions of simulated jurors: A moral dilemma. *Journal of Applied Social Psychology*, 1973, *3*, 345−353.

Sue, S., Smith, R. E., & Gilbert, R. Biasing effects of pretrial publicity on judicial decisions. *Journal of Criminal Justice*, 1974, *2*, 163−171.

Thayer, R. E. Attitude and personality differences between potential jurors who could return a death verdict and those who could not. *Proceedings of the 78th Annual Convention of the American Psychological Association*, 1970, *5*, 445−446.

Thomas, E. A. C., & Hogue, A. Apparent weight of evidence, decision criteria, and confidence ratings in juror decision making. *Psychological Review*, 1976, *83*, 442−465.

Vidmar, N. The other issues in jury simulation research: A commentary with particular reference to defendant character studies. *Law and Human Behavior*, 1979, *3*, 95–106.

Weiten, W., & Diamond, S. S. A critical review of the jury simulation paradigm: The case of defendant characteristics. *Law and Human Behavior*, 1979, *3*, 71–93.

Wigmore, J. A programme for the trial of jury trial. *Journal of the American Judicature Society*, 1929, *12*, 166–170.

Wolf, S., & Montgomery, D. A. Effects of inadmissible evidence and level of judicial admonishment to disregard on the judgments of mock jurors. *Journal of Applied Social Psychology*, 1977, *7*, 205–219.

Zanzola, L. *The role of pretrial publicity in the trial process and jury deliberations.* Unpublished study, Northern Illinois University, 1977.

chapter

The Social Psychology of Jury Deliberations: Structure, Process, and Product

Garold Stasser
Norbert L. Kerr
Robert M. Bray

The jury occupies an almost hallowed place in the American system of justice. However, its symbolic impact is perhaps more important than its actual impact in adjudicating cases. Cole (1975) estimates that only about 8% of criminal cases are decided by a jury, but argues that the anticipated reaction of a jury guides

221

THE PSYCHOLOGY
OF THE COURTROOM

decisions at various stages of the criminal justice process. Decisions to arrest, indict, and enter into plea bargaining are made, in part, by anticipating the probable outcome of a jury trial. Kalven and Zeisel (1966) express this notion well:

> Thus, the jury is not controlling merely the immediate case before it, but also the host of cases not before it which are destined to be disposed of by the pre-trial process. . . . In a sense the jury, like the visible cap of an iceberg, exposes but a fraction of its true volume [pp. 31–32].

In view of the jury's far-reaching impact, there has been considerable interest in understanding the social processes of deliberation and in predicting jury decisions. However, understanding and prediction are not easy in light of the complexity of the jury decision-making process. A jury's deliberation reflects the full dynamics of social interaction: the give-and-take of information and opinion, the discomfort of disagreement and conflict, the emergence of norms and roles in a group, and so forth. These phenomena have captured the interest and imagination of many researchers of group process. Thus, it is not surprising that the jury has been a focal point of the interplay between social psychologists and legal scholars. Many issues (e.g., whether juries should be required to reach unanimous agreement; whether juries with fewer than 12 members should be used) raise both practical and legal questions as well as questions of relevance to psychological theories.

In this chapter, we review, summarize, and organize research that has focused on the jury as a collective decision-making body. We also identify gaps in knowledge and suggest possible new directions for research. Because both ethical and legal restraints keep jury deliberations hidden from the inquiring eye of the social scientist, much of the research we review has examined mock juries rather than actual juries. Our review is not exhaustive; we have attempted to sample representative studies and issues. We also avoid an in-depth coverage of the research concerned with jury size and assigned decision rule; the interested reader is referred to Saks' Chapter 11, this volume.

In organizing this research literature, we have distinguished between the jury's structure, process, and product (cf. Saks & Hastie, 1978). The primary structural question we consider is one of leadership in the jury: who is selected foreman and how is that person selected? In the next section of this chapter, we review research on the deliberation process itself. Of particular interest will be an analysis of verbal interaction during deliberation, looking at who says what to whom. This section will also consider the effect of voting procedures on the course of group deliberation. Our final section will focus upon the product of jury deliberation. Our primary concerns will be with how well these group decisions can be predicted, the effects of group deliberation on individual preferences, and the implications of these findings for understanding the social influence processes at work in the jury.

THE STRUCTURE OF THE JURY

Foreman Selection

The initial task of a jury in the deliberation chambers is usually to select one of its members to act as foreman, if that has not been done already by court-room procedure. Due to the foreman's unique role of performing certain "house-keeping" functions such as guiding the deliberations and recording the final verdict, he or she may become a leader in the group and exert greater influence over the verdict than do other jury members. The data on the selection process do not indicate elaborate efforts by jurors to obtain the foremanship. In fact, usually only 1 or 2 minutes are spent in the rather perfunctory selection process (Hawkins, 1960; Simon, 1967), although there are occasional reports to the contrary (e.g., Wanamaker, 1977, reported a case that required approximately an hour and a half to choose a foreman). Generally, the first person nominated is chosen without formal vote (Bridgeman & Marlowe, 1979; Hawkins, 1960; Strodtbeck, James, & Hawkins, 1957) and there is a tendency for the first person who speaks to be chosen (Strodtbeck et al., 1957, observed this in about one-third of their 49 mock juries; see also Gordon, 1968).

In spite of the seemingly offhanded manner in which the foreman is chosen, several factors appear to facilitate a juror being selected. For example, males are selected more often than females. This bias is evident even in recent studies where females might be expected to be selected about as often as males in view of the changing emphasis on women's roles. An older study by Strodtbeck et al. (1957) using 49 mock juries drawn from actual jury roles reported that females were only about one-fifth as often as might be expected by chance. In a fairly recent study using archival data from 179 actual cases tried in 1975, Kerr, Harmon and Graves (in press) found a strikingly comparable figure: Female foremen were still selected only 22% as often as would be expected by chance. In a number of mock jury studies (Bray, Struckman-Johnson, Osborne, McFarlane, & Scott, 1978; Davis, Kerr, Atkin, Holt, & Meek, 1975; Gordon, 1968; Hawkins, 1960), the percentage of juries with male foremen has never dropped below 78%. Apparently, the label fore*man* is still appropriate.

Seating patterns have also been related to foreman selection with the foreman chosen significantly more often from the end positions of a rectangular table than would be expected by chance. Hawkins (1960) found that in 69 12-person mock juries, 49% of the foremen were chosen from the ends while only about 17% would be expected by chance. Similarly, using 12-person juries, Strodtbeck and Hook (1961) reported nearly identical results, with 46% of their 69 foremen selected from the end seats. More recent data with 6-person juries shows the same pattern. In the Bray et al. (1978) study, 56% of 50 foremen sat in the end positions while only 33% would be expected by chance. The fact that males and people sitting at the ends of tables tend to become foremen, hints that males may sit in end positions more often than females. Nemeth, Endicott, and

Wachtler (1976) report that this was clearly the case in their 6-person mock juries, with 47% of males choosing an end seat compared to 15% of females.

Another variable related to foreman selection is occupational status. The general finding is that the higher one's occupational status, the more likely one's selection as foreman. Three studies from the Chicago Jury Project (Hawkins, 1960; Simon, 1967; Strodtbeck et al., 1957) classified subjects as proprietors, clerical workers, skilled workers, or laborers (housewives were also included in two studies). Proprietors were selected as foremen on the order of two to two-and-a-half times as often as expected by chance.

Finally, prior experience as a juror has been related to selection as foreman. Informally, Hawkins (1960) noted that mock jurors mentioned prior experience as a specific criterion in choosing a foreman, as did actual jurors in their posttrial interviews with Broeder (1965). More recently, systematic data by Kerr et al. (in press) confirms this conjecture. Using archival data on actual 12-person juries, they found that experienced jurors were selected as foreman 51% of the time compared with a chance expectation of only 40%.

Taken together, these research findings suggest the most likely portrait of a jury foreman would be a male proprietor who begins the deliberation, sits at the end of the table, and has served on a jury before. Nonetheless, we still know very little about the dynamics and causes underlying the selection process. That is, we have useful descriptive data about factors that are correlated with foreman selection, but we are as yet unable to explain the critical causal features. For example, is the foreman usually selected from the end of the table because the end position implies leadership or because jurors who perceive themselves as leaders tend to sit in the end position and are picked because of the personal confidence (or some other feature) that they display? Clearly, more research is needed to isolate the critical features of the foreman-selection process.

Factional Structure

Besides the distinction between the foreman and regular jurors another feature of the jury's structure is its division into factions favoring different verdicts. Since emergence and change of these factions seems closely bound up in the deliberation process itself, a discussion of jury factions will be taken up in the following section on the deliberation process.

THE PROCESS OF JURY DELIBERATION

A question that has been used to organize some reviews of the attitude change literature is, "Who says what to whom?" We pose the same question to organize our review of research on the verbal communication process during jury deliberation.

Who Speaks?

Who speaks during deliberation and for how long? Which characteristics of the group, the trial, and the jurors themselves affect the distribution of verbal participation among jury members?

GROUP AND TRIAL CHARACTERISTICS

A common observation in small group discussions of all sorts is that participation is not uniformly distributed across members of the group. This seems to be equally true for jury deliberations where members are equals, at least in principle. The most systematic observation of this pattern was made by Strodtbeck *et al.* 1957) in one of the jury deliberation studies of the University of Chicago Jury Project. These investigators report that in 82% of their juries, the three most active participants accounted for at least one-half of the total verbal acts. Verbatim (Simon, 1967, Appendix A) or summarized (e.g., Chester, 1970; Zerman, 1977) accounts of mock and actual jury deliberations also suggest that talking time is monopolized by relatively few jurors.

Research on discussion groups (e.g., Stephan & Mishler, 1952) suggests that this uneven participation pattern is generally more pronounced in large discussion groups. Jury size would likely have a similar effect on the distribution of participation; that is, in larger juries, proportionally fewer members would tend to dominate the discussion. Kessler (1973) compared 6- and 12-member mock juries deliberating an auto negligence suit. She reported that only 2 of 48 members (4%) of her 6-person groups failed to participate at all, whereas 24 of 96 members (25%) of her 12-person groups were silent throughout their juries' deliberations. Using criminal cases, Saks (1977) also compared participation in 6- and 12-person mock juries. For both a sample of undergraduate psychology students and a sample of former jurors from an Ohio county court, he found that the variability in communication rates across jury members was significantly greater in the 12-person juries than in the 6-person juries. Also, both the total number and the rate of verbal messages delivered during deliberation were lower in the smaller juries, although the number of unique arguments generated during deliberation did not differ significantly for the two jury sizes.

Participation rates also seem to be related to the factional structure of the jury. In one study demonstrating this effect, Hawkins (1962) determined the average percentage of participation of each faction as a function of the faction's size for 22 mock juries from the Chicago Jury Project. He found that as the size of the majority grew, its share of the total participation also grew, but at a slower rate than one would expect if the faction's share of discussion time equalled the relative size of the faction. The implication of these data, corroborated by transcripts of deliberations (e.g., Simon, 1967, Appendix A; Chester, 1970), is that minority factions attempt to "trade" arguments with the majority faction, but that they "take better than they give." That is, the numerically superior faction tends to generate more verbal acts than the minority responds with, and this imbalance grows as the majority faction gets bigger.

The total length of deliberations would appear to be simply regulated: Discussion halts whenever the group achieves the prerequisite consensus (typically unanimity). Interestingly, the Supreme Court argued otherwise as partial justification for its ruling permitting nonunanimous verdicts (*Johnson* v. *the state of Louisiana*, 1972). The Court's dissenters feared that if nonunanimous decision rules were permitted, minority factions might be outvoted before they could fully air their views. However the Court's majority felt that the larger faction would not necessarily halt deliberation upon achieving the necessary consensus, but would conscientiously address the doubts of minority members until it became clear that further deliberating was pointless. Several studies carried out since the Court's ruling (Davis *et al.*, 1975; Hans, 1979; Kerr *et al.*, 1976; Nemeth, 1977; Saks, 1977) have shown that mock juries assigned a nonunanimous rule frequently do quit deliberating as soon as they obtain enough votes. For example, Kerr *et al.* (1976) report that of the 43 mock juries that were assigned a simple majority rule and were not initially unanimous nor become hung, 24 quit deliberating upon reaching the necessary majority. Those juries which continue into what Saks (1977) terms the *epilogue interval* do not continue deliberation until unanimity is reached, but eventually outvote the unconvinced minority (although the epilogue interval is occasionally quite lengthy; see Saks, 1977). Thus, it is common for deliberation in mock juries to stop as soon as the decision rule is satisfied; when deliberation does continue it rarely produces any further progress toward consensus. It remains unclear, however, whether this readiness to ignore dissenters also characterizes the deliberations of actual juries.

INDIVIDUAL DIFFERENCES IN PARTICIPATION

We may distinguish two classes of juror characteristics that have been reliably related to the amount of juror participation: demographic or personality characteristics that jurors bring with them to deliberation and characteristics that jurors acquire during deliberation (e.g., the role of foreman).

Generally speaking, the foreman is usually among the most active members of the jury. Several Chicago Jury Project studies report that on average the foreman is responsible for between one-fourth to one-third of all verbal acts (Hawkins, 1960; James, 1957; Simon, 1967; Strodtbeck *et al.*, 1957; Strodtbeck & Hook, 1961). Early research (Strodtbeck & Hook, 1961) indicated that seating position and amount of juror participation were also associated, with jurors in end seats most active, and those in the "corner" or "flank" positions least active. However, subsequent research (Hawkins, 1960) suggests that this relationship may be a spurious result of the relationship between seating position and foreman selection.

Several studies have examined the relationship between juror sex and amount of participation. Some of the initial work indicated that male mock jurors participated significantly more than females (James, Strodtbeck, 1959; et al., 1957). However, this work was inconclusive because no control was applied for the disproportionate number of male foremen in these studies. Except for one early study (Hawkins, 1960) that preceded the movement toward greater awareness of women's rights, no one has reported significantly greater participation by male jurors who are not foremen than by female jurors who are not foremen (Bray et al., 1978; Nemeth et al., 1976; Simon, 1967).

Other individual difference variables have produced more consistent patterns. Occupational status and amount of participation appear to be positively related for nonforemen (Strodtbeck et al., 1957; Hawkins, 1960; Simon, 1967). Similarly, better-educated jurors appear to participate more actively than less well educated jurors (James, 1959), even when one controls for occupational and foreman status (Hawkins, 1960). On the other hand, there appears to be no association between juror age and participation (Strodtbeck et al., 1957; Hawkins, 1960), and there is only fragmentary evidence on the effect of juror race on participation rates. Hawkins (1960) reports a nonsignificant ($p < .10$) trend for black jurors who are not foremen to participate less than nonblacks for a civil case deliberation (nonblacks = 7.1% of total participation, per juror, blacks = 5.5% of total, per juror). As is the case in many actual courts (cf. Hans & Vidmar, Chapter 3, this volume), blacks constituted a small minority in Hawkins' sample (29 of 440 subjects were black) and hence, were always greatly outnumbered by nonblacks on these juries.

SUMMARY

In principle, there are no differences in status or power between jurors and each has the same right and obligation to speak. In practice, however, it seems that this egalitarian ideal is rarely, if ever, realized. At least for the traditionally large (i.e., 12-person) jury, participation seems to be dominated by a relatively small subgroup of jurors, of whom the foreman is usually the most active. Furthermore, the jury setting does not necessarily erase inequalities of ability and predisposition to speak; jurors who have less education and lower occupational status tend to participate less.

Unequal participation in deliberation counters attempts to obtain equal representation (cf. Hans & Vidmar, Chapter 3, this volume); a constituency adequately represented on the jury in terms of numbers of members may still be underrepresented in discussion. However, we are ill prepared to recommend procedural changes that will facilitate equal participation. For example, little is known about the causal basis for social status effects (cf. Hawkins, 1960). Do higher status jurors talk more because of greater ability and experience at such tasks? Do the lower status members simply defer to high status jurors or encourage them to speak by being more attentive and responsive to their input? Answers to such questions must await further research.

Who Is Spoken To?

There is relatively less evidence on the target of jurors' comments than on their source. This is due, in part, to the difficulty of unambiguously identifying the target, since many comments seem to be directed to no one juror in particular. Also, the target of comment is usually not coded with Bales Interaction Process Analysis (IPA), the coding scheme most widely used in this area of research. Nevertheless, certain patterns have emerged. They can be usefully summarized in terms of the sequential stages or phases of small group discussion. Several stage models have been proposed (Bales & Strodtbeck, 1951; Bennis & Shepard, 1956; Fisher, 1970; Scheidel & Corwell, 1964; Tuckman, 1956) that are all fairly similar. According to these models, the group begins its work with an *orientation phase* during which the nature of its task is defined and initial ideas and personal preferences are tentatively revealed. If differences of opinion emerge, the group moves into an *open conflict phase*, during which group members tend to take sides and become committed, actively defending their own views and attacking the views of opposing positions. Eventually, and with luck, the group enters a period of *conflict resolution* in which a mutually acceptable decision begins to emerge. After sufficient movement, the outcome (or the impossibility of consensus) becomes evident to the members of the group and there follows a concluding *reconciliation phase*. Here the members converge and mutually support one another, attempting to heal the wounds of conflict and to establish group solidarity and commitment to the final decision (or perhaps, if consensus is not possible, to a mutually agreed upon truce).

The channeling of communication in the deliberating jury seems to follow such a sequence. As the jury begins deliberation, jurors may direct many comments to the group as a whole and to members of their own faction as they try to determine the nature and strength of one another's views. As the factions are identified, more and more of the communication is directed to the opposing faction(s). If and when enough members have shifted their positions for the final outcome to become evident, comments again are more likely to be directed to the whole group. Transcripts of actual (e.g., Chester, 1970; Zerman, 1977) and simulated (Simon, 1967, Appendix A) jury deliberations appear to conform to this general pattern. Hawkins (1960) has provided a case study showing this pattern explicitly. He divided the deliberation of a mock jury into four phases, roughly paralleling the phases of the generic model outlined above. The proportion of communications between members of opposing factions rose steadily from the first (53%) to the second (60%) to the third phase (67%). The proportion of comments directed toward members of a juror's own faction and toward the whole group simultaneously dropped. During the final phase, after the group outcome had become evident, the proportion of between-faction communication dropped sharply (to 46%) while the amount directed to the whole group rose sharply (from 17% during the third to 33% during the fourth phase).

A second pattern suggested by the literature is that those who speak more are themselves more likely to be spoken to. This pattern again reflects the fact that deliberation consists largely, and literally, of the exchange of views. For example, James (1957) found that the foremen of her juries not only initiated the most comments but were also the targets of the largest number of comments. Similarly, Nemeth *et al.* (1976) found that not only did men tend to talk more than women, but they also tended to be the targets of more communications.

What Is Said?

We now shift our focus to the content, temporal flow, and patterning of verbal interaction during deliberation. How does the jury sound? What kinds of ideas are expressed? How is discussion organized? The common impression of those who have listened to many mock juries deliberate or who have participated in actual deliberations is that deliberation tends to be rather erratic and disorganized. Consider Chester's (1970) description of the deliberation of his actual jury:

> The discussion now tended to wander from one point to another, depending on which juror managed to command our attention. The deliberation turned into a process of "thinking out loud," with one or another juror giving voice to something that bothered him, or that he thought particularly significant, or that was simply irrelevant. His statement often induced a comment from another juror on the same point or it simply served as a stimulus for a series of unrelated statements from other jurors [p. 131].

Kalven and Zeisel's (1966) characterization of their mock juries deliberation is graphic and, based on our own observations, quite accurate.

> There is at first, in William James' phase about the baby, the sense of buzzing, booming, confusion. After a while, we become accustomed to the quick, fluid movement of jury discussion and realize that the talk moves with remarkable flexibility. It touches an issue, leaves it, and returns again. Even a casual inspection makes it evident that this is interesting and arresting human behavior. It is not a formal debate; nor, although it is mercurial and difficult to pick up, is it just excited talk [p. 486].

GENERAL CONTENT ANALYSES

A few investigators have attempted the extremely difficult task of picking up and analyzing the content of deliberation. The most extensive content analyses have been conducted by Rita James Simon (1967; James, 1959). These analyses are based on 10 mock juries deliberating a housebreaking case. Comments were classified into five general categories. Table 8.1 lists these along with the distribution of comments observed in Simon's sample.

Much, but by no means all, of the deliberation focused on the evidence of the case itself (44% for testimony and opinions on evidence). The percentage of comments dealing with instructions may be atypically high for this case, since the court's definition of insanity and instructions on the role of expert psychiatric testimony were central issues for this case. Simon also rated the quality of

TABLE 8.1
Relative Content Usage in Jury Deliberation[a]

Content category	Percentage (%)	Percentage of high quality[b]
References to testimony	15	77
Opinions on facts of case	29	82
References to court's instructions	8	62
Comments on deliberation procedure	26	76
Experiences from personal and daily life	22	57

[a] Adapted from R. James, Status and competence of jurors, *American Journal of Sociology*, 1959, *64*, 563–570 by permission of The University of Chicago Press.
[b] Percentage of comments in each content category judged by James (1959) to be of high quality.

jurors' comments. Comments about instructions and testimony were classified as accurate or inaccurate, personal experience and opinion comments were classified as pertinent or nonpertinent for the jury's task, and procedural comments were classified as facilitative or nonfacilitative. In Table 8.1, the percentages of *high quality* (i.e., accurate, pertinent, or facilitative) comments are presented for each content category. These data show that the jurors comments were usually of a high quality. Kessler's (1973) data tend to corroborate this sanguine conclusion. Lawyers and law students classified each issue raised by deliberating mock jurors as either legally relevant or irrelevant. The great majority (82%) of the issues discussed were judged to be legally relevant. However, jurors' comments often appeared to have no immediate implication for the guilt or innocence of the defendant; James (1959) found that 64% of all her juries' comments were "neutral" in this sense. Finally, she found that it was more common for a juror to express ideas or opinions than to agree with those of another juror (62% were of the former type).

CONTENT ANALYSES BY SOURCE CHARACTERISTICS

Surprisingly, there are virtually no systematic content analyses of the comments of the most obvious source, the jury foreman. Nonetheless, the foreman does seem more likely to discuss deliberation procedure and the judge's instructions than does a nonforeman (James, 1957; Hawkins, 1960). There also appears to be considerable variation in the roles imposed on or accepted by foremen; some become highly directive and active; others closely approximate the "average" juror; others seem to purposely assume a nonactive, "neutral" role (Hawkins, 1960).

The sex of a juror seems to influence not only the amount of participation but its content as well. Strodtbeck and Mann (1956) examined the Bales's IPA profiles separately for male and female members of 12 mock juries. Males were found to devote proportionally more of their time to the categories "gives opinion" and "gives information" than did female jurors, whereas females devoted proportionally more of their comments than male jurors to "positive reactions" (that is, the pooled Bales's categories "shows solidarity," "shows tension release," and "agrees"). Strodtbeck and Mann concluded that the traditional sex role differentiation (e.g., Strodtbeck, 1951) of the family also characterized jury deliberation. Male jurors seemed more likely to assume the "task-leader" roles, whereas females seemed relatively more likely to assume "socio-emotional" leader roles (Slater, 1955).

At least two interesting external validity questions emerge from Strodtbeck and Mann's research. First, do these sex role differences observed in an adult sample during the 1950s persist today after considerable effort has been devoted to achieving equality for women? The second question relates to the sex composition of Strodtbeck and Mann's juries, where women never outnumbered men. It is unclear whether women would still gravitate to the reactive, supportive role if they were not outnumbered by males.

We have noted previously that sex bias in foreman selection persists in contemporary juries and that there is much evidence in nonjury settings that traditional sex roles persist (e.g., Bem & Bem, 1970; Wyer & Malinkowski, 1972). Furthermore, Nemeth *et al.* (1976) have recently replicated the pattern of Strodtbeck and Mann's (1956) results with modern college students, a population that might be assumed to hold less traditional ideas about sex roles than did Strodtbeck and Mann's sample. Yet the proportion of females' remarks that were "agreements" was significantly higher than males', whereas more of males' talking time was devoted to "giving opinions" and "giving information." Recent work by Piliavin and Martin (1978) speaks to the second issue about sex composition of juries. They varied the sex composition of groups discussing a set of social problems, and coded the groups' interaction using the IPA system. Their results showed the same sex role differentiation reported by Strodtbeck and Mann and by Nemeth *et al.*, and, somewhat surprisingly, such differentiation was strongest in same-sex groups.[1] Interaction in mixed-sex groups tended to moderate sex role differentiation. Thus, it seems likely that the effect observed by Strodtbeck and Mann probably continues to characterize jury deliberation today, and that the closer the jury comes to being all male or all female, the more pronounced the role differentiation becomes. Hence, Strodtbeck and Mann's findings appear not to be limited to the predominately male juries they observed.

Jurors' education also appears to be related to the content of their comments. The least well educated of James' (1959) mock jurors devoted proportionally fewer of their comments to the judge's instructions and the procedures the jury should use than did the better-educated jurors,[2] and the comments they offered turned out to be, respectively, less accurate and more disruptive in these categories. These jurors, whose formal education had ended in grammar school,

---

[1] Since there were no foremen in Piliavin and Martin's groups, their results also ruled out the confound of jurors' sex and foremen status that clouded previous findings.

[2] This relationship held even after the foreman's input was removed.

tended to focus proportionally more of their comments on testimony, personal experiences, and their opinions of the trial. They were also more likely to passively express acceptance of another's view than would their better-educated colleagues.

It appears, then, that jurors who are more active (e.g., males, better-educated jurors) also have different things to say than their less vocal colleagues. Another demonstration of this was provided by Strodtbeck and Mann (1956) who found that a significantly greater proportion of the active jurors' comments were devoted to asking questions, expressing negative reactions (e.g., disagreeing, showing antagonism), and giving information. Altogether, the results suggest that higher status, active jurors devote relatively more of their input to actively solving the jury's task, while the lower status, relatively inactive jurors are more likely to limit themselves to following and supporting.

EFFECTS OF CASE OR PROCEDURE ON DELIBERATION
CONTENT

How do factors which affect the verdicts of individual jurors affect the group deliberation process? Can observed effects on jury decisions plausibly be traced to differences in what is discussed during deliberation? Such questions have stimulated the research examined in this section. In some of this work, the pattern is straightforward. For example, Saks (1977) found that the negligible effects of jury size on verdicts were paralleled by negligible differences in deliberation content. And Borgida (1980) found that providing more admissible evidence on a rape victim's prior sexual history both reduced the likelihood of conviction and the frequency with which the victim's consent was discussed during deliberation. In some studies, one can establish that some case or procedural variable indeed affected both deliberation content and verdict, but the link between the two is rather fuzzy—see, for example, Nemeth's (1977) research on assigned decision rule, or Hans and Brooks' (1977) work on corroboration instructions in rape cases.

One interesting line of research has shown that juries often discuss matters prohibited by the judge's charge to the jury. For example, a majority of Klein and Jess's (1966) and Miller and Fontes's (1979) mock juries discussed evidence that had been ruled inadmissible by the court. As yet another example, both mock (e.g., Hans & Doob, 1976; Simon, 1967) and actual (e.g., Chester, 1970) juries sometimes discuss the consequences of conviction for the defendant, even though this is not legally part of their responsibility (see also Kalven & Zeisel, 1966).

Sometimes features of the evidence seem to influence the thinking of the jurors (and hence, their deliberation) in ways contrary to the court's intention. Hans and Doob (1976) examined the effect of revealing a previous conviction on jury deliberations and verdicts. The usual legal rationale is that such information may help jurors assess the credibility of the defendant's testimony. While prior record strongly influenced verdicts, there was no parallel effect on discussion of the defendant's credibility. However, Hans and Doob's content analysis revealed that knowledge of a prior record led to more frequent assertions that the evidence against the defendant was strong and to more frequent mention of those facts most damaging to the defendant's case, and similiarly, to less frequent dismissal of damaging evidence. Interestingly, jurors frequently maintained, both during and after deliberation, that the defendant's prior record should not and did not affect their guilt judgments.

Foreman Influence: Polling the Jury

Although it is clear that foremen talk more than their fellow jurors, it is not at all clear whether this greater activity translates into greater influence on the jury's decision. Several studies bear on this issue (Bevan, Albert, Loiseaux, Mayfield, & Wright, 1958; James, 1959; Simon, 1967; Strodtbeck et al., 1957), but they are characterized by inconsistent results and serious methodological problems (e.g., extremely small samples, very indirect analyses, use of confederate foremen). As a consequence, there is little reliable evidence on the relative power of the foreman to influence the jury's verdict directly.

The foreman does seem to influence the procedures under which the jury operates (Hawkins, 1960; Simon, 1957), probably because the court prescribes little of the jury's procedure and the foreman occupies the only formal position of leadership. We consider one particular aspect of this power to govern procedure: when and how the jury is polled. Our discussion, drawn primarily from Hawkins (1960), first describes the variety of polling procedures and then shows how these may be related to the deliberation process and product.

Hawkins (1960) examined the deliberations of 46 mock juries considering a civil case. Four different polling methods were observed: (a) the go-around, in which each juror in turn announced his or her verdict preference with or without comment, (b) the secret ballot, (c) the show of hands, and (d) the verbal dissent, in which only those opposing a proposition registered a verbal vote. Juries used the go-around and secret ballot methods most often (a little over one-third of all polls by each method). The show of hands and verbal dissent methods were used only about one-half as often. When the faction split was nearly even and the group was far from unanimity, the go-around and secret ballot methods were used almost exclusively, but as the jury approached unanimity, the use of the show of hands and verbal dissent methods became more common. Final polls took one of the following three forms (in order of decreasing usage): voting (i.e., a formal polling); switching, in which the last holdouts verbally gave in and joined the majority; and announcement, in which the foreman announced a verdict after concluding from jurors' comments that no differences in opinion existed.

More interesting than these descriptive results are the relationships Hawkins found between the method and timing of polling and the deliberation process and product. First, juries that hung were significantly more likely to have used the ballot technique than juries that managed to reach a verdict. Secondly, the timing of the first poll was predictive of the speed (but not the outcome) of deliberation. Juries that took a poll before beginning to discuss the case were the fastest to finish; juries that took a delayed poll were next fastest, and juries that delayed voting until unanimity had been reached were the slowest. Hawkins organized these findings by suggesting that early polling speeds the transition from what we referred to earlier as the orientation phase into the open conflict phase, by creating an open alignment of opposing factions. Secret balloting may have made it more difficult for the majority to identify, and hence, pressure and/or persuade the minority during this conflict phase, resulting in more hung juries. In line with these conjectures, Hawkins observed that the majority faction favored frequent and public polling more than the minority faction. A final bit of corroborative evidence comes from Kerr (1981). Mock juries that were privately polled by the experimenter at 1-min intervals tended to deliberate faster and to hang less frequently than juries that were not polled. Altoghether these results suggest that the foreman may, perhaps unknowingly, be able to hasten deliberations and increase the power of the majority by taking a public poll (a go-around or show of hands) as early in deliberation as possible.

THE PRODUCT OF JURY DELIBERATION: THE ROAD TO CONSENSUS

Our review of research on the deliberation process has said little about the probable outcome of that process. The goal of our review up to this point has been primarily descriptive, and has emphasized verbal communication. However, if we shift our sights to predicting the outcome of jury deliberation and to understanding the nature of the social influence processes leading to that product, we must recognize that "what is said to whom" is not the only, nor perhaps the most informative, way to characterize the jury's deliberation. Kalven and Zeisel (1966), for reasons to be described, even suggest in their classic study of the jury that the content of jury deliberation may nearly always be irrelevant to the outcome of the process. Descriptions of communication pattern and verbal content may be very much like descriptions of the scenery along a route traveled, with little mention of landmarks that indicate the route or the final destination.

It is perhaps apparent but worth emphasizing that the jury is a task-oriented group; its task is to decide the outcome of a trial. This entails fashioning a collective decision out of the opinions of its members. That is, the jury must achieve the requisite consensus from the preferences of its members, even hough these preferences may be quite disparate at the onset of the deliberation. Borrowing an analogy from Godwin and Restle (1974), we could characterize the deliberation process as the group's "road to agreement"; the destination is a decision about the guilt or innocence of the defendant in a criminal case or the legal responsibility of a defendant in a civil case. The origin of the journey can be characterized in terms of the preferences, facts, opinions, and/or predispositions that jurors bring to the deliberation. This section will focus on charting the road to agreement from origin to destination. To what degree is the destination (i.e., the final decision) determined by where the jury starts? What path does the jury take from initial disagreement to consensus? What signposts along the route indicate the probable destination?

Of course, such questions cannot be considered without reference to process. In a sense, this section is a natural extension of the preceding discussion of communication process. However, in focusing on process as leading to product, we shall characterize process in a somewhat different way than we did in the previous section. *Process*, in the broadest sense of the word, can refer to any behaviors that occur during the group's interaction. Communicative acts—who says what to whom—are one class of behaviors that can define process. Process might also include nonverbal behaviors (e.g., gestures, glances, or facial expressions) and cognitive events occuring within group members such as changes of opinion and interpersonal attraction. The behaviors that we choose to represent process ultimately depend on our purposes. In focusing on product and the process leading to the product, we shall describe process in various ways that reflect the conceptual views of different investigators of jury decision making. However, many of these representations of process incorporate, in one way or another, the individual verdict preferences of the jury's members. This emphasis is not surprising; the link between the product or decision of the jury and the preferences of its members is obvious.

The way in which individual preferences have been used to predict the jury's product has varied. Social decision scheme theory (Davis, 1973, 1980; Davis *et al.*, 1975; Davis, Kerr, Stasser, Meek, & Holt, 1977; Kerr, Stasser, & Davis, 1979) emphasizes the relationship between the initial distribution of preferences in the jury and the final verdict. Other approaches have charted the patterns of preference changes between the initial distribution of preferences and the final decision (Davis, Stasser, Spitzer, & Holt, 1976; Stasser & Davis, 1977; Kerr, in press). Kerr, in press, and Hawkins (1960) have suggested that the first change of preference by a jury member may be very informative; once a jury member defects from an initial faction, that faction rarely prevails. We shall now review the evidence for these positions.

Stasser, Kerr, and Davis (1980) have suggested that the preference distribution of jury members over the decision alternatives is particularly useful for describing process and predicting the final verdict because that distribution is closely related to social influence processes occurring in the group. Deutsch and Gerard (1955) contended that opinion change or acquiescence can result from either *informational influence* based on the exchange of information relevant to the task, or *normative influence*, based on compliance with the expectations or desires of others. Stasser *et al.* argued that the nature of both informational and normative influence in a decision-making group such as a jury may be linked to the relative number of supporters for each of the decision alternatives. The one constant in these approaches to the process leading to the product is that the preference distribution of jury members over the decision alternatives is an important and informative unit of analysis.

Simultaneous examination of the distribution of initial juror preferences and the final jury verdict has shown two common findings: a *majority effect*, which is the tendency for juries to decide on the position initially favored by a majority of members; and a *leniency bias* which is the tendency for deviations from the majority effect to favor the defendant. We now turn to a consideration of these two findings, first discussing several studies that document the majority effect and analyze the social influence processes and patterns of opinion change that underlie it. Our analysis counters the oversimplified and pessimistic view that majority effects reflect the tyrannical power of a majority or the "spinelessness" of the minority. We next examine the leniency bias and conclude by speculating on some of the possible explanations for it.

The Majority Effect: The Importance of Where the Jury Starts

A jury can be characterized by the initial preference distribution of its members. In the case of a criminal trial with a charge of only a single count, we can simply count the number of jurors who favor guilty or not guilty at the onset of deliberation. To what degree does this initial configuration of opinion dictate or predict the final verdict?

INITIAL VOTES AND FINAL VERDICT

Kalven and Zeisel (1966) concluded their classic study of judge and jury disagreements with "a radical hunch about the function of the deliberation process [p. 489]." Their "hunch" is expressed in an often-quoted analogy: "The deliberation process might well be likened to what the developer does for an exposed film: it brings out the picture, but the outcome is predetermined [p. 489]." By reconstructing first-ballot votes from posttrial interviews of jurors for 225 criminal trials, Kalven and Zeisel documented a strong relationship between these initial votes and the final verdict. Of the 215 juries that contained an initial majority (10 juries were split six to six for guilty and not guilty), only 6 reached a final decision that did not have majority support on the initial ballot. Thus, the storybook picture of a strong and vocal minority that sways the jury by eloquent, emotional, or well-reasoned debate seems to be a rarity.

Nemeth (1977) approached the problem in a different manner by composing six-person juries that contained a four-to-two configuration of initial opinions. In 19 juries, the four-person majority favored guilty, whereas in the remaining 18 juries, the four-person majority favored not guilty. Consistent with the majority-effect hypothesis, 16 of the 18 groups with an initial not-guilty majority reached a verdict of not guilty; only 1 group reached a guilty verdict, and the remaining group hung. However, the results for the juries that initially contained a majority favoring guilty present a somewhat different picture. Of these 19 groups, 7 reached a guilty verdict, 7 reached a not guilty verdict, and 5 were hung. Thus, a majority of four in a six-person jury was much less likely to prevail when it favored guilty. This result anticipates an important qualification to the majority effect—there seems to be a leniency bias in the deliberation process favoring acquittal. Nemeth speculated, "it is likely that the position of 'not guilty' may be easier to defend, all other things being equal, since it is easier to raise a 'reasonable doubt' than to convince a person beyond such a doubt [p. 54]." We will consider later this and other possible reasons for a leniency bias in the deliberation process. For the present, we will examine in more detail the evidence for a majority effect arising from applications of a general model of group decision making.

SOCIAL DECISION SCHEMES

Social decision scheme theory (Davis, 1973) explicitly incorporates in a stochastic model the notion that the final decision of a group can be predicted, from the initial preference distribution of group members.[3] Several components of the theory deserve elaboration. In a simple criminal trial, two decision alternatives typically exist—verdicts of guilty or not guilty. Social decision scheme theory represents a particular group in terms of the number of members initially favoring each decision alternative (called a distinguishable distribution). If r_G and r_{NG} are the number of jury members initially favoring guilty and not guilty, respectively, then the distinguishable distribution of a jury may be denoted as (r_G, r_{NG}). Of course, many distinguishable distributions are possible; given two verdict alternatives and a jury size of r, $r + 1$ distinguishable distributions are possible. For example, the members of a six-person jury ($r = 6$) can distribute themselves over the two alternatives, guilty and not guilty, in seven ways: (6,0), (5,1), (4,2), (3,3), (2,4), (1,5), or (0,6).

Whereas the jury member may favor or vote for either guilty or not guilty, the jury deliberation may result in one of three outcomes: guilty, not guilty, or a hung jury (i.e., no decision). Social decision scheme theory attempts to specify the probability of each of these outcomes for every possible distinguishable distribution. That is, for each of the $r + 1$ possible configurations of initial opinions within the jury, what is the probability of the jury (a) reaching a verdict of guilty, (b) reaching a verdict of not guilty, and (c) failing to reach a verdict (i.e., being hung)? These probabilities are the entries in the social decision scheme matrix, D, that summarizes the decision processes of a sample or

---

[3] See Penrod & Hastie (1979) for a review of several other models of the jury decision-making process.

population of juries. Some examples will help clarify the concept and role of a social decision scheme.

Table 8.2 illustrates several idealized social decision schemes that might apply to six-person juries. The D matrix on the left represents a "pure majority" process in that any initial distinguishable distribution containing a majority position will decide in favor of that majority with a probability of 1.0. Note, however, that the "majority wins" rule is not sufficient to cover all possibilities: The (3,3) distinguishable distribution does not contain a majority. For this (3,3) case, a subscheme must be invoked. The D matrices at the left and middle of Table 8.2 both have a primary decision scheme of "pure majority" but contain different subschemes for the nonmajority (3,3) case. The D matrix on the left predicts that all juries with an initial (3,3) split will be hung ("otherwise hung" subscheme), whereas the middle D matrix invokes a subscheme in which (3,3) juries have a reasonably high probability of deciding not guilty, with much lower probabilities of deciding guilty or being hung ("otherwise, leniency bias" subscheme). These simple examples should serve to illustrate two points. First, even straightforward notions such as "majority wins" are not adequate to account for all possible distinguishable distributions that may occur. Second, the D matrix can represent subtly different decision processes that are not easily captured by verbal labels or descriptions.

The D matrix on the right in Table 8.2 further illustrates the versatility of Social decision scheme notation. This decision scheme incorporates a modified majority effect in which the majority, if it exists, is likely to prevail; however, the majority effect is stronger for not guilty decisions than for guilty decisions. That is, a not-guilty majority never fails; whereas, a guilty majority may fail and, given failure, the jury will decide not guilty.

One could, or course, generate many other social decision scheme matrices either representing slight variations on those given in Table 8.2 or incorporat-

TABLE 8.2
Idealized Social Decision Scheme Matrices, D, Representing Various Theories of Decision Process in Six-Person Juries

$r_{G}r_{NG}$	Pure majority; otherwise hung			Pure majority; otherwise, leniency bias			Modified majority/ leniency bias		
	G	NG	H	G	NG	H	G	NG	H
6, 0	1.0	0	0	1.0	0	0	1.0	0	0
5, 1	1.0	0	0	1.0	0	0	.9	.1	0
4, 2	1.0	0	0	1.0	0	0	.8	.2	0
3, 3	0	0	1.0	.2	.6	.2	.1	.6	.3
2, 4	0	1.0	0	0	1.0	0	0	1.0	0
1, 5	0	1.0	0	0	1.0	0	0	1.0	0
0, 6	0	1.0	0	0	1.0	0	0	1.0	0

TABLE 8.3
Obtained Social Decision Scheme Matrices from Studies of Six-Person Mock Juries Employing Various Assigned Rules

Initial distinguishable distribution	Jury verdicts			Jury verdicts[b]		
r_G, r_{NG}	G	NG	H	G	NG	H
Simple majority rule assigned	Davis *et al.* (1977)			Kerr *et al.* (1976)		
6, 0[a]	—	—	—	1.00	0	0
5, 1	.93	.07	0	.88	0	.12
4, 2	.84	.16	0	.85	.15	0
3, 3	.16	.68	.16	.20	.40	.40
2, 4	.06	.94	0	.11	.89	0
1, 5	0	1.00	0	0	1.00	0
0, 6	0	1.00	0	0	1.00	0
Unanimity rule assigned	Kerr (in press)			Kerr *et al.* (1976)		
6, 0	1.00	0	0	1.00	0	0
5, 1	.78	.07	.16	1.00	0	0
4, 2	.44	.26	.30	.25	.33	.42
3, 3	.09	.51	.40	.25	.33	.42
2, 4	.04	.79	.17	0	.43	.57
1, 5	0	.93	.07	0	.50	.50
0, 6	0	1.00	0	0	1.00	0

[a] No juries were observed in this initial distinguishable distribution.
[b] Copyright 1976 by the American Psychological Association. Reprinted by permission.

ing other notions of process. However, these examples should sufficiently illustrate the use of social decision schemes in representing the process leading to the product. We will examine the results of several studies using social decision scheme representation. More comprehensive reviews may be found in Davis (1980) and Kerr *et al.* (1979).

Table 8.3 summarizes the obtained social decision scheme matrices from selected studies using six-person mock juries. The table has been organized in terms of the decision rule that juries were *assigned* for reaching a verdict. The distinction between an assigned decision rule and a decision scheme deserves some mention. The decision rule stipulates the degree of consensus, as evidenced by some formal or informal voting process, required for a group to reach a decision. Thus, for example, a unanimity decision rule requires that on the terminal vote all members vote in favor of the group's decision. On the other hand, a decision scheme represents the decision process by relating the initial preference configuration to the final group decision. The decision scheme need not correspond to the decision rule. For example, it is conceivable that juries may evidence a pure majority decision scheme while deliberating under a unanimity decision rule. This result would obtain if the decision alternative preferred by the initial majority eventually received the vote of all members (because of opinion change or acquiescence to the initial majority position). It has been of interest to examine possible differences in decision schemes as a function of assigned decision rules for a number of theoretical and practical reasons (cf. Kerr *et al.*, 1979).

Overall, the obtained social decision scheme matrices in Table 8.3 suggest a majority process modified by a leniency bias. The majority process is particularly evident for juries containing an initial not-guilty majority and deliberating under a simple majority assigned rule. Even under an assigned unanimous decision rule, initial not-guilty majorities rarely convict, although the jury may be hung. On the other hand, initial guilty majorities are often unsuccessful when they contain a small majority of only four out of six and are assigned a unanimity rule.

The most consistent trend across the different assigned rules is the increasing frequency of hung juries as the degree of required consensus to reach a verdict increases from a simple majority to unanimity.[4] As a result, the majority effect is reduced primarily because of the frequency of hung juries. (See Saks, Chapter 11, this volume, for further discussion of the effects of varying assigned rules.) Other applications of social decision scheme analyses have also obtained evidence for some form of a majority process (e.g., Saks, 1977; Davis *et al.*, 1975).

If we ignore hung juries for the moment, there is considerable evidence for a majority process in the social decision schemes given in Table 8.3. We might characterize the process as follows. A simple majority for guilty wins whereas a 5/6 majority for not guilty wins. The leniency bias appears most strongly in the (4,2) and (3,3) cases. In the (4,2) case, the initial simple majority for guilty often reaches a decision of not guilty. When the jury is initially split (3,3) it is more likely to decide not guilty than guilty. Thus, where a jury starts on the road to agreement seems to tell a lot about where it is likely to end up. Kalven and Zeisel's (1966) "radical" hunch that "the real decision is often made before the deliberation begins [p. 488]." does not appear so radical in retrospect. But what are we to make of it?

One implication is that the evidence presented in a trial functions primarily to affect the likelihood that various distinguishable distributions will occur at onset of deliberation. Once the groups are formed and the initial configurations of preference established, the outcomes of deliberation follow a predictable pattern. Does this mean that the jury somehow abrogates its role of discussing and evaluating the evidence in reaching its decision? Or are we to assume that if a sufficient consensus exists at the onset of deliberation, minority members merely acquiesce to meet the explicit requirements of the assigned decision rule through some conformity process (e.g., Asch, 1956)? We think not. Although social conformity is probably involved, we hesitate to characterize such con-

---

[4]The tendency for an increase in the incidence of hung juries as more stringent decision rules were employed was probably fostered, in part, by the imposition of time limits on deliberation in all of these studies.

formity as nothing more than the undisciplined and unthinking acquiescence of minority members. The leniency bias, itself, suggests that the deliberation is more than a simple conformity process. Something more complex than the sheer weight of numbers must be operating to give the defense position an advantage. Furthermore, the initial majority does not always win; in one sense, it fails when the jury ends up being hung. As previously indicated, the failure of the initial majority by virtue of not reaching a verdict is likely when the jury must obtain unanimous agreement and time for deliberation is limited. The implication is that majorities need time to convince minority members to change their vote. Minority members do not automatically nor immediately defect to the majority position. Certainly, there is "strength in numbers," but that strength must accrue from social processes that occur over time.

En Route to a Verdict: Wherein Resides the Power of the Majority?

In an attempt to understand the majority effect, as well as the accompanying leniency bias, we will consider events that occur during the deliberation. One approach is to analyze the nature of social influence processes that lead to opinion change and acquiescence during group discussion. Another approach is to describe the pattern of opinion change over time. In essence, what is the route by which agreement is reached?

SOCIAL INFLUENCE IN DECISION MAKING GROUPS

Deutsch and Gerard (1955) distinguished between informational and normative social influences. Informational influence occurs when a change of opinion results from socially mediated information bearing on the issue at hand. One function of the jury's deliberation is to pool, highlight, and interpret information that is relevant to the jury's decision task. This information may take the form of facts, logical argument, common sense, or personal experience. On the other hand, normative influence occurs when a person changes an opinion in order to comply with others' expectations about what one should or ought to do.

Stasser et al. (1980) suggest that generally both informational and normative influences are operating during group discussion. Discussion may serve to express expectations about what others should do as well as convey information relevant to the decision to be made. Stasser et al. argue, additionally, that the potential for both informational and normative influences may be linked to the configuration of opinion that exists within a group. Both types of influence may underlie the strength that derives from numbers. The Stasser et al. position is that the ability of a faction to exert informational influence depends on the amount of unique and relevant information it introduces in discussion. Except in the unusual case in which all proponents of a position base their opinion on identical sets of information, each proponent will be able to contribute additional information supporting the faction's position. Furthermore, as faction size increases, the faction dominates more of the discussion (cf. Hawkins, 1962). In this way, the number of proponents of a position affects not only the available supporting information but also the likelihood that the information will actually be introduced during discussion.

The relationship between normative influence and the strength-in-numbers effect is a little less obvious, but just as plausible. Any expression of opinion in a group carries a normative message—"I believe such and such and think you should too." At one level, compliance with these normative expectations may be viewed as a selfish attempt to gain social approval or avoid social disapproval (Schachter, 1951). Even such selfishly motivated acquiescence would likely reinforce a strength-in-numbers effect; social disapproval by many is worse than social disapproval by few. However, at another level, normative influence may result from a more egalitarian motive. A jury is, as any decision-making group, a task-oriented group; its goal is to successfully resolve a legal dispute. Being hung is, in one sense, a failure to reach this mutually shared goal. As expressed by Stasser et al. (1980), "to the degree that group members agree on a particular alternative, that alternative becomes identified as a fair and reasonable choice of the group [p. 435]." Thus, it is likely that only a great deal of confidence in the correctness of their position will motivate minority members to maintain their stance and risk ultimate failure in reaching a resolution. Furthermore, as the majority faction gains additional proponents, the remaining minority members undoubtedly recognize the diminishing viability of their position.

In summary, it is likely that the effects of informational and normative influence converge to fuel the strength-in-numbers effect. Whether opinion change occurs because of information exchanged during discussion or because of normative pressures, the majority faction tends to have the advantage in recruiting new adherents. However, Stasser et al. (1980) note the possibility that such a tendency may be modified by the nature of the task. If one position is less easily defended or requires a higher degree of subjective certainty to endorse, it may require relatively more proponents to acquire an advantage in the social influence process. Such may be the case for the guilty position in criminal trials (cf. Nemeth, 1977) and may account for the aforementioned leniency bias.

Because of the concise representation of social decision schemes such as those given in Table 8.3, one is tempted to view the processes they represent in a mechanical way. For example, if a verdict of not guilty occurs with virtual certainty when a simple majority favors not guilty at the onset of deliberation, one might conclude that the deliberation is incidental to the decision-making process; that is, that the decision is a foregone conclusion once the initial majority is obtained. However, another interpretation might be that even when verdicts follow with near certainty, the emergence of the final verdict still depends strongly upon social influence processes that take place during deliberation. In other words, a simple social decision scheme such as "majority wins" does not imply a simple decision process. The majority may win but only because complex informational and normative social influence processes are biased in its favor. There are several ways of exploring the dynamics associated with the deliberation process. One approach is to focus on the content of discussion and the relationship of content to final verdict. Such an approach obviously emphasizes the importance of informational social influence.

THE CONTENT OF DISCUSSION

The notion that opinion change in a group is related to the content of discussion is hardly new or surprising. Several theorists have emphasized the role of informational content. One often-cited finding is that group discussion leads to more extreme opinions or judgments. This tendency has been labeled *group polarization* (cf. Myers & Lamm, 1976). Vinokur and Burnstein (1974; see also Burnstein & Vinokur, 1973; Ebbesen & Bowers, 1974) have argued that opinion shifts that underlie the group polarization phenomena are largely a function of the number, persuasiveness, and uniqueness or originality of arguments that can be introduced in group discussion. Others have modeled opinion change during group discussion using information integration theory (Anderson, 1974; Anderson & Graesser, 1976; see also Kaplan, 1977, for a jury-related application).

However, more germane to our present examination of the process leading to the product is the valence model of Hoffman and Maier (1967, 1964; Hoffman, 1979). The valence model suggests that support for a particular alternative accumulates during discussion. The valence for a particular alternative at any time is simply the cumulative number of statements made in its support. Once the valence of a particular alternative exceeds the valence of its closest competitor by a critical value (adoption threshold), that alternative will eventually emerge as the group's decision. Thus, by keeping a running total of the number of comments supporting each position, one can potentially predict the final decision. Once one position obtains a critical advantage in this cumulative tally, the decision is functionally made regardless of balance of support during the remainder of the discussion.

Nemeth (1977) applied a valence analysis to the deliberation of mock juries. She found that once the difference between the valences for guilty and not guilty exceeded seven, the alternative with the higher valence was the group's final verdict in 36 of 37 cases. Furthermore, this critical difference was attained relatively early in deliberation for most juries. Nemeth defined the time taken to reach a critical difference in valence as *functional deliberation time*. In her data, mean functional deliberation times (for different experimental conditions) ranged from 8.0 to 25.6 min whereas the means for actual deliberation times to final verdict ranged from 29.8 to 68.3 min. In other words, by simply cumulating the number of supporting statements made for each alternative, the final verdict of most juries could be predicted quite early in the deliberation. This result underscores the importance of discussion in determining the final verdict. The implication is that the position supported most frequently in the early stages of discussion will likely be the group's decision. But what factors will result in a position accumulating relatively more support early in a jury's deliberation? One obvious factor is the number of available arguments favoring a position. Thus, the relative amount of testimony and facts presented in the trial favoring a position should be considered. However, as already mentioned, a large percentage of a discussion consists of opinions and personal experiences (James, 1959). As a result, merely keeping a "box score" of the testimony and evidence is probably not sufficient. There may be relatively few pieces of testimony and evidence presented in a trial to support a position, but the evidence may be bolstered or augmented by many interpretive opinions and personal experiences.

Clearly, another factor that may affect the number of arguments made in support of a position is the number of jurors advocating that position. As a result, the relative impact of number of arguments versus number of advocates remains unclear. Put simply, do majorities win because they generate more supporting arguments, or does the position with the most supporting arguments win because it typically has the most supporters? Kaplan (1977) suggests that the number of unique arguments is the critical variable (see also Kaplan & Miller, 1977). In Kaplan's study, the number of sources to which arguments were attributed had no discernible effect on his mock jurors' judgments of guilt. However, jurors did not engage in face-to-face debate ("discussion" consisted of sharing arguments written on index cards) nor were they required to reach a consensus. The dynamics of such minimal social interactions are undoubtedly quite different from those accompanying a jury's deliberation to consensus. Thus, it is premature to conclude that the majority effect is solely a result of the majority's advantage in generating arguments.

INITIAL SHIFTS OF OPINION

In addition to the content of discussion, initial shifts or changes of opinion seem to be an informative characteristic of deliberation for forecasting the final verdict. Hawkins (1962) noted that his mock jurors never switched their votes more than once on public polls. That is, once a juror publicly defected from an initial faction, he or she never returned. Of course, this result alone does not preclude the possibility that jurors privately changed their opinion more than once or that a faction could replace its loss of a member by convincing another opposing juror to switch. Hawkins further examined switching patterns by considering both public and secret ballots. Returning to the notation of the social decision scheme model, we can characterize a jury in terms of its vote split or distinguishable distribution (r_G, r_{NG}). Whereas social decision scheme theory used only the initial distinguishable distribution, we can examine the patterns of vote shifts by noting changes in the distinguishable distribution from one ballot (whether secret or public) to the next. Using this notation, an increase in r_G (and concomitant decrease in r_{NG}) would indicate movement of the jury toward a guilty verdict. Similarly, an increase in r_{NG} (and decrease in r_G) would constitute movement of the jury toward a not guilty verdict. Hawkins (1962) found that with only one exception, juries never moved in one direction and then subsequently in the other. For example, a 12-person jury that moved from an initial (8,4) split to a (7,5) split would not return to (8,4), although it might move further in a not guilty direction, such as to a (6,6) split.

The interesting implication of Hawkins' data is that the final verdict of all his nonhung juries could be predicted by knowing the direction of the first vote switch. Kerr (in press) examined further the predictive value of initial vote shifts. Of the 328 mock jury deliberations studied, 299 involved initially nonunanimous juries. Seventy-five of these initially nonunanimous juries failed to reach a decision in the time allotted; however, the remaining 224 did successfully resolve their initial nonagreement and reach a verdict. The first shift of vote correctly predicted the final decision of 215 (96%) of these 224 verdicts. In other words, the first faction to lose a supporter rarely prevailed. In this way, the first shift of opinion or vote during deliberation seems to be a harbinger of things to come.

To summarize briefly, the early stages of deliberation potentially contain several signposts charting the road to agreement. The initial configuration of opinions as expressed in the distinguishable distribution may be sufficient in many cases to predict the final verdict. Simply knowing the majority position at the onset of deliberation is highly informative. Moreover, the informational content of early discussion may be adequate to predict the final outcome, particularly if one position receives a disproportionately large number of supporting statements. Finally, the first change of opinion seems to set the pattern for further progress toward consensus during deliberation.

CHARTING THE ROAD TO AGREEMENT

Even though the initial majority, the content of early discussion, and the initial vote shifts may predict the outcome of deliberation, we have noted that deliberation often continues for some time after the outcome seems to be a foregone conclusion as indicated by these predictors. Members of minority factions, or factions that are apparently predestined to lose by virtue of an initial defection, either do not sense that their position will be defeated or choose to persevere in the face of insurmountable odds; or, perhaps, the juror is not as preoccupied as is the social scientist with predicting the outcome but is more concerned with playing the game. For example, the one holdout in a (5,1) jury, if asked to objectively assess the situation, recognizes the virtual impossibility of prevailing (Kerr & Watts, 1981) and probably does not typically choose to persevere merely to demonstrate autonomy. One suspects that holdouts feel that it is the responsibility of the majority to convince them of the correctness, reasonableness, or defensibility of its position. At any rate, the emergence of a consensus takes time, whatever the motivations of the dissenters may be. In order to better understand what happens with the passage of time, it is useful to examine the patterns of opinion changes throughout the course of the deliberation.

Davis *et al.* (1976) solicited the current opinions of jurors on private ballots at 1-min intervals during deliberation. Thus, the current distinguishable distribution (r_G, r_{NG}) of each jury was available at regular time intervals. Using these data, they represented the process of opinion change by the relative frequency with which juries moved from one distinguishable distribution to another during the 1-min intervals.

Several patterns are evident in their results. First, movement of the consensus was not rapid. During any given 1-min interval, most juries remained in the same distinguishable distribution. Second, when movement occurred, it did not typically occur in large leaps. That is, it was extremely rare for more than one member of a group to change during the same 1-min interval. Thirdly, movement toward not guilty occurred more frequently than movement toward guilty. This trend is most clearly illustrated by considering (3,3) juries in which neither position has a majority advantage. Overall, (3,3) juries moved toward not guilty about twice as often as they moved toward guilty. Finally, juries tended to move in the direction of an existing majority. A notable exception to this trend occured for (4,2) juries; in these cases, the overall leniency bias seemed to outweigh the advantage of having a two-thirds majority in favor of guilty. This exception corroborates nicely the results of Nemeth (1977) and the Social Decision Scheme analyses contained in Table 8.3; a minimal majority for guilty is not always sufficient to counteract the social influence advantage held by supporters of the not guilty position.

Kerr (in press) has also found that majorities are more likely to gain rather than lose members and that majorities favoring acquittal are more likely to gain supporters than comparable majorities favoring conviction. Additionally, Kerr found evidence for a momentum effect. Movement of a jury in one direction (toward either a greater number of advocates favoring guilty or a greater number favoring not guilty) increased the likelihood that the jury would subsequently move further in that direction. For example, a jury that moved from a (3,3) to a (2,4) split would be more likely to subsequently move to a (1,5) split than would a jury that had started with a (2,4) split. Thus, a faction's acquisition of a new proponent at one point in time may enhance its ability to attract additional supporters during subsequent deliberation.

In summary, the majority effect observed by Kalven and Zeisel (1966), Nemeth (1977), Saks (1977), and the Social Decision Scheme studies shown on Table 8.3 does not seem to be due to an automatic and precipitous acquiescence by the minority. Rather, support for the minority position is eroded throughout the course of deliberation by a sometimes slow but usually sure advantage to the majority. However, this advantage is qualified by a bias for the not guilty position. We have already speculated briefly on possible explanations for this leniency bias. In the following section we explore these explanations more systematically.

Leniency Bias: The Road to Not Guilty Is Less Rocky

We have reviewed several sources of converging evidence for a leniency bias in the deliberation of juries. To this evidence we add two other frequently documented trends: All other things being equal, jurors acting individually are more likely to convict than are juries, and jurors are more likely to favor conviction before than after deliberation (cf. Bray & Noble,. 1978; Bray *et al.*, 1978 Davis *et al.*, 1975, 1977; Davis, Spitzer, Nagao, & Stasser, 1978; Rumsey, Allgeier, & Castore, 1975; Stasser & Davis, 1977). These two trends are particularly pronounced when the preponderance of opinion before deliberation is for acquittal; however, such leniency shifts are not restricted to cases and populations in which a majority favor acquittal before deliberation. For example, Stasser (1977) found that 64% of his individual mock jurors endorsed conviction before deliberation but only 49% favored conviction after deliberation.

On the other hand, there is some evidence to suggest that if the case against the defendant is sufficiently strong, the leniency shift may be reversed. Myers and Kaplan (1976) found that jurors' ratings of the degree of guilt shifted in a more guilty direction as a result of discussion for cases with very incriminating evidence. The conflicting shift patterns can be reconciled as instances of group polarization.

It might also be noted parenthetically that Kalven and Zeisel's (1966) data on disagreements between judge and jury might be due to the leniency bias accompanying deliberation. In the approximately 3500 criminal cases that they examined, the jury convicted the defendant in 64% of the cases, while the presiding judge would have convicted in 83% of the cases. One wonders how much of the reduced conviction rate for juries was due to a leniency bias during deliberation rather than to a difference between jurors' and judges' predeliberation judgments.

GROUP POLARIZATION

The existence of choice shifts or characteristic shifts in judgment as a result of group interaction is hardly new to the study of group process. Myers and Lamm (1976) reviewed evidence from a variety of decision tasks that support a "group polarization hypotheses: The average post-group response will tend to be more extreme in the same direction as the average of the pregroup responses [p. 603]." As they point out, polarization is defined in terms of a decision or judgment along a bipolar continuum containing a subjective neutral point (e.g., judgments along a pro–con attitudinal scale). The usual findings suggest that if prediscussion individual opinions fall predominately in one direction from a neutral point, group discussion and/or decision tend to shift individual opinions to a more extreme position on the continuum.

The choice shifts in verdicts described can be organized in terms of group polarization with some additional assumptions. First, group polarization requires decision tasks for which alternatives can be arrayed along a bipolar continuum, whereas the jury is typically faced with a dichotomous choice. However, we might conceive a continuum of likelihood of guilt underlying the dichotomous choice between guilty and not guilty verdicts. Secondly, the overall pattern of results suggests that the "neutral" point on this continuum with respect to polarization is not its midpoint (i.e., .5 probability of guilt) but rather corresponds to a rather high likelihood of guilt (perhaps near the level required to satisfy the beyond a reasonable doubt criterion). Therefore, guilty shifts may be unusual in the literature because resarchers have chosen to use cases in which the evidence is neither strongly incriminating nor exonerating. Such relatively "balanced" cases afford the greatest opportunity to study social influence processes that accompany deliberation but may not be sufficiently incriminating to establish a predominance of predeliberation opinion on the guilty side of the "neutral" point.[5]

Explanations for group polarization may also guide us in examining possible bases for the frequently observed leniency bias. These explanations fall into two theoretical perspectives: informational influence and normative processes (cf. Myers & Lamm, 1976; Stasser *et al.*, 1980).

INFORMATION EXCHANGE BIAS

The exchange of information and resulting opinion change may be biased in one of several ways. Arguments for acquittal may be more numerous or persuasive; the not guilty position may be more easily defended in debate. Or, arguments may emphasize the risks entailed in a conviction—particularly the risk of convicting an innocent person, (cf. Kerr, 1978) which may become more salient during group discussion.

Number and persuasiveness of arguments

Vinokur and Burnstein (1974) suggest that the direction and amount of opinion shift resulting from group discussion depends on the number, persuasiveness, and originality of arguments introduced for each position. Thus, opinions will tend to shift to that position for which more numerous, compelling, and

---

[5] This polarization hypothesis predicts (barring floor or ceiling effects) that an effect observed in individual jurors should be even larger when juries (rather than jurors) are examined (cf. Kerr, 1978). However, one should also note Kaplan's suggestion (see Kaplan, Chapter 7, this volume) that jury deliberation tends to attenuate juror effects. While we favor the former polarization hypothesis, there is not, as yet, sufficient data upon which to base a direct competitive test of these two opposing hypotheses.

unique arguments can be generated. Such an explanation of the leniency bias seems most plausible for cases in which the weight of evidence initially favors acquittal. However, it does not seem adequate, in and of itself, to account for leniency shifts when the majority of prediscussion opinions are for conviction (presumably, this would occur only if the weight of evidence in the case favored conviction) unless arguments for acquittal were generally more persuasive than arguments for conviction.

Defensibility

As Nemeth (1977) suggests, the not guilty position may be more easily defended in deliberation. The concept of reasonable doubt and the burden of proof borne by the prosecution may combine to make a guilty position more vulnerable to attack (cf. Kerr et al. 1976). The prosecution and its supporters in deliberation must demonstrate the plausibility of a set of necessary premises to establish guilt (e.g., motive, opportunity, lack of alibi). Furthermore, they must discredit all possible alternative explanations (i.e., refute all reasonable doubts). On the other hand, the defense need seriously challenge only one of the essential elements in the prosecution's arguments to raise a reasonable doubt; they need only generate one plausible alternative explanation of the facts. Viewed in this way, the supporters of conviction are in a more vulnerable position; they need not only more arguments but also more convincing arguments to successfully establish the validity of their position. The advocates of acquittal need only focus their attention on a weak link in the opposition's rationale.

Reevaluation of risk

Several theorists (e.g., Feinberg, 1971; Kerr, 1978; Kerr et al., 1976) have emphasized the opposing risks attending a choice between a guilty and not guilty verdict. Put simply, a decision to convict runs the risk of punishing an innocent person, whereas a decision to acquit risks freeing a guilty person and placing society in further jeopardy. A decision to convict or acquit may involve some assessment, either formally or informally, of the costs of these opposing risks.

"Law and order" arguments would emphasize the risks to society in freeing large numbers of guilty persons, whereas libertarian arguments would focus on the injustice of punishing an innocent person. Clearly, our justice system emphasizes the risks entailed in conviction by invoking the criterion of reasonable doubt and by placing the burden of proof on the prosecution. Jury deliberation may serve to emphasize further the disutilities of an erroneous conviction. In this manner, the advantage to the advocates of acquittal may accrue by focusing not on the evidence but on the consequences of the jury's verdict.

If reevaluation of risks is crucial, one might suspect that juries containing a large number of law and order advocates would not be as susceptible to a leniency bias. There is mixed support for this notion. For example, Bray and Noble (1978) composed juries of high authoritarians who are generally thought to be more punitive and predisposed to endorse law and order arguments. The postdeliberation verdicts shifted towards acquittal to an equal degree for high and low authoritarians. However, high authoritarians recommended more severe sentences after deliberation than before, whereas low authoritarians decreased the severity of their sentence recommendations as a result of deliberation.

Similarly, one might argue that the studies demonstrating a leniency bias have predominately used college students, who are typically more libertarian than are other segments of the population (Cvetkovick & Baumgardner, 1973; Saks, 1977; Simon & Mahan, 1971). Bray et al. (1978) used two types of juries: one made up of students and one composed of community volunteers randomly selected from voting registers. Community jurors and student jurors were both more likely to endorse a guilty verdict before deliberation than after deliberation, and the size of this leniency shift did not vary with subject population. Thus, there is little direct evidence that the leniency bias is limited to a particular type of population. Of course, this conclusion does not rule out the possibility that reevaluation of risks occurs.

NORMATIVE PROCESSES

In addition to informational influence, there is ample opportunity for normative pressures to be exerted during face-to-face discussion typical in jury deliberations. How might such normative pressure be biased in favor of acquittal?

Idealized norm for defendant protection

As already noted, our system of justice incorporates several safeguards for the ˙efendant. These safeguards may reflect and/or reinforce an ideal norm of ᴜefendant protection. In an argument similar to social comparison explanations of group polarization (cf. Myers & Lamm, 1976; Pruitt, 1971), people may tend to see themselves as being as fairminded as or even more fairminded than their peers. Thus, a juror favoring guilty who encounters several other jury members who favor acquittal might experience a discomforting threat to his or her self-perception of fairmindedness. Cognitive consistency theories in social psychology (e.g., Festinger, 1957) hold that such a disconfirmation of a self-perception will by itself motivate opinion change.

Although the idealized-norm hypothesis may be plausible in the abstract, empirical evidence for its applicability to jury deliberation is lacking. If interpersonal comparisons relative to an idealized norm were responsible for the leniency bias, one would expect that groups that differed in their adherence to individual rights ideals would likewise differ in their susceptibility to the leniency bias. But, as concluded in the earlier reevaluation of risks discussion, there is scant evidence for such differential susceptibility.

Reasonable doubt and social comparison

Social comparison theory (Festinger, 1954) suggests that in the absence of objective criteria, people are motivated to validate their opinions by comparing with others. Opinions are validated by agreement and invalidated by disagreement. Certainly, in most trials of interest, the evidence is sufficiently ambiguous to leave some uncertainty about the best or correct decision. Thus, according to this theory, the individual juror must rely to some extent on peers to validate personal judgments based on the evidence. However, the individual juror may apply the criterion of reasonable doubt to social as well as objective validation. Just as a few inconsistent facts may raise a reasonable doubt, so may a few dissenters create sufficient doubt to dissuade the individual from maintaining a guilty position.

Reasonable doubt as a group standard

As others have suggested (e.g., Saks, 1977; Kerr *et al.*, 1976), reasonable doubt may not only be a criterion by which to judge one's subjective certainty but also one to judge the consensus necessary within a group for reaching a guilty jury verdict. As our discussion of social influence processes suggests, jurors share a mutual goal of successfully resolving a legal dispute. In a society that embraces collective decision making, continued dissent in the face of an emerging consensus may be viewed as unfair or unreasonable, particularly if the reasons for dissent are not easily articulated. In fact, there may be an implicit norm that once a sufficient number of group members have agreed upon a verdict, it is incumbent on the remaining dissenters either to give an acceptable account of why they continue to hold out, or to acquiesce. Doing neither invites social disapproval and censure. However, the implicit norm regarding the sufficient number to define the fair and equitable group decision may be sensitive to the criterion of reasonable doubt. For example, perhaps 10 of 12 members must agree on guilty before the dissenting not guilty advocates are seen as violating the norm, whereas 8 of 12 members may be sufficient to define not guilty as the fair decision of the group.

It is apparent that these normative explanations of the leniency bias are conceptually related and that the isolation of their potential contributions to a jury's deliberation is a challenging methodological task. Because little direct evidence exists, much of our discussion of both informational and normative explanations of the leniency bias has been speculative.

Process and Product: Summary

Our discussion of the process leading to the product serves to make at least one important point. We may be able to predict the outcomes of deliberations quite accurately and reliably by knowing the initial configuration of opinions, the first vote shift, or the balance of proconviction and proacquittal arguments.

Such prediction is useful and may be adequate depending on our purposes. Furthermore, we may be able to describe the emergence of consensus by examining opinion changes over time. Such description undoubtedly aids our intuition in understanding how juries function and reach a decision. However, there is still much to be learned about what kinds of interpersonal and personal dynamics push the jury along the road to agreement. Whether one is interested in social engineering or a theoretical understanding of group process, the unanswered questions about process leading to product are intriguing. Is the jury primarily an information-processing mechanism, immune to normative dynamics? Or is the information exchange process merely a front disguising the operation of more subtle normative pressures? We suspect that jury deliberation entails both informational and normative influences in various forms and mixes.

STRUCTURE, PROCESS, PRODUCT, AND POLICY

There are several patterns that emerge from the "buzz and hum" of the jury's deliberation. Tradition and expedience require that one member be chosen to occupy the role of foreman. Even though, in principle, every member is a viable candidate for the job, certain members, by virtue of their sex, occupational status, and prior jury experience are more likely to be chosen. Once chosen, foremen speak and are spoken to more often than nonforemen. Furthermore, jurors with higher status and more education seem to participate more actively than their counterparts with less status or education. An inevitable question is whether such patterns of differential participation are desirable.

The question is not easily answered. One interpretation of the phrase "a jury of peers" implies that the jury constitutes a representative body in which the various viewpoints of a cross section of the community are heard and considered. Differential participation threatens this function of jury deliberation. A more rational model of the jury would argue that certain kinds of participation are more acceptable than others. Direct references to testimony and court instructions may be preferred to anecdotal references to personal experience; logical arguments may be preferred to emotional appeals; and certainly discussion that perpetrates inaccurate information is to be avoided. By these criteria, the participation of certain kinds of jurors (e.g., the more educated ones) may be better in quality and should be facilitated. Thus, the demonstration of differential participation, in and of itself, does not imply the need for procedural change; one must decide by some criteria if the documented patterns of differential participation are desirable.

In a similiar vein, certain characteristics of juries and the early portions of the deliberation process seem to anticipate the jury's decision. The apparent power of the initial majority in determining the final outcome may undermine the confidence that derives from the requirement of unanimous consensus. Similarly, the seemingly irreversible nature of an initial defection suggests that the ball game may be over when the first point is scored. One might entertain procedural reforms to lessen the impact of initial majorities and initial defections on the course of deliberation. For example, should early balloting be discouraged to reduce the salience and identity of an initial majority? Should jurors be asked to refrain from stating their preferred decision in early discussion? Should all balloting be private to reduce the potential for normative pressures? The answers, again, are not clear. Our understanding of the dynamics underlying such patterns as the majority effect is far from perfect. Which, if any, procedural changes would mitigate or erase the apparent power of the majority, for example, are not obvious. Furthermore, it is not a foregone conclusion that the interpersonal dynamics mediating the relationships between initial majorities and/or initial defections and final decisions are necessarily undesirable. Our conclusions require both a better understanding of these dynamics and a more clearly articulated and agreed upon model of the ideal jury.

Clearly, the large body of research we have reviewed provides input into procedural and policy debates; however, by itself, the literature recommends nothing. As Davis (1980) has argued, it is useful to regard such empirical studies as "demonstrations" that can challenge and modify our beliefs about the nature of jury decision making. In this way, the empirical literature may serve as a guide in making and evaluating policy when the overriding objectives and goals are clearly understood. However, even when the empirical literature identifies clearly undesirable characteristics of jury decision making, it would usually not anticipate other unwanted side effects of remedial procedural or policy changes. For example, one important function of the jury may be to bolster community confidence in our system of justice. We would be ill-advised to implement procedures which ensure more equal participation or which reduce the power of the majority if these procedures also materially erode public confidence and satisfaction with the process of jury decision making.

In summary, the social scientist's task is to clarify the processes by which juries make decisions. Even though the literature is extensive, we have identified many gaps in our understanding. The policymaker's task is to use the empirical literature judiciously, carefully noting its limitations, to guide the development and revision of policy and procedure.

REFERENCES

Anderson, N. H. Cognitive algebra: Integration theory applied to social attribution. In L. Berkowitz (Ed.), *Advances in experimental social psychology* (Vol. 7). New York: Academic Press, 1974.

Anderson, N. H., & Graesser, C. An information integration analysis of attitude change in group discussion. *Journal of Personality and Social Psychology*, 1976, 34, 210–222.

Asch, S. E. Studies of independence and submission to group pressure: I. On minority of one against a unanimous majority. *Psychological Monographs* 1956, 70 (9 Whole No. 417).

Bales, R. F., & Strodtbeck, F. Phases in group problem-solving. *Journal of Abnormal and Social Psychology*, 1951, 46, 485–495.

Bem, S. L., & Bem D. J. Training the woman to know her place: The power of a nonconscious ideology. In D. J. Bem (Ed.), *Beliefs, attitudes, and human affairs.* Belmont, California: Brooks/ Cole, 1970.

Bennis, W., & Shepard, H. A theory of group development. *Human Relations,* 1956, *9,* 415–437.

Bevan, W., Albert, R., Liseaux, P., Mayfield, P., & Wright, G. Jury behavior as a function of the prestige of the foreman and the nature of his leadership. *Journal of Public Law,* 1958, *7,* 419–449.

Borgida, E. *A process analysis approach to jury deliberation.* Paper presented at the meeting of the Law and Society Association, Madison, June 1980.

Bray, R. M., & Noble, A. M. Authoritarianism and decisions of mock juries: Evidence of jury bias and group polarization. *Journal of Personality and Social Psychology,* 1978, *36,* 1424–1430.

Bray, R. M., Struckman-Johnson, C., Osborne, M., McFarlane, J., & Scott, J. The effects of defendant status on decisions of student and community juries. *Social Psychology,* 1978, *41,* 256–260.

Bridgeman, D. L., & Marlowe, D. Jury decision making: An empirical study based on actual felony trials. *Journal of Applied Psychology,* 1979, *64,* 91–98.

Broeder, D. Previous jury trial service affecting juror behavior. *Insurance Law Journal,* 1965, *506,* 138–143.

Burnstein, E., & Vinokur, A. Testing two classes of theories about group induced shifts in individual choice. *Journal of Experimental Social Psychology,* 1973, *9,* 123–137.

Chester, G. *The ninth juror.* New York: Random House, 1970.

Cole, G. F. *The American system of criminal justice.* North Scituate, Massachusetts: Duxbury, 1975.

Cvetkovich, G., & Baumgardner, S. Attitude polarization: The relative influence of discussion group structure and reference group norms. *Journal of Personality and Social Psychology,* 1973, *26,* 159–165.

Davis, J. H. Group decision and social interaction: A theory of social decision schemes. *Psychological Review,* 1973, *80,* 97–125.

Davis, J. H. Group decision and procedural justice. In M. Fishbein (Ed.), *Progress in social psychology.* Hillsdale, New Jersey: Erlbaum, 1980.

Davis, J. H., Kerr, N. L., Atkin, R., Holt, R., & Meek, D. The decision processes of 6- and 12-person mock juries assigned unanimous and ⅔ majority rules. *Journal of Personality and Social Psychology,* 1975, *32,* 1–14.

Davis, J. H., Kerr, N. L., Stasser, G., Meek, D., & Holt, R. Victim consequences, sentence severity, and decision process in mock juries. *Organizational Behavior and Human Performance,* 1977, *18,* 346–365.

Davis, J. H., Spitzer, C. E., Nagao, D. H., & Stasser, G. Bias in social decisions by individuals and groups: An example from mock juries. In H. Brandstatter, J. H. Davis, & H. Schuler (Eds.), *Dynamics of group decisions.* Beverly Hills, California: Sage, 1978.

Davis, J. H., Stasser, G., Spitzer, C., & Holt, R. Changes in group members' decision preferences during discussion: An illustration with mock juries. *Journal of Personality and Social Psychology,* 1976, *34,* 1177–1187.

Deutsch, M., & Gerard, H. A study of normative and informational social influences upon individual judgment. *Journal of Abnormal and Social Psychology,* 1955, *51,* 629–633.

Ebbesen, E. B., & Bowers, R. J. Proportion of risky to conservative arguments in a group discussion and choice shift. *Journal of Personality and Social Psychology,* 1974, *24,* 216–327.

Feinberg, W. E. Teaching the Type I and Type II errors: The judicial process. *The American Statistician,* 1971, *25,* 30–32.

Festinger, L. Motivations leading to social behavior. In M. R. Jones (Ed.), *Nebraska symposium on motivation.* Lincoln: Univ. of Nebraska Press, 1954.

Festinger, L. *A theory of cognitive dissonance.* Stanford, California: Stanford Univ. Press, 1957.

Fisher, B. Decision emergence: Phases in group decision making. *Speech Monographs,* 1970, *37,* 53–66.

Godwin, W. F., & Restle, F. The road to agreement: Subgroup pressures in small group consensus processes. *Journal of Personality and Social Psychology,* 1974, *30,* 500–509.

Gordon, R. *A study in forensic psychology: Petit jury verdicts as a function of the number of jury members.* Unpublished doctoral dissertation, Univ. of Oklahoma, 1968.

Hans, V. P. *The effects of the unanimity requirement on group communication processes.* Paper presented at the meeting of the Western Psychological Association, San Diego, California, April, 1979.

Hans, V. P., & Brooks, N. Effects of corroboration instructions in a rape case on experimental juries. *Osgood Hall Law Journal,* 1977, *15,* 701–716.

Hans, V. P., & Doob, A. N. Section 12 of the Canada Evidence Act and the deliberations of simulated juries. *Criminal Law Quarterly,* 1976, *18,* 235–253.

Hawkins, C. *Interaction and coalition realignments in consensus seeking groups: A study of experimental jury deliberations.* Unpublished doctoral dissertation, University of Chicago, Illinois, 1960.

Hawkins, C. Interaction rates of jurors aligned in factions. *American Sociological Review,* 1962, *27,* 689–691.

Hoffman, L. R. *The group problem solving process: Studies of a valence model.* New York: Praeger, 1979.

Hoffman, L. R., & Maier, N. R. F. Valences in the adoption of solutions by problem-solving groups: Concept, method, and results. *Journal of Abnormal and Social Psychology,* 1964, *69,* 264–271.

Hoffman, L. R., & Maier, N. R. F. Valence in the adoption of solutions by problem-solving groups: II. Quality and acceptance as goals of leaders and members. *Journal of Personality and Social Psychology,* 1967, *6,* 175–182.

James, R. *Jurors' reactions to definitions of legal insanity.* Unpublished doctoral dissertation, Univ. of Chicago, Illinois, 1957.

James, R. Status and competence of jurors. *The American Journal of Sociology,* 1959, *64,* 563–570

Johnson v. The State of Louisiana. United States Reports, 1972, *406,* 356–403.

Kalven, H., & Zeisel, H. *The American jury.* Boston, Massachusetts: Little, Brown, 1966.

Kaplan, M. F. Discussion polarization effects in a modified jury decision paradigm: Informational influences. *Sociometry,* 1977, *40,* 262–271.

Kaplan, M. F., & Miller, C. G. Judgments and group discussion: Effect of presentation and memory factors on polarization. *Sociometry,* 1977, *40,* 337–343.

Kerr, N. L. Severity of prescribed penalty and mock jurors' verdicts. *Journal of Personality and Social Psychology,* 1978, *36,* 1431–1442.

Kerr, N. L. Social transition schemes: Charting the group's road to agreement. *Journal of Personality and Social Psychology,* in press.

Kerr, N. L. Social transition schemes: Model, method, and applications. In H. Brandstatter & J. H. Davis (Eds.), *Group decision making processes.* New York: Academic Press, 1981.

Kerr, N. L., Atkin, R., Stasser, G., Meek, D., Holt, R., & Davis, J. H. Guilt beyond a reasonable doubt: Effects of concept definition and assigned decision rule on the judgments of mock jurors. *Journal of Personality and Social Psychology,* 1976, *34,* 282–294.

Kerr, N. L., Harmon, D., & Graves, J. Independence of verdicts by jurors and juries. *Journal of Applied Social Psychology,* in press.

Kerr, N. L., Stasser, G., & Davis, J. H. Model-testing, model-fitting, and social decision schemes. *Organizational Behavior and Human Performance,* 1979, *23,* 339–410.

Kerr, N. L., & Watts, B. *Faction size and pre-discussion generation/evaluation of arguments.* Unpublished manuscript, Michigan State Univ., 1981.

Kessler, J. An empirical study of six- and twelve-member jury decision-making processes. *University of Michigan Journal of Law Reform,* 1973, *6,* 712–734.

Klein, F., & Jess, P. Prejudicial publicity: Its effect on law school mock juries. *Journalism Quarterly,* 1966, *43,* 113–116.

Miller, G. R., & Fontes, N. *Videotape on trial: A view from the jury box.* Beverly Hills, California: Sage, 1979.

Myers, D. G., & Kaplan, M. F. Group-induced polarization in simulated juries. *Personality and Social Psychology Bulletin,* 1976, *2,* 63–66.

Myers, D. G., & Lamm, H. The group polarization phenomenon. *Psychological Bulletin*, 1976, *83*, 602–627.

Nemeth, C. Interactions between jurors as a function of majority vs. unanimity decision rules. *Journal of Applied Social Psychology*, 1977, *7*, 38–56.

Nemeth, C., Endicott, J., & Wachtler, J. From the '50s to the '70s: Women in jury deliberations, *Sociometry*, 1976, *39*, 293–304.

Penrod, S., & Hastie, R. Models of jury decision making: A critical review. *Psychological Bulletin*, 1979, *86*, 462–492.

Piliavin, J., & Martin, R. The effects of sex composition of groups on style of social interaction. *Sex Roles*, 1978, *4*, 281–296.

Pruitt, D. G. Choice shifts in group discussion: An introductory review. *Journal of Personality and Social Psychology*, 1971, *20*, 339–360.

Rumsey, M. G., Allgeier, E. R., & Castore, C. H. *Group discussion, sentencing judgments and the leniency shift*. Unpublished manuscript, Purdue Univ., Indiana, 1975.

Saks, M. *Jury verdicts: The role of group size and social decision rule*. Lexington, Massachusetts: Lexington, 1977.

Saks, M., & Hastie, R. *Social psychology in court*. New York: Van Nostrand-Reinhold, 1978.

Schachter, S. Deviation, rejection, and communication. *Journal of Abnormal and Social Psychology*, 1951, *46*, 190–207.

Scheidel, T., & Crowell, L. Idea development in small discussion groups. *Quarterly Journal of Speech*, 1964, *50*, 140–145.

Simon, R. J. *The jury and the defense of insanity*. Boston, Massachusetts: Little, Brown, 1967.

Simon, R. J., & Mahan, L. Quantifying burdens of proof: A view from the bench, the jury, and the classroom. *Law and Society Review*, 1971, *5*, 319–330.

Slater, P. Role differentiation in small groups. *American Sociological Review*, 1955, *20*, 300–310.

Stasser, G. *A model of social influence during group discussion: An application with four- and six-person mock juries*. Unpublished doctoral dissertation, Univ. of Illinois, Urbana-Champaign, 1977.

Stasser, G., & Davis, J. H. Opinion change during group discussion. *Personality and Social Psychology Bulletin*, 1977, *3*, 252–256.

Stasser, G., Kerr, N. L., & Davis, J. H. Influence processes in decision-making groups: A modeling approach. In P. B. Paulus (Ed.), *Psychology of group influence*. Hillsdale, New Jersey: Erlbaum, 1980.

Stephan, F., & Mishler, E. The distribution of participation in small groups: An exponential approximation. *American Sociological Review*, 1952, *17*, 598–608.

Strodtbeck, F. L. Husband–wife interaction over revealed differences. *American Sociological Review*, 1951, *16*, 468–473.

Strodtbeck, F., & Hook. L. The social dimensions of a twelve-man jury table. *Sociometry*, 1961, *24*, 397–415.

Strodtbeck, F. L., James, R., & Hawkins, C. Social status in jury deliberations. *American Sociological Review*, 1957, *22*, 713–719.

Strodtbeck, F. L., & Mann, R. Sex role differentiation in jury deliberations. *Sociometry*, 1956, *19*, 3–11.

Tuckman, B. Developmental sequence in small groups. *Psychological Bulletin*, 1965, *63*, 384–399.

Vinokur, A., & Burnstein, E. The effects of partially shared persuasive arguments on group induced shifts: A group problem solving approach. *Journal of Personality and Social Psychology*, 1974, *29*, 303–315.

Wanamaker, W. B. Trial by jury. *University of Cincinnati Law Review*, 1977, *46*, 191–200.

Wyer, R., & Malinowski, C. Effects of sex and achievement level upon individualism and competitiveness in social interaction. *Journal of Experimental Social Psychology*, 1972, *8*, 303–314.

Zerman, M. *Call the final witness: The People v. Darrell R. Mathes as seen by the eleventh juror*. New York: Harper 1977.

chapter

9

The Psychology of Judging

Anthony Champagne
Stuart Nagel

THE PSYCHOLOGY
OF THE COURTROOM

The purpose of this chapter is to discuss the psychology of judging, including references to some of the key literature on the subject. In order to understand better the psychological aspects of judging, the chapter first discusses the broader context in which judging occurs with regard to court structure at the state and federal level, judicial selection, the representativeness of judges, the role of interest groups, and occupational pressures. Next we consider explanations for variations in judicial behavior including personality factors, the socialization process, judicial attitudes, judicial roles, judicial interaction, and how various explanatory variables can be combined into behavioral predictive schemes. Finally the chapter examines decision-making models that particularly view judicial decision makers as seeking to maximize perceived benefits minus costs. That perspective is used to deduce how judges might behave when the relevant benefits or costs are changed, and it is employed to suggest policies for improving the decision making of judges or jurors when they are making decisions on guilt and innocence or liability and nonliability.

COURT STRUCTURE

State Courts

Prior to examining the psychology of judges, we think it is necessary to understand the structure of the courts, the characteristics of judges, their training, and their tasks. It should be kept in mind that the American judicial system is a maze of judicial offices and jurisdictions. No two states have exactly the same judicial system. And to add to the complexity, the federal judicial system often shares jurisdiction with the states.

In general, the lowest paid and the poorest trained judges are at the lowest levels of the states' judicial hierarchies. These magistrates or justices of the peace are also the judges who most frequently come into contact with citizens, handling the most petty crimes and civil disputes.

The second level in the states' judicial hierarchy can be labeled the lower special courts. These courts may have any number of names, such as county courts, circuit courts, municipal courts, district courts, or common pleas courts. These courts most frequently hear misdemeanor crimes and fairly small civil cases, often involving less than $5000 or $10,000. Such lower special courts may have a number of specialized components such as family courts, juvenile courts, and probate courts.

The next level of state courts are the states' higher trial courts. They are called superior courts in some states, district courts in other states, and, in still others, circuit courts. These courts hear felony criminal cases and major civil cases.

The appellate courts are frequently divided into an intermediate appellate court and a supreme court that is at the top of the judicial pyramid. These appellate courts usually hear only arguments and decide appeals on the basis of legal briefs and oral arguments. Such courts do not hold trials and no witnesses or defendants appear (Abraham, 1968; Jackson, 1974).

Federal Courts

The structure of the federal judicial system is considerably more simple than that of the judicial system found in many states. The federal courts hear cases involving federal constitutional questions, federal statutes, some conflicts among citizens of different states, and cases where the federal government is a party. Thus, some state cases can be appealed to federal courts. In general, the federal courts can be divided into three types: the federal district courts, the courts of appeals, and the Supreme Court. The federal district courts are the trial courts of the federal government. They hear both civil and criminal cases, although the docket of the federal courts is overwhelmingly civil. The vast majority of criminal cases, involving violation of state rather than federal laws, are handled by the state courts. Above the district courts are the courts of appeals, each with responsibility for a geographic region. Most cases receive their final hearing in these appeals courts, since the Supreme Court, for the most part, has discretionary jurisdiction and refuses to hear most cases (Wasby, 1978).

Judicial Selection

Methods of judicial selection vary greatly among the states, and, in some cases, within states. Nevertheless, it is possible to isolate four major forms of selection: (*a*) appointment, (*b*) nonpartisan election, (*c*) partisan election, and (*d*) merit selection. Judicial appointments usually involve gubernatorial nomination of persons to fill judicial vacancies and confirmation of those appointments by the upper house, the State Senate, of the state legislature. This judicial selection method is most common in the East and is found in some form in many states. Federal judgeships are also appointive positions that require nomination by the president and confirmation by the Senate. With the nonpartisan ballot, candidates for judicial offices are not identified by party affiliation, though they may be nominated by political parties. The nonpartisan ballot is a particularly common form of judicial selection in the West and Midwest. Other states use the partisan ballot, on which judicial candidates are identified by party affiliation. Since many of these states are in the South, where the Democratic Party candidate most often wins the election, the Democratic primary, rather than the election, is frequently the key contest. Finally, merit selection plans are used in about one-fifth of the states, mostly the prairie and mountain states. Merit selection plans vary, but one popular plan requires that the governor select a candidate from a list developed by a judicial commission.

After a period of time, the judge's name will be placed on the ballot, without opposition, for a decision by the voters as to whether the judge should be retained in office (Abraham, 1968, 1975; Schmidhauser, 1979).

The debate over the advantages and disadvantages of these systems of selection is an ongoing one. In part, this debate is unresolvable due to difficulty in defining judicial "quality." Without a clear, widely agreed upon definition, it is impossible to determine which system produces the "best" judges. One concern of the advocates of some judicial selection systems, such as merit selection and the nonpartisan ballot, is that judges should be removed from politics. However, it is clear that no selection system completely removes a judge from the political process.

Judicial Responsibilities

The main responsibilities of trial court judges are the resolution of conflicts by the identification of "facts" or events that led to the dispute and the application of law to those facts. It is generally assumed that trial judges, rather than appellate judges, are best able to determine facts, since they can observe witnesses and consider their demeanor in determining their truthfulness. On those rare occasions when a jury sits in a trial, the jury will take on the trial judge's role of determining facts. The trial judge, however, will remain responsible for the application of law to those facts. The trial judge usually sentences convicted defendants in criminal trials. Appellate judges are generally restricted to determining if the trial judge properly applied law to the facts of the case.

It is difficult to evaluate judges given the subjectivity of their decisions. Who can say with certainty that a judge has improperly determined the facts or law in a case? Nevertheless, it is clear that judicial decisions can have consequences that affect important political and social interests. These consequences make judicial behavior and the influences upon judicial decisions very important considerations.

THE JUDICIAL ENVIRONMENT

Judges as Representatives

Judges' group affiliations, religion, ethnic affiliations, political party, geographic identification, and sex may often play a role in their appointment or election. In part, these variables are considered important in judicial selection because judges represent groups in society. That is, judgeships provide symbolic rewards for politically significant groups. Thus, Justice Powell provided representation for the South on the Supreme Court and Justice Field provided it for the West. Justice Brandeis was a Jewish representative; Justice Butler, a Catholic representative. Justice Thurgood Marshall provided black representation on the Court and, no doubt in the near future, a woman will be seated on the Court. Though such symbolic rewards are most obvious on the higher, more visible courts, the same process occurs in all American courts (Abraham, 1974; Chase, 1972; Nagel, 1969).

Symbolic rewards are provided to significant groups through this representation concept, but substantive rewards are also provided. One who has been socialized as a member of a particular group can be expected to better represent that group's interests on a court bench. A black judge, for example, would be expected to have greater understanding of the problems of racism than a white judge. Although the Supreme Court decision in *Brown* v. *Board of Education* (1954) was unanimous, the attacks on Justice Black were among the most vehement. As an Alabamian, Black had been expected to reflect the views of white southerners, but he failed to conform to that expectation (Black, 1975). Such criticism can defeat a judicial candidate for reelection or, more subtly, modify the judge's nonconforming views.

Interest Groups and the Judiciary

As actors within a political environment, judges are affected by the activities of interest groups. If the decisions of judges displease interest groups, the judges can expect criticism and opposition from those groups. When John J. Parker, for example, was nominated to the Supreme Court, he was successfully opposed by the American Federation of Labor and the National Association for the Advancement of Colored People. Both groups opposed Parker because they perceived him as opposed to their interests (Peltason, 1955).

Interest groups also compete within the legal process for the support of judges (Truman, 1951). Sorauf (1976), for example, examined court cases dealing with separation of church and state and found a great deal of interest group involvement in them. Of 67 cases dealing with the establishment of religion clause of the First Amendment, three major interest groups sponsored 20 cases. In another 21 cases, the groups got involved after the litigation had begun. In 10 cases they functioned as friends of the court. Only in 16 cases were the groups not involved.

Occupational Pressures

Judges are generally under occupational pressures. The case loads of most judges are quite large and, as a result, a primary goal of judges must be to hear cases as quickly as possible. This emphasis on expeditious case handling encourages efforts to reduce the number of trials, creating pressure on judges to allow plea bargaining and to urge lawyers to make out-of-court settlements in civil cases (Blumberg, 1967; Ross, 1970). As a result, a complete courtroom trial is an uncommon event. Only 10% of criminal cases actually go to trial and trials in civil cases are at least as rare.

Judges are also part of a social network. The primary members of this network are judges, attorneys, and prosecutors, although police, probation officers, and court clerks also play a role. Lack of cooperation by any member of the network can create a log jam of cases. Thus, judges must usually cooperate with prosecutors and agree with their recommendations. Similarly, judges have a strong incentive to cooperate with attorneys in both criminal and civil cases. Lawyers may engage in dilatory motions and other dealying tactics that will make the judges' work more difficult (Blumberg, 1967).

EXPLAINING JUDICIAL BEHAVIOR

The Study of Judges' Personalities

In this section, we consider the various attempts to explain judicial behavior, one of which involves the study of judges' personalities. This approach suggests that judicial behavior cannot be fully understood without reference to the many different dimensions of judges' personalities. Winick, Gerver, and Blumberg (1961) argue that a judge's "possible interest in dominance, his needs, his self concept, his ways of achieving security, and his use of unconscious defense mechanisms like projection, rationalization, sublimation, repression, and suppression may all be important [p. 136]" in explaining judicial behavior.

A concern for the influence of personality on judicial behavior has been evident for many years. One of the first scholars to show an interest in the effect of personality was Schroeder (1918). Schroeder suggested that psychoanalysis would be a fruitful method for studying judges and that such study would uncover hidden human impulses for judicial decisions. To illustrate this point, he analyzed the decision of a judge in an obscenity case. The judge sustained an objection made by the defendant's attorney. The objection claimed that a pamphlet published by the defendant was not obscene even though it contained charges relating to sexual misbehavior of a guardian in connection with his ward. In his opinion, the judge contrasted the case with another case that involved a question of obscenity where there had been a finding that the material was not obscene. This case, involving prostitution, was discussed by the judge in unusually strong and emotional language. This puzzling, opinionated behavior, according to Schroeder, suggested that the judge "had no special emotional conflict or personal fear as to sexual perversioñ, but must have had a strong personal fear of a prostitution 'skeleton' [p. 107]."

Lasswell (1948) actually psychoanalyzed three judges whom he identified as Judges X, Y, and Z. Judge X manifested a compulsive personality in both his private and public life. He was preoccupied with detail and appeared to be tense and irritable. Judge X lacked warmth, displayed contempt for others, and tended to be unusually fussy. Judge Y, on the other hand, was relaxed and easygoing. He was free of compulsiveness and was remarkably sensitive to others and able to anticipate political consequences. Judge Z had a mercurial temper that was evident in his dealings with counsel, parties, and witnesses. Judge Z demanded deference and had driving ambition. He tended to play an agitational role.

Judge X was prone to deciding cases in a progovernment direction, except in antitrust cases where he was reluctant to break up businesses or hold businessmen criminally responsible. He also tended to be antiunion and pro-civil liberties. Nevertheless, in criminal cases, Judge X was very severe with offenders and tended to impose high fines and long prison terms. Judge Y, on the other hand, was viewed as more benevolent, and less severe in sentencing than Judge X, and less legalistic in taxation and business cases than Judge Z. Judge Y also tried to take a middle way in labor and management cases. Judge Z was quite soft with youthful offenders, severe with the middle aged, and very easy on the aged. Judge Z also could be very antigovernment, and was somewhat biased against large corporations. In later life, he strongly favored a large and strong government.

These decisional propensities reflected the distinctive, complex personalities of the judges. Judge X, for example, displayed such a compulsive personality that he evidenced despotic behavior. Judge Y conceived of himself as a strong, benign authority. Judge Z evidenced an agitational personality type. He was the most sensitive to the emotions of others, the most eager for notoriety, and the most erratic. Such a psychoanalytical approach, according to Lasswell, was necessary to understand the "developmental links between character type, political type, and political role [p. 64]."

Smith and Blumberg (1967) used participant observation of trial judges to create a typology of trial judge types. They identified the personality types as (*a*) the intellectual scholar, (*b*) the routineer hack; (*c*) the political adventurer-careerist, (*d*) the judicial pensioner, (*e*) the hatchet man, and (*f*) the tyrant-showboat-benevolent despot. These six personality types were based on observations of nine judges who sat on one city court. The typology might best be understood as a way of summarizing differences in behaviors of a single sample of judges. Other studies might expand the typology or modify the description.

The workhorses of the court were the first two personality types. The intellectual scholar was well educated and intelligent. He handled over one-third of the case load of the court. The routineer hack was a traditional political figure with a strong political background who handled slightly less than one-third of the court's caseload. Two judges were classified as political adventurer-careerists. They saw the bench as a temporary stepping stone to other offices and had no interest in law or judicial administration. Those judges classified as judicial pensioners obtained judgeships late in life and regarded their positions as sinecures. For all practical purposes, they had retired. The hatchet man was a former district attorney who continued to maintain close ties with the prosecutor's office. He was called upon to handle cases involving scandal and notorious behavior. This judge was politically sensitive and maintained an image as a dispenser of swift justice. He made it clear that defendants should cooperate with the authorities. The tyrant—showboat—benevolent despot was a sadistic exhibitionist. He was deeply hostile, frustrated, and ambition-ridden, and could be cruel or kind, severe or soft, depending on his mood.

It does seem clear that the relationship between personality and judicial behavior is a significant area for research; yet little research has been done in it. As Becker (1970), in offering an overall assessment of research on judicial personalities, concluded, "though the notions of personality occasionally surface in contemporary theorizing about the causes of judicial decisions, it is still not a very popular or deeply researched theory. In the main, it is given lip service or brushed over lightly [p. 87]." It is one thing to recognize an area as an important one for research; another to do research in that area. Study of judicial personalities is probably hindered by the difficulty in getting cooperation from judges. Murphy and Tanenhaus (1972) have pointed out the lack of psychological and psychoanalytical training of judicial scholars, which probably is responsible for the dearth of personality-oriented judicial research. An additional factor is that such research is a slow process. Even at the expiration of years of effort, the product will yield highly speculative conclusions, difficulties in accounting for much variance in behavior, and an analysis of a very limited number of judges. Such problems make it easy to understand the lack of research on judicial personalities.

The Socialization Process

An area of research related to personality research deals with the socialization of judges, and in particular, the effects of their backgrounds on their behavior. A fundamental assumption of legal scholars is that the backgrounds of judges influence their decisions. This assumption flows from a recognition that judicial decisions are human ones as well as strictly legal decisions. The primary way scholars have attempted to study the influence of judges' backgrounds on their decisions is to correlate background characteristics with judicial decisional propensities. For example, such research has correlated the political party affiliations of judges with their tendency to vote in a liberal or conservative direction (Goldman, 1975). Other background variables have also been explored, such as religious affiliations of judges, their occupations prior to becoming judges, their organizational affiliations, age, tenure, and class backgrounds (Goldman, 1975; Murphy & Tanenhaus, 1972; Nagel, 1969).

The political party variable in particular has been found to reliably correlate with decisional propensities: Democrat judges tend to vote more liberally than Republican judges. Goldman (1975) found the correlation between Democrat judges and liberal voting varied depending on the issue area, but he found several correlations in the .30–.40 range. Other variables (e.g., organizational affiliations, class background, religion, and tenure) also show correlations with liberal decisional propensities, but these correlations are (*a*) less consistently found than the correlation between political party and liberalism, (*b*) considerably smaller than the correlation between political party and liberalism, or (*c*) more limited to specific issue areas.

There is, of course, no reason to believe that background variables affect judicial liberalism in all issue areas in the same way or to the same degree. Variables might be related to liberalism in one area, but not in others. For example, Ulmer (1973) studied Supreme Court voting behavior between 1947 and 1956, examining the effects of three background variables: (*a*) age at appointment, (*b*) federal administrative experience, and (*c*) religious affiliation. Those three variables accounted for 70% of the variance in voting support of federal government prosecution in federal criminal cases. Yet the same variables accounted for only 58% of the variance in state criminal cases. Similarly, Goldman (1975) examined judges' voting behavior on the United States courts of appeals. He examined the effects of such background variables as political party, age, religion, prior political candidacy, prior judicial experience, and years on the court. A stepwise multiple regression with these variables as independent variables and liberalism as the dependent variable produced multiple correlations ranging from .23 to .61 depending on the issue area.

Ulmer (1973) has suggested that one problem with research relating backgrounds to decisions is that scholars have not examined a wide range of background variables. Studies that have examined previously unexplored variables support Ulmer's suggestion. Cook (1973), for example, who was interested in the voting behavior of federal judges in draft evasion cases, examined the influence of judges' families on their voting behavior. Among the variables she examined was one dealing with whether the judge had draft-age sons. She found a tendency for judges who did to be more severe in sentencing draft evaders than judges who did not have draft-age sons. Cook also found that one could extract profiles of the typically severe sentencer and mild sentencer in draft cases. The mild sentencer was an Eastern urban judge who heard cases in a city with a high crime rate. It was likely that the judge would be a Democrat from a Democratic community. The judge would be about 60 years old, a World War II veteran, and a nominal member of the American Legion as well as of the American Civil Liberties Union. His draft case load would likely be a large one. On the other hand, the severe sentencer would probably sit in the South, in a poor, small town. The judge would be about 67, a Republican sitting in a Democratic community. His draft case load would probably be quite low and his court would not have more than one judge sitting. The severe sentencer would be a nonveteran and a member of only local organizations.

Vines (1964) studied the voting behavior of federal district judges in race relations cases after the *Brown* (1954) decision and found a number of variables associated with prointegrationist voting behavior. Southern Republican judges were more prointegration than Democrat judges. This was probably because President Eisenhower's judicial appointments were not restricted by senatorial courtesy since there were no Republican Southern senators, and also because in the 1950s Southern Republicans tended to be more liberal on the race issue than Southern Democrats. The few Catholic judges were all integrationists. There was a tendency for segregationists to be less cosmopolitan than other judges and segregationists were far more likely to have held state political offices. Most interestingly, Vines found that judges were far more likely to be segregationists if their districts contained large numbers of blacks.

Giles and Walker (1975) examined the policymaking of Southern federal judges in school segregation cases. They correlated a number of variables with an index that measured the level of enforcement of desegregation. The variables included social background variables: birthplace, education, religion, political party, previous local political office, and previous state political office. Only slight correlations, ranging between .02 and .16, were found with these variables and the desegregation index. Similarly, only small, statistically insignificant correlations were found between the index and two variables designed to measure environmental influences: (a) percentage black in community (r = .10) and (b) percentage of community voting for Wallace (r = −.10). Two variables were used to measure the court's links to the community: the judge's organizational memberships and court's location within or without the school district. Though organizational memberships showed no correlation with the desegregation index (r = −.02), there was a moderate positive correlation between presence of the court in the school district and the desegregation index (r = .45). Two variables dealing with the school district were also studied. There was a slight, positive, statistically insignificant correlation between the desegregation index and the percentage of black enrollment in the school district (r = .13) and a moderately high positive correlation between district size and the desegregation index (r = .54).

This study conflicts with earlier ones that found correlations between judicial background, environmental characteristics, and judicial behavior in race relations cases. But two things distinguished this study from previous ones—It was made many years after *Brown* (1954) and the index measured degree of desegregation rather than whether or not it should occur. Perhaps the decline in the correlations involving the background and environmental variables is related to the reduction in the intensity of personal and community feelings about desegregation. The authors were uncertain why judges tended to allow more segregation in their own communities. They suggested three possible explanations:

1. The court location variable was a link between the judge and unstudied environmental variables.
2. Desegregation in a judge's own community aroused a judge's personal feelings.
3. A judge might be more sensitive to the feelings in his community.

The size of the school district had a very high correlation with the index, suggesting that the logistics of desegregation were far greater in larger than smaller districts.

Even a traditionally studied variable, such as religion, has proven to be very predictive of judicial voting behavior in some cases. Sorauf (1976), for example, examined judicial voting in cases involving the establishment of religion clause of the First Amendment. He found that Jewish judges were strongly supportive of the claims of those who favored separation of church and state, Catholic judges were very supportive of accommodation between church and state, and Protestants tended to divide between separationist and accommodationist claims. If one looks, for example, at appellate judges in all cases, separationist claims were supported by 58% of Jewish judges, 48% of nonfundamentalist Protestants, 46% of fundamentalist Protestants, and 22% of Roman Catholic judges.

In summary, studies which have attempted to correlate background and environmental variables with judicial decisional propensities have been most valuable in suggesting several aspects of the judicial socialization process that can account for discretionary judicial decision making. Specifically, it has been found that some nonlegal variables are correlated with judicial decisional propensities in some cases. Nevertheless, this socialization approach has its critics. It has been argued, for example, that

1. Attempts to correlate backgrounds to behavior have simply been too crude to produce meaningful results.
2. General background variables cannot capture the richness of the judicial socialization process.
3. Such correlational research is based on the inaccurate assumption that judges have common background experiences and respond to them in the same way.

Finally, it has been suggested that analysis of one or several background variables ignores the effects of precedent and judges' efforts to decide cases without bias. Both efforts would depersonalize judicial decisions (Becker, 1964; Fuller, 1966; Grossman, 1966, 1967). Perhaps the key problem with such research is that explanation tends to proceed in a *post hoc* fashion, where correlations are found and then efforts are made to explain the correlations. But since correlations do not necessarily imply causation, such research findings offer only tentative explanations.

Judicial Attitudes

Socialization research is related to research on judicial attitudes in that the latter are viewed as formed by the former. One of the first studies of the attitudes of trial court judges was by Haines (1922/1964). He noted great disparities in the discharge and dismissal rates of New York City magistrates. In intoxication cases, for example, Haines noted that while the overall conviction rate was 92%, one judge discharged 79% of those cases. In disorderly conduct cases, one judge had almost a 0% discharge rate, another an 18% rate, and a third judge had a 54% discharge rate. Haines argued that such disparities could only be explained by differing attitudes among the judges. He noted that "the process of judicial decision is determined to a considerable extent by the judges' views of fair play, public policy, and their general consensus as to what is right and just [p. 45]."

Other studies of sentencing disparities have also focused on attitudinal differences among trial court judges (Jackson, 1974). Aside from those concerned with sentencing disparities, studies of judicial attitudes have overwhelmingly examined appellate courts. In this research, voting behavior patterns have been identified and can be compared among judges, since appellate courts have many judges who frequently hear the same cases. Some research has ranked judges along a liberal-conservative dimension and has examined the ideological differences among them. (Pritchett, 1948; Schubert, 1965, 1974). For example, justices such as Murphy, Douglas, and Rutledge were found to frequently vote in favor of individuals and against the government. Such justices were labeled liberals and their voting behavior was explained in terms of an underlying liberal ideology. A justice such as Vinson, on the other hand, tended to vote in favor of the government. An underlying conservative ideology was assumed to explain this voting behavior. Since a judge's degree of liberalism is relative to the voting behavior of other judges on the court, this approach is limited to multijudge courts and could not be used for trial courts where only one judge hears a case.

One approach to the study of judicial attitudes on state supreme courts could, however, be applied to the study of the attitudes of trial court judges. Nagel (1969) sent a liberalism questionnaire to state supreme court judges and then related liberalism, as expressed in responses to the questionnaire, to liberal voting behavior by the judge. He found that judges who voted liberally in a variety of issue areas also expressed liberal attitudes on the questionnaire. These judges were much more prodefendant in criminal cases, much more progovernment in business regulation cases, somewhat in favor of the plaintiff in motor vehicle accident cases, and slightly in favor of the employee in employee injury cases.

To summarize, research on judicial attitudes has focused primarily on multijudge, appellate courts, though some attitudinal research has examined sentencing disparities among trial judges. The fundamental assumption of most of this research is that differences in voting behavior among judges reflect ideological differences. Nagel's (1969) research is a useful development in that efforts are now being made to measure attitudes independently from voting behavior. Nevertheless, the nature of the connection between judicial attitudes and voting behavior remains uncertain.

The Judicial Role

Closely related to research on judicial attitudes is research on judicial role perceptions. Becker (1964, 1966, 1970) has argued that attitudinal research is too narrow, that it ignores a significant filter between attitudes and behavior. That filter is the legal socialization process that develops a notion of judicial role. According to Becker, judicial role stresses the importance of reliance on precedent rather than attitudes when judicial decisions are made.

Becker (1964) presented hypothetical cases for decision by both law and nonlaw students. He found that in reaching decisions law students tended to rely more on precedent than did nonlaw students even when it required them to decide cases against their own values. One problem with this research was that Becker was discussing judicial role without using judges in his analysis. As a result, Becker (1966) conducted a similar study that used Hawaiian judges as his sample. Here Becker found great variation in precedent orientation among judges. In fact, he found that the great majority of judges ranked personal factors as extremely important in making decisions. Yet if the judges did have a strong precedent orientation, they were likely to decide hypothetical cases against their personal values and in favor of precedent.

Most notions of judicial role are clearly related to judicial attitudes. One would expect the judges' attitudes interact with role perceptions and that interaction would prove a strong determinant of judicial votes. A recent study by Gibson (1978) sought to examine that relationship between attitude and role. He obtained sentencing severity data on 26 Iowa state court judges and also interviewed judges about their attitudes and their role perceptions, especially whether the judges thought it was proper to allow personal values to influence decision making. Gibson found that judicial attitudes accounted for only about 14% of the variance in sentencing behavior, and role orientation accounted for only about 8%. However, Gibson could explain a remarkable 64% of the variance in sentencing behavior with an interactive model of attitudes and role perceptions. This approach represents one of the most promising developments in the research on judicial attitudes and roles.

Judicial Interaction

Trial court judges work within the structure of the courtroom, and as a result, must interact with others in that setting. That interaction, it would seem, should affect trial decisions. Unfortunately, courtroom interaction is one of the most understudied aspects of the psychology of judges; some research does exist and it does suggest the importance of courtroom interaction.

Blumberg (1967) has argued that the trial is a social network that is primarily composed of the judge and the trial attorneys. These actors emphasize cooperative behavior since cooperation maximizes case productivity for all parties. The judge and the attorneys learn to rely on one another since they function within a structured environment that demands cooperation.

An example of the dependence of judges upon attorneys is found in a recent study of the setting of bail. Ebbesen and Konečni (1975) examined the setting of bail and found that the most important determinant was the prosecutor's recommendation. The defense attorney's recommendation was also of some importance in determining the amount of bail. It is likely that some dependence upon attorneys is also evident in a trial setting, though the main predictors of sentences appear to be the probation officer's recommendation, the prior record of the defendant, and the severity of the crime (Konečni & Ebbesen, 1979).

There is also evidence that defendant characteristics have only a very slight effect on judicial decisions. Hagan (1974) reviewed 20 studies of the relationship between criminal sentencing severity and defendant characteristics. He found only "a small relationship between extra-legal attributes of the offender and sentencing decisions [p. 375]." More specifically, no correlations were found between sentencing severity and age or sex of defendants. No correlation between socioeconomic status and sentencing severity was found if the cases were not capital ones and prior record and type of offense were held constant. No correlation between race and sentencing severity was found if the cases were not capital ones, if there were no prior offenses, and if the type of offense was held constant. Race was related to sentencing severity, although only where there were prior offenses or in interracial capital cases in the South.

Though jury trials are rare, they have generated a considerable body of research. Interestingly, it has been found that juries are somewhat more willing to acquit defendants in criminal cases than are judges. Kalven and Zeisel (1966) compared jury verdicts with the judges' responses to the question of guilt for a total of 3,576 trials. They found that both judge and jury agreed to acquit in 14% of cases, and agreed to convict in 64% of cases. Thus, the total agreement rate between judges and juries was 78%. In only 3% of cases would the judge acquit and the jury convict. In 19% of cases, the judge would convict although the jury voted to acquit.

That juries have a mind of their own is well known among trial attorneys. Sue, Smith, and Caldwell (1973) suggested that juries will readily ignore judicial instructions. Using students as jurors, Sue *et al.* attempted to determine whether the simulated juries would follow judges' instructions to ignore inadmissible evidence clearly damaging to the defendant's case. A 2 × 3 factorial design was used with initial evidence strongly showing guilt for one group of subjects and weakly showing guilt for another group. The additional evidence presented was admissible for some subjects and inadmissible for others, while a third group received no additional evidence at all. Where the initial evidence was weak, the conviction rate for the group hearing no additional evidence was 0%. For the group hearing additional admissible evidence, the conviction rate was 26%; for the group hearing additional inadmissible evidence, the conviction rate was 35%. If the initial evidence of guilt was strong, the conviction rate for the group hearing no additional evidence was 47%. If admissible evidence was heard, the conviction rate was 68%; if additional inadmissible evidence was heard, the conviction rate was 53%. Thus, especially in weak evidence cases, the simulation suggests that juries may not obey judges' instructions to ignore inadmissible evidence of guilt.

Still other research assumes that juries will more likely heed judicial instructions if those instructions are made clearer and more understandable. Sales, Elwork, and Alhni (1977) have applied psycholinguistic theory to improve the understandability of judges' instructions. (See Lind, Chapter 2, this volume, for a more complete discussion of the comprehensibility and effectiveness of judicial instructions.) Other research does suggest that juries are responsive to judges' trial behavior. Kerr (in press) found that the more respectfully judges behaved toward the defense, the more likely that juries would acquit. Similarly, juries tended to respond to the favoritism that judges evidenced toward contesting attorneys. If the judge favored the prosecution, the jury conviction rate tended to be slightly higher than if the judges favored the defense. Kerr speculated that jurors may use judges as models to determine their emotional reactions to the defense. Unfortunately, no measure of the strength of evidence was available so it remained unclear whether the judge's reactions were just incidental effects of the balance of evidence.

Prediction of Judicial Decisions

Psychology has also been used in the prediction of judicial decisions. Because judicial behavior research has primarily been concerned with appellate courts, most predictions are of higher court decisions. Nevertheless, the same theory and some of the methods are applicable to trial courts as well as appellate courts. Though not all methods can be used for single-judge courts, all methods can provide insight into the probable outcome of appeals from trial courts to larger, multijudge appellate courts.

Prediction research requires regular patterns of behavior to anticipate future behavior. Studies clearly show these requisite regular patterns. Justice Hugo Black, for example, voted prolabor in 55 of 59 Fair Labor Standards Act cases decided between 1941 and 1959. Black's voting behavior during this period was more predictable than that of most justices but no justices voted in a completely unpatterned manner. In 60 Federal Employers Liability Act cases decided between 1938 and 1958, Black voted for the worker 59 times. Black found a violation of the Sherman Anti-Trust Act in all 19 cases decided between 1949 and 1959 (Mendelson, 1961). A key assumption is that such patterns in judicial voting behavior are based on the underlying attitudes of judges. Thus, if one can identify the relevant questions in past cases and if those questions exist in future cases, predictions can be made on the assumption that judges' answers to the questions will be the same based on ideological consistency.

Several methods have been used to assign weights to the questions posed by cases. One such method is discriminant function analysis. With this method, the decision is equal to the sum of the weights of each relevant question. Ulmer (1964) identified four relevant questions in previous search and seizure cases decided by the Supreme Court between 1942 and 1962. He was able to correctly predict the outcome of 18 of 19 cases.

Kort (1964) and Lawlor (1963) have used Boolean algebra to predict judicial decisions. An appellate court may state a number of conditions that will result in certain case outcomes. Boolean algebra can reduce these conditions to a simple formulation. In examining right to counsel cases, Lawlor identified 39 relevant conditions. He found that a distinction between pro and con decisions could be provided by the following Boolean equation:

$$D_{\text{pro}} \leftrightarrow (f_{11} \bigvee f_{12}) \bigwedge f_{19} \bigwedge \{L\ (1, S_a) \bigvee L(5, S_b)\}.$$

The equation states that a decision in right to counsel cases is in favor of the defendant if and only if fact 11 or fact 12 (or both), and fact 19, and at least one fact in subset S_a facts, or at least five facts in subset S_b facts, or both, are present. Otherwise, the decision will be against the defendant. Since in Lawlor's study there are 2^{39} combinations of facts, a computer is necessary to obtain the appropriate Boolean equation.

Kort (1964) has used simultaneous equations to predict decisions on multijudge courts. In a highly simplified form, this approach can be illustrated as follows. If the court is a nine-judge court and three facts lead to a seven-judge decision for the aggrieved, the equation is:

$$X_1 + X_2 + X_3 = 7$$

Presence of two facts might lead to the following five-judge majority:

$$X_1 + X_3 = 5$$

In another case where only fact 1 and fact 2 are present, three judges might decide in favor of the aggrieved.

$$X_1 + X_2 = 3$$

Working with simultaneous equations, one can determine that the value of X_1 is 1; X_2 is 2; and X_3 is 4. If in a new case only fact 2 and fact 3 are present, the predicted court majority would be the sum of X_2 and X_3, or 6. Since it is unlikely that a real series of cases will be as elementary as this simple illustration, a computer would normally be essential for this method of prediction. The approach assumes, however, that the facts are scaled along the same dimension and it does not provide for interaction among facts. Both of these assumptions may, of course, be invalid.

Schubert (1968) has used a psychometric model to predict judicial decisions. He developed cumulative scales of the voting behavior of Supreme Court justices and reconstructed them as scale axes in factor space. The result was a mathematical proof that the points at which the justices were located in factor space represented the attitude syndromes of the justices. The distances between these points represented the psychological distances separating the justices. Based on knowledge of the justices' locations in factor space, Schubert made a number of predictions of judicial voting in reapportionment cases in 1962 and 1963. All predictions were confirmed.

All of the above methods require the aid of computers and some knowledge of advanced mathematics or statistics. Nagel (1969), however, has developed a simple prediction method that can be applied without computers and with limited statistical and mathematical knowledge. The method involves the use of simple contingency tables. Predictor variables are dichotomized into the presence or absence of a characteristic (e.g., having an attorney). Likewise, the judicial judgment of interest is dichotomized; for example, into rulings for the prosecution or rulings for the defense. The association between predictor and criterion is determined using the simple regression coefficient between the dichotomized predictor and criterion variables. When working with dichotomized variables in this context, one can algebraically show that the regression coefficient between winning and the presence or absence of any variable is equal to the percentage of cases having the variable present in which the prosecution won minus the percentage of cases having the variable absent in which the prosecution also won. For example, if there are two cases in which a variable is present, and the prosecutor won both cases, those cases would have a victory score of 100%. Likewise, if there are three cases in which the variable was absent, and the prosecutor won only one case, those cases would have a victory score of 33%. The regression coefficient for that variable would thus be +.67, or the difference between 1.00 and .33. This is the situation with variable *s* in Table 9.1. Regression coefficients are more meaningful to use than correlation coefficients because they are so simple to calculate in this context, and because our concern here is with prediction, not the best curve-fitting. In other words, we want to know, for a 1-unit change on a predictor from absent to present, how much the percentage of victory increases.

Predictors with reasonably large regressions should be preferred. In addition, one might choose to reduce the set of predictors by using just one of a highly intercorrelated set of predictors. A composite value is then computed for each case in the sample. This *composite value* is defined as the sum of the coefficients for all predictors that were present for that case. Then the composite values would be rank ordered. Generally, it should be possible to identify two cutoff scores from this rank ordering: that composite score above which the ruling was generally for one position (e.g., the prosecution), and that composite score below which the ruling was generally for the other position (e.g., defense). Between those two cutoff points are cases that are evenly divided between the prosecution and defense, or else an area exists where no cases have been decided. Using the regressions from the original sample, a composite value for any new case of interest could be calculated, and as long as this composite score did not lie between the identified cutoff scores, a prediction of the likely judicial decision in the new case could be made. A single cutoff could also be developed, above which prosecution victories would be predicted, and below which defense victories would be predicted. The single cutoff would be designed to minimize the number of errors when applied to cases in the data base. A series of cutoff scores could also be established, each of which would encompass a set of cases that have a given probability of victory depending on how many of the cases above the cutoff score were decided for the prosecution out of the total number of cases in that subset.

To illustrate this method, let us assume that four predictor variables, $p,q,r,$ and s, were reliably associated with the outcomes of a sample of five cases (A,B,C,D, and E). Table 9.1 depicts a hypothetical set of outcomes, predictor values, and correlations. The composite value for each case is then just the sum of the regressions for all predictors present in that case. So, for example, in Case B, for which all four predictors were present, the composite value would just be the sum of all four regressions, 175. In Table 9.1, the lowest composite score where the prosecution won is 175. The highest composite value where the defense won is 8. Thus, our cutoff points would be 8 and 175. If the composite value of a new case was 175 or higher, a prediction of a prosecution victory would be made; if its composite value was 8 or lower, a defense victory would be predicted. No prediction would be made if the value was between 8 and 175.

The simplicity of this method is most appealing. Additionally, it can be quite successful in predicting case outcomes. Ulmer (1963), for example, reported that application of Nagel's method to 20 facts (variables) in a sample of 19 Supreme Court search and seizure cases resulted in perfect separation of pro and con cases. There are limitations upon these and other similar prediction methods, however, since there is no certain method for identifying relevant variables in past cases. The case to be predicted may have a new variable that will dramatically affect the case outcome. Similarly, such a method assumes

TABLE 9.1
An Illustration of Nagel's (1969) Prediction Method

Case	Predictors[a]				Composite value	Judicial decision
	p	q	r	s		
E	1	0	1	1	242	Prosecution
B	1	1	1	1	175	Prosecution
D	1	0	1	0	175	Prosecution
C	1	1	0	0	8	Defense
A	0	1	0	0	−67	Defense
Regression coefficients[b]	75	−67	100	67		

[a]"1" signifies the presence of the predictor; "0" signifies its absence.
[b]Decimal points have been removed from the coefficients for ease of presentation.

conformity with past decisions and is not useful for predicting a dramatic change from precedent. And there must, of course, be a pattern of decisions in the past cases. Thus, such methods would not be useful for new legal areas for which few cases are available or where patterns in voting behavior have not yet developed. More complicated methods might also be incorporated into this model. For example, partial regression methods might be used to eliminate overlap between predictor variables, and to handle variables with degrees of presence that do not meaningfully dichotomize.

JUDICIAL DECISION-MAKING MODELS

The Models in General

The purpose of this section of the chapter is to analyze applications of decision theory to the judicial process as manifested mainly in the decision making of judges and the related decisions of jurors. By *decision theory* we mean the study of how decision makers do and ought to arrive at decisions designed to maximize perceived benefits minus costs. The "do arrive" refers to the prediction purpose of the decision theory; the "ought to arrive" refers to its optimization purpose. To define decision theory more completely requires a defining of its distinctive methodology as well as its purposes. That methodology involves arriving at conclusions through a deductive reasoning process from premises that have been empirically validated or that are accepted intuitively or as axiomatic by definition. A *model* can be defined as a system of premises and the conclusions that are deduced from them.

The term *decision theory* in this chapter thus refers to the twin concepts of optimization prediction and deductive analysis. A sometimes used but more narrow definition of decision theory focuses on decision making under conditions of risk and uncertainty involving probabilities of contingent events occurring. In this chapter, that kind of optimum choice with probabilities is considered to be one type of decision theory rather than synonymous with decision theory itself.

There are at least seven important criteria of a good deductive model. First, the premises about reality should be empirically validated or at least be consistent with related empirical knowledge. Second, premises about normative goals should be reasonably related to the goals that relevant policymakers are likely to have, or the goals (and probably their source) should at least be explicitly stated. Third, the conclusions that are derived should follow from the premises by logical deduction without requiring outside information. Fourth, the deductive model should serve a causal, prescriptive, or some other useful purpose. Fifth, the model should indicate how its conclusions would change as a result of changes in its empirical and normative premises. Sixth, the model should have broadness in time, geography, and abstractness, but still be applicable to concrete situations. Seventh, the model should be simple and understandable, but still capture the essence of an important and complex phenomenon.

There are various relations worth mentioning between deductive modeling and empirical analysis. One important connection is the fact that the premises about reality can often be empirically tested or at least benefit from relevant empirical data. That may also be true of conclusions about reality, but deduction is often used to draw conclusions as to matters that cannot be directly observed. Purely normative premises (such as that goal Y is desirable) can sometimes be empirically validated if Y has instrumental value for achieving some higher value, but not if Y is an ultimate value. Purely normative conclusions (such as that input X is desirable) cannot be empirically tested, although they can be deductively validated in terms of how they relate to their premises.

Decision theory can be classified into decisions that involve discrete choices or choices along a continuum of alternatives. By *discrete choices* are meant alternatives that have no inherent numerical order, whereas *continuum choices* do have inherent numerical order. For example, the decision to release or hold a defendant in jail prior to trial are discrete choices, as are a set of alternative legislative redistricting plans. The pretrial release decision involves two choices, whereas the redistricting decision involves many choices. A common feature of discrete choices is that there is no inherent order in the choices with which one is confronted. The pretrial release problem, however, involves a choice that is affected by a probability, namely the probability that the defendant will appear in court if released, whereas the redistricting problem involves no contingent probabilities.

Deciding the optimum number of jurors to have, or the optimum allocation of dollars to police, courts, and corrections agencies are examples of choices on a continuum. In both situations the choices have an inherent order; eight jurors is more than seven jurors, and $100 is more than $90. The jury problem, however, is an *optimum level* problem on the single variable of jury size, whereas the allocation problem is an *optimum mix* problem across the three variables of police, courts, and corrections.

Time-oriented models represent another category of decision theory models. Some time-oriented models are concerned with seeking to minimize time consumption, a special kind of cost involving special deductive models such as queueing theory, optimum sequencing, and critical-path flow charts. Other time-oriented models are concerned with predicting the equilibrium position toward which decision makers or events will move. Such models may involve Markov chain analysis or difference equations.

Decision theory as defined above in its various forms has not been extensively applied to the legal process. The first well known application was probably that of Schubert (1958) in his *American Political Science Review* article, where he attempted to deduce the optimizing goals of the 1937 Supreme Court justices by determining what goals were most consistent with their observed decision-making behavior. Other political scientists, such as Krislov (1963), Murphy (1962), Rohde (1972), and Ulmer (1965), subsequently developed different deductive coalition-formation models for the Supreme Court.

Another landmark article was written by economist G. Becker (1968). Entitled, "Crime and Punishment: An Economic Approach," it brought decision theory from the Supreme Court level to the grass roots of the legal process and emphasized optimization rather than prediction. The essence of Becker's analysis was to deduce an optimum level of law enforcement at the point where the sum of the crime-committing costs plus the law enforcement costs are minimized. His benefit-cost analysis was followed by other economists such as Landes (1971) and Ehrlich (1973), and by economics-oriented law professors such as Posner (1973). Tullock (1971) has also contributed related analyses to that literature.

In the middle 1970s, political scientists began a synthesis of the political conflict and prediction perspective of Schubert (1958), and the economic modeling of criminal justice matters associated with Becker (1968). That new perspective, which included an analysis of compliance with Supreme Court decisions and other legal rules in terms of the risky benefits and costs to would-be noncompliers, is illustrated by the work of Stover and Brown (1975) and Rogers and Bullock (1977). The new perspective also showed a concern for modeling the decision-making process in law enforcement, pretrial release, plea bargaining, juries, sentencing, and judicial delay. Political and social scientists doing that kind of modeling include Aranson (1977), Brams and Davis (1976), Church (1976), Grofman (1977), Hennessey, Gray, and Conover (1977), Matheny (1979), Nagel and Neef (1977), and Palumbo, Levine, and Musheno (1977).

Decision theory can serve many purposes when applied to the judicial process and judicial behavior. Two of these purposes are to deduce the effects of system changes before the changes are adopted, and to aid the judicial system in maximizing its goals. The rest of this chapter will provide concrete examples of models fulfilling these two purposes.

Deducing Judicial Results from Decision-making Models

A good illustration of deductive modeling based on an individual decision-making model involves attempting to determine the effect on judicial behavior of publicizing judicial propensities (Nagel & Neef, 1979). For example, the law provides that when in doubt, a judge should release rather than hold a defendant in jail prior to trial. In reality, however, judges stand to lose more by making the mistake of releasing defendants who fail to appear for their court dates or who commit crimes while released, than by making the mistake of holding defendants who would appear and without having committed crimes while released. No one can tell in an individual case that a held defendant would have appeared and without having committed a crime since the held defendant is not given an opportunity to do so. Thus, the rational judge, when in doubt, may tend to hold rather than to release a defendant because the expected cost of holding is less than the expected cost of releasing. The deductive modeling problem involves determining the effect on judicial behavior of publicizing the holding rates of judges in light of this decision-making model.

Publicizing the holding rates of the judges serving in a given area is unlikely to bring those holding rates down. In other words, making it known the trial court judges in a given city hold 60% of all defendants in jail pending trial will not cause any individual judge to decrease the holding rate because publicizing that information still does not increase the expected costs of holding. Likewise, publicizing the holding rates for each individual judge on the court is not likely to lower the holding rates of those whose rates are high because they can justify, at least to themselves, that their high holding rate is needed to decrease nonappearances and crime commission by defendants released prior to trial. If, however, the holding rates of individual judges are publicized along with the appearance rates and the number of defendants who did not commit crimes while released by those judges, then those whose rate of holding is high might come down.

This might be so because empirical studies show that holding rates do vary greatly across judges, but that appearance and non-crime-commission rates tend to be almost uniformly high among judges whose rate of holding is high or low. Thus, Judge Jones, who holds 80% of all defendants, may look bad in comparison with judges like Judge Smith, who holds only 30% of all defendants. Each is likely to have about a 90−95% appearance rate and non-crime-commission rate for those defendants they release. In other words, it looks as if Judge Jones is holding 50% more defendants than he needs to hold in order to have a 90−95% appearance and non-crime-commission rate, even though we cannot tell in which cases Judge Jones has made an error in holding a defendant. That kind of publicizing thereby increases the expected cost of holding to Judge Jones, and is likely to cause him to decrease his holding rate if everything else remains constant. That effect can be further accentuated by also publicizing the undesirable effects and high social costs incurred by holding defendants in jail, such as jail maintenance, lost income productivity, more families on welfare, jail congestion, and the frequency of held defendants being found not guilty or guilty only of crimes involving sentences shorter than the jail time already served awaiting trial.

The same individual decision-making model can be used to deduce the effects of other changes on decreasing the number of decisions to hold. The expected cost of holding relative to releasing is likely to go down if the costs of releasing are decreased by such means as making rearrests easier through pretrial supervision or decreasing the interval from arrest to trial, thereby lessening the time available to defendants to disappear or commit new crimes. The expected cost of releasing also goes down if the probability of appearance and non-crime-commission can be increased through such means as better screening and notification and more vigorous prosecution of those who fail to appear.

Normative Decision-making Models

A good illustration of finding an optimum policy choice is involved in the problem of how a juror should vote with regard to convicting or acquitting a given criminal defendant, and how jurors should be instructed in order to maximize objectivity across jurors and conformity with the principle that convictions should occur only if the defendant is found guilty beyond a reasonable doubt (Nagel & Neef, 1979).

Rational jurors should vote to convict or acquit depending on which choice will give them the highest expected value, although expected value calculations are done implicitly rather than explicitly. The expected value of each choice equals the perceived benefits minus costs, discounted by the probability of their being received. The probability in this context is the probability that the defendant is actually guilty. To obtain the highest expected value, a juror should vote to acquit if the perceived probability of guilt is below a threshold probability, and vote to convict if the perceived probability of guilt is above a threshold probability. The threshold probability can be determined by knowing the relative value a juror places on avoiding the conviction of an innocent defendant versus the acquittal of a guilty one.

Suppose a legal system would like to stimulate jurors to have both a common threshold probability and a high threshold probability in the high .90s. The .90 figure is the one most often mentioned by judges when surveyed as to their understanding of the guilty "beyond a reasonable doubt" criterion (Simon & Mahan, 1971). To achieve that goal, jurors can be instructed that it is considered 10 times as undesirable to convict an innocent defendant as it is to acquit a guilty one (i.e., the 10-to-1 trade-off instruction). Merely instructing them that the standard of guilt is "beyond a reasonable doubt" or that a conviction requires a .90 probability does not generate a common or high threshold probability. For example, male and female students at the University of Illinois were given diverse instructions on how to decide criminal cases, and then their threshold probabilities in rape cases were determined by asking them questions about their relative satisfaction or dissatisfaction from convicting a guilty defendant, convicting an innocent defendant, acquitting a guilty defendant, or acquitting an innocent defendant. The results were roughly as follows (Nagel, Neef, & Lamm, 1981):

Type of jury instruction	Threshold probabilities (in rape cases)	
	Males	Females
No instruction	.70	.50
Beyond reasonable doubt	.75	.60
.90 probability	.85	.75
10-to-1 trade off	.90	.90

With no instruction, there is considered divergence between the two groups and both groups are substantially below the desired .90 threshold probability. A verbal instruction increases both objectivity and conformity with the law, but not by enough. A quantitative instruction makes for an improvement, but not as much as the 10-to-1 trade-off instruction.

Although the optimum choice seems to be the 10-to-1 instruction, the empirical reality is often no instruction. The difference between the empirical and the optimum here may possibly be caused by judges' awareness that a 10-to-1, .90, or verbal instruction will make convictions more difficult to obtain, a result they do not want. In other words, many judges have decided on the no-instruction choice, and we suggest that it is because they perceive that convictions will be more difficult to obtain if jurors are given the instructions we recommend. We thereby deduce that their values must generally be oriented toward keeping the conviction rate up, since there seems to be no other value position capable of reconciling the decision reached with the assumed factual perception.[1] This illustrates how optimizing analysis can often relate back to making deductions about decision-making behavior, just as deductions about decision-making behavior can often serve as the premises for an optimizing model.

CONCLUSIONS

The organization of this chapter indicates trends in the analysis of the judicial process and points toward some future directions. Studying judges formerly involved an almost exclusive concern with the legal structure under which they operate. An increased concern subsequently developed for the role of judges in the political process, including judicial selection, judicial representativeness, and the role of interest groups. Parallel to those political concerns has been the development of a public administration perspective on judging that tends to emphasize case load pressures and how to efficiently handle them.

[1] If it is true that judges are aware that convictions would be reduced by calling jurors' attention to the standard of "beyond a reasonable doubt," and the judges still refuse to call the jurors' attention to the standard, then one might argue that they are refusing for some reason other than not wanting to reduce convictions. Perhaps another reason is that they have no choice because pattern jury instructions generally require not giving a definition of "beyond a reasonable doubt." The pattern jury instructions, however, are developed by judges, rather than by legislators. Thus, blaming the lack of beyond a reasonable doubt (BRD) instructions on the pattern jury instructions system is just moving the motivation question back a step from the trial court decision making to the appellate court decision making that develops the required jury instructions. Another reason may be that alternative instructions are too vague, and judges are seeking to avoid vagueness by not giving the reasonable doubt standard instructions, rather than seeking to avoid nonconvictions. That reasoning, however, assume that it is impossible for judges to develop reasonably clear instructions on the need to find guilt beyond a reasonable doubt, or that they do not have the authority to replace the vague instructions with clear ones. Neither assumption, however, is true. Appellate judges could institute the 10-to-1 instruction mentioned in the text.

The behavioral movement within political science and the other social sciences has manifested itself in studying judges as individuals rather than in terms of the legal, political, and administrative context in which they operate. That type of analysis has sometimes involved psychoanalytical case studies of individual judges to explain their behavior. More often, it has involved the quantitative analysis of behavioral patterns across judges, such as relations between judicial decisions and judicial backgrounds, ideological attitudes, role perceptions, and small group interactions. It has also involved the quantitative prediction of judicial decisions from such variables and from factual elements in the court cases.

The latest developments relevant to the psychology of judging include the attempt to establish deductive models whereby one can deduce how judicial behavior would change given certain changes in aspects of judging that influence perceived benefits and costs of alternative behaviors. Those developments also include the attempt to establish deductive models to deduce prescriptions or policies relevant to the judicial process for maximizing or achieving given goals.

Such deductive models represent a synthesis of the two prior perspectives: the legal-political and behavioral perspectives. The legal-political process provides goals or values to which judging is supposed to adhere and that serve as the normative premises for deductive models. The behavioral research provides a body of empirically validated propositions that can serve as the empirical premises for such deductive models. What thus may be especially needed for future work on the psychology of judging is a clarification of the legal-political values, a growth of the behavioral propositional inventory, and a building of more powerful models for deductively predicting and prescribing judicial behavior.

REFERENCES

Abraham, H. *Justices and presidents.* London and New York: Oxford Univ. Press, 1974.
Abraham, H. *The judicial process* (2nd ed.). London and New York: Oxford Univ. Press, 1968. (Originally published, 1962.)
Abraham, H. *The judicial process* (3rd ed.). London and New York: Oxford Univ. Press, 1975. (Originally published, 1962.)
Aranson, P. The simple analytics of sentencing. In G. Tullock & R. Wagner (Eds.), *Deductive reasoning in the analysis of public policy.* Lexington, Massachusetts: Lexington, 1977.
Becker, G. Crime and punishment: An economic approach. *Journal of Political Economy,* 1968, 76, 169−217.
Becker, T. *Political behavioralism and modern jurisprudence.* Chicago, Illinois: Rand McNally, 1964.
Becker, T. A survey study of Hawaiian judges: The effects of judicial role variations. *American Political Science Review,* 1966, 60, 677−680.
Becker, T. *Comparative judicial politics.* Chicago, Illinois: Rand McNally, 1970.
Black, H., Jr. *My father: A remembrance.* New York: Random House, 1975.
Blumberg, A. *Criminal justice.* New York: Quadrangle, 1967.
Brams, S., & Davis, M. A game-theory approach to jury selection. *Trial,* 1976, 12, 47−49.

Brown v. *Board of Education, Supreme Court Reporter*, 1954, 74, 686–693.

Chase, H. *Federal judges: The appointing process.* Minneapolis: Univ. of Minnesota Press, 1972.

Church, T. Plea bargains, concessions and the courts: Analysis of a quasi-experiment. *Law and Society Review*, 1976, *10*, 377–402.

Cook, B. Sentencing behavior of federal judges: Draft cases—1972. *University of Cincinnati Law Review*, 1973, *42*, 567–633.

Ebbesen, E., & Konečni, V. Decision making and information integration in the courts: The setting of bail. *Journal of Personality and Social Psychology*, 1975, *32*, 805–821.

Ehrlich, I. Participation in illegitimate activities: An economic analysis. *Journal of Political Economy*, 1973, *81*, 521–565.

Fuller, L. Science and the judicial process. *Harvard Law Review*, 1966, *79*, 1604–1628.

Gibson, J. Judges' role orientations, attitudes and decisions: An interactive model. *American Political Science Review*, 1978, *72*, 911–924.

Giles, M., & Walker, T. Judicial policy-making and southern school segregation. *Journal of Politics*, 1975, *37*, 917–936.

Goldman, S. Voting behavior on the U.S. Courts of Appeals revisited. *American Political Science Review*, 1975, *69*, 491–506.

Grofman, B. Jury decision-making models. In S. Nagel (Ed.), *Modeling the criminal justice system.* Beverly Hills, California: Sage, 1977.

Grossman, J. Social backgrounds and judicial decision making. *Harvard Law Review*, 1966, *79*, 1551–1564.

Grossman, J. Social backgrounds and judicial decisions: Notes for a theory. *Journal of Politics*, 1967, *29*, 334–351.

Hagan, J. Extra-legal attributes and criminal sentencing: An assessment of a sociological viewpoint. *Law and Society Review*, 1974, *8*, 357–383.

Haines, C. General observations on the effects of personal, political, and economic influences in the decisions of judges. In G. Schubert (Ed.), *Judicial behavior.* Chicago, Illinois: Rand McNally, 1964. (Originally published, 1922.)

Hennessey, T., Gray, C., & Conover, C. Choosing among corrections alternatives: A political economy perspective. In S. Nagel (Ed.), *Modeling the criminal justice system.* Beverly Hills, California: Sage, 1977.

Jackson, D. *Judges.* New York: Atheneum, 1974.

Kalven, H., & Zeisel, H. *The American jury.* Boston, Massachusetts: Little, Brown, 1966.

Kerr, N. Trial participants' characteristics/behaviors and juries' verdicts: An exploratory field study. In V. Konečni & E. Ebbesen (Eds.), *Social psychological analysis of the legal system.* San Francisco: W. H. Freeman, in press.

Konečni, V., & Ebbesen, E. External validity of research in legal psychology. *Law and Human Behavior*, 1979, *3*, 39–70.

Kort, F. Simultaneous equations and Boolean algebra. In G. Schubert (Ed.), *Judicial behavior.* Chicago, Illinois: Rand McNally, 1964.

Krislov, S. Power and coalition in a nine-man body. *American Behavioral Scientist*, 1963, *6*, 24–26.

Landes, W. An economic analysis of the courts. *Journal of Law and Economics*, 1971, *14*, 61–107.

Lasswell, H. *Power and personality.* New York: Norton, 1948.

Lawlor, R. Computer aids to legal decision-making. *Modern Uses of Logic in Law*, 1963, *63*, 98–114.

Matheny, A. *Plea bargaining in organizational perspective.* Unpublished doctoral dissertation, University of Minnesota, 1979.

Mendelson, W. *Justices Black and Frankfurter.* Chicago, Illinois: Univ. of Chicago Press, 1961.

Murphy, W. Marshaling the Court: Leadership, bargaining and the judicial process. *University of Chicago Law Review*, 1962, *29*, 640–672.

Murphy, W., & Tanenhaus, J. *The study of public law.* New York: Random House, 1972.

Nagel, S. *The legal process from a behavioral perspective.* Homewood, Illinois: Dorsey, 1969.

Nagel, S., & Neef, M. *The legal process: Modeling the system.* Beverly Hills, California: Sage, 1977.

Nagel, S., & Neef, M. *Decision theory and the legal process.* Lexington, Massachusetts: Lexington, 1979.

Nagel, S., Neef, M., & Lamm, D. Decision theory and jury decision-making. In B. Sales (Ed.), *The trial process.* New York: Plenum, 1981.

Palumbo, D., Levine, F. J., & Musheno, M. Individual, group, and social rationality in controlling crime. In S. Nagel (Ed.), *Modeling the criminal justice system.* Beverly Hills, California: Sage, 1977.

Peltason, J. *Federal courts in the political process.* Garden City, New York: Doubleday, 1955.

Posner, R. An economic approach to legal procedure and judicial administration. *Journal of Legal Studies*, 1973, *2*, 399−458.

Pritchett, C. *The Roosevelt court.* New York: Macmillan, 1948.

Rodgers, H., & Bullock, C. School desegregation: A cost benefit longitudinal analysis. In J. Gardiner (Ed.), *Public law and public policy.* New York: Praeger, 1977.

Rohde, D. Policy goals and opinion coalitions in the Supreme Court. *Midwest Journal of Political Science*, 1972, *16*, 208−224.

Ross, H. *Settled out of court.* Chicago, Illinois: Aldine, 1970.

Sales, B., Elwork, A., & Alfini, J. J. Improving comprehension for jury instructions. In B. Sales (Ed.), *Perspectives in law and psychology*, (Vol. 1): *The criminal justice system.* New York: Plenum, 1977.

Schmidhauser, J. *Judges and justices: The federal appellate judiciary.* Boston, Massachusetts: Little, Brown, 1979.

Schroeder, T. The psychologic study of judicial opinions. *California Law Review*, 1918, *6*, 89−113.

Schubert, G. The study of judicial decision-making as an aspect of political behavior. *American Political Science Review*, 1958, *52*, 1007−1025.

Schubert, G. *The judicial mind.* Evanston, Illinois: Northwestern Univ. Press, 1965.

Schubert, G. Judicial attitudes and voting behavior. In T. Jahnige & S. Goldman (Eds.), *The federal judicial system.* Hinsdale, Illinois: Dryden, 1968.

Schubert, G. *The judicial mind revisited.* London and New York: Oxford Univ. Press, 1974.

Simon, R., & Mahan, L. Quantifying burdens of proof: A view from the bench, the jury, and the classroom. *Law and Society Review*, 1971, *5*, 319−330.

Smith, A., & Blumberg, A. The problem of objectivity in judicial decision-making. *Social Forces*, 1967, *46*, 96−105.

Sorauf, F. *The wall of separation.* Princeton, New Jersey: Princeton Univ. Press, 1976.

Stover, R., & Brown, D. Understanding compliance and noncompliance with law. *Social Science Quarterly*, 1975, *56*, 363−375.

Sue, S., Smith, R., & Caldwell, C. Effects of inadmissible evidence on the decisions of simulated jurors: A moral dilemma. *Journal of Applied Social Psychology*, 1973, *3*, 345−353.

Truman, D. *The governmental process.* New York: Knopf, 1951.

Tullock, G. *The logic of the law.* New York: Basic Books, 1971.

Ulmer, S. Quantitative analysis of judicial processes: Some practical and theoretical applications. *Law and Contemporary Problems*, 1963, *28*, 164−184.

Ulmer, S. Discriminant analysis and an error criterion. In G. Schubert (Ed.), *Judicial behavior.* Chicago, Illinois: Rand McNally, 1964.

Ulmer, S. Toward a theory of sub-group formation in the United States Supreme Court. *Journal of Politics*, 1965, *27*, 133−152.

Ulmer, S. Social background as an indicator to the votes of Supreme Court justices in criminal cases: 1947−1956 terms. *American Journal of Political Science*, 1973, *17*, 622−630.

Vines, K. Federal district judges and race relations cases in the South. *Journal of Politics*, 1964, *26*, 338−357.

Wasby, S. *The Supreme Court.* New York: Holt, 1978.

Winick, C., Gerver, I., & Blumberg, A. The psychology of judges. In H. Toch (Ed.), *Legal and criminal psychology.* New York: Holt, 1961.

PART IV

PROBLEMS AND PROSPECTS FOR RESEARCH ON THE PSYCHOLOGY OF THE COURTROOM

chapter

10

Methodological Considerations in the Study of the Psychology of the Courtroom

Robert M. Bray
Norbert L. Kerr

THE PSYCHOLOGY
OF THE COURTROOM

The large number of current articles, reviews, and books devoted to the psychology of the courtroom reveals a substantial and lively interest in this topic by practitioners and researchers alike. And in recent years, social science research on psycho-legal issues has been drawn on increasingly by the judiciary (Loftus & Monahan, 1980; Suggs, 1979). Since research findings are tied to the methods used to obtain them, it is vital in interpreting the validity of results to understand the strengths and limitations of various research strategies. In most of the extant research, particularly that on juror and jury behavior, simulations have emerged as the primary research vehicle. Despite their popularity, simulations have become the target of increasing criticism (Bermant, McGuire, McKinely, & Salo, 1974; Colasanto & Sanders, 1976; Dillehay & Nietzel, 1980, 1981; Foss, 1975; Konečni & Ebbesen, 1979; Konečni, Mulcahy, & Ebbesen, 1980; Miller, Fontes, Boster, & Sunnafrank, 1977; Weiten & Diamond, 1979). While such criticisms have raised important issues that deserve thoughtful consideration, there seems to be a need for an analysis that identifies and balances the simulation's many strengths against its weaknesses.

In this chapter we discuss alternative methodologies for studying the psychology of the courtroom, with special attention devoted to the use of laboratory experiments and simulations. We begin by examining the range of procedures actually in use for one topic area, juror/jury research. This is followed by a general consideration of laboratory, simulation, and field methodologies coupled with an examination of their strengths and limitations. Special emphasis is given to the problem of establishing generality. In the next two sections of the chapter, we examine basic themes inherent in the current methodological criticisms of simulation studies and offer responses to those criticisms. Finally, we draw several conclusions and present some recommendations regarding the study of the psychology of the courtroom.

EXPERIMENTAL PROCEDURES OF MOCK TRIAL RESEARCH

Because mock trials are the most widely used research strategy in the study of the courtroom and because they have drawn considerable criticism, it is of interest to elaborate the range of procedures employed with this method. For our analysis, we consider investigations of juror/jury behavior, the most active area of research in the psychology of the courtroom.

To grasp the procedural variations of mock trial research we examined 72 studies[1] conducted during the past two decades (although over 60 have ap-

[1]Our selection of studies was based on research cited in the jury literature reviews (Davis, Bray, & Holt, 1977; Elwork & Sales, 1980; Gerbasi, Zuckerman, & Reis, 1977) combined with more recent works that have appeared subsequently. While our review is not exhaustive, it is substantial enough to be representative of the techniques utilized.

peared since 1970) and classified them along the six dimensions noted in Table 10.1. The first dimension of variation is the subject population. Participants were classified into three populations: (a) college students, usually undergraduates but including some graduates, and in one study, high school students, (b) actual jurors drawn from a jury pool who were serving a term of jury duty, and (c) others, with this category generally representing adults obtained from voter registration lists, jury roll lists, evening school classes, and the like.

The second column in the table identifies the setting or location where the resarch experiment was conducted. There are three settings: the classroom, the experimental laboratory, and the courtroom. The category *classroom* refers to the fact that the data were collected during the regular activity of a course or as a class demonstration. Some studies classified as *laboratory* also made use of classroom facilities, but not during a regularly scheduled class period.

The third dimension of comparison is the stimulus mode of presenting the simulation. Four modes are identified in the third column: (a) a brief, written case summary (called a *fact summary* in the table), (b) an audiotaped presentation in which actors play the role of trial participants, (c) a videotaped reenactment of a trial, generally with actors taking the parts, and (d) a live presentation by a troupe of actors (often including judges, attorneys, and other courtroom figures portraying their official roles). A few studies not included in the table (Diamond & Zeisel, 1974; Dillehay & Nietzel, 1981) have compared responses of mock jurors present in the audience at an actual trial with those of the actual jurors. Dillehay and Nietzel prefer the term *alternative jurors* to distinguish their method from the mock trial approach.

The fourth column in the table lists trial elements included in the simulation. Six usual trial elements are listed: (a) voir dire or pretrial jury selection, (b) opening statements by counsel, (c) witness testimony, (d) closing arguments, (e) judge's charge and instructions to the jury, and (f) deliberation by the jury. We also included another element, fact summary, to indicate that in certain studies information was presented to jurors in summary form without attention to the usual courtroom sequence.

The fifth column identifies dependent (response) variables most commonly used. Studies frequently included additional measures that are not listed to assess effectiveness of manipulations, evaluations of various aspects of the trial, believability of witnesses, and so on. One can also infer from this dimension of comparison whether the trial was criminal or civil.

Finally, Table 10.1 indicates whether the unit of analysis was individual jurors or entire juries. Even though a number of studies included group deliberation as a trial element, they did not always focus on the jury as the unit of analysis.

To assess regularities across the dimensions of Table 10.1, a series of frequency tables were computed, and the results are summarized in Table 10.2. Since a comprehensive categorization of all dimensions resulted in numerous

TABLE 10.1
Mock Trial Studies Classified by Experimental Procedures

Investigator	Juror population	Experimental location	Stimulus mode	Trial elements	Dependent measures	Unit of analysis
Becker et al. (1965)	S	C	A	T, J, D	CG	I
Berg & Vidmar (1975)	S	L	W	FS	CG, S[1]	I
Bevan et al. (1958)	O	CR[a]	L	O, T, C, J, D	DG, A	I, J
Boehm (1968)	S	C	W	FS	DG	I
Bray & Noble (1978)	S	L	A	O, T, C, J, D	DG, S[1]	I, J
Bray & Struckman-Johnson (1977)	S, O	L	A	O, T, C, J, D	DG[b], A	I, J
Bray et al. (1978)	S, O	L	A	O, T, C, J, D	DG, S[1]	I, J
Broeder (1959)	P	CR	A	O, T, C, J, D	DG, A	I, J
Davis et al. (1975)	S	L	A	O, T, C, J, D	DG, CG	I, J
David et al. (1977)	S	L	V	O, T, C, J, D	DG, CG	I, J
Davis et al. (1978)	S	L	V	O, T, C, J, D	DG, CG, S[1]	I, J
Davis et al. (1976)	S	L	V	O, T, C, J, D	DG, CG	I, J
DeJong & Hogue (in press)	O	L	W	FS	S[1]	I
DeJong et al. (1976)	S	L	W	FS	S[1]	I
Doob & Kirshenbaum (1972)	O	L	W	FS	CG	I
Efran (1974)	S	L	W	FS, J	CG, S[1]	I
Erickson et al. (1978)	S	L	W[c], A	O, T, C, J	DG[b], A	I
Foss (1976)	S	L	W	FS, D	CG, S[1]	I, J
Gleason & Harris (1976)	S	L	W[c]	O, T, C, D	CG	I
Gordon & Jacobs (1969)	S	L	W	FS	DG	I
Griffitt & Jackson (1973)	S	L	V[d]	FS	CG, S[1]	I
Hamilton (1978)	O	L	A[e]	NR, D	DG, CG, S[1]	I
Hans & Doob (1976)	S, O	L	W	FS, J, D	DG	I, J
Hawkins (1962)	P	CR	A	O, T, C, J, D	I	I, J
Hoiberg & Stires (1973)	S[f]	L	A	O, T, C	CG	I
Izzett & Leginski (1974)	S	L	W	FS, D	CG, S[1]	I
James (1959)	P	CR	A	O, T, C, J, D	I	I
Jurow (1971)	O	L	A	O, T, C, J	DG	I

Reference						
Kagehiro & Werner (1977)	S	L	W	FS, J	DG, CG	I
Kaplan (1977a)[g]	S	L	W	FS, D[h]	CG, S[i]	I
Kaplan & Kemmerick (1974)	S	L	W	FS	CG, S[i]	I
Kaplan & Miller (1977)	S	L	A	FS, D	DG, CG	I
Kaplan & Miller (1978a)	O	L	W	FS	CG, S[i]	I
Kaplan & Miller (1978b)	S, O	L, CR[a]	W, L	FS, O, T, C, J, D	CG, S[i]	I
Kerr (1978a)	S	C	W	FS, J	DG, CG	I
Kerr (1978b)	S	L	W[c]	O, T, C, J	CG, S[i]	I
Kerr et al. (1976)	S	L	V	O, T, C, J, D	DG, CG, S[i]	I, J
Kerr et al. (1979)	S	L	W[c]	O, T, C, J, D	DG, CG, S[i]	I, J
Kerr et al. (in press)[g]	S	C	W	FS, J	DG, S[i]	I
Kessler (1973)	S	L	V	O, T, C, J, D	DG[b], I	I, J
Kirby & Lamberth (1974)	S, O	CR[a]	L	V, O, T, C, J, D	DG, A	I
Landy & Aronson (1969)	S	L	W	FS	S[i]	I
Lineberry et al. (1977)	S	L	W	FS	DG, S[i]	I
Miller et al. (1975)[g]	S, P, O	CR, L	V, L	O, T, C, J	DG[b], A	I
Mitchell & Byrne (1972)	S	L	W	FS	CG, S[i]	I
Mitchell & Byrne (1973)	S	L	W	FS	CG, S[i]	I
Myers & Kaplan (1976)	S	L	W	FS, D[i]	CG, S[i]	I
Nemeth (1977)[g]	S	L, CR	W, L	FS, V, O, T, C, J, D	DG, I	I, J
Nemeth & Sosis (1973)	S	L	W	FS	S[i]	I
Ostrom et al. (1978)	S	L	W	FS	CG	I
Padawar-Singer & Barton (1975)[g]	P	CR	A	V, O, T, C, J, D	DG	I, J
Rumsey et al. (1978)	S	L	W	FS, D	S[i]	I
Rumsey & Rumsey (1977)	S	L	W	FS, J, D	CG, S[i]	I
Sealy & Cornish (1973)	O	L	A	O, T, C, J, D	DG	I
Shaffer et al. (1976)	S	L	W	FS	CG	I
Sigall & Ostrove (1975)	S	L	W	FS	S[i]	I
Simon (1966)	O	L	A	O, T, C, J	DG	I
Simon (1967)	P	CR	A	O, T, C, J, D	DG, I	I, J
Simon (1970)	S	L	A	O, T, C, J	DG, CG	I
Simon & Mahan (1971)	S, P	L, CR	A	O, T, C, J, D	DG, CG	I, J

Investigator	Juror population	Experimental location	Stimulus mode	Trial elements	Dependent measures	Unit of analysis
Stephan (1974)	S	L	W	FS, D	CG, S^1	I
Strodtbeck et al. (1975)	P	CR	A	O, T, C, J, D	I	I
Strodtbeck & Mann (1956)	P	CR	A	O, T, C, J, D	I	I
Sue et al. (1973)	S	C	W	FS	DG, S^1	I
Thibaut et al. (1972)	S	L	W	FS	CG^j	I
Thomas & Hogue (1976)	S	L	W	FS, D	DG^j	I
Thornton (1977)	S	C	W	FS	DG, S^1	I
Valenti & Downing (1975)	S	L	W, A	FS, D	DG	I, J
Vidmar (1972a)	S	C	W	FS	DG, CG	I
Vidmar (1972b)	O	C	W	FS, D	CG, S^1	I, J
Walker et al. (1972)	S	L	W	FS	CG^j	I
Williams et al. (1975)	O	CR	W^c, A, V, L	V, O, T, J	A	I
Wilson & Donnerstein (1977)[g]	S	L	W	FS	DG, S^1	I

Note: Juror population: S = student; P = jury pool; O = other. Experimental location: C = classroom; L = laboratory; CR = courtroom. Stimulus mode: W = written summary; A = audiotape; V = videotape; L = live. Trial elements: V = voir dire; O = opening arguments; T = testimony; C = closing arguments; J = Judge's charge; D = deliberations; FS = fact summary; NR = not reported. Dependent Measures: DG = dichotomous guilt scale (i.e., guilty or not guilty); CG = continuous guilt scale (e.g., 7-point guilt scale); S^1 = Sentence; A = amount of damage award; I = interaction patterns. Unit of analysis: I = individual jurors; J = juries.

[a] Mock trial room at a law school was used.

[b] A civil case was used; subjects gave verdicts about the defendant's negligence rather than guilt.

[c] Written transcript rather than fact summary was used.

[d] The videotape consisted of a person reading a written summary.

[e] Audiotape was accompanied by slides.

[f] Subjects were high school students.

[g] Reports a series of experiments. Labels represent a composite of procedures used across all studies.

[h] Discussions consisted of sharing information by passing index cards.

[i] Brief 2-1/2-min discussions for each of eight cases.

[j] Subjects gave judgments about lawfulness of defendant's actions.

TABLE 10.2
The Distribution of Mock Trial Studies across Experimental Procedures[a]

| Population | Location | Mode of presentation | | | | Total |
		Written[b]	Audiotape[c]	Videotape[c]	Live[c]	
	Classroom	8.33	1.39	0	0	9.72
Student	Laboratory	37.50[d]	9.72[e]	8.33[f]	0	55.56
	Courtroom	0	0	0	1.39	1.39
	Classroom	0	0	0	0	0
Jury pool	Laboratory	0	0	0	0	0
	Courtroom	0	11.11	0	1.39	12.50
	Classroom	1.39	0	0	0	1.39
Other	Laboratory	6.94	6.94	0	0	13.89
	Courtroom	0	0	0	5.55	5.55
		54.17	29.17	8.33	8.33	

[a]Table entries are percentages; total N = 72. The Hamilton (1978) study did not report sufficient information to be classified. Small differences between the sum of cell entries and their marginal totals are due to rounding error.
[b]All but three studies used an abbreviated fact summary.
[c]All but three studies included several trial elements.
[d]Three studies used trial transcripts rather than the abbreviated fact summary.
[e]Two studies used audiotape to present a summary of the facts.
[f]One study used videotape to present a summary of the facts.

empty cells, Table 10.2 presents the distribution of studies only for the dimensions of population, location, mode, and trial elements.[2]

As shown in Table 10.2, the modal strategy (37.5%) in these studies has been students responding to a written summary of the facts in the experimental laboratory. Table 10.2 also shows that the laboratory has been the setting for approximately 70% of the studies and that the written (54%) and audiotape (29%) modes of presentation have been most widely used. There has been, of course, additional variation within the modes that is not reflected in our tables, in the amount of detail and information presented (e.g., some audiotape trials lasted 30 min whereas others took 90 min).

[2]In constructing Table 10.2, two conventions were adopted. The first was that whenever a dimension contained more than a single entry, we classified the study along the more "realistic" aspect of that dimension (i.e., the one most closely approximating the jury behavior system). For example, an experiment using both students and other participants was tabulated as "other" participants. Similarly, a study using both written and live stimuli was tabulated as live. The second convention was combining trial elements with mode of presentation. As inspection of Table 10.1 shows, in the majority of cases when the fact summary appears, the other trial elements do not (exceptions are a few instances of jury deliberations and/or the judge's charge) and it occurs primarily with the written mode of presentation. Thus in Table 10.2 fact summaries are within the written mode category. The audiotape, videotape, and live modes signify use of "other" trial elements.

Our analysis of the trial elements revealed several other items of interest. First, voir dire was used in only 5.48% of these studies. Second, whenever the mode was not the written summary, most of the trial elements have been included. Third, jury deliberations have often been omitted (48% of the studies) but even when included, researchers frequently have not utilized group data in their analyses. The jury appeared as the unit of analysis (always along with individual jurors) only 28.77% of the time.

Examination of the dependent variables showed that dichotomous guilt scales and continuous guilt scales were each used in 52.06% of the studies sampled (sometimes in separate studies, sometimes in the same study). Sentencing was used 43% of the time while civil suit awards and analysis of interaction patterns each occurred 9.59% of the time. As is clear from Table 10.1, most studies used some combination of these measures.

Considered together, the investigations examined here illustrate a range of procedures in research on juror/jury behavior. A few mock trials have been quite "realistic" (i.e., live presentation in a courtroom with jury pool or other jurors) in their simulation of the jury behavior system. However, nearly one-half of the studies have been highly "unrealistic" (i.e., students responding to a written summary in the classroom or laboratory) and characterize the familiar laboratory experiment. The remaining studies fall between these extremes.

When considering other topics of research in the psychology of the courtroom, this same range of procedures from the highly artificial (i.e., laboratory) to the highly realistic (i.e., field) is also evident. Some topics place even greater reliance on artificial methods (e.g., eyewitness testimony, witness credibility) than observed in the jury literature, whereas other topics place greater emphasis on the field methods (e.g., judges' and attorneys' behavior, courtroom innovation). In general, it seems to be the case that when behavior is largely governed by formal legal rules, procedures, or strong social norms, then research should and does rely less on artificial laboratory or simulation methods and more on field methods. For example, a judge's behavior is probably best studied in the field, since in laboratory or simulated conditions judges may be inclined to give responses in line with legal and social norms about how they are supposed to make judgements. In contrast, when there are few formal rules that specify behavioral expections, then more highly controlled and hence artificial methods may and have been employed. For instance, there seems to be little reason to suspect that drastically different processes will be at work in a study of eyewitness reliability if it is posed as a memory task in the laboratory or classroom rather than as an eyewitness task at a crime.

METHODOLOGICAL COMPARISONS OF SIMULATION, LABORATORY, AND FIELD RESEARCH

As we have already discussed, simulation and laboratory experiments are widely used research strategies in the study of jury behavior as well as in the study of the behavior of other courtroom participants. In addition, although not nearly as prevalent, many field studies and experiments have been conducted. In fact, field research is generally the corrective preferred by critics of simulation and laboratory research. In this section, we first contrast the simulation strategy with its most commonly proposed alternative, the field study. Then we consider the advantages of laboratory research and "unrealistic" simulations to understand better why they have been so widely used. We conclude by addressing the major limitation of nonfield research—the problem of establishing generality.

First, however, it is useful to draw some broad distinctions among the simulation, laboratory, and field methods of research. In an experimental simulation, according to Runkel and McGrath (1972), the researcher seeks to construct a behavior setting that mirrors in certain respects some naturally occurring behavior system (e.g., the jury system). Thus, a simulation has as a focus the imitation of a specific existing behavioral system and in that sense represents a *particular* class of events. This contrasts with the laboratory experiment which is concerned with a generic or *abstract* class of systems that are deliberately isolated from any particular behavioral system. For example, a jury simulation might study the influence of defendant attractiveness of judgments of guilt or innocence. A laboratory experiment, in contrast, would be more concerned with the general processes of making judgments (on any variety of dimensions) about others as a function of their attractiveness (regardless of the particular setting).

The most popular alternative research strategy to the simulation and experiment is the field study, in which the systematic observation of behavior takes place in a naturally occurring behavior system (as opposed to the artificial ones created by the experiment or simulation). In the present discussion we mean by *field studies* any form of systematic observation of the behavior of courtroom participants. Thus, we include direct in-court observations, postdeliberation interviews with jurors, analyses of court records or archives, and so on. By *realistic* experimental simulations we mean those that closely reconstruct the actual behavior setting. For example, a model realistic simulation of the jury task would draw its participants from actual jury rolls and would present an entire actual case using live actors (or actual judges, lawyers, etc.) in a courtroom setting. Further, it would collect group verdicts after a deliberation period unconstrained by time limitations, from a jury that believed its verdict would have real consequences for the defendant. (The studies by Miller *et al.*, 1975, and Williams, Farmer, Lee, Cundick, Howell, and Rooker, 1975, include many aspects of such a realistic simulation.)

As we will show, each of these research strategies has particular strengths and limitations (see Runkel & McGrath, 1972, Chapter 4, for a detailed discussion). Unfortunately, a strength of one strategy is often a limitation of another. Regardless of which method is used, researchers always face dilemmas in that they cannot (in a given study) simultaneously maximize (a) realism (i.e., the concreteness of the behavioral system), (b) precision of control and measurement, and (c) generality over actors, behaviors, and situations. A decision to strengthen one feature, such as precision, by the adoption of a particular strategy, such as the laboratory experiment, automatically weakens one or both of the other features (i.e., generality or realism).

Advantages of Experimental Simulations over Field Studies

The advantages of experimental simulations over field studies are both methodological and practical. Methodological advantages are the familiar ones implied by the term *experimental control*. Foremost among these is the ability to obtain unconfounded replications (cf. Strodtbeck, 1962). Since no two actual trials are exactly alike, each courtroom behavior is a response to a unique and highly complex stimulus. A comparison of the outcomes of pairs (or sets) of trials that are demonstrably different on some variable of interest is constantly plagued by the strong likelihood that they also differ on some other variables as well. For example, one study that compared the sentences received by black and white defendants (Bullock, 1961) seemed to show that blacks received longer sentences than whites for interracial crimes. Another study (Green, 1964), however, suggested that these effects may have been attributable to differences in the prior criminal history of the defendants and the seriousness and repetitiveness of their criminal act, and not to the defendant's race per se. Usually it is possible to guess at the existence of some such confounding variables, but one can rarely anticipate, control, and/or measure all of them. Thus, establishing empirical relationships with a high degree of confidence is difficult to impossible in field studies. In the experimental simulation, however, one can construct trial elements so that they differ only on the variable(s) of interest.

A related methodological advantage is the ability to perform multiple replications. Thus, for example, the same simulated case can be shown to *many* jurors or juries, whereas it is possible to observe the response of only one single jury to any unique actual trial. By performing multiple replications, the effects of extraneous subject characteristic variables can be removed (e.g., juror personality variables) through random assignment and at the same time, the reliability of observed differences can be statistically assessed.

Another familiar advantage of the experimental method is the ability to establish causal relationships. By comparing experimental conditions whose only differences are created by the experimenter prior to the performance of the behavior of interest, one can conclude with some confidence that these created differences caused any obtained behavioral differences.[3] In theory, of course, it is possible to manipulate factors of interest in the courtroom setting (i.e., to do field experiments on courtroom behavior or bring the laboratory into the court-

---

[3]The problem of multiple confounds in field research can often be dealt with, in part, through sophisticated methods of analysis (e.g., multiple partial correlations, log-linear models). Only rarely and indirectly (e.g., by the use of cross-lag panel correlation techniques, path analysis, structural equation models) can field data be analyzed to establish causal relationships firmly.

room). In practice, however, there may be many serious legal, ethical, and practical barriers. For example the constitutional requirement of equal protection under the law requires an equal treatment of defendants that would prohibit experimentation on procedural questions. Furthermore, the courts have their own traditional methods of analysis and evaluation which are not, by and large, experimental in nature. Thus, the decision and policymakers whose cooperation would be essential for field experimentation in the courts (e.g., judges, legislators, lawyers) are often neither familiar with nor reliant upon the experimental method of analysis.

Even when it is possible to win the active cooperation of the court and avoid serious ethical difficulties, a variety of thorny problems still exist. For example, adequate experimental control may be compromised in unpredictable and uncontrollable ways; organizational procedures may come into conflict with experimental requirements; decision makers may exercise discretionary powers in selective or arbitrary ways; or court leadership or cooperativeness may change in the middle of the experiment. (See Ross & Blumenthal, 1975, for a description of an attempted field experiment on sentencing that provides an excellent illustration of the difficulty of field experimentation, even under ideal conditions.)

A final important aspect of the utility of experimental control for the study of several topics in the psychology of the courtroom is the investigator's greater ability to observe in the experimental simulation. For example, many interesting aspects of actual jurors' behavior are inaccessible to observation. Jurors may not discuss their opinions of the case during a trial, and jury deliberations by tradition and by law are also secret. Attempts to question jurors directly during a trial or secretly observe their deliberations are both illegal and unethical. One notorious attempt to tape-record jury deliberations clandestinely (Strodtbeck, 1962) precipitated a storm of protest and the federal law barring such observation. Other topics where simulations afford greater ability to observe than does the actual setting include plea bargaining (e.g., to examine the impact of alternate strategies), fairness of lineups (e.g., to see what variables are related to selection bias), and eyewitness behavior (e.g., to determine the factors that limit accuracy).

Several less direct methods of assessment have been applied with some degree of success. These include posttrial interviews with trial participants (e.g., Broeder, 1959), asking some knowledgeable participants what they think influenced the behavior of other participants (e.g., Kalven & Zeisel, 1966, who surveyed judges' inferences about jury behavior), correlating assessments of in-court behavior (e.g., Kerr, 1981, did a study on the relationships between attorney and judge behaviors and jury verdicts), and archival analyses (e.g., Dillehay & Nietzel, 1981; Kerr, Harmon, & Graves, in press; Konečni & Ebbesen, 1979). However, each of these methods is typically subject to serious difficulties of measurement reliability and validity. For example, posttrial interviews with jurors run the risk of jurors forgetting or distorting their recollection of their predeliberation opinions and jury deliberations; juror's conclusions about other jurors' motives are usually subjective inferences based on fragmentary information; and judges' inferences of the basis for a jury's verdict (e.g., Kalven & Zeisel, 1966) are probably based on even less information.

In contrast to these drawbacks, the experimental simulation permits systematic examination of any private or public behavior of interest. One may observe not only the product of individual and group judgment, but may also examine the processes of individual and group decision making which lead to those judgments. This is particularly crucial when attempting to test competitively theories of individual or group decision making.

Besides the methodological problem we have been considering, there are also serious practical drawbacks to field studies. All of the field study methods mentioned above tend to be very costly. Archives are often inaccessible and are rarely organized in ways that yield the desired data without laborious and expensive distillation; comprehensive in-court observation is difficult and time-consuming; courtroom participants may be hard to contact, set meetings with, and interview; and working with expert observers (e.g., judges or lawyers) can be very expensive in terms of the time and expense of cultivating contacts. Because the complexity of real trials produces so much "noise," field studies require many more observations than experimental simulations to detect the signal of actual relationships. After initial laboratory setup costs, the experimental simulation tends to have far lower cost per replication.

Advantages of "Unrealistic" Simulations/Laboratory Studies over "Realistic" Simulations

The foregoing discussion focused on the advantages of an experimental over a field methodology for the study of the psychology of the courtroom. However, even if persuaded of the merits of an experimental approach, one may still question why an experimental simulation should or should not be "realistic." Whereas the most compelling reasons for choosing an experimental over a field strategy are methodological ones, the popularity of "unrealistic" simulations and laboratory experiments seems to rest more on practical considerations.

The key practical considerations are the cost and ethics of the research. For example, the ready accessibility of a student population to academicians often governs the choice of subjects. The expense of using samples more representative of real courtroom participants is prohibitive for many investigators. Likewise, the widespread use of classrooms or laboratory rooms instead of actual or simulated courtrooms is attributable to their greater accessibility and lower cost. Highly artificial stimuli (e.g., written case summaries, staged crimes for eyewitnesses) are the mode chosen for similar reasons. The equipment, production, and personnel costs of stimulus preparation and presentation usually increase rapidly as one moves from more to less artificial stimuli (e.g., written to audiotaped to videotaped to live trial enactments). The brevity of most simulated case materials may be traced both to the costs of producing lengthy trials and of having subjects sit through them. If groups (e.g., judicial panels, juries rather than individual jurors) are used as experimental replicates, the cost per replicate increases by a factor of n (equal to the group size) at the minimum; this cost is further inflated by the additional expense of scheduling groups and by subject loss (when fewer than n subjects appear at an experimental session). Finally, one can lead subjects to believe that their decisions have real consequences, but the deception required must be very thorough and elaborate, especially for student subjects familiar with experimental deception (Kerr, Nerenz, & Herrick, 1979; Miller et al., 1977). Besides the material costs in doing this, there are several significant ethical questions raised by the use of what is likely to be an elaborate deception about a personally significant behavior for the subject (e.g., see Elwork & Sales, 1980; Kelman, 1967).

Of course, in addition to the practical reasons there are several good methodological reasons for the use of the unrealistic simulation. One reason concerns stimulus mode. The most realistic mode of stimulus presentation, a live trial, can never be replicated exactly. Like a stage play, a live trial simulation can vary from performance to performance, conceivably in ways that may alter the behavior under study. One may have all subjects attend a single live presentation, but this approach still has problems that the use of recorded trials can avoid.[4]

Another methodological reason for using abbreviated transcripts or case summaries is to increase the impact of an experimental manipulation; the less complex and lengthy the case materials are, the more sharply the independent variables will typically stand out.[5] This is particularly desirable when one's primary research objectives are to demonstrate whether some variable can have an effect, or to test a hypothesis of a psychological theory or model.

Judgments other than or in addition to those normally rendered in a trial (e.g., sentence recommendations or probability of guilt judgments from mock jurors rather than verdicts) are commonly collected for several methodological reasons:

1. The statistical analysis of dichotomous dependent variables can present difficulties, especially for multifactored designs although recent statistical advances (e.g., log-linear models) have made this less problematic.
2. Multivalued or continuous response scales should, in general, be more sensitive than simple dichotomous one.
3. Much theory guided research has sought to test hypotheses framed in terms of conceptual variables (e.g., punitiveness), for which several operationalizations are reasonable.

[4]For example, even with this procedure, the live trial can never be reproduced by the same or different experimenters hoping to replicate and extend the original findings. Furthermore, the presence at a trial of large numbers of jurors or juries creates another kind of artificiality with potentially important effects (Kerr et al., 1979).

[5]While we view this as an asset, others count it a liability. We will return to this issue when we discuss reactions to simulation research.

Of course, the unit of analysis should be dictated by the purpose of the research. Naturally, individual mock jurors rather than juries have been studied where theories of individual juror decision making are being tested (e.g., Kaplan & Kemmerick, 1974; Ostrom, Werner, & Saks, 1978; Thomas & Hogue, 1976).

Finally, for some situations the use of an unrepresentative population for subjects may be preferred over the use of a more representative population (e.g., college students rather than actual jury panel members). This may be the case, for example, when some types of materials are used, such as paper and pencil response measures or written case materials, due to one population's greater familiarity and facility with such materials. Students, for example may show greater comprehension and reading speed than actual jurors.

Strengths of Experiments and Simulations: Summary

In summary, there are a number of practical and methodological reasons for the use of simulations instead of field studies and for the greater popularity of laboratory experiments and unrealisitc simulations over realistic simulations. The practical advantages are primarily associated with available resources and research costs in securing subjects, stimulus materials, facilities, and the like. Methodological advantages include the ability to obtain unconfounded and multiple replications, to effect precision and control in establishing causal relationships, to more thoroughly observe all individual and group behavior of interest, to increase the impact of explanatory variables, and to use measures maximally sensitive to statistical methods.

Disadvantages of Experiments and Simulations— Establishing Generality

The main limitation of experiments and simulations concerns the extent to which results obtained from these methods will generalize to actual courtroom behaviors of interest. That is, is the control and affordability of these methods purchased at too high a price? To address this leads us to consider the problem of establishing the generality of research findings.

A widely known distinction proposed by Campbell (1957) is a useful one for the present discussion. He suggests that there are two fundamental problems with drawing inferences from experimental studies. The first problem is establishing with confidence that the effects observed in the experiment can be attributed to the experimental treatment. The more firmly this link is established, the greater the *internal validity* of the study. One can specify many threats to internal validity, such as variables confounded with the experimental treatment, procedural or instructional artifacts, experimental demand characteristics (Orne, 1962), experimenter effects (Rosenthal, 1964), and so on. A quite separate problem is establishing that the effects observed in an experiment will generalize beyond the particular conditions of that experiment. The more broadly the results will generalize, the greater the *external validity* of the study.

Although these two problems are distinct, they are related. An experiment must have high internal validity to have high external validity. As Carlsmith, Ellsworth, and Aronson (1976) put it, "if random or systematic error makes it impossible for the experimenter to draw any conclusions from the experiment, the question of the *generality* of these conclusions never arises [p. 85, italics in original]." On the other hand, high internal validity is never sufficient to establish high external validity; there may be a genuine effect that occurs only under the particular conditions of the experiment. (See Cook & Campbell, 1979, for an expanded discussion of these distinctions.) The issue presently at hand is how to establish the external validity of experimental and simulation research on the psychology of the courtroom. Our discussion draws extensively from that of Runkel and McGrath (1972).

Runkel and McGrath conceptualize the science of behavior as dealing with *actors* engaging in *behavior towards an object* in a *context*. This view suggests that one must be concerned with generality in three forms. The first is the concern with generality over actors, that is, with the range of people over whom results will obtain. For example, we need to be concerned whether the results found with college student mock jurors will also occur in the general population of actual jurors and juries. The second is the concern with the generality over variations in the particulars of experimental treatment and measurement. For example, will the physical attractiveness of a defendant in a live trial have a similar effect to that of a photographed defendant in a written trial summary? We might also include in this category questions concerning variation over the type of response (e.g., dichotomous verdicts versus continuous ratings of guilt versus sentences), and the significance of the response to the subject. Finally, one needs to be concerned with the extent of generality across contexts or settings. For example, will a phenomenon which obtains during a regularly scheduled university class also obtain in a criminal courtroom?

Before specifying ways to establish generality across actors, behaviors, and contexts, two fundamental points should be made. They are obvious, perhaps, but frequently seem to be lost sight of in evaluations of experimental and simulation research. The first point is that one can firmly establish that a result will or will not generalize from one investigated set of conditions (e.g., an experimental jury simulation) to another set of conditions (e.g., an actual trial situation) only by investigating the phenomenon in question under the new conditions. In other words, external validity must ultimately be established empirically. The second point is that high external validity cannot be established within the confines of a single study. Since any study is necessarily carried out under particular conditions (actors, contexts, and behavior toward objects) one can assume with confidence that its results hold only under those particular conditions. Runkel and McGrath (1972) put it in the following way:

> Any single study, even the most grandly planned, can yield only a very limited degree of external validity. If, in an initial study, we obtain a substantial and interesting finding within an internally valid experiment, we can be proud of

having composed a hypothesis that predicted the fall of the data. However, our finding cannot have any practical influence on the wider world until this first study is followed by other studies that explore the range of treatment, . . . measurements, . . . and actors over which the obtained results will hold. . . . Only after we have demonstrated that the effect holds over a range of variations in treatments, observations, and actors can we begin to have confidence that it will hold in other cases under conditions not yet tested. And even then, we cannot know with certainty that it will hold under any given set of not-yet-tested conditions [pp. 46–47].

This second point warrants some discussion. Obviously, it is impractical to test empirically the generality of an effect over all conceivable conditions of interest. Strictly speaking, since no two observations are *exactly* alike, it is impossible to test in principle. Such certainty is precluded by the inductive nature of scientific reasoning. We can never be absolutely certain that a result will generalize to new conditions (or even, for that matter, recur under conditions as unchanging as we can make them), although we can take steps to increase our confidence that it will.

Nonetheless, there are at least two ways to increase our confidence in a result's external validity within the confines of a single study. The first approach is to increase the diversity of the populations of actors, contexts, and behaviors toward objects from which an investigator randomly samples. For example, instead of using a single criminal case, as is the norm in experimental jury simulations, a random sample of such cases could be used. Obtaining comparable results across cases would increase confidence that the results were not case specific.[6] The second approach is to vary the actor, context, or behavior toward objects systematically within the study, rather than permitting them to vary unsystematically. For example, one might include a case factor with several levels (e.g., rape, murder, robbery, and burglary) as a variable in the experimental design. If the same effect obtained with each type of case, the external validity of the result would be increased; if not, then something about the limits of generalization has been learned.

Despite the promise of these methods for increasing a study's external validity, both are costly. Increasing the diversity of actors, contexts, or behaviors toward objects in a study also increases the error variation and hence reduces the power of the study's tests. The power can be restored, but only by increasing the number of observations, and hence, the cost. Likewise, for any particular total sample size, the more design factors included, the lower the number of observations per experimental treatment, and the lower the power of the experiment to detect effects. Thus, increases in external validity of a study are purchased at the cost of the study's power to detect any effects at all.

---

[6]It is not justified to assume that the observed effects will be identical or even similar for all of the cases in the sample or population. By random sampling of cases (or subjects, treatments, etc.) one estimates only the "average" response for the entire population of cases.

Of course, one need not nor rarely does attempt to establish a result's external validity within the confines of a single study. Rather, normally a systematically planned series of studies would be carried out. Consider an example of the relationship between a criminal defendant's physical attractiveness and the punitiveness of jurors established in an experiment or unrealistic simulation (e.g., Efran, 1974; Sigall & Ostrove, 1975). A first step in external validation would be an attempt to replicate with a longer videotaped trial, with mock juries instead of mock jurors, and with subjects solicited from current jury rolls. This might be followed (or preceded) by a field study to test for an association between an actual defendant's attractiveness and jury verdicts. The results of such a series of investigations would provide the data needed to assess the limits of external validity. Unfortunately, the cost considerations that militate against "grandly planned" single studies have also discouraged this kind of systematic work among those interested in jury behavior.[7] Consequently, attempts at external validation have been undertaken only rarely (see Ebbesen & Konečni, 1975, and Kerr *et al.*, in press, for modest exceptions to this rule).

Given that research in this area is very costly (particularly field studies or realistic simulation research), it seems evident that only the most important simulation research findings could be externally validated in anywhere near thorough fashion. What then besides our intuition is to guide us in judging how complete or accurate an understanding of actual courtroom behavior is provided by the experimental and simulation literature? One general principle is that the more similar two situations (i.e., actors behaving toward objects in a context) are, the more likely it is that results obtained in one will also obtain in the other. This principle lies at the heart of the frequently heard exhortations that more realistic simulations be used in jury research. Of course, one must keep in mind that apparent similarity is neither a sufficient nor a necessary condition for the generality of a result.

Another springboard for the inferential leap from examined to unexamined conditions is psychological theory (see Davis, 1980). It is often possible to extend a well-validated theory or model to as yet unstudied or practically unexaminable conditions. Psychological theory can also suggest limitations on the external validity of a result. One concrete illustration is the research on jury size using Davis's (1973) social decision scheme model. Application of this model involves specifying a combinatorial role or *social decision scheme* that summarizes a group's (e.g., a jury's) movement from disagreement to consensus. A number of studies have suggested that some kind of high order majority decision scheme can fairly well account for the distribution of student mock juries' verdicts (Bray, 1974; Davis, 1973; Davis, Kerr, Atkin, Holt, & Meek, 1975; Davis, Kerr, Stasser, Meek, & Holt, 1977; Kerr *et al.*, 1979).[8]

[7]Other important factors are many investigators' basic theoretical (rather than applied) interests and a widespread and unfortunate attitude that because such external validation research lacks originality it also lacks value.

[8]See Chapter 8, this volume, for a brief review of the social decision scheme literature.

This type of decision scheme has direct implications for the effect on verdicts of changing jury size. For example, it has been shown (Davis *et al.*, 1975) that if juries operate under such decision schemes, permissible variation in jury size between 6 and 12 members (Ballew v. Georgia, 1978; Johnson v. Louisiana, 1972) should have only very small effects on jury verdicts. Furthermore, the model predicts that the effect of jury size should depend upon such factors as the strength of the prosecution and defense cases. Of course, theoretical predictions of this sort must make several assumptions, the most central of which is the validity and generality of the theory itself. Before we can confidently pursue the predictions of the theory, its predictive power must be demonstrated. In the case of the social decision scheme model, one is encouraged by the number and consistency of its findings, corroborative results from jury field research (Kalven & Zeisel, 1966, Chapter 38), and the confirmation of some of its predictions (e.g., Myers & Kaplan, 1976, and the polarization prediction that jury verdicts will be more extreme than prediscussion juror sentiment, but in the same direction).

Establishing Generality: Summary

In summarizing the establishing of generality or external validity, it must first be recognized that such discussions presume that the research of interest is internally sound or valid (i.e., results are attributable to experimental treatments rather than to uncontrolled or confounding factors). External validity must be demonstrated empirically in the final analysis, but it cannot be established by any single study employing particular actors, contexts and behaviors. Nonetheless, we can increase our confidence in the generality of any single study's findings by (a) sampling a diverse set of actors, contexts, and behaviors toward objects and/or (b) systematically incorporating the variation of actors, contexts, and behaviors into the experimental design rather than letting them vary randomly. Such elaborations of a study, however, are often constrained by cost considerations. An alternate and more favored approach to establishing generality is to conduct a series of carefully planned studies that collectively provide data that determine the limits of generalizability. Regrettably, the high costs of such a research program often limit the number of issues that will be thoroughly assessed. When systematic data are unavailable, a well-validated psychological theory may provide useful information about the likelihood and limits of the external validity of research findings.

BASIC THEMES IN CRITICISMS OF SIMULATION RESEARCH

With few exceptions (e.g., Kaplan, 1977b; Sigall & Ostrove, 1975), most of those who have evaluated the experimental simulation methodology for the study of the psychology of the courtroom have been highly critical of it. In this section we outline the most common themes running through this criticism; in the next section we discuss some of the key assumptions and implications of these themes.

Experiments and Simulations Tell Us Little about Actual Courtroom Behavior

The artificiality of most laboratory experiments and experimental simulations has led many observers to argue that the findings of this literature are of limited or no value in describing or understanding actual behavior in the courtroom. For example, Miller *et al.* (1977), in discussing the common use of student mock jurors, state that "researchers should stop deluding themselves with the wishful thought that the exclusive reliance on the species akademia moros will yield empirical generalizations which will meet the predictive tests of the judicial marketplace [p. 8]." Likewise, in their discussion on the common use of brief, nondetailed case materials, Miller *et al.* (1977) conclude that "it strikes us as an act of scientific and social folly to read much practical import into the findings of such truncated simplified studies [p. 17]."

Some writers question the utility of simulation research because subjects are often asked to play the role of trial participants. Dillehay and Nietzel (1980), for example, note that

> In the experimental research on jurors/juries, subjects are sometimes asked to behave "as if" they were real jurors. This is role playing research. As a method it has generated a share of debate (e.g., Freedman, 1969; Greenberg, 1967) and generally appears to be inadequate to the task of understanding real juries [p. 250].

Similarly, Weiten, and Diamond (1979), in critiquing the jury simulation paradigm, say:

> In jury simulations, subjects are asked to speculate about how they would behave *if they were real jurors.* Thus role-playing represents the very essence of the jury simulation paradigm. Yet, role-playing has been the target of much criticism (Aronson & Carlsmith, 1968; Freedman, 1969), which has questioned the premise that subjects can predict with substantial accuracy how they would behave in various situations [p. 81, italics in original].

Such reservations about typical simulation research are fairly representative of social scientists who have criticized such simulations. The skepticism that characterizes such critics, who are well versed in research methodology, often becomes outright dismissal among those less grounded in the social sciences. For example, Justice Powell of the Supreme Court asserted in *Ballew* v. *Georgia* (1978) that the many studies of jury size (see Lempert, 1975, for a review) "merely represent the unexamined findings of persons interested in the jury system [p. 246]."

Typical Simulation Treatments are Worthless or Misleading

Several observers (e.g., Colasanto & Sanders, 1976; Dillehay & Nietzel, 1981; Elwork & Sales, 1980) have pointed out that experimental treatments sometimes fail to recognize legal realities. For example, some researchers have examined the effects of types of evidence that are excluded from actual trials by the rules of evidence (e.g., see critiques of the Landy & Aronson, 1969 study, by Colasanto & Sanders, 1976; and by Dillehay & Nietzel, 1981), and many researchers have collected sentences from mock jurors, a judgment that few actual juries make.

A second complaint is that the experiment's independent variable is often more prominent in the simulation than in actual trials, either because the accompanying trial materials are very abbreviated or because the variable is accentuated in an unrepresentative fashion. This causes concern for several reasons. It has been asserted that studies with unduly prominent treatments may well arouse strong demand characteristics (i.e., provide clues that allow subjects to figure out the hypothesis or purpose of the study), especially if their subjects are experimentally sophisticated (Miller et al., 1977). Jurors' evaluation of the independent variable might also be altered, qualitatively or quantitatively, by the complexity and content of the context within which it is presented (Miller et al., 1977). Therefore, an effect obtained within one bare bones context might not obtain or might be altered in a more complicated context.

Finally, when the experimental treatment is highly prominent, the effect it produces on behavior may be much stronger than the effect it would have in actual trials. This may occur either because the variable does not show as much variation in actual trials or because the manipulation constitutes a disproportionate share of the total stimulus in the simulation (see Colasanto & Sanders, 1976; Konečni et al., 1980; Miller et al., 1977). The basic thrust of this argument is that the proportion of behavioral variance accounted for by the experimental treatment may not accurately estimate the proportion of variance this variable accounts for in actual behavior.

"Unrealistic" Simulations or Laboratory Experiments Are Inappropriate to Study Applied Questions

Several observers suggest that because psycho-legal research has an obvious potential for application, simulations or experiments that contain artificial elements are not appropriate research methods. At the heart of this argument is the premise that applied issues require different ways of choosing a problem and conducting research than are appropriate for basic research. For example,

Miller *et al.* (1977) argue that "in an applied area such as juror behavior, research should aim for results which shed light on the consequences of various policy alternatives [p. 2]."

Or, as an anonymous reviewer of one of our jury simulation studies says,

> [my] objection is the implicit assumption that one can understand complex, real-life events by doing laboratory research using "rigorous experimental control" and then "adding up" the results. This assumption is widely made among experimental social psychologists, and it may be appropriate for study of certain psychological "processes." But the raison d'etre of research on jury decision making is to understand better the behavior of actual jurors making decisions which will affect participants in court cases.

Interestingly, such critics of the typical simulation differ on the "correct" method for doing "applied," "real-life" research. Some seem to favor field studies. As Konečni *et al.* (1980) said:

> to the extent that one's goals are to understand the actual [legal] system and possibly feed information back to the participants, it would seem more reasonable to *begin* by studying the real-world stysem and then go back to the laboratory to study the specifics (given ample time, funds, and human resources), rather than *vice versa* [p. 91, Italics in original].

Others, like Colasanto and Sanders (1976), seem to favor realistic simulations: "We hope to show that typical simulation methods do indeed greatly distort the laboratory findings, and that a clearer conception of how real juries decide may *only* be obtained through more realistic simulation and refined conceptualization [p. 2, italics added].

But all would probably agree with the reviewer who stated "I think that the *minimum* starting point for research intended to be directly generalized to the real world is an experiment modeled after the "actual" conditions [italics added]."

Some critics suggest that the method and the type of research being conducted require certain matches. Dillehay and Nietzel (1981), for example, argue that experiments and simulations are acceptable methods for research aimed at testing basic psychological theory (in which all reference to legal terms should be avoided) or theory specific to the psychological and social processes of the courtroom (the bases of which are derived from astute observation in actual courtrooms), but see little value in most mock trial research because it may not do either of these. Further, they find these same methods unacceptable for applied research with policy implications.

Similarly, Lind and Walker (1979) say that if a (presumably) general theory guides one's research, then the closely controlled laboratory method is an acceptable and even necessary research strategy. Without such theory, however, realism is needed.

"Unrealistic" Simulations or Laboratory Studies Should Not Be Done

A number of critics have prescribed the specific conditions under which experiments or simulation methods can provide useful information. For example, Miller *et al.* (1977) advance the following methodological caveat: "If simulations are to provide much practical guidance concerning juror behavior, they should use persons whose demographic characteristics and perceptual and attitudinal sets approximate those of actual venire persons [p. 8]." Miller *et al.* also advised that simulations should be "conducted under informational and presentational conditions approximating the actual courtroom trial [p. 17]."

Different critics identify different features as essential to a truly realistic or satisfactory simulation. For example, Colasanto and Sanders (1976) emphasize the importance of deliberations in studying juries: "our feeling is that having a deliberation is by far the most crucial consideration in the design of a jury simulation (beyond the obvious necessity of a proper simulation) [p. 31]." Weiten and Diamond (1979) indicate that "insofar as future researchers are interested in the generalizability of their findings, they should procure more representative samples, employ more realistic trial simulations such as lengthy and complex audio and videotaped trials, and focus more on collective verdicts arrived at by deliberating juries [p. 83]." Most critics would probably agree with Colasanto and Sanders (1976) that unrealistic simulations are proscribed:

> If researchers are going to try to exert influence in areas outside of social psychological theory, they must begin to conduct their research more responsibly and be aware of the requirements of external validity before making broad generalizations from their results. If this research is to be done, it must be done *correctly* [p. 32, italics added].

ASSUMPTIONS AND IMPLICATIONS OF CRITICISMS

The themes we have outlined above run through most of the critical discussions of simulation methods. They all share a single implication of discouraging the continued use of laboratory research or nonrealistic simulations, at least as they are currently conducted (see Table 10.1). From personal experience, we also know that these themes are often overriding concerns of journal editors, journal reviewers, and the members of advisory panels to funding agencies. Thus, they represent more than considerations in individual investigators' choice of research method; they may fundamentally affect the funding and dissemination of research in this area. Hence, these themes deserve careful scrutiny and evaluation. We will now examine what we perceive as the key questions arising from these themes.

When Is a Difference Important?

As our overview of the existing literature has documented, the usual jury simulation study is different from an actual courtroom trial in many ways. Many critics of the simulation method conclude that this makes generalization impossible. Some are bothered by the large *number* of differences, while others argue that *any* differences make generalization impermissible. In a strict sense they are correct, since, as noted previously, a study's results are always conditional on the particular choice of actors, contexts, and behaviors towards objects.

But some of these critics go one step further. They imply that the very existence of such differences makes it implausible or impossible that results *will* generalize. They fail to recognize that identifying such differences only raises the question of generalizability but does not settle it. In fact, in some instances the arguments raised against use of the controlled simulations turn out on closer inspection to be less serious than portrayed. A case in point is the criticism that jury simulations are not useful because subjects are merely roleplaying or anticipating how they might behave as jurors in a real trial (Dillehay & Nietzel, 1980; Weiten & Diamond, 1979). Since such estimations often turn out to be considerably different from actual behavior, the roleplaying results are deemed questionable. (For example, Milgram, 1965, found large discrepancies between subjects' estimates of how many individuals would administer 450 volts of shock to a learner and the number that did.)

One should, however, keep in mind the important distinction between active roleplaying and passive roleplaying (Mixon, 1977). In active roleplaying, the participants do more than passively speculate about how they might behave— they actively engage in the behavior. As Krupat (1977) has noted:

> By having subjects actively participate in a situation, active role playing envelopes [sic] them in a set of circumstances which elicits the high degree of realism and spontaneity which critics have found missing in other role playing models. In active role playing subjects do not sit passively and predict what they might do in a situation that is selectively summarized and interpreted for them as in what Mixon calls role taking or non-active role playing. Rather, they actively participate, they "go to the moon" [p. 501].

Our own experience with mock jury research strongly suggests that simulated jurors typically engage in active, rather than passive role playing; they become highly involved and take very seriously their role as jurors. Simon (1967) has offered a similar observation. "The mock jurors became so involved in defending their own interpretation of the case and in convincing others of the correctness of their views that they forgot that their verdicts would have no practical significance [p. 38]." Even though our experience with role playing jurors results in more optimism than expressed by critics (and one may imagine that subjects who simulate other courtroom participants such as witnesses or attorneys may similarly engage in active role playing), the question of external validity cannot and should not be settled by intuition; it must be demonstrated empirically. In this regard, recent data by Kerr *et al.* (1979) offer encouragement that active role playing may not be a serious threat to external validity, at least for mock jurors (see Bray & Kerr, 1979).

The question of external validity is not dissimilar to the problem of ruling out alternative explanations for an experimental result. One can, with a little thought, come up with alternatives to almost any explanation for a result. But an experimenter with foresight and a carefully planned study will gather the necessary data or obtain it in subsequent research to rule out the really plausible alternatives to the proposed explanation. The point is that our confidence in the validity of alternative explanations rests on their *plausibility* and not their mere existence. In the same way, one can always identify differences (if only temporal) between any study and the settings to which it is intended to generalize. But in the absence of direct empirical comparison, our confidence in a result's external validity largely depends upon whether it is plausible that such differences limit its generality, in the light of what else we know. When there are many differences, our confidence is lowered, just as our confidence in an explanation is lowered when there are many, instead of a few, alternative explanations. But even when there are many differences, we can still have some confidence that the result may generalize if existing theory and data erect few plausible obstructions.

Do existing theory and research plausibly suggest that any or all of the artificialities of the standard courtroom simulation limit its value for describing actual courtroom behavior? There is little doubt that college students often behave differently from the general adult population, that individual behavior often differs from group behavior, and so on. The null hypothesis is rarely if ever valid. But which of these differences represent plausible reasons to question the informativeness of the simulation's results? Or, as the title of this section asks, when is a difference important?

Some differences are much more important than others, in our judgment. To illustrate, let us imagine a simulation study that examines the effect of the defendant's physical attractiveness on mock jurors' verdicts. Furthermore, let us suppose we have here our generic "unrealistic" simulation: college students reading brief, written trial summaries with photos of the defendant and making individual judgements. Finally, let us assume, for the sake of argument, that there are no internal validity problems with the study. Suppose we find that the mock jurors are more likely to convict the unattractive than the attractive defendant. Now, the question is, what kind of difference between our unrealistic juror's behavior and realistic mock or actual juror's behavior would be important? The first, and least important kind of difference would be if the latter were more (or less) likely to convict; that is, there could be a main effect on a "realness" factor. This would be least important because it would suggest that the jurors in both settings are reacting to attractiveness similarly, both qualititatively and quantitatively, although they do differ in their general evaluation of the case or perhaps in their criteria for reasonable doubt (Simon & Mahan, 1971).

The second and next most important difference might be a "realness by attractiveness" interaction indicating that attractiveness and acquittals were positively related in both settings, but that the relationship was stronger in one of the two settings. Here the relationship differs in degree but not in kind. It may suggest that attractiveness was manipulated more powerfully, that it was noticed more, or that there were other more powerful factors operating in one of the settings. But the *way* the attractiveness information is utilized is apparently the same. Much of the research on the differences between individual and group decisions seems to follow this pattern (e.g., Bray & Kerr, 1979; Kerr *et al.*, 1976).

A third kind of difference could be an interaction which shows an attractiveness effect for the unrealistic conditions but no effect for the more realistic ones.[9] This might indicate that the attractiveness factor is salient in the one condition but not in the other.[10] This type of outcome is illustrated by Kerr's (1978b) finding that the severity of the prescribed penalty affected verdicts but not judgments of the probability of guilt.

The fourth and most serious difference we might find is an interaction indicating that the jurors in the two settings both react to attractiveness, but in opposite ways. This difference is the most serious because it suggests that the attractiveness information may be evaluated and/or processed differently in the two settings. For example, Konečni and Ebbesen (1979) observed a number of such crossover effects in their study of judges' sentencing decisions that compared several different research methods. Results based on interviews, questionnaires, experimental simulations, and archival records each suggested that a different overall pattern of factors influenced judges' sentencing decisions (although some of the same factors emerged from several methods).

Given the pattern of results obtained by Konečni and Ebbesen (1979), the interesting methodological issue is to consider the conditions under which these serious types of reversals are likely to be a problem in the study of the psychology of the courtroom. Although it is difficult to provide an exhaustive catalog of conditions, we believe that the most serious type of problems will occur when the data-gathering process includes reactive measurement effects (Webb, Campbell, Schwartz, & Sechrest, 1966). In reactive situations, subjects' awareness or sensitivity to their participation in a research project often systematically influences or affects their responses.

In the psychology of the courtroom, reactive situations appear most prob-

---

[9]Or, as occurred in the Scroggs study (1976), we may find the reverse to be true.

[10]Of course, it may also just mean that there are many other powerful factors at work in the actual trial.

lematic for behaviors such as those of judges or lawyers that are governed by rules or norms and for which there are a clear set of socially desirable responses. For example Konečni and Ebbesen's (1979) questionnaire and interview methods that ask judges to identify the factors that influenced their sentencing decisions may have elicited responses about the factors judges thought they were *expected* to employ (such as severity of the crime, prior record, family background, etc.). In contrast, Konečni and Ebbesen's finding from the archival analysis, that judges relied primarily on the recommendation of the probation officer (who relied on the factors of prior record, severity of the crime, and status), may reflect a strategy judges use to deal with the pressures of heavy case loads in the courtroom. Of course, as Saks (see Chapter 11, this volume) points out, models of judicial behavior may fail to incorporate certain factors that occur infrequently (e.g., resisting arrest, defendant injuring a child) due to their extreme skewness. Nonetheless, the very rarity with which these factors occur may cause them to become salient to a judge in those particular cases.

The research methods compared by Konečni and Ebbesen (1979) basically distinguish self-report (e.g., interview, questionnaire, simulation) and behavioral measures (or some trace evident in archival records). These researchers favor the latter as reliable but decry the former as questionable. We agree that when strong norms exist that are likely to result in reactive situations (e.g., in the study of judges' decisions), then behavioral or unobtrusive measurement, such as archival analyses, are generally to be favored over self-report or laboratory methods (see Webb *et al.*, 1966). But we disagree with the implication that because different methods produced different results in the study of a given behavior (e.g., judge's sentencing decisions) that different methods will necessarily produce different results for all behaviors in the courtroom. In particular, the behavior of jurors, juries, and eyewitnesses do not seem to engage the strong social desirability norms apparent for judges' behavior. There are few rules, for example, that dictate how jurors are to behave. Prior to deliberations, jurors are prohibited from discussing the case; during deliberations they are sheltered from any intrusions; after deliberations they are protected from any sanctions relative to their verdicts. Thus we find a greater range of methods permissible for the study of such behaviors, including laboratory and simulation methods.

To date, reviews assessing the external validity of portions of the mock jury literature (Bray & Kerr, 1979; Weiten & Diamond, 1979) have indicated very few factors that consistently produce either the less serious or the more serious kinds of differences previously noted (use of sentences rather than verdicts is one, possibly; see Bray & Kerr, 1979). Given the current state of research, it clearly seems premature to dismiss entirely the utility of standard simulations (i.e., to assume that serious differences are the rule). In this same regard, it is important to note that it is no more reasonable to conclude that simulation studies of legal systems are often misleading, based on a single study that does find a serious difference (cf. Colasanto & Sanders, 1976, p. 14; Konečni *et al.*,

1980, p. 89), than it is to conclude that simulation studies are usually not misleading, based on a single study that fails to find a serious difference.

Is There a Right Way and Wrong Way to Study Juries?

Runkel and McGrath (1972) have suggested that

> the choice among the [research] strategies should be made with an eye to their respective advantages and weaknesses and on the basis of (1) the nature of the problem the investigator wants to study, (2) the state of prior knowledge about this problem, and (3) the amount and kind of resources available to the investigator [p. 89].

Much of the criticism of the standard jury simulation is implicitly founded on the assumption that all those who use it are or should be concerned with the same problem, that is, how juries behave *in situ*. If this is indeed one's sole or overriding objective, the importance placed upon simulation realism is well founded. However, there are many other legitimate objectives being pursued in such research. Some investigators are testing a psychological theory or model for which juries are but one interesting application. Others hope to test the validity of some of the psychological assumptions of the law or court procedure, and may or may not have wanted also to determine the probable extent or impact of the violation of that assumption on the operation of the real system. Still others have been doing basic research on more general psychological processes that are also manifest in juries. Many, including ourselves, have pursued *both* theoretical and applied interests and (if not able to kill) have tried to wound two birds with one stone. We disagree with those who feel that experimenters must always choose either one objective or another in their research (e.g., Dillehay & Nietzel, 1980) and suggest that useful knowledge about courtroom behavior as well as general psychological knowledge can often be gained from several objectives simultaneously.

But even if objectives are to be purely applied, we disagree with the notion that there exists an optimal research method. To borrow a metaphor from Runkel and McGrath (1972), researchers are continually faced with a multihorned dilemma. In choosing to avoid one horn, they invariable are gored by another. The investigator who chooses the field setting to maximize realism must sacrifice experimental control and opportunity for observation. The investigator who chooses the standard simulation buys control, opportunity to observe, and affordability, but at a cost of realism. No choice of method is free from such compromises, including the realisitic simulation. Making a jury simulation more realistic by removing such artificialities as predeliberation polling of jurors, experimenter observation of deliberation, nonspontaneous testimony, and knowledge that verdicts have no real consequences, requires sacrifices of control, opportunity to observe, or ethical principles. Runkel and McGrath (1972) make our key point well: "The trick is not to search for the 'right' strategy but to pick the strategy that is best *for your purposes and circumstances* and then use all the strengths of that strategy and do whatever can be done to limit or offset its inherent weaknesses [p. 117, italics in original]." Given the range of objectives and resources of those interested in the study of the courtroom, many strategies, including the standard simulation, can be "optimal."

Triandis (1978) suggests a similar view in arguing the need for basic research when studying applied problems. "As soon as you break a practical problem into its more basic elements you are faced with numerous fundamental question, requiring basic research. You cannot make progress in the situation of the practical problem unless you solve the basic problems [p. 385]." In proposing a general paradigm for conducting research in applied areas, Triandis advocates both basic laboratory research which is usually emphasized more during the study of the initial phases of a problem, and field research which is usually more prevalent later in the study of the problem.[11]

Finally, there is the implicit (sometimes explicit, e.g., Konečni *et al.*, 1980) assumption that the relevance of basic laboratory research for relatively concrete and well-defined "real world" systems (like the jury) is not as great as it is for more general and diffuse topics (e.g., aggression). There are differences between the two, to be sure. One difference is that the jury is certainly a much more specific, delimited system. Another difference may be a greater temptation to apply laboratory results prematurely since the potential for application is so tangibly manifest. Clearly there is a need for greater caution in discussing findings for an area like jury research.[12] However, we are not persuaded that there are basic differences in the suitability or utility of the various research methodologies for delimited, applied topics and for more abstract topics. The relative concreteness of courtroom behavior only makes external validation of laboratory research more tractable. Rather than presenting an impediment to laboratory research, this concreteness presents, in our opinion, an opportunity for checking the generality of such research to the real world settings of interest.

Must a Useful Simulation Be "Realistic"?

We have already touched upon some aspects of the question of whether the usefulness of a simulation depends on its realism. While the usefulness relates

[11]Saks (1978) has also recently lauded the contributions of basic research in applied settings drawn from his experience serving on a Senate subcommittee.
[12]Such caution, of course, is manifested differently depending on the audience. Research published in scientific journals for an audience trained in research methodology should not require constant reminders of the limits of generalization. Research described in law journals or the

largely to the use to which the simulation is to be put, the question of external validity is unanswered as yet empirically. We would like to make just one additional point. There is no single standard against which to judge the realism of a simulation (cf. Davis, 1980). There are features that all or most trials have in common, but within these broad limits there is enormous variety, and any simulation, even the most realistic, is directly comparable only to a subset. (For that matter, most field studies examine only one court, type of trial, juror population, and the like.) To be sure, matching the simulation with the common features of most jury trials increases our confidence that the results will generalize to most trials, but again one can directly generalize with high confidence only to that identical and perhaps quite small subset.

Is Half a Loaf Better than None?

Several critics have argued that if psycho-legal research cannot be done "correctly" (i.e., with realistic simulations or in the field) it should not be done at all. This is a philosophy of "no loaf is better than half a loaf." But, as we have noted previously, different researchers may (straining our metaphor) have very different tastes or nutritional needs, and in any case, one can never buy the whole loaf in a single purchase. Some (e.g., Konečni *et al.*, 1980) argue that the simulation's power to test and develop psychological theory is of little use in describing legal decision makers. In effect, they argue that this part of the loaf has no nutritional value: "We do not question the *possibility* of generating 'mediational' explanations for the decisions under study but merely doubt that they *add* anything to the ability to predict and understand the future behavior of the participants in the real legal system [p. 90, italics in original]." In an even stronger statement, Konečni and Ebbesen (1979) seem to reject all but field research as acceptable.

> It is impossible for researchers to be present during jury deliberations and it is extremely difficult to obtain access to files containing information that leads to certain decisions (e.g., prosecutor's files). Many would probably think that simulation research in these cases is fully justified even if all of our criticisms are correct. A more cautious point of view, and one that we favor, is that erroneous information obtained by scientific methods (and therefore having an aura of truth) *is more harmful than no information at all* . . . especially when

---

popular press should probably draw conclusions much more carefully. Caution in describing findings, however, should not preclude discussion of potential implications for actual jury behavior suggested by those findings. Some (e.g., Ellsworth & Ross, 1976) have counseled social scientists to preempt misinterpretation and misapplication of their findings by actively disseminating their research findings among the appropriate policymakers. This suggestion has much to recommend it when the strength of the data justifies such an advocacy role.

issues as sensitive as legal ones are being dealt with, and people's futures are quite literally at stake [p. 68, italics added].

Others argue that increased quality of the purchase justifies a drop in quantity. For example, Miller *et al.* (1977) noted that the production of more realistic simulations

> is sure to increase the economic and energy costs of conducting research; the sheer volume of research conducted is likely to shrink dramatically. This reduction in quantitative output can be justified by the added potential for ecological validity. Although researchers may not know as much, they should be able to place more confidence in the social applicability of what they do know. In an applied area such as juror behavior, we view this change in priorities as a step in the right direction [p. 17].

These viewpoints suggest that the body of knowledge of courtroom behavior can best grow on a steady diet of realistic research. We feel, on the other hand, that theory development is essential for moving beyond description to an explanation of behavior, and that abandonment of the controlled research methods upon which such theory development relies is no wiser than complete reliance on highly controlled and thus unrealistic methods.

Also, as Runkel and McGrath (1972) noted, one's choice of research strategy must inevitably take into account "the amount and kind of resources available to the investigator [p. 89]." We do not stand to gain much knowledge by prohibiting all research except that which is restrictingly expensive for most investigators. We concur with Kalven and Zeisel's (1966) view that "in new efforts it must be better to learn something, however imperfectly, than to withdraw from inquiry altogether when preferred methods are as a practical matter not available [p. 39]." In other words, a good half loaf is better than none. We are not applying the drunkard's logic of looking for his key under a distant streetlamp because the light is better there when he knows he lost it by his darkened doorway. That is, we are not advocating employing a method with no value just because it is all we can afford. Rather, we are suggesting that beginning one's inquiry where the light is good (i.e., where research is practical and powerful) is a reasonable strategy when it can provide useful clues to the key's location.

Can "Unrealistic" Simulations Be Informative?

Naturally, this issue will be fully resolved only through a great deal more research, but we think that the results of experimental simulations can make several valuable contributions to our understanding of courtroom behavior. As we have noted previously, much of this research has added to our general body of knowledge and to theory development on the processes of interpersonal perception, attribution, group decision processes, and so on, which are part and parcel of jurors', judges', witnesses', and lawyers' tasks. The small scale and quickly conducted simulation study can also be an efficient way of developing and checking tentative, working hypotheses about actual behavior; in essence, they can serve as pilot studies for more amibitious simulations or field studies. Davis, Bray, and Holt (1977) have also suggested that such studies can be viewed "as 'demonstrations' that may reveal that assumptions inherent in the law do not always hold or that the legal system works in a way other than that officially prescribed [p. 327]." Finally, we are not persuaded that simulation studies must accurately estimate the strength of an effect or that the effects must account for large amounts of variability in the behavior of actual courtroom actors in order to be interesting or useful. If our interest is exclusively predictive, weak effects may not be terribly useful. But if our interest extends to the ability of courtroom participants to carry out their responsibilities, even small or infrequently applied biases may be important, particularly when they are based on extralegal factors or might be remedied through minor procedural safeguards. Nor is it essential that an experimental treatment in a simulation study accurately mirror the range in variation or prominence of the independent variable in "typical" trials. In this regard, one might draw an analogy between strong manipulations in simulations and feeding massive doses of a substance to laboratory rats to determine possible carcinogenic effects of that substance. Even if saccharine is not a major cause of human bladder cancer, demonstrating that massive saccharine doses reliably lead to bladder cancers in rats can alert us to possible risks and can guide future research. Demonstrations that artificially powerful treatments reliably affect courtroom behavior can serve similarly valuable functions.[13]

---

[13]Dillehay and Nietzel (1980) have objected to our use of this analogy as applied to mock jury research (see Bray & Kerr, 1979). "A close examination of this analogue reveals significant differences from the experimental juror/jury research. A main difference concerns the inducing agent or treatment variable. In drug research using animal models the drug of interest, not a substitute or facsimile, is used as the inducing agent. In experimental juror/jury research typically there is low fidelity to the events of the trial that are targeted for research [p. 252]."

Their criticism seems based on their failure to distinguish between passive and active roleplaying (discussed earlier). In jury simulations we maintain that the stimuli that subjects are exposed to are in fact real and not a substitute or facsimile. For example, if defendant attractiveness is manipulated, it is accomplished by actually exposing subjects to defendants of varying attractiveness, not by asking them to *imagine* a defendant who is attractive or unattractive, as would be the case in passive roleplaying. It is true that the laboratory presentation does not always mirror what occurs in the courtroom (e.g., pictures of defendants may be used instead of live defendants), but the extent to which that difference is a serious problem is the issue of external validity. In defense of our analogy, we would also point out that there are a number of differences between the way a drug is administered in research settings and how it is handled in real settings (e.g., the size and frequency of dosage, the method of ingestion). Despite these differences, which primarily exploit the advantages of control offered by the laboratory, such research is still considered useful.

CONCLUSIONS AND RECOMMENDATIONS

The fundamental conclusion of the present chapter is that the mock trial simulation (both the unrealistic or laboratory experiment and the realistic) is one of several viable methods for the study of courtroom behavior. Although it clearly would not be the preferred method in all or many situations, we maintain that social scientists should not, in their zeal for realism, dismiss the utility of closely controlled experimental simulations, nor be unmindful of the practical and methodological drawbacks of more realistic methods. Realizing that our research methods are imperfect tools for answering empirical questions, we recommend methodological diversity in the study of the psychology of the courtroom. This point of view also leads us to urge rejection of the increasing counsel to limit the range of "acceptable" methods. Unless the need for such closure can be established empirically, we urge mutual tolerance of differences in research methodologies since these reflect honest differences in research objectives, resources, and style.

A second conclusion, related to the first, is that the study of the psychology of the courtroom is not qualitatively different from the study of other social phenomena, although the potential for application of the findings may be considerably greater. To prevent misapplication or misinterpretation of findings, we recommend that investigators be as explicit as possible about the objectives of their research and use great care in noting the limits on generalization of their results. Findings derived from unrealistic simulations should be appropriately qualified (depending on the audience and outlet for the material) and should not be forwarded as the primary basis for policy changes. This does not mean, however, as some have suggested (Dillehay & Nietzel, 1980) that investigators must be so cautious that they fail to explore *potential* implications of the data.

The need for explicitness of purpose and qualification of findings seems particularly important given that the potential consumers of such research crosscut the disciplines of social science and law. That members of both disciplines share a joint interest in the courtroom setting leads to our recommendation for greater education of and cooperation between participants in both camps. Social scientists with clear applied interests need training in the law and legal realities while legal professionals need greater sophistication in the methods and theories of social scientists. It is our hope that such training may help us view, in proper perspective, the value of data obtained through all methods.

REFERENCES

Ballew v. Georgia. *United States Reports*, 1978, *435*, 223–246.

Becker, T. L., Hildum, D. C., & Bateman, K. The influence of jurors' values on their verdicts: A courts and politics experiment. *Southwestern Social Science Quarterly*, 1965, *45*, 130–140.

Berg, K. S., & Vidmar, N. Authoritarianism and recall of evidence about criminal behavior. *Journal of Research in Personality*, 1975, *9*, 147–157.

Bermant, G., McGuire, M., McKinley, W., & Salo, C. The logic of simulation in jury research. *Criminal Justice and Behavior*, 1974, *1*, 224–233.

Bevan, W., Albert, R. S., Loiseaux, P. R., Mayfield, P. N., & Wright, G. Jury behavior as a function of the prestige of the foreman and the nature of his leadership. *Journal of Public Law*, 1958, *7*, 419–449.

Boehm, V. Mr. Prejudice, Miss Sympathy and the authoritarian personality: An application of psychological measuring techniques to the problem of jury bias. *Wisconsin Law Review*, 1968, 734–750.

Bray, R. M. *Decision rules, attitude similarity, and jury decision making.* Unpublished doctoral dissertation, University of Illinois, Urbana, 1974.

Bray, R. M., & Kerr, N. L. Use of the simulation method in the study of jury behavior: Some methodological considerations. *Law and Human Behavior*, 1979, *3*, 107–119.

Bray, R. M., & Noble, A. M. Authoritarianism and decisions of mock juries: Evidence of jury bias and group polarization. *Journal of Personality and Social Psychology*, 1978, *36*, 1424–1430.

Bray, R. M., & Struckman-Johnson, C. *Effects of juror population, assigned decision rule and insurance option on the decisions of simulated juries.* Paper presented at the meeting of the American Psychological Association, San Francisco, August 1977.

Bray, R. M., Struckman-Johnson, C., Osborne, M. D., McFarlane, J. B., & Scott, J. The effects of defendant status on decisions of student and community juries. *Social Psychology*, 1978, *41*, 256–260.

Broeder, D. W. The Univesity of Chicago jury project. *Nebraska Law Review*, 1959, *38*, 744–761.

Bullock, H. A. Significance of the racial factor in the length of prison sentences. *Journal of Criminal Law, Criminology, and Police Science*, 1961, *52*, 411–417.

Campbell, D. T. Factors relevant to the validity of experiments in social settings. *Psychological Bulletin*, 1957, *54*, 297–312.

Carlsmith, J. M., Ellsworth, P. C., & Aronson, E. *Methods of research in social psychology.* Reading, Massachusetts: Addison-Wesley, 1976.

Colasanto, D., & Sanders, J. *From laboratory to juryroom: A review of experiments on jury decision-making.* Unpublished manuscript, University of Michigan, 1976.

Cook, T. D., & Campbell, D. T. *Quasi-experimentation: Design and analysis issues for field settings.* Chicago, Illinois: Rand McNally, 1979.

Davis, J. H. Group decision and social interaction: A theory of social decision schemes. *Psychological Review*, 1973, *80*, 97–125.

Davis, J. H. Group decision and procedural justice. In M. Fishbein (Ed.), *Progress in social psychology.* Hillsdale, New Jersey: Erlbaum, 1980.

Davis, J. H., Bray, R. M., & Holt, R. W. The empirical study of decision processes in juries: A critical review. In J. L. Tapp & F. J. Levine (Eds.), *Law, justice, and the individual in society: Psychological and legal issues.* New York: Holt, 1977.

Davis, J. H., Kerr, N. L., Atkin, R. S., Holt, R., & Meek, D. The decision processes of 6- and 12-person mock juries assigned unanimous and 2/3 majority rules. *Journal of Personality and Social Psychology*, 1975, *32*, 1–14.

Davis, J. H., Kerr, N. L., Stasser, G., Meek, D., & Holt, R. Victim consequences, sentence severity, and decision process in mock juries. *Organizational Behavior and Human Performance*, 1977, *18*, 346–365.

Davis, J. H., Spitzer, C. E., Nagao, D., & Stasser, G. T. Bias in social decisions by individuals and groups: An example from mock juries. In H. Brandstatter, J. Davis, & H. Schuler (Eds.), *Dynamics of group decisions.* Beverly Hills, California: Sage, 1978.

Davis, J. H., Stasser, G., Spitzer, C. E., & Holt, R. W. Changes in group members' decision preferences during discussion: An illustration with mock juries. *Journal of Personality and Social Psychology*, 1976, *34*, 1177–1187.

DeJong, W., & Hogue, A. Effect of an escaped accomplice on juridic judgment: The role of jurors' emotional reaction to a crime. *Catalog of Selected Documents in Psychology*, in press.

DeJong, W., Morris, W. N., & Hastorf, A. H. Effects of an escaped accomplice on the punishment assigned to a criminal defendant. *Journal of Personality and Social Psychology*, 1976, *33*, 192–198.

Diamond, S. S., & Zeisel, H. A courtroom experiment on juror selection and decision-making. *Personality and Social Psychology Bulletin*, 1974, *1*, 276–277.

Dillehay, R. D., & Nietzel, M. T. Constructing a science of jury behavior. In L. Wheeler (Ed.), *Review of personality and social psychology*, Beverly Hills, California: Sage, 1980.

Dillehay, R. D., & Nietzel, M. T. Conceptualizing mock jury–juror research: Critique and illustrations. In K. S. Larsen (Ed.), *Psychology and ideology*. Monmouth, Oregon: Institute for Theoretical History, 1981.

Doob, A. N., & Kirshenbaum, H. M. Some empirical evidence on the effect of s. 12 of the Canada evidence act upon an accused. *Criminal Law Quarterly*, 1972, *15*, 88–96.

Ebbesen, E. B., & Konečni, V. J. Decision making and information integration in the courts: The setting of bail. *Journal of Personality and Social Psychology*, 1975, *32*, 805–821.

Efran, M. G. The effect of physical appearance on the judgment of guilt, interpersonal attraction, and severity of recommended punishment in a simulated jury task. *Journal of Research in Personality*, 1974, *8*, 45–54.

Ellsworth, P., & Ross, L. Public opinion and judicial decision making: An example from research on capital punishment. In H. A. Bedau & C. M. Pierce (Eds.), *Capital punishment in the United States*, New York: AMS Press, 1976.

Elwork, A., & Sales, B. D. Psychological research on the jury and trial processes. In C. Petty, W. Curran, & L. McGarry (Eds.), *Modern legal medicine and forensic science*. Philadelphia, Pennsylvania: Davis, 1980.

Erickson, B., Lind, E. A., Johnson, B. C., & O'Barr, W. M. Speech style and impression formation in a court setting: The effects of "powerful" and "powerless" speech. *Journal of Experimental Social Psychology*, 1978, *14*, 266–279.

Foss, R. D. *A critique of jury simulation research*. Paper presented at the meeting of the American Psychological Association, Chicago, August 1975.

Foss, R. D. Group decision processes in the simulated trial jury. *Sociometry*, 1976, *39*, 305–316.

Gerbasi, K. C., Zuckerman, M., & Reis, H. T. Justice needs a new blindfold: A review of mock jury research. *Psychological Bulletin*, 1977, *84*, 323–345.

Gleason, J. M., & Harris, V. A. Group discussion and defendant's socio-economic status as determinants of judgments by simulated jurors. *Journal of Applied Social Psychology*, 1976, *6*, 186–191.

Gordon, R. I., & Jacobs, P. D. Forensic psychology: Perception of guilt and income. *Perceptual and Motor Skills*, 1969, *28*, 143–146.

Green, E. Inter- and intra-racial crime relative to sentencing. *Journal of Criminal Law, Criminology, and Political Science*, 1964, *55*, 348–358.

Griffitt, W., & Jackson, T. Simulated jury decisions: The influence of jury-defendant attitude similarity-dissimilarity. *Social Behavior and Personality*, 1973, *1*, 1–7.

Hamilton, V. L. Obedience and responsibility: A jury simulation. *Journal of Personality and Social Psychology*, 1978, *36*, 126–146.

Hans, V. P., & Doob, A. N. S.12 of the Canada Evidence Act and the deliberations of simulated juries. *Criminal Law Quarterly*, 1976, *18*, 235–253.

Hawkins, C. H. Interaction rates of jurors aligned in factions. *American Sociological Review*, 1962, *27*, 689–691.

Hoiberg, B. C., & Stires, L. K. The effects of several types of pretrial publicity on the guilt attributions of simulated jurors. *Journal of Applied Social Psychology*, 1973, *3*, 267–275.

Izzett, R., & Leginski, W. Group discussion and the influence of defendant characteristics in a simulated jury setting. *Journal of Social Psychology*, 1974, *93*, 271–279.

James, R. M. Status and competence of jurors. *The American Journal of Sociology*, 1959, *64*, 563–570.

Johnson v. *Lousiana. United States Reports*, 1972, *406*, 356−403.

Jurow, G. L. New data on the effect of a "death-qualified" jury on the guilt determination process. *Harvard Law Review*, 1971, *84*, 567−611.

Kagehiro, D. K., & Werner, C. M. *Effects of authoritarianism and inadmissibility of evidence on jurors' verdicts.* Paper presented at the meeting of the Midwestern Psychological Association, Chicago, May, 1977.

Kalven, H., Jr., & Zeisel, H. *The Amererican jury.* Boston, Massachusetts: Little, Brown, 1966.

Kaplan, M. F. Discussion polarization effects in a modified jury decision paradigm: Informational influences. *Sociometry*, 1977, *40*, 262−271. (a)

Kaplan, M. F. Judgments by juries. In M. Kaplan & S. Schwartz (Eds.), *Judgment and decision processes in applied settings.* New York: Academic Press, 1977. (b)

Kaplan, M. F., & Kemmerick, G. D. Juror judgment as information integration: Combining evidential and nonevidential information. *Journal of Personality and Social Psychology*, 1974, *30*, 493−499.

Kaplan, M. F., & Miller, C. E. Judgments and group discussion: Effect of presentation and memory factors on polarization. *Sociometry*, 1977, *40*, 337−343.

Kaplan, M. F., & Miller, L. E. Effects of jurors' identification with the victim depend on likelihood of victimization. *Law and Human Behavior*, 1978, *2*, 353−361. (a)

Kaplan, M. F., & Miller, L. E. Reducing the effects of juror bias. *Journal of Personality and Social Psychology*, 1978, *36*, 1443−1455. (b)

Kelman, H. C. Human use of human subjects: The problem of deception in social psychological experiments. *Psychological Bulletin*, 1967, *67*, 1−11.

Kerr, N. L. Beautiful and blameless: Effects of victim attractiveness and responsibility on mock jurors' verdicts. *Personality and Social Psychology Bulletin*, 1978, *4*, 479−482. (a)

Kerr, N. L. Severity of prescribed penalty and mock jurors' verdicts. *Journal of Personality and Social Psychology*, 1978, *36*, 1431−1422. (b)

Kerr, N. L. Trial participants' characteristics/behaviors and juries' verdicts: An exploratory field study. In V. Konečni & E. Ebbesen (Eds.), *Social psychological analyses of legal processes.* San Francisco, California: W. H. Freeman, 1981.

Kerr, N. L., & Anderson, A. B. *Defendant-juror religious similarity and mock jurors' judgments.* Paper presented at the meeting of the American Psychological Association, Toronto, August 1978.

Kerr, N. L., Atkin, R., Stasser, G., Meek, D., Holt, R., & Davis, J. H. Guilt beyond a reasonable doubt: Effects of concept definition and assigned rule on judgments of mock jurors. *Journal of Personality and Social Psychology*, 1976, *34*, 282−294.

Kerr, N. L., Harmon, D. L., & Graves, J. K. Independence of verdicts by jurors and juries. *Journal of Applied Social Psychology*, in press.

Kerr, N. L., Nerenz, D., & Herrick, D. Role playing and the study of jury behavior. *Sociological Methods and Research*, 1979, *7*, 337−355.

Kessler, J. B. An empirical study of six- and twelve-member jury decision-making processes. *University of Michigan Journal of Law Reform*, 1973, *6*, 712−734.

Kirby, D. A., & Lamberth, J. *The lawyers' dilemma: The behavior of authoritarian jurors.* Paper presented at the meeting of the Midwestern Psychological Association, Chicago, May, 1974.

Konečni, V. J., & Ebbesen, E. B. External validity of research in legal psychology. *Law and Human Behavior*, 1979, *3*, 39−70.

Konečni, V. J., Mulcahy, E. M., & Ebbesen, E. B. Prison or mental hospital: Factors affecting the processing of persons suspected of being "mentally disordered sex offenders." In P. D. Lipsitt & B. D. Sales (Eds.), *New directions in psycholegal research.* New York: Van Nostrand-Reinhold, 1980.

Krupat, E. A re-assessment of role playing as a technique in social psychology. *Personality and Social Psychology Bulletin*, 1977, *3*, 498−504.

Landy, D., & Aronson, E. The influence of the character of the criminal and his victim on the decisions of simulated jurors. *Journal of Experimental Social Psychology*, 1969, *5*, 141−152.

Lempert, R. O. Uncovering "nondiscernible" differences: Empirical research and the jury-size cases. *Michigan Law Review*, 1975, *73*, 643−708.

Lind, E. A., & Walker, L. Theory testing, theory development, and laboratory research on legal issues. *Law and Human Behavior*, 1979, *3*, 5−19.

Lineberry, M. D., Becker, L. A., & Lammers, H. B. *The influence of evidence on punitiveness and attraction.* Paper presented at the meeting of the Midwestern Psychological Association, Chicago, May, 1977.

Loftus, E., & Monahan, J. Trial by data: Psychological research as legal evidence. *American Psychologist*, 1980, *35*, 270−283.

Milgram, S. Liberating effects of group pressure. *Journal of Personality and Social Psychology*, 1965, *1*, 127−134.

Miller, G. R., Bender, D. C., Boster, F., Florence, B. T., Fontes, N., Hocking, J., & Nicholson, H. The effects of videotape testimony in jury trials. *Brigham Young University Law Review*, 1975, *1975*, 331−373.

Miller, G. R., Fontes, N. E., Boster, J., & Sunnafrank, M. *Methodological issues in jury research: What can simulations tell us?* Paper presented at the meeting of the American Psychological Association, San Francisco, August, 1977.

Mitchell, H. E., & Byrne, D. *Minimizing the influence of irrelevant factors in the courtroom: The defendant's character, judge's instructions, and authoritarianism.* Paper presented at the meeting of the Midwestern Psychological Association, Cleveland, May 1972.

Mitchell, H. E., & Byrne, D. The defendant's dilemma: Effects of jurors' attitudes and authoritarianism on judicial decisions. *Journal of Personality and Social Psychology*, 1973, *25*, 123−129.

Mixon, D. Temporary false belief. *Personality and Social Psychology Bulletin*, 1977, *3*, 479−488.

Myers, D. G., & Kaplan, M. F. Group-induced polarization in simulated juries. *Personality and Social Psychology Bulletin*, 1976, *2*, 63−66.

Nemeth, C. Interactions between jurors as a function of majority vs. unanimity decision rules. *Journal of Applied Social Psychology*, 1977, *7*, 38−56.

Nemeth, C., & Sosis, R. H. A simulated jury study: Characteristics of the defendant and the jurors. *The Journal of Social Psychology*, 1973, *90*, 221−229.

Orne, M. T. On the social psychology of the psychological experiment: With particular reference to demand characteristics and their implications. *American Psychologist*, 1962, *17*, 776−783.

Ostrom, T. M., Werner, C., & Saks, M. J. An integration theory analysis of jurors' presumptions of guilt or innocence. *Journal of Personality and Social Psychology*, 1978, *36*, 336−450.

Padawar-Singer, A. M., & Barton, A. H. The impact of pretrial publicity on jurors' verdicts. In R. J. Simon (Ed.), *The jury system in America: A critical overview.* Beverly Hills, California: Sage, 1975.

Rosenthal, R. Experimental outcome-orientation and the results of the psychological experiment. *Psychological Bulletin*, 1964, *61*, 405−412.

Ross, H. L., & Blumenthal, M. Some problems in experimentation in a legal setting. *American Sociologist*, 1975, *10*, 150−155.

Rumsey, M. G., Allgeier, E. R., & Castore, C. H. Group discussion, sentencing judgments and the leniency shift. *The Journal of Social Psychology*, 1978, *105*, 249−257.

Rumsey, M. G., & Rumsey, J. M. A case of rape: Sentencing judgments of males and females. *Psychological Reports*, 1977, *41*, 459−465.

Runkel, P. J., & McGrath, J. E. *Research on human behavior: A systematic guide to method.* New York: Holt, 1972.

Saks, M. J. Social psychological contributions to a legislative subcommittee on organ and tissue transplants. *American Psychologist*, 1978, *33*, 680−690.

Scroggs, J. R. Penalties for rape as a function of victim provocativeness, damage, and resistance. *Journal of Applied Social Psychology*, 1976, *6*, 360−368.

Sealy, A. P., & Cornish, W. R. Juries and the rules of evidence. *Criminal Law Review*, 1973 (April), 208−223.

Shaffer, D. R., Sadowski, C., & Hendrick, C. *Effects of withheld evidence on juridic decisions.* Paper presented at the meeting of the Southeastern Psychological Association, New Orleans, 1976.

Sigall, H., & Ostrove, N. Beautiful but dangerous: Effects of offender attractiveness and nature of the crime on juridic judgment. *Journal of Personality and Social Psychology*, 1975, *31*, 410–414.

Simon, R. J. Murder, juries, and the press. *Trans-action*, 1966, *3*, 40–42.

Simon, R. J. *The jury and the defense of insanity.* Boston, Massachusetts: Little, Brown, 1967.

Simon, R. J. "Beyond a reasonable doubt"—An experimental attempt at quantification. *Journal of Applied Behavioral Science*, 1970, *6*, 203–209.

Simon, R. J., & Mahan, L. Quantifying burdens of proof: A view from the bench, the jury and the classroom. *Law and Society Review*, 1971, *5*, 319–330.

Stephan, C. Sex prejudice in jury simulation. *The Journal of Psychology*. 1974, *88*, 305–312.

Strodtbeck, F. Social processes, the law, and jury functioning. In W. M. Evan (Ed.), *Law and sociology: Exploratory essays.* New York: Free Press, 1962.

Strodtbeck, F. L., James, R. M., & Hawkins, D. Social status in jury deliberations. *American Sociological Review*, 1957, *22*, 713–719.

Strodtbeck, F. L., & Mann, R. D. Sex role differentiation in jury deliberations. *Sociometry*, 1956, *19*, 3–11.

Sue, S., Smith, R. E., & Caldwell, C. Effects of inadmissible evidence on the decisions of simulated jurors: A moral dilemma. *Journal of Applied Social Psychology*, 1973, *3*, 344–353.

Suggs, D. L. The use of psychological research by the judiciary: Do the courts adequately assess the validity of the research? *Law and Human Behavior*, 1979, *3*, 135–148.

Thibaut, J., Walker, L., Lind, E. A. Adversary presentation and bias in legal decisionmaking. *Harvard Law Review*, 1972, *86*, 386–401.

Thomas, E. A. C., & Hogue, A. Apparent weight of evidence, decision criteria, and confidence ratings in juror decision making. *Psychological Review*, 1976, *83*, 442–465.

Thornton, B. Effects of rape victim's attractiveness in a jury simulation. *Personality and Social Psychology Bulletin*, 1977, *3*, 666–669.

Triandis, H. C. Basic research in the context of applied research in personality and social psychology. *Personality and Social Psychology Bulletin*, 1978, *4*, 383–387.

Valenti, A. C., & Downing, L. L. Differential effects of jury size on verdicts following deliberation as a function of apparent guilt of a defendant. *Journal of Personality and Social Psychology*, 1975, *32*, 655–663.

Vidmar, N. Effects of decision alternatives on the verdicts and social perceptions of simulated jurors. *Journal of Personality and Social Psychology*, 1972, *22*, 211–218. (a)

Vidmar, N. *Group-induced shifts in simulated jury decisions.* Paper presented at the meeting of the Midwestern Psychological Association, Cleveland, May, 1972. (b)

Walker, L., Thibaut, J., & Andreoli, V. Order of presentation at trial. *Yale Law Journal*, 1972, *82*, 216–226.

Webb, E. J., Campbell, D. T., Schwartz, R. D., & Sechrest, L. *Unobtrusive measures: Nonreactive research in the social sciences.* Chicago, Illinois: Rand McNally, 1966.

Weiten, W., & Diamond, S. S. A critical review of the jury simulation paradigm: The case of defendant characteristics. *Law and Human Behavior*, 1979, *3*, 71–93.

Williams, G. R., Farmer, L. C., Lee, R. E., Cundick, B. P., Howell, R. J., & Rooker, C. K. Juror perceptions of trial testimony as a function of the method of presentation: A comparison of live, color video, black-and-white video, audio, and transcript presentations, *1975*, 375–421.

Wilson, D. W., & Donnerstein, E. Guilty or not guilty? A look at the "simulated" jury paradigm. *Journal of Applied Social Psychology*, 1977, *7*, 175–190.

chapter

11

Innovation and Change in the Courtroom

Michael J. Saks

Thinking people think about change. The status quo, being already present, requires no thought.

        —E. G. Boring, A History of Experimental Psychology *(1950)*

Many—probably most—social psychologists who are interested in the law, the legal system, or the legal process are interested because they wish to con-

THE PSYCHOLOGY
OF THE COURTROOM

tribute to productive change in this institution. This chapter is about the problem of change. The first quarter of the chapter discusses three aspects of innovation and change: the nature of these concepts and their role in the courts as institutions: the real or potential contributions of social psychologists to the "scientific-technical" substance of innovation and change; and the real or potential contributions of social psychologists to the problem of how the judicial process changes or fails to change, that is, to understanding what causes or inhibits change in legal institutions as social organizations. The remainder of the chapter reviews three technically well-studied innovations that have been adopted by some or many courts: changes in jury size and social decision rules, the advent of sentencing guidelines, and the development of videotape technology. Each of these innovations is reviewed to offer a flavor of the kinds of issues and charges with which the courts must concern themselves, a summary of the major findings of research on the scientific-technical aspects of these innovations, and an examination of what they teach us about the legal-political-organizational context of innovation and change.

INNOVATION AND CHANGE

What Is Innovation and Who Wants It?

Science is in large part the business of change, of revising—if not revolutionizing—our comprehension of the way things work. Applied science is concerned mostly with the business of bringing those revised understandings to bear on changing what we make and what we do, including the structure of our institutions and the conduct of our affairs. As we know, scientific progress can go on without becoming manifest in a society's life, and change can take place without the benefit of society's comprehension. My belief is that science can benefit when its intended fruits include improving a society's life, and surely planned change benefits when it is founded on a base more solid than the seat of one's pants (see Kidd & Saks, 1980).

The courts are one institution well aware of the need for improvement, and that unavoidably means change. A nearly ubiquitously shared truism in the world of the judiciary is that things are not as good as they should be (Fetter, 1978). The judiciary committees of state and federal legislatures teem with reform proposals or altogether new judicial articles. Government and private organizations, such as the Federal Judicial Center, the National Institute of Justice, the National Center for State Courts, the Office for Improvements in the Administration of Justice (within the United States Department of Justice), the American Judicature Society, the Institute for Court Management, the American Bar Foundation, and others, exist to facilitate positive change in the courts. Nearly every court system has committees of judges and support staffs and holds annual judicial conferences in part to consider problems and proposed solutions. Despite unprecedented activity in this sphere, it is not clear that improvement is being made.

Some problems are cyclical, such as those involved in new areas of litigation. Current examples include the growth of scientific and complex commercial subject matter that challenge the intellectual capacity of judges and juries, and the claims of rights by groups that previously suffered in silence. Some problems are created by solutions to other problems, such as the anticipated transfer of a large body of litigation from the federal courts to state courts. Some problems have been with the courts seemingly forever. The most discussed problem of today's courts is that of delay and backlog. It is said that justice delayed is justice denied. The Speedy Trial Act (1974) mandates that criminal cases be tried within a limited number of days or be dismissed. That mandate urging the disposition of criminal cases in turn exacerbates backlogs in processing civil cases (Church, Lee, Tam, Carlson, & McConnell, 1978). We are occasionally reminded by quantitative historical studies that this backlog problem was with us a century ago (e.g., Heumann, 1975). And in his "To be or not to be" soliloquy, Hamlet counts "the law's delay" among the inescapable calamities of human experience (right next to "the pains of [rejected] love"). Thus by 1602 the courts already had a reputation for being less than expeditious.

In the pursuit of solutions, the courts, by definition, strive to innovate. Even if we adopt a neutral and broad definition of innovation as *any* alteration in established structure or procedures, we have a problem in deciding what is an innovation and what is an established structure or procedure. The problem is temporal. Innovation is easiest to perceive when it does not yet exist; that is, when it is contemplated, part of the future. Of past changes, where do we draw the line between the established and the reformed? Today's introduction of computerized calendaring and case management is an innovation. But what of last year's abolition of justices of the peace? Or the promulgation of the "new" Federal Rules of Evidence (1975)? Or the advent of juvenile courts (1899)? Indeed, we easily overlook that courts themselves are an innovation over feudal systems, the concept of *parens patriae*, and so on. This is the evolution of law that Sir Henry Maine characterized as the move from status to contract: where the ownership of people by the king and his lords, and the rights and duties that attach to owning or being owned, were replaced by systems of (contractual) agreements which, from time to time, had to be interpreted and enforced by courts. Today, some hold that the abolition of juvenile courts would be a step forward. In a trial and error world, it may never be clear what we are moving toward and what we are moving away from. At some point, people begin to perceive an old innovation as no innovation at all, but as an established part of a current problem. A comprehensive study of innovation would address the problem of innovation as a social process worthy of study in its own right. Such a study might clarify when an element of a social institution will be regarded as in need of overhaul, and what kinds of changes will be seen as "innovative."

The innovations examined in this chapter are not "old," and yet have been in effect in some places long enough to generate both evaluation studies and criticism of such studies. For example, Lempert (1980) has criticized such innovation evaluation as backward looking and status quo oriented and therefore something less than the best that social science has to contribute to the process of change. On the other hand, as we move closer to basic research, we simultaneously become more forward looking as well as less "relevant" and more "academic." For researchers interested in contributing to innovation and change in an important and struggling institution, one must ask where the research should be aimed; at what stage of innovating research can make the most positive contributions; if innovation can mesh intelligently enough with the social, organizational and historical context of change that it can be felt; and what the roles of long-range planning research, research and development of an about-to-be implemented reform should be. When is an innovation still "experimental" enough to be modified, when is it so much in place that it must be left alone until it eventually is again seen as ripe for a change? These are some of the issues considered in this chapter along with substantive discussions of three relatively well circumscribed contemporary innovations, and their social-psychological content.

Innovation and Change as a Scientific-Technical Problem

Innovations in the courtroom can be regarded, at one level, as highly similar to any other "technological" change. They usually involve some sort of organizational restructuring or procedural alteration, and sometimes the introduction of machine technology (e.g., communications equipment, computers, new record management systems, other business machinery). Organizational modifications can include administrative changes in everything from the way personnel (including judges) are selected, trained, assigned, and replaced to the structure of state courts (unified and tightly administered, or composed of a number of semiautonomous units.) Organizational modifications can also include changes that aim more clearly at the conduct of cases: for example, abolishing juries in complex civil cases (as Chief Justice Burger proposed in 1979); reducing or expanding the experts' testimony, enlarging or contracting the use of challenges to the composition of juries, or regulating judicial discretion in sentencing by introducing flat sentencing, indeterminate sentencing, or sentencing guidelines. Of course, there are myriad other innovations recently introduced or still on the drawing board somewhere in the judicial drafting room.

All of these innovations may in principle be treated like any other problem in applied science. The innovation must be defined and described with enough operational precision so that interested people can try to implement it or can tell if they are looking at it when they come upon a court that has (or purports to have) it. Specification of an innovation is no small matter for a researcher or reformer. Each incarnation of an innovation will likely vary from some ideal model, sometimes so much so that it ceases to be an example of the innovation. In addition to specifying the attributes of the innovation, the setting into which it is introduced must be understood. And finally, the class or classes of events upon which the innovation is supposed to have an impact must be identified. The design of an innovation could benefit from a consideration of existing relevant knowledge from social psychology and other fields, but this is rarely done well (or at all), whether the reformers are court administrators, legislators, or Supreme Court Justices. The knowledge, nevertheless, often exists and probably would contribute to a more thoughtful innovation and fewer surprises and disappointments down the road.

The methodological tool that has the most obvious relevance is evaluation research. Only after an innovation has been introduced (and ideally has been in place long enough so that its start-up chaos has settled) can one assess the degree to which it in fact meets its intended goals. Perhaps at no other point is a social science contribution more necessary and likely to be definitive. And, indeed, evaluation research has come to be valued by judges and court administrators about as highly as has been any social science contribution to court administration and reform. Formative evaluation can assist in implementing a new program and serve as a kind of management information system. Summative evaluation may then answer the critical question of whether the new structures or procedures live up to the visions of their proponents.

Experimental and quasi-experimental methods are unusually well suited to the problem of evaluating innovation and change. The changes are easily likened to experimentally manipulated independent variables. They are introduced under administrative control, and can, if desired, be introduced at times and in ways that permit useful comparisons (controls) that facilitate relatively unconfounded assessments of their effects. Of course, the introduction of changes never works as smoothly as one might hope (or is accustomed to in the laboratory); supplemental methods help ensure that problems that may arise in the evaluation can be tested or statistically adjusted for. That is, assumptions of randomness are often not safe—selection confounds, differential attrition, reactivity, and other effects are possible and perhaps likely (Campbell & Stanley, 1963; Cook & Campbell, 1979). Such difficulties make the experimental method no less attractive on inferential grounds, and experimental or quasi-experimental approaches to research in the courts are not at all uncommon.

Innovation and Change as a Legal-Political-Organizational Problem

Thus far, we have discussed innovation and change as a scientific-technical problem, much like the development of a new empirical phenomenon, a new surgical technique, or a new kind of camera. The innovation is defined, made conceptually digestible and feasible, its operation and effectiveness are assessed, and these steps are gone through again until the innovation is recognized as desirable and is adopted or is recognized as fit only for abandonment. This final point is the focus of the present section. All research, especially applied research on social institutions and behavior, involves more than questions of the empirical attributes of the subject under study. Somehow the information of the innovation's existence must be disseminated among those people and institutions who might be interested in it, perceived by them as desirable, adopted, and accepted by those who must change their former ways and live with it. The problem of innovation and change is also a problem of law, of politics, of change in the attitudes and behavior of individual human beings and changes in organizations; in short, innovation is a problem of social as well as technical change. A newly recognized empirical phenomenon must come to be accepted by the relevant scientific community before it "exists" for them; a new surgical technique must become recognized by the relevant community of surgeons as worth learning and doing; a new camera must not only have the confidence of the company's management or an inventor's financial backers, but must also be marketed successfully among consumers. And of course, an innovation in the courts must not only be technically and scientifically sound, but must also win the acceptance and support of judges, lawyers, legislators, court administrators, and perhaps the public. (Yankelovich, Skelly, & White, Inc. 1978).

The problem of social change and the role of technical knowledge in that change is itself a researchable question and has in fact been the subject of some study by social scientists (e.g., Coleman, Katz, & Menzel 1966; Katz & Kahn 1966; Weiss 1972; and the work of the Center for Research in the Utilization of Scientific Knowledge). As social scientists become increasingly involved in bringing about change, they also have become increasingly aware of the value of studying the social process of change as well as the technical substance of the changes themselves. This resurgence of interest in organizational and political change has paralleled (and, I believe, has been caused by) increasing involvement in applied research. Many social psychologists seem surprised to discover that their research findings accounted for only a modest proportion of the variance in policy decision making. They became frustrated and fascinated by the "irrationality" of organizations and policymakers who were driven more by constituent prejudices, political deals, popular wisdom, or the "wrong" goals than by systematic, empirical, credible data on the effects of some policy options versus others (Weiss, 1972). The frustration is illustrated more clearly by an example from a community which might be expected to be more "rational," less "political," and have more agreed upon goals and methods than do legal policymakers: physicians. Research finds that the conventional manner of treating disease X is no more effective than a vastly cheaper and easier alternative with fewer harmful side effects. Or, a new method of treating disease Y is found to be more effective than the conventional approach. Upon reading these findings in medical journals, do the relevant physicians (rationally) begin using the innovative methods? Dissemination is slow (because they do not learn from the standard sources of dissemination, but rather through informal social networks), and adoption is slower. Once a medical innovation is demonstrated to be effective, it may become the profession's treatment of choice only many years later, perhaps a generation of physicians later (Cochrane, 1974).

Fortunately for social scientists, the very phenomena that slow down acceptance and adoption of innovations are themselves appropriate subjects of study and susceptible to the social scientist's theories and methods. Applied social researchers confronted with resistant political and organizational responses have, it seems, begun not only to lament the situation, but also to carry out research on it. Indeed, understanding the process of change in the courts and related institutions might be a pivotal contribution to facilitating the more orderly and effective assessment and acceptance of innovation by the courts. What causes acceptance or rejection of reforms—what characteristics of the reform itself, its informational surround, the organization to be changed, the social and historical context, and so on? What are the prospects for successful change when the changes are obligatory versus optional? What are the sources of resistance to (technically positive) change? What is the role of scientific-technical knowledge in the policymaking process? Under what conditions is the knowledge likely to have a greater or lesser impact? These questions are increasingly the subject of study by applied and change oriented social researchers (Caplan, 1976; Saks & Baron, 1980; Weiss, 1977).

CONTEMPORARY INNOVATIONS AND CHANGES

Jury Size and Decision Rule

Reducing the requisite size of juries and abolishing the requirement for a unanimous verdict may not seem like startling "innovations," but they do satisfy our definition. Moreover, these two changes have, in the past decade, commanded the attention of state legislatures, national legal organizations, the Supreme Court (in seven cases) and quite a few social scientists. (Therein may lie an important lesson about innovation in the courts.)

For hundreds of years of English common law history and nearly 200 years of United States constitutional history, the jury consisted of 12 people required to reach a unanimous verdict. But in the 1970s, that changed. In *Williams v. Florida* (1970) the Supreme Court ruled that juries could be smaller than 12 and in *Apodaca, Cooper, and Madden v. Oregon* and *Johnson v. Lousiana* (both 1972) that the requirement for unanimity was constitutionally superfluous. Congress and state legislatures were now free to reduce jury size and relax the unanimity requirement, and did so to an extent that what was nearly unheard of a decade ago is now to be found in virtually every federal district and state court. This is institutional change of a rapid and widespread order.

What brought this change about? Although it is difficult to know precisely, the following scenario is probably not unfair, and certainly captures something of the political, social, and organizational context in which these changes took place. In the years leading up to the 1970s, the nation's perenially underfunded courts (Baar, 1975) were learning to take management, administration, and finance seriously, and to organize themselves in the interest of court modernization and reform. Another threat of the times was the rising crime rate and public and government demands that something be done, with the judiciary receiving much of the vague and generalized criticism. A third underlying theme was a long-standing and respectable view among some lawyers and judges that juries were simply no good (Frank, 1930, 1949). These latter views persisted, despite landmark research by Kalven and Zeisel (1966) that disconfirmed a number of the assumptions and arguments put forward by some commentators, whose speculation is nevertheless still quoted today (e.g., Burger, 1979). Several state codes provided for juries of fewer than 12 and decision rules permitting less than unanimous verdicts. This innovation appeared to solve a number of problems at once, some financial (e.g., fewer jurors require fewer dollars), some political (e.g., smaller juries were popularly believed to offer some advantage to prosecutors), some ideological (e.g., smaller juries are a step closer to no juries at all). The legal question, however, was whether the Constitution permitted such alterations. Several persons convicted under such relaxed conditions brought important appeals of their cases.

In *Apodaca, Johnson,* and especially *Williams,* the Supreme Court laid out its jury function test under which it found that the reductions in jury size and the existence of nonunanimous decision rules did not offend constitutional standards. The court reasoned that the Constitution itself was silent on these two characteristics of the jury, and that the legislative history was ambiguous. The issue then was the jury's *function.* The structure of the institution did not matter; whether it served its function was the issue. A jury's size and shape could be altered, so long as its function was not vitiated. The Court in *Williams* went on to specify the jury function:

> The performance of this rule is not a function of the particular number of the body that makes up the jury. To be sure, the number should probably be large enough to promote group deliberation, free from outside attempts at intimidation and to provide a fair possibility for obtaining a representative cross-section of the community. But we find little reason to think that these goals are in any meaningful sense less likely to be achieved when the jury numbers six, than when it numbers twelve [p. 100].

> In short, neither currently available evidence nor theory suggests that the 12-man jury is necessarily more advantageous to the defendant than a jury composed of fewer members [p. 101].

This language of the court translates itself into the language of experimental social psychology as an independent variable (jury size or decision rule) having (or not having) an effect upon a set of dependent variables (quality of deliberation, verdicts, cross-sectional representation of the community, etc.).

In *Williams* the Court held that the jury function was only "negligibly" altered by reducing its size to six and, likewise in *Apodaca* and *Johnson*, the Court held that decision rules as thin as 8 of 12 would not affect the jury's process or product. These conclusions obviously make some strong assertions about the scientific-technical nature of these innovations: that structural changes within the given limits do not alter function. The court's basis for this conclusion was terribly weak. To support its conclusion that "there is no discernible difference between the results reached by the two different-sized juries (p. 102)" the opinion cited a series of "studies" that were, on examination, merely a collection of speculative writings, or irrelevant references to the general issue of size. To support its conclusion that numerical minorities in small juries would be as resistant to majority pressure as they were in large juries, the courts cited Asch (1952), Kalven and Zeisel (1966), and a Yale Law Journal article, "Comment: On instructing deadlocked juries" (1968). The problem here was that each of these sources concluded essentially the opposite of what the opinion said they concluded. The Court believed that a minority's response to majority pressure is unchanged so long as the ratios stay the same. Thus, according to the Court, a jury divided ten to two (83%:17%) would be the functional equivalent of a jury divided five to one (83%:17%). As each of the cited authorities points out, the lone juror in the five-to-one jury is under far more psychological pressure to yield than are the two minority jurors in the 12-person jury, since each of the two has an ally. The Yale Law Journal piece even suggests a logarithmic relationship—glaringly at odds with the Court's claims about it, and strikingly in line with Latané's (Latané & Nida, 1980) recent findings regarding social impact in groups. Finally, to support its conclusion that reduced size has no effect on how representative of the community the jury will be, the court offered its own intuitive sampling theory:

> While in theory the number of viewpoints represented on a randomly selected jury ought to increase as the size of the jury increases, in practice the difference between the 12 man and the six-man jury in terms of the cross-section of the community represented seems likely to be negligible. [p. 102]

The Court's conclusion is precisely what an intuitive decision maker, implicitly believing in a "law of small numbers" would conclude (Saks & Kidd, 1980–1981; Tversky & Kahneman, 1971). But it is simply wrong. For example, suppose a community was stratified 90–10% on some demographic characteristic. Under the Court's own assumptions, the arithmetic of sampling theory tells us that 72% of the 12-person juries, but only 47% of the 6-person juries, would contain at least one representative of the 10% minority (Zeisel, 1971).

The response of the scientific and scholarly community to this display was almost unanimously critical. The errors in relying on nonstudies, on intuitive statistics, and in misread studies, were widely elucidated and condemned (e.g., Saks, 1977; Zeisel, 1971). One commentator summed up the Supreme Court's performance in these cases as "an embarrassment" (Saks, 1974, p. 18). Some researchers noted, as the Court did not, the absence of direct research on the issues and proceeded to conduct some well-aimed empirical studies, notably on the group-size question, to test the Court's conclusion.

In 1973, in *Colgrove v. Battin* the Court had another opportunity to address the question of jury size. In reaffirming the position taken in *Williams*, the Court cited four empirical studies carried out in response to that earlier opinion, all of which found no effect as a function of group size. Unfortunately for all concerned, the studies suffered from a number of classic methodological flaws, in some instances glaring ones (see review in Saks, 1977). Prominent among these were confounding errors—by selection and by history, inadequate sample size, and lack of variance in the dependant variable. Perhaps the Court thought that it had covered itself this time, but its reward was another scorching lesson in the use of empirical data to guide policy: Once real empirical studies are in hand, their methodology has to be assessed (i.e., a finding is only as good as the methods used to find it).

A variety of critiques, new empirical studies, and mathematical models (These are cited in *Ballew v. Georgia*, 1978 and Sperlich, 1979) followed the *Colgrove* decision, mostly deploring it and providing further evidence of the Court's error. Methodological problems had to do with the subtlety of the effects, at least with regard to the dependent variable of verdicts. Although mathematical models, based on most reasonable assumptions, showed that small effects result from change in group size (Davis, Kerr, Atkin, Holt, & Meek, 1975), empirical studies generally failed to detect these effects at reliable levels (reviewed in Saks, 1977). An optimizing approach demonstrated that the "best" size, that is, the one that minimizes total weighted errors made by juries, varied according to such factors as the relative weight to be given errors of false conviction versus errors of false acquittal, the unknowable true distribution of guilty and innocent defendants brought to jury trial, and so on (Nagel & Neef, 1977). On other dependent variables, however, there was ample demonstration of differences as a function of size reduction, such as the effect of sample size on jury representativeness. But even here, the optimal size depends upon the distribution of relevant attributes in the population from which juries are to be sampled. One of the few studies to examine group process as well as product found some advantages for each kind of jury (12-person, 6-person, unanimous verdict rule, nonunanimous verdict) and that the choice of any one meant the loss of the advantages of the others (Saks, 1977; also see Davis *et al.* 1975; Kerr, Atkins, Stasser, Meek, Holt, & Davis, 1976). Such complicating realities do not make a policymaker's life any easier. Rather than showing *the* way to a solution, research can make the world seem less clear and the solution more elusive. The studies, as a group, left little doubt that there were differences between 12- and 6-person juries. The conclusion of Saks (1977) was that consideration might be given to devising an innovative new jury structure that could capture the best features of both size juries and both decision rules. The illustration given by Saks (1977) was:

> A jury of size twelve (to provide better community representation), directed to self-select into two twin juries of six each for the deliberation (providing more involvement per juror as well as more total communication by having two juries deliberating simultaneously, and better proportional recall of arguments), each jury required to come to at least 4/6 consensus (more communication per jury per unit time, better recall of arguments, and virtually no hung juries), and both twin juries must agree on guilt independently for the verdict to be guilty, otherwise the verdict becomes not guilty (eliminating hung juries without introducing increased error into the decision process, requires more certainty and consistency, and has the added virtue of making explicit the underlying variability in jury decision making [p. 107].)

This solution, however is most likely *too* innovative.

In light of the Supreme Court decisions, it became constitutionally permissible to have smaller juries in state and federal trials, and nearly every federal district and most states quickly adopted the change. The Court explicitly declined to set lower bounds on jury size, saying only that "whatever the minimum may be, six is not below it (*Williams*, 1970)." Inevitably, some states would test the limits. In 1978 the Supreme Court decided *Ballew* v. *Georgia*, in which a criminal jury of five was challenged as unconstitutional. The State of Georgia argued, with the indomitable logic of whole numbers, that "if six is above the minimum, five can not be below it. There is no number in between" (cited in Sperlich, 1979). But the slide downward had stopped. In *Ballew* the Court held that no further reductions in size would be permitted (Sperlich, 1979).

The Court's opinion in *Ballew* is noteworthy on several grounds. It brought a halt to a trend that research indicated was not supported by the facts, as the Court had once mistakenly believed. Moreover, the Court's opinion in *Ballew* reflects an extensive acquaintance with the research and writing that its decisions earlier in the decade had prompted, including the critiques of those earlier decisions. This opinion is, in fact, by far the Supreme Court's most thoroughgoing consideration and discussion of social science research to date. The opinion reads like a *Psychological Bulletin* article, organized by the empirical questions and reviewing the studies germane to those questions.

The *Ballew* opinion could be faulted on a few relatively minor grounds, such as its treatment of statistically nonsignificant differences as though they were significant, and its treatment of data generated by a mathematical model as though they were empirical. The more interesting problem is that after reviewing these studies, the majority opinion reached two conclusions. First, "these writings do not draw or identify a bright line below which the number of jurors would not be able to function as required by the standards enunciated in

Williams. On the other hand, they raise significant questions about the wisdom and constitutionality of a reduction below six." And secondly, the Court announced that "we adhere to, and reaffirm our holding in *Williams v. Florida.*" Recall that the research on jury-size effects was stimulated by the *Williams* and *Colgrove* décisions. All but one of these studies compare juries of 12 with juries of 6. Thus, on the basis of studies comparing 12 with 6, and finding some adverse effects, the Court was able to reaffirm the correctness of its original reduction to 6 while becoming concerned about a reduction from 6 to 5. Clearly, something more than evidence and logic are in command here (Sperlich, 1979). For the record, several other studies of the effects of jury size have been conducted (Bermant and Coppock, 1973; Davis *et al.,* 1975; Institute of Judical Administration, 1972; Kessler, 1973; Mills, 1973; Valenti & Downing, 1975), but they have been widely criticized on methodological grounds (see Diamond, 1974; Lempert: 1975; Saks, 1974, 1977; Sperlich, 1979; Zeisel & Diamond, 1974; and the opinion of the Court in *Ballew* v. *Georgia,* 1978).

The size reduction innovation stands on untenable technical-scientific ground. A demonstration of *no effect,* the acceptance of a null hypothesis, carries unusual demands in the logic of decision theory, even if the studies had no masking artifacts, which the major null studies certainly seem to. The Court could have reversed its earlier error, which it was obviously aware of, as can be seen in *Ballew,* but it chose only to halt further reductions of jury size. Speculative attribution of motives is always a risky exercise, but I shall venture it. The technical-scientific findings became generally known and felt. So had the reaction of the bar and public commentators to past jury size decisions. The limits had now been set; the Supreme Court had gone about as far as it could without giving up the jury altogether ("a line has to be drawn somewhere [p. 245]," wrote Justice Powell in his concurring Opinion in *Ballew*), and without looking awfully foolish in light of the technical-scientific data available. But the reductions already had been adopted widely throughout the nation. To reverse now and order a return to a jury of 12, would be unpopular and disruptive, and would make the Court look even more uncertain of its facts by admitting it had been in error only a few years before. The safest course, then, was the course adopted, even though it required embracing an irrational position. The line, however, has been drawn on how small a jury may be.

Changes in jury decision rules have been less widespread and commanded less attention than the change in jury size. Perhaps the most intriguing way to contemplate the available empirical research on decision rule effects is to compare the findings of that research to the theory of jury deliberation put forth by the majority in the Supreme Court's decisions in *Apodaca* and *Johnson.* The majority argued that jurors recognize their obligation to listen seriously to and be open to influence by minority viewpoints, even if the minority's votes are mathematically superfluous to the verdict. The deliberation, it was argued, would be no less vigorous and thorough.

Of the handful of studies conducted on the matter of decision rule (Bray, 1974; Bray & Struckman-Johnson, 1977; Davis *et al.,* 1975; Hans, 1978; Kerr *et al.*, 1976; Nemeth, 1977; Saks, 1977), none found a significant effect on the distribution of verdicts. But the studies constitute a consensus on the deliberation process, and those findings contradict the Supreme Court's theory of jury decision making. Each of the following findings was reported in at least two of the studies, and was contradicted by none of the other investigations: Under unanimous decision rules (in comparison to five-sixths or two-thirds majorities), the deliberation took a longer time, juries were more likely to become hung, minority factions shared more equally in the communication, more communication occurred in total, and jurors were more certain of the correctness of their verdicts. In addition, each of the following findings was reported by one or another of the studies and contradicted by none: In unanimous rule juries, members of minority factions were more satisfied with the deliberation, more conflict was generated, more opinion change occurred, more jurors felt that "justice was done," and there was more minority influence. Majority rule juries did, indeed, continue to deliberate past the point where the minimum number of votes required to conclude was obtained, but no members of the majority changed their vote once that consensus was reached. A related study (C. E. Miller, 1974), though not focused on the jury unanimity issue, compared groups operating under majority rule, oligarchy, and dictatorship. Even under these divergent rules, no differences were found in the distribution of decisions. But minority acceptance of the group decision was greater as the opportunity for legitimate participation was afforded by the rule. The only finding favoring the majority decision rule was that jurors operating under that rule recalled more of the arguments generated during the deliberation. The small group research evidence regarding group process, and the Supreme Court's speculations on the deliberation process, contrast sharply.

The difference in the enthusiasm with which the equally legal and implementable innovations of jury size and decision rule have been adopted might tell us something about the institutional motivations behind the changes. Both are popularly thought to lend an advantage to prosecutors. But reduced jury sizes, more than a relaxation of the unanimity requirement, reduces the management burden and some of the costs associated with the jury system. Those who saw anti-civil liberties conspiracies may have misinterpreted the forces behind the changes. Those who would promote change might consider the lessons that can be extracted from past changes (or failures to adopt changes). The line on decision rules remains to be drawn clearly, although a decision by five of a six person jury has been unceremoniously declared unconstitutional (*Burch v. Louisiana*, 1979). Far less social-psychological and statistical research exists on the decision rule question, compared to the matter of jury size. The Supreme Court has some delicate paths yet to trace.

Sentencing Guidelines

The second innovation to be considered has to do with the problem of how judges combine information about a convicted defendant to decide on a sentence. If a person's job were defined by the kind of tasks performed and the amount of time spent on them, it would be concluded that a criminal trial judge's job is to assign sentences to convicted criminals. Trials are infrequent events; the vast majority (well over 90%) of defendants plead guilty, and so obviate a trial (Cole, 1975). Most defendants who seek trial are found guilty; a result that becomes increasingly skewed as prosecutors exercise greater care in screening cases (declining to prosecute weak cases, sweetening the bargain in questionable cases, allowing only strong cases to go to trial). Judges spend a large portion of their time reading (perhaps) presentence reports and brooding, one hopes, over whether or not to incarcerate the convicted defendant and, if so, for how long. While statutes place some bounds on the decisions and the prosecutor controls the charge, the judge usually has considerable discretion. Some of the problems that have come to be recognized in the sentencing process are different aspects of the same problem: Sentences are too unpredicticable, decisions made by different judges differ too widely, similarly situated defendants convicted of the same offense may receive sentences that differ disturbingly, with one placed on probation and the other incarcerated for a long period (Partridge & Eldridge, 1974; O'Donnell, Churgin, & Curtis, 1977). A national trend is under way to restructure and control the sentencing process, so that these inequities are reduced. What made this movement focus on this problem at this time is an interesting question of social innovation that we will do no more than pose here. The various efforts at solution have included flat or determinate sentencing, mandatory sentencing, presumptive sentencing, and institution of sentencing guidelines. Most states have either adopted one of these strategies or have been seriously considering them.

The sentencing guidelines approach has been introduced in five cities in which extensive and systematic research evaluating the execution and impact of the technique has been undertaken (Rich, Sutton, Clear, & Saks, 1980). These cities are Denver, Chicago, Newark, Philadelphia, and Phoenix. (Other cities and states have adopted the approach on their own but are not part of the national evaluation.)

The essence of the concept of sentencing guidelines is that judges have at hand some device that specifies for them a fairly narrow sentence range, given certain characteristics of the offense and the offender. The judge is free to choose a sentence from within the range or to go outside of it, but in the latter case usually is asked to provide a written explanation. The guidelines device practiced thus far has consisted of a set of tables specifying the characteristics of the offense and the offender, and recommended sentences. (Other approaches could employ an equation or algorithm, computed manually or by computer.) The contents of the guidelines are derived in part normatively and in part empirically. Norms could be obtained simply by asking the judges of the given jurisdiction to argue out a set of consensual guidelines based on law, jurisprudence, philosophy, and personal views. This purely normative approach has been advocated by Partridge and Leavitt (1979) but is thought to be inadequate by those who have developed existing guidelines. The empirical component of the guidelines attempts to describe past sentencing behavior and with that description inform judges of what their past implicit sentencing policies have been. To do so offers several advantages. Judges may be unaware or unwilling to acknowledge some of the bases for their sentencing practices. By building new guidelines on a base of past behavior, change should either seem less radical (and therefore more acceptable), or a radical change will have consequences that are more predictable (and because there will be fewer surprises, the changes might be easier to sustain). Certain variables that may have influenced sentencing in the past but ought not to have (e.g., race) can be deliberately excluded from guidelines and projections can be made of the impact this will have. It might be noted that studies of noncapital cases spanning over 50 years have failed to find general effects of extralegal variables once legal variables are controlled (Hagan, 1974). This does not ensure, however, that in particular sites there is no such general bias or that individual judges do not rely on improper cues in making their decisions. Sentencing guidelines are constructed separately for each jurisdiction in which they are to be used, and are thus free to vary in accord with the laws, norms, and practices of varying jurisdictions. What they seek to do, then, is to reduce judges' discretionary power to sentence within a jurisdiction.

The most technical-scientific aspect of developing and implementing sentencing guidelines, then, is the prior development of a model of judges' sentencing behavior, which will then shape the guidelines that are written. If the model is deficient (i.e., fails to predict well because it employs the wrong variables or wrong structure, or applies the wrong weights; or the model predicts well but for the wrong reasons) judges may find that in practice the guidelines that emanate from it depart too widely from their intuitions and therefore they will depart widely from the guidelines. If, however, the model is deficient, but judges adhere to it nonetheless, then something worse may occur. Policy will have been made in part by some quantity of irrational statistical noise. Other scientific-technical, as well as organizational-social issues also exist. These include the operation, acceptance, and impact of the guidelines on the rest of the justice system and on offenders and society at large. It is thought, for example, that making sentencing policies more explicit will increase not only the actual fairness of sentencing but also the perception of its fairness by clarifying the basis for discretion. Discretion will still exist, but it will be tethered, elastically, within certain normative borders. As systems examples, sentencing guidelines it is thought, by reducing discretion, will also alter the exchange relationships that play a large role in the criminal justice system, and may (in combination with legislative changes) contribute to reduction of the prison system's control over how long a person is incarcerated. (The criminal justice system is marked throughout by a high degree of discretion; see Abt & Stewart, 1979). The most crucial impact, of course, is whether the advent of sentencing guidelines reduces the disparity in sentencing. All other things being equal, the variance in sentencing for similar offenses and circumstances should be smaller after the introduction of sentencing guidelines than it was before.

In the remainder of this section, I will summarize the research findings on these two scientific-technical questions: How adequate the models of judicial sentencing decision making were, and what the impact of the guidelines was in the five focal cities mentioned earlier (Rich *et al.* 1981).

The guidelines construction research was conducted in the focal cities as a single project by the same workers (Calpin, Kress, & Gelman, 1979). Data were gathered on past cases that resulted in conviction (of which virtually all, of course, were by guilty plea). Files were coded for dozens of variables describing (*a*) the offense (e.g., what it was, whether a gun was involved, whether it involved injury to anyone), (*b*) the offender (e.g., educational background, income, number of dependents), (*c*) the victim (e.g., whether the victim was a person, a business, or the state, or whether the crime was victimless), and of course (*d*) the sentencing decision (placement on probation, imposition of some nonincarcertive alternative, or incarceration, and if so, for how long and whether in jail or prison). The analytic task then was to try to account for the sentencing decisions with the available predictor data. The developers did this by screening in variables that had a least some zero order correlation (rarely above .20) with the criterion variables, or had some "theoretical" importance, and then regressing the sentencing decisions on the candidate predictors in stepwise fashion. Variables that appeared in the resulting regression equation became serious candidates for inclusion in the eventual guidelines. The findings of the data analyses were presented to the judges; through a series of meetings alternative sets of guidelines were considered. Accommodations were made between what the judges *wanted* to influence their sentences and what the data suggested currently *did* influence their sentences. The resulting guidelines can be used as a prediction equation and a comparison can be made between what the judges had been doing and what they will be doing, assuming they operate within the guidelines. In subsequent years modifications can be made, in accord with changing laws or shifting sentencing philosophies, or perhaps there will be only narrowing or widening of the recommended sentence ranges so as to reduce or enlarge the acceptable exercise of discretion.

To the extent that the empirical description of past sentencing behavior is important to the specification of guidelines, the adequacy of the predictive/descriptive mathematical model is a central issue. A variety of methodological deficiences may be pointed out—such as unrepresentative sampling of cases, much missing data, sample sizes that are sometimes too small to begin with, poor measurement of particular variables, failure to consider interactions, and so on. These deficiencies are, in principle, correctable; they are not problems inherent in the approach. Whatever its cause, the most obvious flaw is that the final regression equations accounted for no more than about 30% of the variance in sentencing decisions. As a means of informing judges and the criminal justice community about past sentencing practices, this leaves a good deal of room for improvement; it tells us there is considerably more that we do not know than we do know. Several reasons exist to suggest that a regression approach, relatively simple and convenient though it may be, is unlikely to predict judges' decisions much better than in these instances.

First, many variables that may be important are so skewed that in a regression analysis they make no contribution. Only a handful of defendants injure a child, resist arrest, assert that they look forward to their next crime, and so on. Because these are such infrequent events, they will share little variance with the dependent variable. Yet they may, in part *because of their rarity*, be salient to a judge. This potentially important information is largely or completely thrown away in a standard regression analysis. Another problem is that different judges may have well practiced, consistent, and *different* cognitive algorithms for making sentencing decisions. When these are jumbled into a single data set, a potentially powerful variable is ignored: the judge. If sentencing decisions do, indeed, have a substantial idiographic component, a far better approach would be to construct a separate description of the behavior of each judge. These could be pooled to yield predictions for the court. And in developing consensual guidelines, it might be better to describe the individual differences accurately, and invite the judges to resolve their differences in arriving at consensual norms, instead of offering them an excessively aggregated model that does not sound quite right to any one judge, and does not predict well for the group. Another major possibility is that a simple linear weighted averaging model just is not analogous to the way judges decide on sentences. For example, there is reason to believe that sentencing is a two-stage or bifurcated process. First, the judge decides whether or nor to incarcerate. If the decision is to incarcerate, then a "separate" decision is made as to length. If this is indeed the decision process (and no one yet knows this although it obviously would be helpful to find out), the decision at each stage may be determined by quite different sets of information or at least by quite differently weighted sets. Indeed, by doing *separate* regression analyses for the in-out decision and the length decision, we have found that different partially overlapping sets of variables do the best job of predicting the two decisions. Even if the predictions were accurate, that is, high R^2, we still have the problem of determining whether they are accurate for the right reasons, that is, because the model is correct. One problem is the familiar correlation-causation issue. These are correlational data. For a variable to predict sentencing decisions does not mean it does so because the judge made the decision in response to that variable.

Now, given that guidelines were developed, even if the development rested on poor models of past sentencing, what impact did the guidelines innovation have on the sentencing behavior of judges? In a word, the sentencing guideline program evaluated was ineffectual. Judges did not modify their sentencing decisions in the direction of the guidelines, did not reduce disparity in sentencing, and showed no change in overall level of severity in sentencing. Compliance was assessed by comparing judges' actual in-out decisions with the guidelines recommendations. In addition to examining overall compliance rates, lenient and severe deviations were examined separately, and compliance rates were examined over time for 64 months. The overall compliance rate (about 70%) was lower than claimed by the guidelines developers, was no different from the preguidelines "compliance," and did not change over time from 24 months before implementation through 36 months after. Also, rates of lenient and severe deviations from guidelines remained strikingly similar before and after implementation. Similarly, sentence length was unaffected by the guidelines; compliance was greatest where statutory constraints preordained the result; where legal constraints did not limit discretion, deviations were not restrained by the guidelines.

Disparity was examined with respect to the effects of race, sex, and the exercise of waiver of trial rights. In path analyses, the relationship of these variables to sentencing was examined, controlling for legally relevant variables. Any effect found should have been reduced after the implementation of guidelines. No effect of race was found before the guidelines were implemented, and the result was no different after guidelines. Before guidelines, males had a slightly higher probability of incarceration; this did not change after guidelines. Another way to think about "disparity" is as the amount of unexplained variation in sentences. According to this approach, if guidelines guide sentencing, sentences should be more explainable after guidelines than they were before. Using multiple regression analysis and examining total explained variance (R^2), only negligible change occurred in the proportion of explained variance, and the change was in the direction of less explained variance after guidelines.

By examining the slopes and intercepts of the regression lines formed by regressing sentencing decisions on predictor variables before and after guidelines, it was possible to assess trends in severity as a function of the guidelines. Again, the data suggest that the guidelines did not result in changes in overall severity of sentences (For details, see Rich et al., 1981).

The availability of these findings, assuming they are replicated by other researchers, ought to have some effect on the adoption of methods of reducing disparity in sentencing. Rationally, other methods would be preferred or the causes for the lack of efficacy of these guidelines would be sought. Federal financial support and the "marketing" of guidelines by their proponents are forces advancing their use. The scientific-technical information developed by evaluation research is another force. The topic of sentencing guidelines might lend itself to the study of how innovation is adopted or diverted or how competing forces resolve themselves in the choice of innovations to clear up a problem the courts are already motivated enough to do something about.

Videotaped Presentation of Trials

One of the clearest innovations in the 1970s was the adoption by some courts of electronic technology (in contrast to purely social technology), and, in particular, videotape recording. Videotape has been recognized as having the potential to facilitate a number of trial activities, including the presentation of evidence to judge or jury, the preservation of a trial record (as an alternative to stenographic recording), and the taping of trials for public broadcast. This section deals only with the first of these applications, presentation of evidence.

Consider some of the advantages of using videotape to bring testimony and other evidence to jurors. Some witnesses may find it inconvenient or costly to appear at a trial, or, because of the inconvenience, the cost to litigants, or scheduling difficulties, may not appear at all. Conventionally, depositions would be taken at various locations prior to the trial, a typed transcript made, and appropriate portions read to the fact finders at the trial. With videotape recording, the testimony of these witnesses can be taken at one time, held for use as needed, and played back at the trial, in portions, as needed. In addition, inadmissible testimony can be excised from the tape in advance, according to the judge's rulings, and the judge need not make evidentiary rulings on the spot. Time at the trial is saved and jurors are prevented from hearing information that they otherwise would have to be later instructed to disregard. Visits to the scene of a crime or accident can be reduced to videotape and brought to the court, instead of bringing the court to the scene. Traditional live trials may either be supplemented with videotaped portions, or may be entirely supplanted by full trials edited together out of videotape. These are known as *PRVTTs* for *prerecorded videotaped trials.*

The convenience, increased flexibility in orchestrating trial participants, and reduction in time and cost are attractive possibilities. (See McCrystal, 1973, 1977, for still others.) And, indeed, these increases in efficiency and the reduction of delay are among the major benefits associated with the innovation. Although the anticipated savings are not the concern of this review, they have become the subject of some debate, suggesting that relevant time and cost studies have a necessary place in the policy discussion. The major social-psychological concern here is the same one we see in many efficiency-oriented innovations, and which we saw in the jury size debate. Do changes in procedure which enhance efficiency accomplish this good without vitiating the trial's major function, just resolution of disputes? Not surprisingly, then, most of the studies and debate about the development of videotape recording focus on testing the equivalence of various modes of presentation (primarily live versus videotape recorded) with respect to such concerns as verdicts, awards, amount of information gained and retained, judgements of credibility of attorneys and witnesses, and so on. Change of medium (especially from live) might be expected to have powerful social-psychological consequences; information transmission is not all that goes on at a trial. In addition, concern has been raised about the consequences of seriously altering these symbolic or ritual aspects of the trial (Bermant, 1975), or removing the arousal that accompanies the presence of live disputants, victims, defendants, and attorneys. Were it found that the videotape medium altered the fact finder's conclusions, or perhaps even altered the information processing without altering the conclusions, the wisdom of increased use of videotape would be called into question (e.g., Doret, 1974).

Numerous studies have been conducted addressing these and other questions (e.g., Bermant, Chappell, & McGuire, 1973; Bermant et al., 1975; "Comment: Opening Pandora's Box," 1975; Miller et al., 1975; Short, Florence, & Marsh, 1975; Western S.L.R., 1974; Williams, Farmer, Lee, Cundick, Howell, & Rooker, 1975). In general, the studies find no effect of the videotape medium on verdicts or awards, and some effects on retention of information, physiological responses, and attitudes toward and judgments about attorneys, judges, and witnesses. The surveys of lawyers and jurors find generally positive attitudes toward the use of videotape and its technical aspects, but include some suggestion that it produces more juror fatigue and some concerns about impersonality and emotional response. We will focus on this core issue of juror responses as a function of medium of presentation and will review the research in light of the nature of the social institution that is a trial, the policy questions to be answered, and the role and requirements of data in providing answers.

The longest, largest, and best-funded study of the effects of videotaped trials on jurors is that of Miller and his colleagues (Miller et al., 1975; Miller, Bender, Florence, & Nicholson, 1974; Miller & Boster, 1977: Miller, Fontes, & Dahnke, 1978; Miller & Siebert, 1975). Their research approach was straightforward and in most respects exemplary (Bermant, 1975). An automobile negligence case was edited slightly and reenacted live in an actual courtroom in Michigan before 52 jurors. At the same time, the reenactment was taped by a battery of videotape cameras. The judge told the jurors that the trial was real and that their verdict was binding, that 52 jurors were hearing the trial as part of the court's experiment on jury size, and that the cameras were present to make a record of the trial for possible later appeal.[1] The videotape was subsequently shown to other groups of people (jurors, other adults, students) as a full-screen image, a triple-camera split-screen image, in black and white, or in color. In regard to the major policy relevant empirical questions, the researchers tell us that *mode of presentation* (live versus split-screen videotape "did not significantly influence" attributions of negligence, damage awards, perceptions of attorney credibility, retention of information, or juror interest in the trial.

What can we make of these findings? (Incidentally, if we pick on this program of research, it is only because it is the best and most comprehensive research on the matter.) Bermant (1975) offers an exceptionally good critique; my critique covers overlapping ground and disagrees with none of Bermant's comments but pushes the criticism a bit farther and arrives at a more cautious conclusion. One major problem is that of contemplating acceptance of the null

---

1. Notwithstanding the desired verisimilitude the cover story may have secured, the fact that a judge lied to jurors in a court is a serious ethical matter. I will not pause to go into this except to note that the ethical question should not be overlooked (Bermant, 1975).

hypothesis as a serious outcome of a study. In policy relevant studies of innovation, this is a common event; the researchers are testing the innovator's key assumption of equivalence on major variables. (Whether this is what researchers should be doing in light of the logical impossibility of doing so will be taken up later; the fact is that it is what they do.) If acceptance of the null hypothesis is to be contemplated, there ought to be as great a concern about the probability of committing Type II error (i.e., erroneous failure to reject the hypothesis of no difference) as about the probability of committing Type I error (i.e., erroneous rejection of the hypothesis of no difference) when entertaining possible rejection of the null hypothesis. If research is designed—due to its measures, sample size, choice of statistical tests, and the like—so that it has no hope of rejecting the null hypothesis, that fact ought to be known in advance so that the inconvenience of conducting the study can be avoided. A power analysis is indispensable here (Cohen, 1969); that is, an assessment of a study's ability to reject the null hypothesis when it is in fact false. Where important policy decisions may flow from the results of a study, the nature of those decisions may dictate the need for statistical power higher than the conventional .80. These choices result from judgments about the relative value of efficiency versus the preservation of the litigant's right to a fair judicial decision. The real issue in such research, however, is in what direction the differences go and the size of their magnitude. Is the magnitude so great as to cause concern? The significance test tells only whether the observed direction of difference is reliable. Failure to find statistical significance may indicate only that insufficient power was employed to know what the direction of difference was; and that the confidence limits around each mean were too wide. In this applied context, to look only at a probability level and not at the magnitude of an effect misses the point of asking data to inform policy.

Where acceptance of the null hypothesis is the desired result, as in model testing, researchers customarily set alpha at $p = .20$, thus making their analysis more sensitive to differences and, in the given context, appropriately more conservative. In this line of research, the "model" videotaped trial is being tested for differences against the standard of the live trial, and the innovators (like mathematical modelers) hope the researchers find no difference. Had Miller and his colleagues employed this convention, they would have found that the verdicts did indeed "differ significantly" at $p = .20$. Defendant negligence was less likely to be found in a live trial than in any of the videotaped trials. These observed differences are not of a modest magnitude. In the live trial condition, the defendant was more likely to be found not negligent, by a ratio of .70:1 (verdicts for the plaintiff:verdicts for the defendant). In all of the various videotaped trial conditions, the plaintiff was more likely to prevail, by ratios of 1.34:1, 4.13:1, 1.71:1, and 1.41:1. These differences are probably overlooked because of insufficient power to reject the null hypothesis (also see Williams *et al.*, 1975, p. 383). Thus, on the same data on which the original Miller researchers find the comfort of equivalence, I and Williams *et al.* are able to find cause for concern. In fairness to these researchers, it should be pointed out that in later stages of their project and in later writing (Miller & Fontes, 1979) Miller did not overlook the question of statistical power.

A second issue I will raise with the basic approach of the study by Miller and his colleagues is whether, despite the judge's cover story, the 52 jurors in the live trial with the cameras really believed they were about to decide a real case.[2] If one effect of prerecorded videotaped trials (PRVTTs) is to create a sense of unreality, a lack of urgency and weightiness to the decision to be made, that would only be detected in comparison with a live trial that elicited such involvement. The "nondifferences" observed could be a reflection of the failure of the cover story to erase any doubts jurors had about the reality of the trial they were hearing. Just how this possiblity would be tested is a methodological dilemma, and to believe it is a problem or not is, with present information, unfortunately, a matter of faith. The ideal solution, of course, would be for courts that are using PRVTTs to do so on a truly experimental basis, so that genuinely important decisions are being made in both videotaped and live trials.

Miller and his colleagues also reported that in comparing live to monochromatic and color videotaped trials, there were declines in information retention over the course of the trial. This drop was slightly steeper in a live trial; slightly greater retention was found in the black-and-white than in the color videotape condition; and no effect was found upon juror perceptions of witness or attorney credibility. In this lengthy study, the researchers then had a choice of replicating earlier findings, or moving onward using new conditions and subject populations. They chose the latter course, studying such matters as introduction of taped material into otherwise live trials, deletion of inadmissible testimony, different editing techniques, use of paralinguistic and nonverbal cues on jurors' evaluations of witness credibility, and effects of certain production techniques on verdicts and perceptions of trial participants. The conclusion of this massive body of work is that videotape recording creates no serious problems for trial equivalence except differences due to use of black and white versus color, various editing techniques, and type of camera shots. As indicated above, the hypothesis testing criteria used leave me less sanguine. Additional concerns will be mentioned following a brief review of other studies.

Williams *et al.* (1975) presented a mock trial through different modes (live, black-and-white videotape, color videotape, audiotape only, or transcript) to groups of 26 to 28 jurors in each mode. The jurors filled out lengthy questionnaires giving their reactions under the different media conditions. A variety of statistically reliable differences, but nearly always small in magnitude, were obtained. Importantly, none of the dollar awards differed significantly com-

2. It might be noted that on consideration of this issue, Miller is satisfied that it is not a matter for concern. Based on posttrial conversations with a number of jurors and other court personnel, he believes that the jurors were convinced they were sitting on an actual trial (Miller, personal communication, 1980).

pared to the mean award of the group seeing a live trial. This study found, not surprisingly, that reading transcripts was less clear, less interesting, and more fatiguing than watching videotaped presentations; thus, as a means of presenting evidence from a deposition, videotape seems to have much to recommend it.

In addition, a whole genre of how-to studies and reports exists (e.g., National Center for State Courts, 1974), and decisions in appellate cases concerning the permissibility of videotaped evidence form yet another body of literature on the subject (e.g., *Carson v. Burlington Northern Inc.*, 1971; *People v. Moran*, 1974). It is noteworthy that these other literatures quickly outpace the social-psychological and communications research. Innovations become doable and legal and have influential advocates leading the way (e.g., McCrystal, 1973) long before definitive research can be done on the innovation's effects on justice.

The available studies suggest that there may be as much variation among alternative forms of videotaped trials as between live trials and any one kind of viodiotaped trial. As Bermant (1975) points out, this means that comparisons between videotaped trials and live trials are uniformative for policymaking unless one can specify and regulate the particular kind of videotaped trial. Were a conclusion to say that videotape is acceptable, people could then construct particular kinds of videotaped trials that might not be acceptable at all. Thus, the how-to guides can be important if they are sensitive to the effects of medium and production variations (if any) on the fact finder's responses.

Another issue of research into policy that pervades the videotaped trial research is the choice of a standard for comparison. I have implied, and Williams *et al.* (1975) make the argument directly, that the live trial is the only proper benchmark. They take that benchmark seriously enough so that when Miller and his colleagues found certain enhancements due to videotape (such as improved recall), Williams *et al.* cite the difference as a reason to be wary of videotaped trials. The Miller team, looking only for decrements, do not view the enhancements as problems. Are these innovations to operate solely on the administrative (time, cost, and convenience) aspects of a trial, and to slavishly recreate the status quo? Or might such innovations be looked to as a way of enhancing the substantive legal process as well? If we agreed on just what we wanted a trial to do, what the *processes* of justice are supposed to be, then those normative standards could be the benchmarks, and the administrative innovations could be tested for the capacity to improve on justice, and not merely as potential sources of damage.

The final issue of concern is the problem of the trial as a contest. The studies on which I have focused seem vaguely aware that what matters in a trial is the relative impact of one side versus the other on the fact finder. Thus, it is of little practical importance to the outcome of individual trials if one medium compared to another increases the overall perception of credibility of lawyers or witnesses. What matters, and matters centrally, is whether one side presents a more potent case than the other. Thus, main effects of medium are of little interest. If the relative differences between the parties remain constant, overall changes in many dependent variables are of no importance.[3] The point is that what ought to be of central, not secondary, concern to videotaped trial researchers are the interactions between medium of presentation and particular trial elements. Examples of such interactions have been found (Miller *et al.*, 1978). For example, perceived credibility of the "strong witness" was exaggerated further in the black-and-white compared to the color videotape. To the extent that the medium alters the relative advantages to one party or the other, it alters what ultimately matters in a trial, just as the advent of "talkies" ended some actors' careers and catapulted others to stardom. If such interaction effects really exist, they would lead to a change in the effectiveness of some attorneys relative to others and eventually to changes in trial tactics such as selection of witnesses and decisions to put some witnesses on live and others on tape. For researchers, the possibility of interactions suggests a different strategy than the ones heretofore employed. Instead of sticking with one or two mock trials, a wide and systematically varied range of trials would be needed. Are small live differences between parties magnified or nullified by tape? What kinds of witnesses or attorneys come across better on what kinds of videotape productions? Some of these effects might be large but cannot be detected at all unless trials tapping the range of variables are tried. Important systematic interaction effects might have policy implications (e.g., permit videotape recording in some kinds of cases but not others), and would certainly affect the tactics of knowledgeable attorneys. Again, a solution is to carry out such research in actual courtrooms, where cases could (in principle) be matched on important variables and then randomly assigned to one or another medium of presentation. As noted earlier, the adoption or rejection of the innovation does not wait for the research and the eventual research findings may have to overcome recently accepted practices.

CONCLUSIONS

There is little cause for great celebration in either the innovations reviewed, the research done in support of them, or the legal community's capacity to deal critically and intelligently with the innovations and research on them. My informal impression is that what I have to say in this paragraph, in light of the innovations reviewed, is representative of courtroom innovation generally.

The innovations seldom go beyond tinkering, and usually are aimed only at trimming dollars or minutes. Often the tinkering is ineffective. The research is aimed at assessing whether the tinkering will do unintended damage and in

---

3. I hedge in saying this, because something that might matter would be, for example, recall of facts. A main effect improvement here would constitute an enhancement of the justice producing machinery.

that respect Lempert's (1980) criticism of its lack of forwardlookingness is well taken. Why not design innovations, if only on a demonstration basis, that boldly advance efficiency *and* justice at once?

The research is often disappointing—not just because it may be poorly done, but because the nature of the empirical questions makes definitive research difficult or impossible. Many different studies, in different places, on different variables, yet overlapping enough to replicate each other, would be necessary to yield data on which policy could, with confidence, be made. Even the few studies done present a potpourri of findings that are difficult to assess clearly and confidently (Bermant, 1975).

Since a finding of fact is no better than the methods used to find it, a close examination of the research methods (design, measurement, data analysis) is necessary. Few legal policymakers are equipped or have the time or staff to do this. Moreover, busy policymakers prefer concise conclusions and hate detail (Staats, 1980). Thus, some of Miller's conclusions that I have argued are probably Type II errors, will be passed on uncritically to policymakers because in the final report they are presented in the brief, convenient, detailless form that policymakers like. Several cities instituted sentencing guidelines without seeing any of the data supposedly generating them. This is a real dilemma of policy-oriented research. The needs of policymakers for digestible conclusions is at odds with the requirements of critical evaluation of research findings (Saks & Stapleton, 1980). In appropriate situations, I would urge funders not to issue their checks unless a power analysis has been made part of the proposal, nor should refereed journals publish, nor should readers pay any attention to studies lacking such information.

Policy-oriented research, because it embodies so many considerations, including "trans-science" (Weinberg, 1972) issues, is exceedingly difficult to do. Insufficient methods for assessing policy exist, but even those that do are not often enough used. Researchers and policymakers are not as helpful to each other as they could be. Exhortations such as the present one may goad some researchers into improving their performance, but the overall policy process, which gives innovations the green or the red light, has some distance yet to go (Abt, 1980).

REFERENCES

Abt, C. C. *Problems in American social policy research.* Cambridge, Massachusetts: Abt, 1980.

Abt, L. E., & Stuart, I. R. *Social psychology and discretionary law.* New York: Van Nostrand-Reinhold, 1979.

Apodaca, Cooper, and Madden v. Oregon, United States Reports, 1972, *406,* 404–415.

Asch, S. E. Effects of group pressure upon the modification and distortion of judgments. In G. Swanson, T. Newcomb, & E. Hartley, (Eds.), *Readings in social psychology* (Rev. ed). New York: Holt, 1952.

Baar, C. *Separate but subservient: Court budgeting in the American states.* Lexington, Massachusetts: Heath, 1975.

Ballew v. *Georgia, United States Reports,* 1978, *435,* 222–245.

Bermant, G. Critique—Data in search of theory in search of policy: Behavioral responses to video tape in the courtroom. *Brigham Young University Law Review,* 1975, *1975,* 467–485.

Bermant, G., Chappell, D., & McGuire, M. Liggons v. Hanisko: *Juror reactions to videotaped trial testimony in California.* (Unpublished manuscript, Battelle Memorial Institute, Seattle, Washington, 1973.

Bermant, G., Chappell, D., Crockette, G., Jacoubovitch, M., & McGuire, M. Juror responses to pre-recorded videotape trial presentations in California and Ohio. *Hastings Law Journal,* 1975, *26,* 975–998.

Bermant, G., & Coppock, R. Outcomes of six- and twelve-member jury trials: An analysis of 128 civil cases in the State of Washington. *Washington Law Review* 1973, *48,* 593–596.

Boring, E. G. *A history of experimental psychology* (2nd ed.). New York: Appleton, 1950.

Bray, R. M. *Decision rules, attitude similarity, and jury decision making.* University of Illinois, at Urbana-Champaign (Unpublished dissertation), 1974.

Bray, R. M., & Struckman-Johnson, C. *Effects of juror population, assigned decision rule and insur-ance option on the decisions of simulated juries.* Paper presented at the meeting of the American Psychological Association, San Francisco, August, 1977.

Burch v. *Lousiana, United States Reports,* 1979, *441,* 130–139.

Burger, W. Speech before the Conference of Chief Justices, Flagstaff, Arizona, August, 1979.

Calpin, J. C., Kress, J. M., & Gelman, A. M. *Sentencing guidelines structuring judicial discretion, Volume III: The analytical basis for the formulation of sentencing policy.* Albany, New York: Criminal Justice Research Center, 1979.

Campbell, D. T., & Stanley, J. C. *Experimental and quasi-experimental designs for research.* Chicago: Illinois: Rand McNally, 1963.

Caplan, N. Social research and national policy: What gets used, by whom, for what purposes, and with what effects? *International Social Science Journal,* 1976, *28,* 187–194.

Carson v. *Burlington Northern Inc.,* 1971, *Federal Rules Decisions, 52,* 492–493.

Church, T. W., Lee, J. Q., Tam, T., Carlson, A., & McConnell, V. *Pretrial delay: A review and bibliography.* Williamsburg, Virginia: National Center for State Courts, 1978.

Cochrane, A. *Effectiveness and Efficiency.* (Nuffield Provincial Hospitals Trust). London: Burgess and Son, Ltd., 1972.

Cohen, J. *Statistical power analysis for the behavioral sciences.* New York: Academic Press, 1969.

Cole, G. F. *The American system of criminal justice.* North Scituate, Massachusetts: Duxbury, 1975.

Coleman, J. S., Katz, E., & Menzel, H. *Medical innovation: A diffusion study.* Indianapolis, Indiana: 1966.

Colgrove v. *Battin, United States Reports,* 1973, *413,* 149–188.

Comment: On instructing deadlocked juries. *Yale Law Journal,* 1968, *78,* 100–142.

Comment: Opening Pandora's box: Asking judges and attorneys to react to the videotape trial. *Brigham Young University Law Review,* 1975, *1975,* 487–527.

Cook, T. D., & Campbell, D. T. *Quasi-experimentation: Design & analysis issues for field settings.* Chicago, Illinois: Rand McNally, 1979.

Davis, J. H., Kerr, N. L., Atkin, R. S., Holt, R., & Meek, D. The decision processes of 6- and 12-person mock juries assigned unanimous and 2/3 majority rules. *Journal of Personality and Social Psy-chology,* 1975, *32,* 1–14.

Diamond, S. S. A jury experiment reanalyzed. *University of Michigan Journal of Law Reform,* 1974, *7,* 520–532.

Doret, D. Trial by videotape—Can justice be seen to be done? *Temple University Law Quarterly,* 1974, *47,* 228.

Federal Rules of Evidence, Pub. L. 93–595, Jan. 2, 1975, 88 Stat. 1929.

Fetter, T. J. (Ed.), *State courts: A blueprint for the future.* Williamsburg, Virginia: National Center for State Courts, 1978.

Frank, J. *Law and the modern mind.* New York: Brentano's, 1930.

Frank, J. *Courts on trial.* Princeton, New Jersey: Princeton Univ. Press, 1945.

Hagan, J. Extra-legal attributes and criminal sentencing: An assessment of a sociological viewpoint. *Law and Society Review*, 1974, *8*, 357–383.

Hans, V. P. *The effects of the unanimity requirement on group decision processes in simulated juries.* Unpublished doctoral dissertation, University of Toronto, 1978.

Heumann, M. A note on plea bargaining and case pressure. *Law and Society Review*, 1975, *9*, 515–528.

Institute of Judicial Administration. A comparison of six- and twelve-member juries in New Jersey Superior and County Courts. New York: Institute of Judicial Administration, 1972.

Johnson v. Lousiana, United States Reports, 1972, *406*, 356–40.

Kalven, H., & Zeisel, H. *The American jury.* Boston, Massachusetts: Little, Brown, 1966.

Katz, D., & Kahn, R. L. *The social psychology of organizations.* New York: Wiley, 1966.

Kerr, N. L., Atkin, R. S., Stasser, G., Meek, D., Holt, R. W., & Davis, J. H. Guilt beyond a reasonable doubt: Effects of concept definition and assigned decision rule on the judgments of mock jurors. *Journal of Personality and Social Psychology*, 1976, *34*, 282–294.

Kessler, J. An empirical study of six- and twelve-member jury decision-making processes. *University of Michigan Journal of Law Reform*, 1973, *6*, 712–734.

Kidd, R. F., & Saks, M. J. What is applied social psychology? In R. F. Kidd & M. J. Saks (Eds.), *Advances in applied social psychology* (vol. 1). Hillsdale, New Jersey: Erlbaum, 1980.

Latané, B. & Nida, S. Social impact theory and group influence: A social engineering perspective. In P. B. Paulus (Ed.). *Psychology of group influence.* Hillsdale, New Jersey: Erlbaum, 1980.

Lempert, R. O. Uncovering "nondiscernible" differences: Empirical research and the jury-size cases. *Michigan Law Review*, 1975, *73*, 643–708.

Lempert, R. O. Remarks made at a meeting of the National Jury Project, New York City, January 4, 1980.

McCrystal, J. Videotape trials: Relief for our congested courts. *Denver Law Journal*, 1973, *49*, 463–488.

McCrystal, J. The promise of prerecorded videotape trials. *American Bar Association Journal*, 1977, *63*, 977–979.

Miller, C. E. *The effects of group decision rules on interpersonal attraction and other psychological variables.* Unpublished doctoral dissertation, University of Michigan, 1974.

Miller, G. R., Bender, D. C., Boster, F., Florence, B. T., Fontes, N., Hocking, J., & Nicholson, H. The effects of videotape testimony in jury trials. *Brigham Young University Law Review*, 1975, *1975*, 331–373.

Miller, G. R., Bender, D., Florence, T., & Nicholson, H. Real vs. reel: What's the verdict? *Journal of Communication*, 1974, *24*, 99–111.

Miller, G. R., & Boster, F. J. Three images of the trial: Their implications for psychological research. In B. D. Sales (Ed.), *Psychology in the legal process.* New York: Spectrum, 1977.

Miller, G. R., Fontes, N. E., & Dahnke, G. L. Using videotape in the courtroom: Four year test pattern. *University of Detroit Journal of Urban Law*, 1978, *55*, 655–698.

Miller, G. R., & Fontes, N. E. *Videotape on trial: A view from the jury box.* Beverly Hills, California: Sage, 1979.

Miller, G. R., & Siebert, E. *Effects of videotape testimony on information processing and decision-making in jury trials: Final report.* Unpublished monograph, Department of Communication, Michigan State University, 1975.

Mills, L. Six-member and twelve-member juries: An empirical study of trial results. *University of Michigan Journal of Law Reform*, 1973, *6*, 671–711.

Nagel, S. S., & Neef, M. G. *Legal policy analysis.* Lexington, Massachusetts: Heath, 1977.

National Center for State Courts. *Video support in the criminal courts.* Williamsburg, Virginia: National Center for State Courts, 1974.

Nemeth, C. Interactions between jurors as a function of majority vs. unanimity decision rules. *Journal of Applied Social Psychology*, 1977, *7*, 38–56.

Note: What the California legal community thinks about the use of videotapes in judicial proceedings. *Western State Law Review*, 1974, *2*, 188–192.

O'Donnell, P., Churgin, M. J., & Curtis, D. E. *Toward a just and effective sentencing system: Agenda for legislative reform.* New York: Praeger, 1977.

Partridge, A., & Eldridge, C. *The second circuit sentencing study: A report to the judges of the second circuit.* Washington, D.C.: Federal Judicial Center, 1974.

Partridge, A., & Leavitt, M. R. *The feasibility of a national sentencing policy. A critique* (FJC Staff Paper). Washington, DC: Federal Judicial Center, 1979.

People v. *Moran, California Reporter,* 1974, *114,* 413—424.

Rich, W. C., Sutton, L. P., Clear, T. R., & Saks, M. J. *Sentencing guidelines: An evaluation of the initial experiences.* Williamsburg, Virginia: National Center for State Courts, 1981.

Saks, M. J. Ignorance of science is no excuse. *Trial,* 1974, *10,* 18—20.

Saks, M. J. *Jury verdicts: The role of group size and social decision rule.* Lexington, Massachusetts: Heath, 1977.

Saks, M. J., & Baron, C. H. *The use/nonuse/misuse of applied social research in the courts.* Cambridge, Massachusetts: Abt, 1980.

Saks, M. J., & Kidd, R. F. Human information processing and adjudication: Trial by heuristics. *Law and Society Review,* 1980—81, *51,* 123—160.

Saks, M. J., & Stapleton, W. V. Eliminating bureaucratic impediments to social reality testing. In C. C. Abt, (Ed.) *Problems in American social policy research.* Cambridge, Massachusetts: Abt, 1980.

Short, E. H., Florence, B. T., & Marsh, M. A. An assessment of videotape in the criminal courts. *Brigham Young University Law Review,* 1975, *1975,* 423—465.

Speedy Trial Act of 1974, Pub. L. 93—619, Jan. 3, 1975; 88 Stat 2076 (1974).

Sperlich, P. Trial by jury: It may have a future. In P. Kurland & G. Casper (Eds.), *Supreme Court review 1978,* Chicago, Illinois: Univ. of Chicago Press, 1979.

Staats, E. B. Why isn't policy research utilized more by decision makers? (Or why do researchers talk only to each other?) In C. C. Abt, (Ed.) *Problems in American social policy research.* Cambridge, Massachusetts: Abt, 1980.

Tversky, A., & Kahneman, D. Belief in the law of small numbers. *Psychological Bulletin,* 1971, *76,* 105—112.

Valenti, A. C., & Downing, L. L. Differential effects of jury size on verdicts following deliberation as a function of the apparent guilt of a defendant. *Journal of Personality and Social Psychology,* 1975, *32,* 655—663.

Weiss, C. H. *Evaluation research.* Englewood Cliffs, New Jersey: Prentice-Hall, 1972.

Weiss, C. H. *Using social research for public policy-making.* Lexington, Massachusetts: Lexington, 1977.

Weinberg, A. M. Science and trans-science. *Minerva,* 1972, *2,* 209—222.

Williams, G. R., Farmer, L. C., Lee, R. E., Cundick, B. P., Howell, R. J., & Rooker, C. K. Juror perceptions of trial testimony as a function of the method of presentation: A comparison of live, color video, black-and-white video, audio, and transcript presentations. *Brigham Young Unveristy Law Review,* 1975, *1975,* 375—421.

Williams v. *Florida,* United States Reports, 1970, *399,* 78—145.

Yankelovich, Skelly, & White, Inc. Highlights of a national survey of the general public, judges, lawyers, and community leaders. In T. Fetter (Ed.), *State courts: A blueprint for the future.* Williamsburg, Virginia: National Center for State Courts, 1978.

Zeisel, H. . . . And then there were none: The diminution of the federal jury. *University of Chicago Law Review,* 1971, *38,* 710—724.

Zeisel, H., & Diamond, S. S. Confincing empirical evidence on the six-member jury. *University of Chicago Law Review,* 1974, *41,* 281—295.

Author Index

Numbers in italics refer to the pages on which the complete references are listed.

Subject Index